07244001

BAT

KT-419-920

BATH COLLEGE OF HIGHER EDUCATION
NEWTON PARK LIBRARY

Please return or renew not later than

B.C.H.E. — LIBRARY

00021955

FOOD SERVICE SYSTEMS

Analysis, Design, and Implementation

ACADEMIC PRESS RAPID MANUSCRIPT REPRODUCTION

The Updated Proceedings from the Seminar
FOOD SERVICE SYSTEMS: ANALYSIS, DESIGN, AND IMPLEMENTATION
Sponsored by Food Science Associates, Inc.,
in Framingham, Massachusetts in 1976

FOOD SERVICE SYSTEMS

Analysis, Design, and Implementation

edited by

G. E. LIVINGSTON

Department of Home Economics and Nutrition
New York University
New York, New York

Food Science Associates, Inc.
Dobbs Ferry, New York

CHARLOTTE M. CHANG

Food Science Associates, Inc.
Dobbs Ferry, New York

BATH COLLEGE OF HIGHER EDUCATION
NEWTON PARK LIBRARY

Stock No.	Class No.
801204	641·57

ACADEMIC PRESS   **1979**
A Subsidiary of Harcourt Brace Jovanovich, Publishers
NEW YORK   LONDON   TORONTO   SYDNEY   SAN FRANCISCO

COPYRIGHT © 1979, BY ACADEMIC PRESS, INC.
ALL RIGHTS RESERVED.
NO PART OF THIS PUBLICATION MAY BE REPRODUCED OR
TRANSMITTED IN ANY FORM OR BY ANY MEANS, ELECTRONIC
OR MECHANICAL, INCLUDING PHOTOCOPY, RECORDING, OR ANY
INFORMATION STORAGE AND RETRIEVAL SYSTEM, WITHOUT
PERMISSION IN WRITING FROM THE PUBLISHER.

ACADEMIC PRESS, INC.
111 Fifth Avenue, New York, New York 10003

United Kingdom Edition published by
ACADEMIC PRESS, INC. (LONDON) LTD.
24/28 Oval Road, London NW1 7DX

Library of Congress Cataloging in Publication Data
Main entry under title:

Food service systems.

    Proceedings of a conference held in Framington,
Massachusetts on April 7--9, 1976.

    Includes index.

    1. Food service -- Congresses. I. Livingston,
Gideon Eleazar   II. Chang, Charlotte M.
TX911.F66   642   79-23152

ISBN 0-12-453150-4

PRINTED IN THE UNITED STATES OF AMERICA

79 80 81 82   9 8 7 6 5 4 3 2 1

CONTENTS

UTILIZING LABOR EFFECTIVELY

EQUIPMENT AND FACILITY PLANNING

INSURING FOOD QUALITY AND WHOLESOMENESS

CASE HISTORIES OF SUCCESSFUL FOOD SERVICE SYSTEMS IMPLEMENTATION

CONTRIBUTORS

Numbers in parentheses indicate the pages on which the authors' contributions begin.

Catharina Y. W. Ang (359)
Richard B. Russell Center, U.S. Department of Agriculture, Athens, Georgia 30604

J. L. Balintfy (155)
School of Business Administration, University of Massachusetts, Amherst, Massachusetts 01002

Frank D. Borsenik (311)
College of Hotel Administration, University of Nevada, Las Vegas, Nevada 89154

Richard E. Bresnahan (189)
Analytic Services, Inc., Arlington, Virginia 22202

Charlotte M. Chang (41, 227)
Food Science Associates, Inc., Dobbs Ferry, New York 10522

Robert V. Decareau (275)
Food Engineering Laboratory, U.S. Army Natick Research and Development Command, Natick, Massachusetts 01760

H. C. Gibbons, Jr. (343)
Dennis–Weingarten Associates, Inc., Prairie Village, Kansas 66208

Richard J. Giglio (201)
Department of Industrial Engineering and Operations Research, University of Massachusetts, Amherst, Massachusetts 01002

Gary L. Hotchkin (179)
Pipers Restaurants, Memphis, Tennessee, 38195

Robert W. Jailer (331, 447)
Systems Sciences Company, Planning Research Corporation, Englewood Cliffs, New Jersey 07632

Sanford Kotzen   *(461)*
    Franklin Square Hospital, Baltimore, Maryland 21237

Rauno A. Lampi   *(101)*
    Food Engineering Laboratory, U.S. Army Natick Research and Development Command, Natick, Massachusetts 01760

G. E. Livingston   *(3, 19, 67, 89, 243)*
    Food Science Associates, Inc., Dobbs Ferry, New York 10522

Thomas Mario   *(413)*
    Food Science Associates, Inc., Dobbs Ferry, New York, 10522

Herbert L. Meiselman   *(127)*
    Food Sciences Laboratory, U.S. Army Natick Research and Development Command, Natick, Massachusetts 01760

Robert A. Phinney   *(219)*
    Sambo's Restaurants, Carpinteria, California 93013

Harold Ratner   *(447)*
    New York State Department of Mental Hygiene, Albany, New York 12219

Gerald L. Schulz   *(101)*
    Food Engineering Laboratory, U.S. Army Natick Research and Development Command, Natick, Massachusetts, 01760

Richard N. Schwartz   *(405, 475)*
    Fairfield Farm Kitchens, Beaver Heights, Maryland 20027

Gerald J. Silverman   *(379)*
    Food Sciences Laboratory, U.S. Army Natick Research and Development Command, Natick, Massachusetts 01760

Robert S. Smith   *(201)*
    Food Engineering Laboratory, U.S. Army Natick Research and Development Command, Natick, Massachusetts 01760

Lawrence E. Symington   *(301)*
    Food Sciences Laboratory, U.S. Army Natick Research and Development Command, Natick, Massachusetts 01760

Joseph W. Szczeblowski   *(101)*
    Food Engineering Laboratory, U.S. Army Natick Research and Development Command, Natick, Massachusetts 01760

John S. Thompson   *(261)*
    John S. Thompson Company, Inc., Los Altos, California 94022

FOREWORD

Real solutions to complex problems may involve applications of systems analysis and, separately or together, operations research techniques. This is particularly true when the problems are in an unstudied field such as food service systems. Food service systems entail interrelationships of customer acceptance, nutritional quality, training and motivation, and many other factors that must be assessed and, if possible, quantitated as part of the analysis.

The main thrust of a cost–benefit analysis is to determine what benefits can be obtained from an existing system, what alternatives or changes to the system will give more benefits, and at what cost. This approach requires benefits and cost projections for the alternatives, and an experimental period that determines actual performance of alternatives prior to implementation. A good alternative or new system is, of course, one that costs less and offers more benefits. An undesirable alternative would be a new system that costs more and gives fewer benefits.

Successful application of this approach has required rigorous definition of costs and benefits. Costs have been relatively easy to define and quantify, even though such costs are not usually available in the form required for proper analysis. On the other hand benefits have proven difficult to define and quantify, especially for military systems. In industry, the definition of system benefit is usually associated with profit and return on investment. If a food service company or facility is making a reasonable profit and return on investment each year, it is considered successful. Military food service, however, has no similar profit motive, and benefits are more difficult to define.

Reasonable applications of a food systems approach, which includes before and after cost and benefit analysis, as supported by actual test results, will ensure that new or changed systems of food service will more than achieve their objectives. A test and evaluation period is essential. Without the proven results achieved through testing, our reports would be gathering dust on shelves rather than generating improved systems of food service.

This volume for the first time brings together, in some detail, the methodology used in recent systems studies. We are happy to share the techniques we have developed, with other workers in the field.

Robert J. Byrne

Operations Research/Systems Analysis Office
U.S. Army Research & Development Command
Natick, Massachusetts

PREFACE

The need for a volume on food service systems has been apparent for some time. Although it has been recognized for some twenty years that complex food service operations must be planned as systems, no serious attempt appears to have been made to incorporate the knowledge relating to the various disciplines required to develop successful food service systems into a single reference book.

In 1976, Food Science Associates, Inc., in commemoration of its twentieth anniversary, conducted a three-day seminar in Framingham, Massachusetts, entitled "Food Service Systems: Analysis, Design, and Implementation." The present book presents the proceedings of this seminar, suitably updated by the participants. It presents a step-by-step approach to the problems of analyzing and optimizing the major elements of food service systems, such as food, labor utilization, facility design, equipment selection, quality control, training, and microbiological and nutritional aspects.

The contributors, all experts in their respective fields, have aimed to provide a comprehensive in-depth treatment of the interrelated elements of food service systems. Each element is approached from the standpoint of its analysis and its design into a new system, with emphasis on the methodology involved. Some actual case histories of successful food service systems designs and implementation are included.

It is our hope that this book will serve both as a text for college and university level courses in Food Service Systems and as a reference work for research workers, consultants, and planners in the field.

G. E. Livingston
Charlotte M. Chang

ACKNOWLEDGMENTS

The authors wish to express their sincere appreciation to Dr. Edward E. Anderson and Dr. Robert J. Byrne of the United States Army Natick Research and Development Command for their support of the FOOD SERVICE SYSTEMS SEMINAR upon which this book is based, and to Mrs. Vivian Servedio for her dedicated work in preparing the camera-ready copy.

SYSTEMS AND THEIR STUDY

CHAPTER 1

DEVELOPMENT OF THE SYSTEMS APPROACH
TO THE DESIGN OF FOOD SERVICE OPERATIONS

G. E. Livingston

I. INTRODUCTION

It was probably inevitable that the "systems approach",
that has been used in attacking other complex problems in our
terrestrial and extraterrestrial environments (e.g. weapon systems, space travel systems, eco systems), would result in the
application of the same concept to the problems in the food
service industry. What does appear to be astonishing is that
the term "food service system" did not come into general use
before the 1950's and that it was not the professional food
service managers, but rather food technologists and industrial
engineers, viewing the problems of the food service industry,
who brought the term into general use. A food service system
has been defined as "an integrated program in which procurement, storage, preparation, and service of food and beverages
and the equipment and methods required to accomplish these objectives are fully coordinated for minimum labor, optimum customer satisfaction, quality, and cost control" (1). Although
one could probably define the term in many ways - and indeed
the term "food service system" is frequently and erroneouly,
used to describe what are, in fact, equipment "subsystems" -
the fact that several workers in the field have used this definition in their publications (2,3) suggests that it is indeed
serviceable.

II. THE INDUSTRIAL REVOLUTION IN FOOD SERVICE

The awareness of mass feeding operations as "food service
systems" developed with the growth of multiunit food service
operations, and the introduction of new methods for increasing
worker productivity. In one form or another, these methods in-

Copyright © 1979 by Academic Press, Inc.
All rights of reproduction in any form reserved
ISBN: 0-12-453150-4

cluded the divorce of food production from food service, either
in time, in place, or in both. This cleavage of two functions,
which historically and traditionally have been joined together
to such an extent that today people still argue that they cannot be separated without considerable loss of food quality,
meant that at long last, the industrial revolution and the food
service industry had met. Like its sister industry, food manufacturing, the food service industry had to succumb to the inevitable logic of economic common sense. As in other fields,
the industrial revolution of the 19th century signaled the
transformation of shop level manufacture to industrial scale
production, and industrial scale food processing such as canning, bottling, and freezing, developed.The food service industry also heard the message of the industrial revolution: goods
no longer need be produced on the same premises in which they
are sold. Production should take place where raw materials and
labor are most plentiful and least expensive, while consumption
can occur at times and places far removed from the food source.
Under the best circumstances, the food service industry, because it is a service industry,is highly labor intensive. Every
rational opportunity should be exploited to increase worker
productivity, especially in those areas where the "human factor
element" of food service, the eyeball to eyeball contact between customer and food service employee, is not lost!

III. MILITARY, SCHOOL FEEDING, AND AIRLINE CONTRIBUTIONS TO
     FOOD SERVICE SYSTEMS

     It would be unfair to suggest that no effort had been made
before the 20th century to divorce food preparation and service. One needs only to point to the invention of canning by
Nicholas Appert in 1809, responding to Napoleon's requirement
for a more dependable way to feed his armies in the field, to
find the first step toward a food service system. Parenthet-
ically, it is interesting to note that only now (with the advent of retort pouches and traypacks) is the full potential of
canning to meet the needs of the food service industry being
recognized and seriously exploited! One could also point to
1790 and the municipal soup kitchen set up in Munich, Germany
for unemployed workmen. It was not long before thousands of
school children were included in this early feeding program,
and thus school feeding in Europe began (4). France opened can-
teens in 1849 with surplus National Guard funds, and these can-
teens received recognition by the Ministry of Public Education
a year later. Within ten years school lunches were made manda-
tory in France as part of a compulsory education law. The provision of Meals Act in 1906 in the United Kingdom, gave the

educational authorities the responsibility for school feeding.
Before World War I, Austria, Belgium, Denmark, Finland, Italy,
Norway, and Sweden had well developed school lunch programs,
and Norway perfected what was called the "Oslo Breakfast," a
cold meal consisting of milk, sandwiches, and a raw carrot,
apple, or orange. In the United States, during the great de-
pression of the 1930's, the Reconstruction Finance Corporation
gave loans to several cities in Missouri to pay for the labor
of preparing and serving school lunches. By 1934, through the
Civil Works Administration and Federal Emergency Relief Administration, similar assistance was being granted in 39 States,
and in 1935, the federal government began to contribute donated
surplus commodities to school lunchrooms under Section 32 of
the School Lunch Law. The importance of school lunch programs
in an historical overview of food service systems development
is well justified because satellite feeding operations, through
the distribution of hot or cold food, probably began within
this sector of civilian institutional mass feeding. (Fig. 1)

If meeting military requirements precipitated the development of food preservation by canning, as it did in France under
Napoleon and subsequently in the United States during the Civil
War, and if the desire to feed school children provided an incentive for the transport of hot soup or food, then one must
also recognize that the concept of systematized food and beverage service to non-institutionalized populations, probably began with the advent of airline feeding which started with box
lunches some forty years ago. Progress in this area can perhaps best be gauged while enjoying a First Class meal in the
upper lounge of a Boeing 747 at 35,000 feet on an interconti-
nental flight, convincing proof indeed that culinary excellence
does not mandate on-premise food preparation!

It is clear though, as one search as the historical record,
that modern food service systems, and the use of the systems
approach in designing such operations, had their origins during
the Second World War. Obviously, the military food service
system, and the various types of operational rations developed
to support it, i.e. the B Rations, the C Rations and the K Rations, effectively provided the means of feeding troops in locations remote from sources of fresh food or kitchen facilities. While such rations certainly permitted feeding military
populations in the field with stable food forms, they by no
means represented a level of quality or variety capable of a-
chieving long term consumer satisfaction. During that period,
therefore, efforts were being made to exploit the possibilities
for greater customer satisfaction offered by precooked frozen
foods.

Prepared frozen meals, produced for the United States Navy
as early as 1944 by the Maxson Company (5), were reheated in
flight using the Maxson Whirlwind Oven which was developed by

FIGURE 1. Public school children in New York City in the early
1960's testing Type A lunches prepared using bulk pack frozen
foods. (Courtesy of New York City Board of Education, Bureau of
School Lunches)

its originator for this purpose, and is the forerunner of the forced hot air convection ovens of today! The Maxson Company was succeeded by the Frigidinner Company, which provided the starting point for the entire frozen dinner industry that we now take for granted (6). The first commercial airline to install the Maxson Whirlwind Oven as part of its own inflight feeding program was Pan American World Airways, which received delivery of its first ovens toward the end of 1945 (7). The oven was small and relatively light, provided a 400°F temperature, and contained a fan that assured an even heat distribution throughout. Each DC-4 and Constellation aircraft was equipped with two ovens, each of which could reconstitute six meals in about fifteen minutes, thus permitting meal service for the approximately 40 passengers, aboard to be completed within an hour. (Fig. 2)

The Strategic Air Command of the United States Air Force became interested in using precooked inflight meals in its B-36 long range heavy bombers in 1948 (5), and a B4 oven, a conduction type unit, was developed for this purpose. During the same period, the application of microwave energy to the cooking of food was being studied by Proctor and Goldblith at the Massachusetts Institute of Technology (8), using a radar oven manufactured by the Raytheon Manufacturing Company, and equipped with a magnetron tube generating microwaves at a frequency of approximately 3000 megacycles with a power input of 2000 watts to the food. These initial studies, however, were concerned with cooking raw foods rather than reheating prepared foods. It is in this latter area that microwave ovens have found their widest food service application in recent years.

With the exception of the W.L. Maxson Company, having packed its first commercial frozen precooked dinners, consisting of meat, vegetable, and potatoes on an especially treated heat resistant blue plate (9), the aluminum tray has dominated the precooked frozen meal scene almost since the beginning. Possibly the first published specification written by an institutional mass feeder for precooked frozen meals was the purchase description issued by the Quartermaster Food and Container Institute in November 1952, covering the procurement of tray and casserole type meals by the United States Air Force (5). On 11 October 1956, Military Specification MIL-M-13966A was issued to describe, "Meal, Precooked, Frozen."

IV. COMMERCIAL DEVELOPMENTS

Pioneering the utilization of precooked frozen foods to supply the needs of restaurants, and one of the earliest developers of a truly modern food service system, was Lyons Limited

FIGURE 2. *Pan American World Airways cabin attendant loading Maxson frozen meals into Whirlwind Oven, and serving heated meals to passengers.* (From The Maxsonite, April 1946)

in the United Kingdom. This company developed the "slab pack" method. In this process, cooked products were frozen in shallow aluminum pans holding about 8 portions each, after which they were removed from the pan and wrapped in wax paper for storage and shipment. At the point of usage, aluminum pans of the same dimensions used for freezing were used for reheating (10). Thus, Lyons was able to supply their fifty London area restaurants with precooked frozen foods out of one central commissary. This method has been used effectively in the United Kingdom since, and is the basis for the "cook-freeze system" developed by Clew and his coworkers at the University of Leeds for hospital and school feeding purposes. In the United States, the slab pack was first exploited by ARA, a major in-plant feeder, and food packed by this method was produced by Seabrook Farms in the 1950's (11).

In reviewing the early history of modern food service systems one may find perhaps three failures for every successful experiment. This is not to say that the concepts used in the systems that failed were not valid concepts. In most instances, however, it can readily be seen that the failures arose because a true systems approach was not used in the design of these systems. In a systems approach, one must carefully investigate every component of the system or subsystem. These subsystems include the food, packaging, equipment for preparation and packaging, distribution, reheating (if required), service, handling methods, training programs, and management information systems. Credit must be given to the people who had the courage to experiment to lay the groundwork for the successes that are now taken for granted!

If systems that failed are cited, it is not to be critical, but rather to give their originators due recognition for their willingness to pioneer when odds were against them, because of lagging technology or insufficient management commitment. The Rock Island Railroad, for example, carried out extensive tests using precooked frozen foods that were successful from a cost standpoint, but failed because of the difficulty in getting the frozen food properly heated for rapid service. Also in the early 1950s, the Pennsylvania Railroad acquired specially designed dining cars equipped with microwave ovens to reheat chilled, precooked foods, in buffet type service (10). Beginning in 1952, the Kaiser Foundation hospitals in California, began to experiment with a centralized tray service operation using insulated containers for transport to the wards (12). The success of this test led to a desire to centralize hot food preparation in one location for the hospital group, freezing the meals for storage, and shipment to the hospitals. Because conventional ovens did not satisfactorily reconstitute the hot meals, microwave reheating was investigated and, in November 1955, the first full scale food service operation using micro-

wave ovens began in a 90-bed Kaiser Foundation Hospital in Wal-
nut Creek, California. Two Raytheon Model 1161A, a two magnetron unit with a power output of 1500 watts at 2450 megacycles, were used. By 1963, the system was in use in five of the
12 Kaiser Foundation hospitals (13).

Starting in 1956, the Swedish Board of Education began to
experiment with the use of precooked, preportioned frozen
foods in school feeding (14). In the initial experiments, carried out in the Uppsala and Huddinge School Districts, food
was prepared in a school with a fairly large kitchen and quick
frozen for use in a satellite. A week's food supply was shipped at a time and stored in a freezer at the receiving school.
Initially, the reheating of the food was done in an oven on top
of a range or in a bainmarie, but in the spring of 1957, the
Swedish "Elektro Helios" Oven, built by Aktiebolaget Elektro
Helios of Stockholm, was successfully introduced into the program. This unit was the first roll-in type, forced hot air
convection oven that has now become commonplace as a reconstitution device in schools throughout the world that are operating a frozen food system. Almost from the beginning, the Swedish Board of Education was concerned about the possible effects of this type of handling on the nutritive value of the
food served. The Board was reassured when it determined that
the vitamin C loss in frozen food was no greater than under ordinary conditions of food preparation in large kitchens, where
the food is held hot in bulk. Later in this same program, the
schools began to be supplied with commercially packed frozen
foods.

In 1957, also working with Pan American World Airways, the
Temperature Engineering Corporation of Riverton, New Jersey,
developed a quartz infrared oven intended for use in new jet
aircraft on order. The oven heated by conduction on the bottom, and by infrared rays on top (7). The initial premise was
that the oven would be capable of reconstituting frozen foods
in seven minutes as indeed it could with certain steaks and
broiled meats. However, in retrospect, it would appear that a
fundamental principle in the development of a food service system based upon convenience food had been overlooked, that being
the relationship of product formulation to mode of reconstitution. The infrared heating caused vegetables to burn and sauces to dry out when the standard packs which Pan American had
developed for use in their ovens, were heated in the infrared
units.

The 1950s were also the period during which various food
processors became interested in the development of convenience
foods for food service systems. As early as 1955, the Research
Department of Swift and Company carried out studies on the reheating of precooked frozen foods, and in 1959, Wilson & Company introduced its "Menu-pak" line of pouch-packed, precooked,

frozen institutional entrees. In conjunction with this development, the Electronics Corporation of America and Chrysler
Zeder Inc., developed special equipment to reconstitute pouch-
packed products (15). This unit, the model 12 "Electronic Chef
Conveyor," a tunnel type unit equipped with a conveyor and an
infrared heat source, was stated to have a throughput of 240
pouches per hour. Another reconstitution device manufactured
by the same company, the Model 4C "Electronic Chef Counter U-
nit", was a device somewhat resembling a waffle iron, containing two sections, each capable of holding a single serving
pouch and heating it independently of the other. The heating
elements were thermostatically controlled. The average heating
time was stated to be two to four minutes.

In 1956, Luchow's Restaurant in New York began to pack its
gourmet "Round-the World"dinners in boil-in-bag plastic pouches for retail sale (16). By 1959, the availability of the
boilable plastic bags and aluminum pouches prompted a number
of companies to introduce precooked frozen foods in individual
portion packs for food service usage. Following the lead of
Wilson and Seabrook, Armour & Co., launched its "Continental
Cuisine" in 1960 (17). This line, which consisted of gourmet
quality entrees, packed in divided two-compartment pouches(one
containing the entree, the other the accompaniment) was primarily intented for a la carte restaurant usage. (Fig. 3)

In 1960 also, the Morton Frozen Food Division of Continental Baking developed a line of individual portion and bulk-
packed entrees, vegetables and starches, packaged in rectangular high-density polyethylene trays with a heat-sealed polyester film cover. The choice of trays over pouches was based on
(1)greater ease of handling when hot as compared with pouches,
(2)ability to use individual container for vending units, (3)
use of trays as disposable dishes, (4)ability to use bulk size
containers as steam table pan inserts, (5) ability to reheat
packages directly in boiling water, steam, microwave, or readily transfer rectangular shape blocks to foil pan for heating
in infrared oven, and (6) relative ease of filling on production line. Unlike the Armour effort, the Morton line was aimed
at fast food operations such as lunch counters and inplant
feeding. To provide the customer the ability to select the
components of the meal, while preventing any food waste, the
individual portion packs of each entree, vegetable, and starch
were formulated to permit one step reheating from the frozen
state in a microwave oven. The concept was tested in five
lunch counters during a one month period in 1961, following a
one month study of the same lunch counters operating with the
same menus prepared on-premise. Using the frozen prepared
foods, lunch counter sales increased by nearly 5%, and it was
determined that the hot food preparation labor,that represented approximately 18.8% of the total labor cost when the stores

FIGURE 3. *Stuffed cabbage rolls with sweet and sour raisin sauce packed by Armour and Company as part of its "Continental Cuisine" line introduced in 1960. (Courtesy of Armour & Co.)*

were cooking on premises, could be eliminated. While it had been expected that labor costs should be reduced through the use of prepared foods a concurrent reduction of nearly 10% in food cost that was also recorded, came as a surprise. The research team attributed it to the reduction in food waste normally resulting from careless serving, spillage, improper handling, or pilferage and spoilage. (Fig.4)

To sum up, contrast these test findings:

	On premise entree preparation	*ChefLine* entrees	Difference
Labor Cost	36.6%	29.7%	-6.9%
Food Cost	41.1%	31.2%	-9.9%
Controllable Costs	6.8%	6.8%	no change
Cross Profit	15.5%	32.3%	+16.8%

FIGURE 4. Results of Morton Frozen Foods market test of "Chef Line" entrees and vegetables in lunch counter operations.

The high degree of consumer acceptance and the economic success of the test notwithstanding, the commercial marketing of the product line was not successful. The reason was simple: due to the high turnover of personnel in the lunch counter operations, it was impossible to maintain a training program to insure that all personnel handling those foods had been correctly instructed in their use and in the proper operation of the microwave ovens. As with many other instances of food service system failures, it was discovered too late that, without total management dedication and support, and without a commitment on the part of the organization to back the program with appropriate personnel training, no convenience food service system can succeed!

Following the 1950's, during which there seemed to be more failures than successes, came the decade of the sixties during which some highly successful systems were developed. Among the significant successes, one must cite the frozen food program of the New York City Board of Education, which started in 1962 and spawned many similar programs elsewhere. Notwithstanding the lack of success of a frozen food system at the Pollack Hospital in Jersey City, another hospital in the same state, the 221 Rahway Hospital, instituted a frozen food system based upon commercially prepared frozen foods and microwave reconstitution. In 1965, during its first year of operation using the system, labor costs at the Rahway Hospital were reduced by over $56,000. Over the years, the Rahway Hospital continued to perfect its frozen food system that is still in use today (18).

In the early 1960s too, the Dutch Pantry chain of restaurants, then consisting of 23 units ranging from Pennsylvania to Florida, developed a centralized food production system in which all the food served at the restaurants, with the exception of milk, lettuce, lemons, and tomatoes were shipped from the central commissary. Meats were either fully precooked, packed in plastic pouches and frozen, or portion cut raw and frozen. All mixes, condiments, sauces, and breads were shipped from the commissary. The net initial result of the system, was a reduction in food and labor cost of 5%. Labor cost, which was 30% when restaurants prepared their own food, dropped to 23%, and the combined food and labor costs totaled 595, or one point below the 60% target set by the chain when it began to develop the system (19).

Other restaurant chains, including Howard Johnsons, The Marriot Corporation, Mannings and Stouffer's established similarly successful programs tailored to their own needs.

V. THE SEARCH FOR AUTOMATION

Even as some organizations predicated their system upon the use of convenience foods, others looked to the use of automated food production equipment to increase worker productivity. The outstanding earliest example of a large scale food service operation that installed continuous food preparation equipment of the type normally used in food manufacturing, was the U.S. Naval Academy at Annapolis, which adopted a system called "Rapid Automatic Food Preparation Techniques" (RAFT), in Bancroft Hall, the midshipmen cafeteria. The goal was to prepare 4000 meals in 30 minutes with a maximum holding time of 45 minutes. This was achieved by utilizing equipment such as continuous infrared broiler, fryers, blanchers, steam kettles, elevators, pumps, and an ingredient room. The result of the RAFT system was that preservice preparation was reduced from 2 hours to 30 minutes. Manpower in the preparation area was reduced by 25 to 30 percent. Significantly, product area was reduced by 28% and travel distance by 75 %, and a need for 2000 square feet of new construction was eliminated. The initial annual labor savings was $ 137,000 (20).

Another system that received a good deal of publicity in the mid 1960s, was the American Machine and Foundry Company's "AMFare" system, which was a fully automated system to handle food ordering, preparation, and billing in a drive-in operation. The heart of this system was the Orbis Unit (ordering

ORBIS*
(2)

MIMS*
(3)

(6) HAMBURGER MACHINE

(7) ENTREE FRYER

The "AMFare System"—   How it works (see flow chart, left):
The orders from curb service or dining room (1) are placed with the
ORBIS* (Ordering and Billing System) operator (2) who confirms them
and relays the data through the MIMS* (Menu Item Memory System—3)
to the automatic check printer (4). MIMS distributes the orders to the
food machines (5–10) where they are prepared and moved by conveyors
(11) to the assembly area (12). The orders are then assembled, and
served.

FIGURE 5.   The American Machine & Foundry Company's "AMFare
System" (Reprinted from Food Technology, Vol. 20, No.5, p.77,
1966. Copyright © by Institute of Food Technologists)

and billing system). The customer phoned his order to an operator, seated at an Orbis Control Panel, who pressed the appropriate buttons on the unit. The control console actuated six menu-producing machines, each capable of preparing one or more of the items on the menu. The latter consisted of broiled hamburgers, cheeseburgers, fried shrimp, chicken, fish, other entrees, onion rings, potatoes, milk shakes, and carbonated beverages. The foods were freshly cooked, one portion at a time by the entirely mechanized system, and traveled down conveyors to an employee who assembled the order on the appropriate trays using the sales ticket printed by the Orbis Units. Unfortunately, the system was too costly for the type of operation for which it was intended. Furthermore, the sophistication of the equipment required a maintenance level that could not be provided in an ordinary drive-in restaurant (1).

VI. RECOGNITION OF THE SYSTEMS APPROACH

By the late 1960s, many food service systems were in operation or in the advanced planning stages. At long last there was general recognition that the design of a successful system requires the use of the systems approach, which mandates the careful identification of all of the relevant aspects that must successfully interface if a system is to function smoothly, achieve customer acceptance, and be economically viable. With this realization came the recognition that only an interdisciplinary team can successfully plan and execute a system study and implement its recommendations. Efforts were often successful because such teams were formed. Some new food service systems failed because they did not take into account all the technological, engineering, economic, and psychological aspects that must inevitably be addressed if success is to be achieved.

VII. REFERENCES

1. Livingston, G. E., *Food Technol. 20,* 76 (1966)
2. Dungan, A. and Lacey, S.,*Cornell Hotel Rest. Admin. Quart. 10,* 6 (1969)
3. Smith, R. S., Bustead, R. L., Prifti, J. K., and Chang, C. M., "An Evaluation of Selected Advanced High Production Feeding Systems," p. 1, U.S. Army Natick Laboratories, Natick, Mass. (1972)
4. Bard, B., "The School Lunchroom: Time of Trial." Wiley, New York (1968)

5. Robertson, E. L., in "Precooked Frozen Foods" (M. Bollman and M. S. Peterson, eds.) p. 4, Nat.Acad.Sci.,Washington D.C. (1955)

6. Tressler, D. K. and Evers, C. F., "The Freezing Preservation of Foods" p. 671, Avi Publishing Co., Westport, Connecticut (1947)

7. Parrott, P. J., *Cornell Hotel & Rest. Admin. Quart. 4*, 83, (1963)

8. Proctor, B. E., and Goldblith, S. A. *Food Technol., 2*, 95, (1948)

9. Williams, E. W. *Quick Frozen Foods 31*, (1), 49 (1968)

10. Logan, P. P., in "Precooked Frozen Foods" (Bollman, M. and Peterson, M. S., eds.) p. 7, Nat.Acad.Sci.,Washington D.C. (1955)

11. Nagel, J. J., "Food Processor Aid Restaurants", *The New York Times,* April 7 (1963)

12. Park, E. R. *Hospitals,* January 16 (1957)

13. Harrington, R. L. *Inplant Food Management,* February 1 (1963)

14. Landry, H. A. "A Survey of the Experimental Program Conducted by the Swedish Board of Education on the Use of Precooked, Preportioned Frozen Foods and its Effect on Kitchen Design, Labor, Space and Equipment Costs as Compared with the Conventional Method of Conducting a School Lunch Program" Board of Education, City of New York, New York, New York (1961)

15. Anon. "At Last! The Way to Heat Frozen Foods. The Electronic Chef," p. 4. Chrysler-Zeder, Inc. New York, New York (1959)

16. Anon. "Heat-in-Bag Industry Mobilizes for Major Expansion", *Food Processing,* May 23 (1961)

17. Anon. *Frozen Food Age,* July, 36A (1962)

18. Van Gemert, G. A., *Modern Hospital, 5,* 160 (1965)

19. Anon. *Quick Frozen Foods, 27,* (6), 109 (1965)

20. Anon. *Institutions, 56a,* (2), 61 (1965)

CHAPTER 2

PLANNING, STAFFING AND IMPLEMENTING THE SYSTEM STUDY

G. E. Livingston

I. INTRODUCTION

If one accepts the notion that institutional or commercial mass feeding is a "system", it appears logical to postulate that a systems approach must be taken in analyzing or developing food service systems. The success of the systems analysis and development efforts required will depend, to a large extent, on the thoroughness with which the project has been planned and the expertise of the project team members.

Before discussing the approach to be taken in planning a systems study,it is well to examine the elements that comprise a food service system. In any food service operation, large or small, there are two principal functions: *production* and *distribution* (Fig. 1). In a traditional restaurant, the kitchen is the site of the production function,and the dining room the site of the distribution function. In a multi-unit food service operation, production may remain on-site, if each serving unit has its own kitchen, or it may be centralized into a "central kitchen", "commissary" or "food preparation facility" with the serving units or satellites representing the distribution function.

In general terms, one can identify the three major functions of the *production* part of the system as being *procurement, preparation* and *transport*. The major parts of the *distribution* function consist of *receiving, holding,* (heating, if chilled or frozen foods are employed), *serving, warewashing* and *waste disposal*.

Procurement can be broken down into *purchasing, receiving* and *storing. Preparation,*depending upon the type of operation, may include *hot food, cold food, salad, dessert,baked goods* or even beverage preparation. The transport function, which in an ordinary cafeteria might simply consist of *filling* hot product into a tray or a pot and bringing it out to a steamtable, becomes,in the large systems, a fairly complex operation. It may

Copyright © 1979 by Academic Press, Inc.
All rights of reproduction in any form reserved
ISBN: 0-12-453150-4

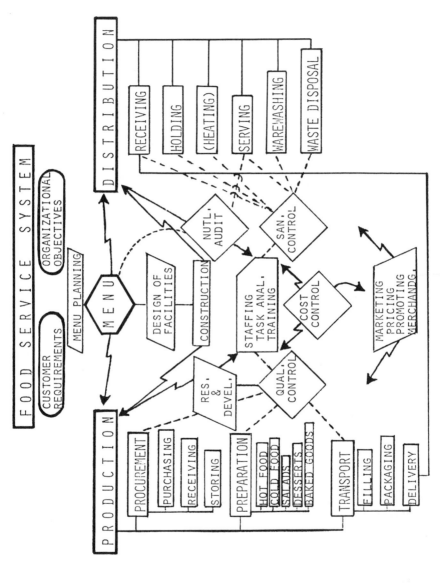

FIGURE 1. Elements of a food service system and their interrelationships to each other.

involve tray assembly lines, as in hospital or airline catering; *packaging* lines, where long life chilled foods or frozen
foods are involved; freezing, chilling and *delivery* under suitable temperature conditions, which may be hot, chilled or frozen. The delivered food is *received* at the serving end and a-
gain is *held* hot, cold or frozen. The *serving* of the food may
be a relatively uncomplicated operation, as in a cafeteria operation, or may be quite complex as in hospital patient feeding. Finally, *warewashing* and *waste disposal* must be considered
essential parts of the system. In elementary terms then, those
are the functional aspects of the food service system.

The question which one must ask at the outset is: "What
drives the system?" The answer is that any food service system
is driven by the *customer requirements* and the *organizational
objectives*. These *objectives* might include budgetary constraints in institutional operations, or desired sales and profit objectives in commercial operations. In either event, this
combination of *customer requirements* and *organizational objectives* is the basis for the planning of the *menu*. The *menu* is
indeed the critical focal point of all the activities in a food
service system. It will dictate what foods are produced, what
foods are distributed and how. It will govern the facilities
that are required, and thus will be reflected in the design of
facilities and their construction.

In turn, the *production* and *distribution* requirements will
determine the *staffing* that is required. The *staffing* should be
detailed by *analyzing the tasks* to be performed by each member
of the staff and in developing *training programs* that will insure that each member of the food service system is indeed performing the task that is expected of him in the most competent
manner possible. Naturally, whether it is identified as such or
not, there will be a *marketing* function involved in any food
service systems operation. While marketing may be more obvious
in commercial systems, it is equally as important in institutional systems. Institutional populations respond to food merchandising and promotion no less positively than do the customers of a commercial operation!

To control the entire food service system, management needs
additional sub-systems. *Cost control* is most critical for no
operation, whether for profit or non-profit, can operate very
long without it. Equally important, however, if the system is
indeed to be a successful one, are *quality control, sanitary
control* and *nutritional auditing* of the menu and the food being
offered. In nearly any large food service system today, there
will also be an identifiable *research and development* function,
for no major system can be or remain successful if it is not
continuously on the look-out for improved methods, improved
products, improved equipment and indeed improved systems. Because these various elements of the food service system have

requirements for different skills, and because of the many interfaces that are involved, it is imperative that systems be
analyzed and developed by interdisciplinary teams.

II. IDENTIFYING THE COMPONENTS OF AN EXISTING OR PROPOSED SYSTEM

If one understands the fact that every operational and management function involved in a food service system is a relevant entity within that system, it becomes possible to identify all of the system components and relate them to each
other. It is absolutely necessary to do so as a first step in
any systems analysis or development project. Naturally, one
must start with the functional aspects of the system as they
relate to each other in a chronological sequence. For example,
Figure 2 shows the stages of the cook-freeze system for school
meals (1). A more complete flow diagram would also show the
interrelationships of procurement, storage and distribution in
a proposed system, such as the system flow diagram prepared
for a central food preparation facility system for the U.S.
Army at Fort Lewis, Washington, illustrated in Figure 3 (2).

III. IDENTIFYING THE SYSTEMS ALTERNATIVES

In any project aimed at improving an existing food service
system or developing a new one, there are a number of logical
alternatives that suggest themselves to the project team.
Based upon the experience of the team members and their knowledge of the available spectrum of operational possibilities,
including those offered by modern food packaging, preservation
and equipment technologies, it is possible to eliminate, by
discussion, alternatives that, for one reason or another, do
not appear to respond in all respects to the requirements of
the system. Having done so, however, one is usually left with
several alternative possibilities which then must be seriously
evaluated, quantified and analyzed for their cost/benefit. For
example, in a study of a proposed central kitchen for a school
district in Florida (Fig. 4), two alternative systems were
identified which had to be fully analyzed in order to determine which would be more advantageous (3). The existing system included a number of schools that were "self-contained",
i.e. contained kitchens capable of preparing meals on premise.
Several high schools, however, had kitchens which supplied
their own needs and, in addition, prepared meals for shipment
to elementary schools which were their "satellites". The food

FIGURE 2. Stages of the cook-freeze system (Reprinted from "The Utilisation of the Cook-freeze System for School Meals", p.18, 1973. Copyright © by University of Leeds).

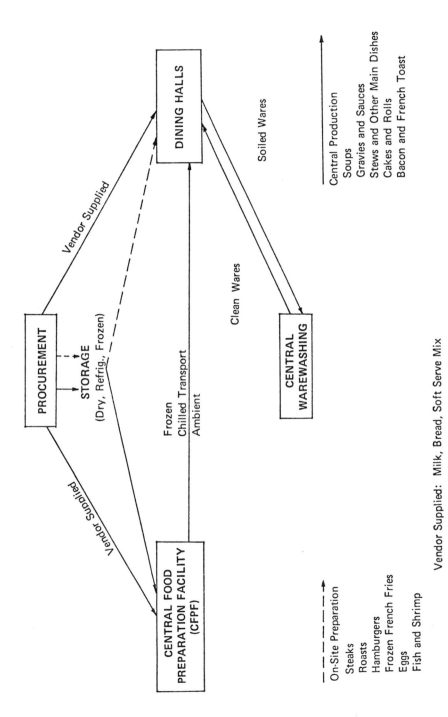

FIGURE 3. System flow diagram for a U.S. Army Central Food Preparation Facility System (2).

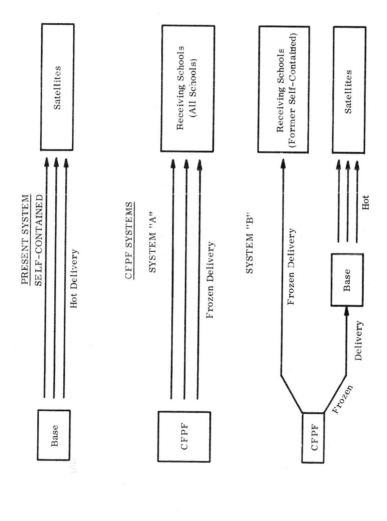

FIGURE 4. Food service system alternatives for a school district in Florida (3).

was shipped hot from the "base schools" to the satellites. Under a central food preparation facility system, one could seriously contemplate eliminating the role of the base school by shipping food from the central facility directly to all the schools. One could contemplate, just as realistically, shipping food from the central facility only to all of the former self-contained schools and to the former base schools, allowing the latter to store and reheat the frozen food and continue to ship it hot to their existing satellites. At a conceptual level, this possibility appeared attractive inasmuch as it would eliminate the need to provide the existing satellite with frozen food storage and heating capabilities.

In a food service system study in the mid 1960's, an international airline investigated the feasibility of a frozen meal system (Fig. 5). For a variety of reasons, which effectively precluded the possibility of the airline manufacturing its own frozen meals, the only system that could be compared with the existing fresh meal system was one involving the procurement of frozen meals made to the airline's specifications at the various stations which it operated in a number of countries. Thus, the system entailed a study of cost comparisons, on a station-by-station basis, when frozen meals were used versus fresh meals; quality evaluation by inflight passenger acceptance tests; and functional benefits accruing from the use of frozen meals (such as the reduction in wasted meals that occurs in a fresh meal system whenever extended departure delays take place and increased flexibility in provisioning aircraft). Naturally, the study also entailed the definition of galley equipment and inflight systems and these, in turn, required time-motion studies and the critical consideration of weight balance. On the other hand, the ground support system required for a frozen meal program involved the development of meal and packaging specifications, the sourcing of suppliers and the definition of storage and transport procedure (4).

IV. DEVELOPMENT OF A PROJECT PLANNING CHART

In recent years, it has become customary in the management of research and development projects to resort to the use of some form of "critical path analysis", "network analysis", or "PERT" (project evaluation and review technique) in planning the project. The analysis and design of food service systems are activities which lend themselves perfectly well to this type of planning.

The first step in developing any kind of planning chart is to correctly identify the steps that will need to be taken and the sequence in which they must take place. For example,

OBJECTIVES:

- Comparison of present fresh meal method versus a frozen meal system:
    1. *Costs*
    2. *Quality (inflight tests)*
    3. *Functional benefits (waste reduction, increased flexibility)*

For such a comparison, the information on the existing system is available, but that on the frozen meal system must be gathered.

- Functional requirements for a TOTAL inflight frozen meal system:
    1. *Galley equipment and system (freezer, ovens, time-motion studies, weight balance)*
    2. *Ground support system (meal and packaging specifications, suppliers, storage and transport)*

SUMMARY RESULTS OF FEASIBILITY STUDY:

- A TOTAL inflight frozen meal system is NOT ADVISABLE at this time because:
    1. *Cost of converting existing galleys is considerable*
    2. *Increase needed in weight of galley is not acceptable for present aircraft*

RECOMMENDATION:

- A PARTIAL system is ADVISABLE to reduce costs in certain stations

IMPLEMENTATION:

- Management approval of use of frozen meals in ground stations:
    . *Designation of stations to be converted*
- Design of flight kitchen facilities:
    . *Selection of high-speed heating equipment to meet station logistical requirement; kitchen layouts*
- Design of Menu:
    . *Meal formulations; specifications*
- Meal procurement:
    . *Supplier contacts; sample evaluation; plant inspections; bids; contracts*
- Continuing functions:
    . *Quality assurance procedures; R&D for menu improvement*

FIGURE 5. System analysis, design and implementation of a a frozen meal system for an international airline (Reprinted from Food Technology, Vol. 22, No. 1, p. 36, 1968. Copyright © by Institute of Food Technologists).

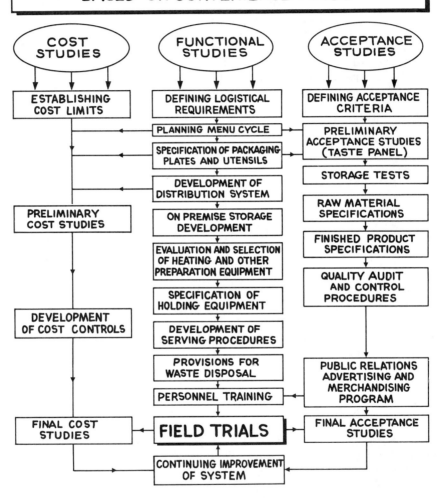

FIGURE 6. Flow diagram for the development of food service systems based on the utilization of convenience foods.

Fig. 6 shows the areas of concern in the development of a food service system utilizing convenience foods. It will be noted that three major areas of consideration are involved: *cost studies, functional studies* and *acceptance studies*. In all three of these areas it is first necessary to define the management goals, i.e. *cost limits, logistical requirements* and *acceptance criteria*. Having done so, one must proceed to plan the *menu* which, in most institutional mass feeding systems is, in fact, a menu cycle. A triple track approach is followed which provides, at all stages of development, the assurance that the steps being contemplated are compatible with the cost limitations and acceptance requirements. It will be noted that all relevant aspects of the system are addressed in this scheme. To attempt to develop a convenience food system without considering each of the areas shown would, most likely, result in an unsuccessful system.

A critical path analysis for the cost study of alternative school food service systems mentioned above is shown in Figure 7. Having defined the *system alternatives* (Fig. 4), one must then proceed to develop the *menu cycle* which will be used in developing all the other requirements. The main track of the study (shown as the center track) requires inputs based upon the study of the *existing system* as well as the analysis of proposed *alternative systems*. From the present system, one must know the current *enrollment* and the rate of school age population growth, in order to project enrollment for the reference year upon which the entire study will be predicated. One must know the *facilities* that are in existence and those that are planned. One must ascertain the *cost of the food* and the *procurement methods* used. One must determine the *staffing* and all of the *direct* and *indirect labor costs* and finally, one must determine all of the *indirect costs* which, in the case of school operations, are not necessarily readily obtained (because the existing cost accounting system may not be allocating to food service its share of overhead expenses such as administration, purchasing, maintenance, utilities, etc).

It is prudent to subject the proposed menu cycle to a computerized *nutritional audit* to insure, as in this particular case, that each meal supplies one third of the recommended daily allowances of essential nutrients. (The original menu cycle proposed by the school district dietitian in this project did not meet this target and the menu therefore had to be revised. See Chapter 21). Using the revised menu as the basis then for all other calculations, it is possible to project the *food costs* for the reference year using current rate of increase in the consumer price index to allow for inflationary increases. In the meantime, the major *systems decisions* must be made. Should the prepared food be *packaged* in *individual meals* or in *bulk packs?* Should they be *transported hot,*

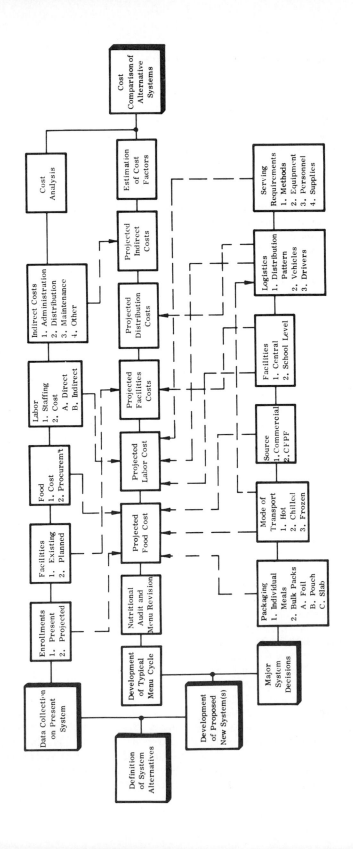

FIGURE 7. Flow diagram for cost comparison of alternative school food service systems (3).

chilled or *frozen?* If frozen bulk packs are selected, should they be in aluminum *foil* half-size steam table pans, in *pouches* or in *slabs?* Should they be secured from outside *commercial* sources or made in a *central food preparation facility* operated by the school district? Once the packaging, shipping mode and source decisions have been made, one can estimate the *packaging costs, shipping costs* and *labor costs* that are involved. One can also plan the *facilities* which are required for the manufacturing of the meals and the shipping, receiving, storing and serving of the meals in the *schools.* The *logistical* aspects of distribution, such as the number of vehicles, the routes that they will take, the distances involved, the number of drivers required and the cost of operating the vehicles, must all be included in projecting the *distribution costs.* At the level of the *schools,* the *serving methods, equipment, personnel* and *supplies* required must be identified, costed and fed into the projections. Thus, with *food, labor, facilities, distribution* and *indirect costs* considered, one can now estimate the costs under the alternative proposed systems and compare these with the costs projected under the present system if it is continued into the same reference year. The cost comparison of the alternative systems then provides a suitable basis for decision-making.

The actual critical path analysis for the Florida study is shown in Figure 8. It will be noted that the decision was made to use frozen bulk packs, prepared in a central food preparation food facility, and the study costed out the systems A and B previously defined (Fig. 4). It may be interesting to note, as shown in Table I, that in this particular instance neither System A nor System B was projected to generate a savings over the existing system. With a cost per meal of 92¢ for the existing system, System A was costed out at $ 1.36 and System B at $ 1.32. The reason is readily evident. The only area in which any significant saving could be generated through the introduction of the new systems based on centralized food preparation is in the direct labor. This savings must therefore be large enough to offset all the increased costs associated with packaging, distribution, depreciation of facilities, etc, if a net savings is to occur. Since the existing system was already providing 11.77 meals per man hour, and Systems A and B could only raise this to 12.85 and 13.30 meals per man hour respectively, neither one of the proposed alternatives could improve the effectiveness of the existing system sufficiently to generate an overall savings.

In developing a project chart for the systems study, one must do more than merely identify the tasks to be performed and the sequence in which they are to be performed. One must determine also which task(s) and event(s) will serve as a limiting factor(s) and will therefore dictate the minimum dura-

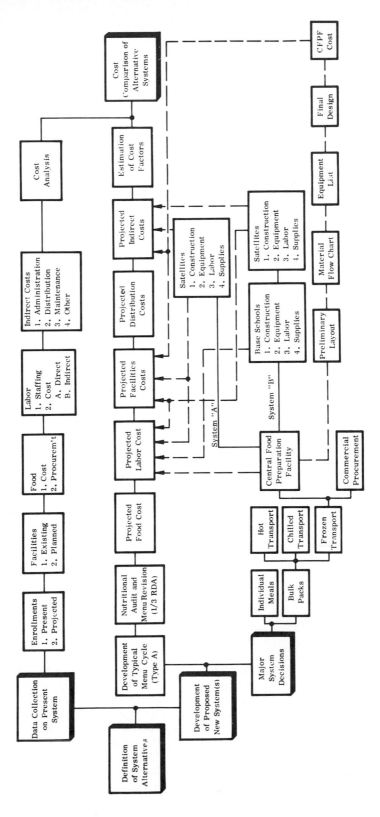

FIGURE 8. Flow diagram for critical path analysis of study of alternative food service systems for a school district (3).

TABLE I. *Cost Comparison of Alternative Systems of Food Service for a School District in Florida, Projected for the Year 1974 – 1975, Based on 3,409,740 Meals per Year (3).*

COST ITEMS	PRESENT SYSTEM		SYSTEM A		SYSTEM B	
	Cost per Year	Cost per Meal	Cost per Year	Cost per Meal	Cost per Year	Cost per Meal
FOOD COST	$1,681,002	$0.4930	$1,681,002	$0.4930	$1,681,002	$0.4930
Non-Food Supplies						
Packaging	-----		88,653		88,653	
Disposables	51,092		98,882		98,882	
Cleaning Supplies	13,103		13,103		13,103	
TOTAL FOOD & SUPPLIES:	$1,745,197	$0.5118 (55.6%)	$1,881,641	$0.5518 (40.6%)	$1,831,641	$0.5518 (41.8%)
LABOR COST						
Direct Labor						
CFPF	-----		$ 202,332		$ 202,332	
Schools	$ 733,122		425,687		361,835	
Distribution	-----		14,164		14,164	
Total Direct Labor	$ 733,122		$ 642,183		$ 578,331	
Indirect Labor						
CFPF	-----		$ 108,794		$ 108,794	
District Office	41,176		4?,176		41,176	
Distribution	7,082		7,082		7,082	
Maintenance	9,350		9,350		9,350	
Total Indirect Labor	$ 57,608		$ 166,403		$ 166,403	
TOTAL LABOR COSTS:	$ 790,730	$0.2313 (25.2%)	$ 808,585	$0.2371 (17.5%)	$ 744,734	$0.2184 (16.6%)
INDIRECT COSTS						
Utilities	$ 55,238		$ 76,667		$ 76,667	
Insurance & Empl. Benef.	48,383		75,869		74,798	
Other	69,559		69,559		69,559	
Depreciation	171,249		573,019		557,481	
Vehicle Operation	8,028		8,753		14,034	
Interest	94,454		427,203		404,226	
Repayment of Bonds	157,424		712,005		673,710	
TOTAL INDIRECT COSTS:	$ 604,339	$0.1772 (19.2%)	$1,943,075	$0.5698 (41.9%)	$1,870,474	$0.5485 (41.6%)
TOTAL COSTS:	$3,140,266	$0.9209	$4,633,301	$1.3587	$4,496,849	$1.3187
System Effectiveness:	11.77 Meals/Man-hour		12.85 Meals/Man-hour		13.30 Meals/Man-hour	

tion of the entire project. In the relatively simple study, of the hospital project in Figure 9, a five month time frame was sufficient to proceed from the initial conference to the delivery of equipment specifications, drawings and schedule to the architect.

Glew and his co-workers have illustrated the complexity of planning a school system (1) operating under the "cook/freeze" system (Fig. 10) and a hospital system (5) operating under the same program (Fig. 11). In network analysis, it is the practice to indicate the earliest likely completion date and latest possible completion date for every event that must take place. This permits the proper sequencing of intermediate steps, review and decision-making in order to meet the targeted completion date. Obviously, considerable thought and effort must go into the make-up of the planning chart if it is to serve as the project management tool which it is intended to be. Above all, it must be based on realism, and sufficient discipline must exist among the team members to abide by the projected timetable.

V. STAFFING THE SYSTEMS STUDY

It has already been pointed out that a systems analysis is an interdisciplinary effort. One should therefore ask: "what are the disciplines required?" At the very least, one would need a "food expert" a "cost expert" and an "engineering expert". The landmark New York City School Lunch Frozen Meal Study in the early 1960's (see Chapter 24) was carried out with just such a three man team and over a decade has elapsed since its successful completion and implementation. Today, however, it is doubtful that such a significant study would be carried out with only a food service expert at the helm, backed by a cost analyst and an engineer. In addition to experience in food service operation, the team must include expertise in food and packaging technology; in nutrition; in microbiology; in menu planning; in food facilities design; and in management systems and industrial engineering.

VI. MANAGEMENT COMMITMENT

It seems almost superfluous to say that a systems study should not be undertaken unless there is a commitment on the part of management to accept the findings of the study and implement the recommendations whose functional or cost effectiveness have been validated by the study. Without management

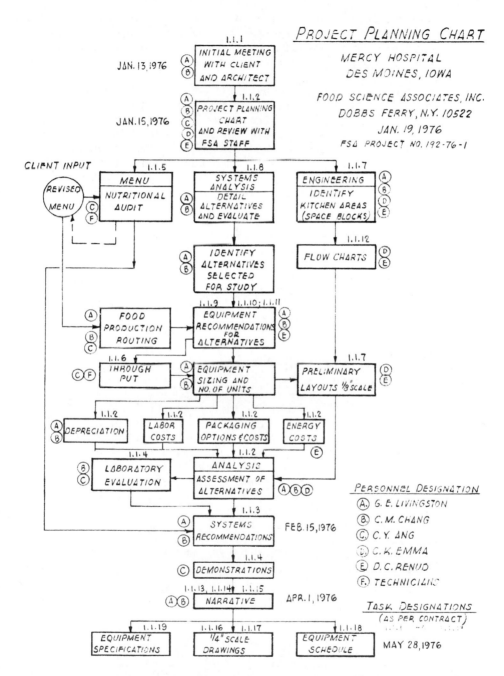

FIGURE 9. Project planning chart for design of food service system and facilities for a 500 bed hospital.

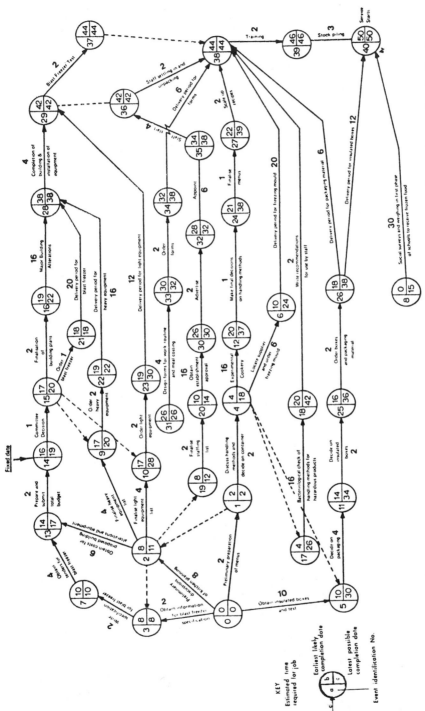

FIGURE 10. Network analysis for the planning, installation and commissioning of a school food service production unit (Reprinted from "The Utilization of the Cook-freeze System for School Meals", p.19, 1973. Copyright © by University of Leeds).

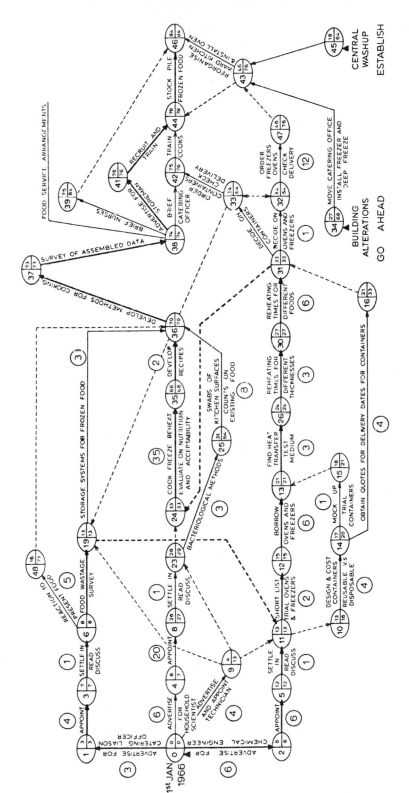

FIGURE 11. Critical path network for design and implementation of a hospital cook-freeze system (5).

backing of food service systems employing new techniques, e-
quipment or concepts, there can be no real hope for ultimate
success. There must be *a priori,* a willingness to "make the
system work", once the decision has been made to opt for the
alternative selected.

A. *Review Team*

A management review team to provide liaison with the project management should be set up from the onset. This liaison
group should be kept fully informed by the project team so
that the conclusions reached by the project team will appear
as inescapably valid to the liaison committee members as they
did to the project team members. Full, complete and enthusiastic concurrence in the findings and recommendations on the
part of the members of the liaison committee is essential if
one is to gain management support and commitment for the implementation of the project.

B. *Pilot Testing*

All food service systems studies should include a provision for pilot testing the recommended alternative. Pilot
tests are costly, cumbersome and time-consuming and it may be
very tempting to decide to proceed with implementation without
one. The annals of food service history are replete with examples of systems that have failed because they were not properly pilot-tested before being implemented!

C. *Training and Motivation*

Along with the pilot testing, there must be a willingness
to provide the training necessary to the personnel that will
operate the new system. In many instances, new systems are
predicated upon the use of convenience foods and new equipment. There is a natural reticence on the part of persons to
change old habits, but if a system is to succeed in fact as
well as on paper, it can only do so if it is supported by
the full and enthusiastic cooperation of every individual involved, from the top administrator to the lowliest dishwasher. Proper task analysis, training and motivation are
critical and they must be built into the project development.

D. *Laboratory Control*

Frequently,modern food service systems require a degree of
technical attention and laboratory control previously unknown
in the food service industry. The need for nutritional audits,
for microbiological audits,for the development and application

of quality control programs, must be identified early in the study and incorporated into the implementation plan.

E. *Management Continuity*

It is imperative that continuity be provided in terms of strong leadership as the project proceeds from the research phase into the pilot phase, and then into the implementation phase. Many projects,that were properly researched and tested, later failed because of a change in management which broke the continuity and robbed the project of the strong and committed leadership it required for successful implementation. On the other hand,in nearly all instances where projects did succeed, one will usually find the element of continuity in the form of one or more committed individuals who saw the project from the research phase through to its fruitful conclusion!

VII. REFERENCES

1. Millross, J., Specht, A., Holdsworth, K. and Clew, G. "The Utilization of the Cook-Freeze Catering System for School Meals", Univ. of Leeds, Leeds, United Kingdom (1973)
2. Bustead, R. L., Byrne, R., Chang, C. M., Cramer, R. W., Fennema, R., Frey, A. E., Hertweck, G., Leitch, D. P., Livingston, E. G., Prifti and Smith, R. S. "A Proposed Modern Food Service System for Fort Lewis, Washington" *Tech. Rep. 73-10-OR/SA,* U.S. Army Natick Lab., Natick, Massachusetts (1972)
3. Res. & Dev. Staff, Project ANSER "Five Country Management Improvement Project. Program Element 3. Facilities Alternative Planning" Project ANSER, Volusia County School Dist., Deland, Florida (1974)
4. Livingston, G. E. *Food Technol. 22,* 33 (1968)
5. Staff, Univ. of Leeds Catering Res. Unit "An Experiment in Hospital Catering Using the Cook/Freeze System", Univ. of Leeds, Leeds, United Kingdom (1970)

CHAPTER 3

IDENTIFICATION AND DEFINITION OF COST FACTORS

Charlotte M. Chang

I. INTRODUCTION

An analysis of systems alternatives for a food service system, whether commercial or institutional, single facility or multi unit, on premise production or central production with satellite distribution, will reveal relative merits (i.e. positive attributes) and disadvantages of the alternatives under consideration. However, unless a system alternative is also shown to be cost effective both in the long term, i.e. allowing for an inflated economy, as well as in the near term, it is not likely that such an alternative will be acceptable. For this reason, as well as from the standpoint of good business management, it is important to identify and quantify all costs that are fully or proportionally attributable to the food service system.

It should be obvious that cost factors involved in a food service operation are numerous and in operations where food service is ancillary to the main objective, such as health care, education or transportation, not necessarily easy either to identify or determine. A step wise evaluation of the components of the system, whether existing or contemplated, should reveal areas requiring data acquisition. Data collection is greatly facilitated through the development of detailed questionnaires. These questionnaires should be structured so as to generate data required for the summary report which will permit the economic analysis of the system alternatives to be carried out. Such a questionnaire for a district level school lunch program is shown in Table I. Data collected can be analysed using a computer in many situations in which the scope of the project justifies the costs of programming and computer time.

Cost factors will vary with the sector of the food service industry in which the system operates. The principal difference between a cost analysis in the commercial food service

Copyright © 1979 by Academic Press, Inc.
All rights of reproduction in any form reserved
ISBN: 0-12-453150-4

TABLE I. Data Collection Questionnaire
for a School District

I. *School Food Service Operating Fund*

A. Evaluation of Program Worth
   in Relation to Operating
   Fund as of _____
                          (Date)
   Cash Balance $_____
   (Verify Bank Statements)
   (Plus) Ending
     Inventory $_____
   (Plus) Re-
     ceivables $_____
   (Less) Pay-
     ables $_____
     Program Worth $_____

B. Expenditures and Fund Use
   (From School Food Service
   Operating Funds Only *- Do*
   Not Include the Value of
   USDA Donated Commodities)

   Beginning Food
     Inventory $_____
   (Plus) Expenditures
     for Food $_____
   (Less) Ending Food
     Inventory $_____
       Food Used $_____

B. *(Cont'd.)*
   Beginning Other
     Inventory $_____
   (Plus) Expenditures
     for Other $_____
   (Less) Ending Other
     Inventory $_____
       Other Used $_____

   Expenditures for
     Labor $_____
   (Plus) Labor
     Incurred But Not
     Yet Paid $_____
   (Less) Labor Paid
     This Period For
     Services Performed
     in Previous
     Period $_____
       Labor Cost
       This
       Period $_____
   (Less) Previous
     Period's Pay-
     ables Paid This
     Period (Food and
     Other) $_____
   (Plus) This Period's
     Payables (Food
     and Other) $_____
       TOTAL OF (B) -
       Fund Use During
       Period $_____

C. Average Monthly Expenditures $ _____
   (Derive by dividing the total
   days in operation into "B"
   above the then multiplying
   that number by 22)

TABLE I.   Data Collection Questionnaire for a
           School District (cont'd)

II. Income Statement

	Milk	Breakfast	Lunch	Other
A. Income - Children	$	$	$	$
B. Income - Reimbursement				
C. Other Income				
D. Total	$	$	$	$

III. Commodity Utilization

A. Value on hand beginning of period $_____

B. Received during period   _____

C. Ending inventory   _____

D. Used ("A" + "B" - "C")   _____

IV. Indirect Costs

(Contribution from Tax or Other Funds to Operate and Support
School Food Service Programs)

A. Utilities (food service costs only, estimate - prorate as
   needed)

                                                    Total
   1. Fuel, hot water, heat and cooling $_____
   2. Electricity - light kitchens, dining
        rooms and power   _____
   3. Water and sewage, dishwashing and
        other kitchen and dining room usage   _____
   4. Garbage and trash   _____
   5. Telephone   _____
   6. Other (specify)   _____

B. Insurance and Employee Benefits

   1. Direct Labor Payments $_____
   2. Hospitalization and Life Plans   _____
   3. Workmen's Compensation   _____
   4. Liability Insurance   _____
   5. Other insurance charges   _____
   6. Terminal pay   _____
   7. Vacation pay   _____
   8. In-service training   _____
   9. Retirement fund matching   _____
  10. Other (specify)   _____

TABLE I.   Data Collection Questionnaire for a
           School District (cont'd)

C. Food Service Supervision (District Wide)

1. Salaries $_____
2. Travel   _____
3. Consultant Services   _____
4. Other (specify) teacher and teacher
   aid supervision of children during lunch   _____

D. Other Administrative Costs - Prorated to Food Service
   Department

1. Purchasing - Food $_____
2. Purchasing - Equipment   _____
3. Personnel Administration   _____
4. Quality Control and Inventory Control   _____
5. Other (specify)   _____

E. Other District-Wide Services

1. Linen $_____
2. Pest Control   _____
3. Armored Car   _____
4. Commodity Delivery   _____
5. Commodity Storage   _____
6. Food Warehousing   _____
7. Equipment Repair and Service   _____
8. Janitorial Services   _____
9. Satellite (transporting) Costs   _____
10. Computer Services   _____
11. Food Service Accounting   _____
12. Food Service Payroll Processing   _____
13. Annual Audit Costs   _____
14. Other (specify)   _____

F. Depreciation for Equipment Replacement (10 years at
   10 % per Annum) $_____

G. Depreciation for New Equipment (10 years at 10 % per
   Annum)   _____

H. Rentals (Legit. as per Federal Regulations) _____

I. Printing   _____

*TABLE I.   Data Collection Questionnaire for a
School District (Cont'd)*

J. *Other (List)*

_____ $_____

_____   _____

_____   _____

K. *Total of IV (Indirect Costs)* $_____

V. *Lunch per Meal Calculations*

A. *Total of I.B. (Page 1) and IV. K.* $_____
                                    Rates Per Meal

B. *Deducts for Other Programs*

    1. *Cost of Special Milk Pro-
       gram Milk*   _____ $_____

    2. *Cost of Breakfast - Food*   _____   _____

    3. *Cost of Breakfast - Labor*   _____   _____

    4. *Cost of Breakfast - Other*   _____   _____

    5. *All Other Meal Costs,
       Including A La Carte and
       Excluding Lunch*   _____

    6. *ECE and Other Section 13
       Programs*   _____

          Total of "B" $_____

C. *Cost Per Lunch   "A" - "B" $ _____
   Divided by _____Lunches = _____ ¢ Per Lunch
          Number   (Including Adult)*

VI. *Sale Prices Charged*
(Most Recent)

	Full Price	*Reduced Price*	*Adult*
Lunch			
Breakfast			
Milk			

        *Signed_____
              (Name and Title of Person
              Completing Report)
       Date_____*

sector and the institutional sector is the fact that in the
commercial sector, all costs associated with the operation
will generally be chargeable to the food service systems,
while in the institutional sector, many of the overhead costs
are not routinely broken out between the primary functions of
the operations and its food service. Under these circumstances, the systems analyst will be required to search out
all relevant indirect and overhead costs and estimate the
fraction of each to be charged to food service.

A. Fixed Costs and Variable Costs

One way to analyze costs is to separate them into two
broad categories: *fixed* and *variable*. *Fixed Costs* are those
that do not vary with output. These include interest on capital, rental expense (plant and equipment), some taxes, salaries of non-dispensable employees, etc. *Variable costs* are
those which change as output changes. These include such
things as raw material costs, depreciation of equipment, the
variable portion of utility charges, and direct labor costs.
It should be noted that while all of the above cost factors
apply to food service systems, each food service situation is
unique in terms of which of these costs factors more significantly impact on system alternatives. In some situations
these cost factors may be those associated with labor, in other situations they may be those associated with packaging
forms, and in some instances one system may be more favorable
in terms of food cost than another.

B. Institutional Food Service Systems

When analyzing costs for institutional food service in the
evaluation of system alternatives it is important to determine
all the costs for these operations. The method of accounting,
especially in non-profit making operations, does not always
make these costs readily apparent since profit is not an overriding motivation, and food service is often only of secondary importance in the overall scope of operations. Frequently, there are separate budgets for food and labor which
can make calculation of total meal cost cumbersome. Depreciation of shared facilities and/or equipment, amortization of
capital outlay, interest expenses to the system, as well as
other allocated expenses must be charged to food service. System analysts in these organizations most likely have responsibilities of higher priority than to extract all relevant
costs, including the peripheral ones which, contribute to the
total meal cost. Remarkable as it may seem, some non-profit
institutions do not in fact, know the true and complete costs
of their meals. However in carrying out an analysis of al-

ternative food service systems, it may be possible to focus only on those factors that are likely to affect costs and, while accurately determining cost differences between system alternatives for the purpose of decision making, to ignore the total costs. For example, a school food service system was analyzed in which several system alternatives were being compared with the present system, one which combined onsite preparation and service with some centralized hot food preparation and transportation to satellite schools. The systems analysis showed that the present system was very cost effective from a labor standpoint and any new system would have to be considerably less labor intensive to be more cost effective. When labor requirements of the new system were compared with those of the present system, only a slight labor cost benefit could be derived in going to one of the system alternatives, i.e. centralized food production. The anticipated labor saving was insufficient to offset the capital outlay that would be required to construct a new facility to implement the new system. The results of this analysis were apparent at the point where it was determined that no significant labor savings could be achieved, and a total systems analysis was, in fact, not required for decision making.

Although one can, at times, limit the study to certain cost aspects one should never, however, shortcut the cost analysis. All costs required should be documented and assumptions made in deriving them clearly spelled out. Only then can one thoroughly evaluate the proposed system alternatives.

C. Commercial Food Service System

As opposed to institutional operations, food service is the principal activity of commercial food service organizations. Thus all costs can usually be attributed to the food service system under study or allocated to a particular system if only one of the organization's systems is being studied. In addition to all the cost factors that are common to both industry sectors, the commercial operations must also consider sales, marketing, and other costs that are necessary in advertising, promoting and selling the concept and/or the establishment to the consumer.

Marketing departments for commercial food operations generally exist at the corporate and/or headquarters level. Their functions usually include advertising and promotion. These departments generally have separate budgets to cover radio, TV or print advertising special, promotions, etc. In franchised operations, cooperative advertising may be based on a set percentage of the unit sales.

Sales costs, where applicable, may include both administrative costs and direct labor. Sales departments for commercial food management companies may include national and regional locations. Sales cost may include salemen's salaries, office overhead and transportation expenses, and in many cases also, bonuses or benefits from sales incentive programs.

Some commercial operations may also pay various fees such as commissions, finder's fees, etc., which must then also be appropriately charged to the food service system.

Multi-unit food operations such as those represented by the fast food chains generally have to allocate indirect expenses at several levels: unit, regional, and national (or international). A regional office would assume responsibility for the units within its area. In making a decision regarding a change at the unit level it is necessary to prorate the regional and headquarter costs to each unit before the impact of the proposed change on any one unit can be assessed.

II. DATA COLLECTION FOR A FOOD SERVICE SYSTEMS ANALYSIS

The following procedural sequence can serve as a guideline for cost data gathering and analysis:

A. *Preliminary Data*

1. Environment. The first step in gathering cost data is to identify and define relevant system requirements in terms of volume of meals to be prepared and served and general conditions of meal service. For example:

a) number of meals per day
b) on premise or satellite service
c) types of meal
d) cafeteria or full service
e) existing facility or new facility to be constructed

2. Reference Period. Establishment of the reference period for the study, for purposes of projecting costs, production volumes, meal usage, etc.

B. *Menu Analysis*

The menu affects all phases of a food service system and should be the starting point for the systems analysis rather than a subject to be addressed after all other elements of the system have been studied. On the menu rest the nutritional characteristics of the system, purchasing patterns, food costs, etc. The state of the art technology for menu analysis by computer makes possible the generation of data quickly and thoroughly and allows an on-going update and analysis.

In institutional food service systems (i.e. hospitals, schools, prisons) and in commercial systems such as industrial cafeterias, menu cycles are in use which dictate the repeat pattern of the menu offerings. The existence of a menu cycle, its duration and offerings should be identified in the first phase of the menu analysis. Should the operation under study be a new one, decisions would have to be made regarding the menu, use of a cycle (and its duration), recipes, product etc. Formulations and production guides would be either collected or newly generated. As important as the menu, are the portion sizes to be offered and these must also be determined. Where a menu cycle is used it provides a logical time frame within which to determine all the costs for the system. When a menu cycle is not in use, and is not anticipated for future use, it is necessary to choose an arbitrary time frame for the cost projection. This time frame should be sufficiently long so that influences such as holidays and seasonal variations do not constrain the validity of the data. In some situations, such as college feeding, gathering data on a yearly basis would be best since the effects of the seasonal factors would be mitigated.

C. Determination of Food Costs

Once recipes have been collected and the time frame chosen it is possible to calculate the quantities of food needed to provide the required number of meals.

In the case of an existing system, invoice prices and current quotations may be used to calculate dollar value. For a totally new system not yet in existence, quotations on current prices would have to be secured from distributors or directly from processors (depending upon quantity of purchase and processors' policies). In all cases, it is desirable to reduce the food cost information to a cost per meal based on calculations made for the reference period. An example of such a food cost calculation for a school lunch study is shown in Table II.

In the case of a proposed alternative system, the effects of any changes resulting from the implementation of the new system have to be considered. For example, it may be feasible in an institutional food service setting for food costs to be reduced in going from on site preparation to centralized food production, as a result of a reduction in food wastage through controlled preparation, and quantity purchasing. However, cooperative (or collaborative) purchasing is already widely used by hospitals, school food service districts and, while such large volume purchasing lowers food costs, the food cost per se is not system dependent. A 500 bed hospital for exam-

TABLE II.   Food Costs for 32,000 School Meals Per Day
Based on a 6-Week Menu Cycle (1)

Meal Component	Cost ($)	
	Total	Cost Per Meal
Desserts other than baked		
(Refrig., frozen, canned)	104,768.81	.109
Baked Desserts	19,367.77	.020
Baked Breads, Rolls, Butter		
pats & Milk	69,852.56	.072
Salads and Vegetables	80,987.59	.080
Main Dishes or Entrees	160,973.56	.167
Total meal (in 1972-73)	435,950.29	.448
Total meal (in 1974-75)[a]	479,545.32	.493

[a]Allowing for 5 % annual inflation as per 1967-1972
Consumer Price Indices.

ple could not significantly decrease its food cost as a result of changing from a fresh food to a cook-chill or frozen
system because only one facility is involved and the number of
meals served is fixed and relatively small. Under any alternative systems, therefore, volumes of food would not change,
nor would waste control be a significant factor in decreasing
food cost. The relative advantages of the systems alternatives would, therefore, have to be based on other cost factors.

D. Nonfood Supplies

Nonfood supplies include disposables and cleaning supplies. If the system alternative includes central food preparation, however, packaging materials must also be considered
and may become a significant expense factor.

1. Disposables. If a proposed system alternative proposes
the use of disposables for meal service the cost of these
disposables must be charged to the new system, including the
cost required for building up an inventory, storing them and
the cost incurred in disposing of them. However, their use
must also be evaluated in terms of the following cost related
factors associated with dishwashing: reduction in labor

cost, equipment, and utilities (See Chapter 18). Costs of disposables for three systems in a school lunch study are shown in Table III.

2. *Cleaning Supplies.* Costs for cleaning supplies must be considered. This cost would increase somewhat for a system alternative including a central food production facility. Cost for cleaning supplies for the aforementioned school lunch study are shown in Table IV.

3. *Packaging Supplies.* Packaging cost may have a substantial impact on total meal costs in comparing onsite food preparation and service with a system in which production is divorced in time and/or place from meal service. Packaging costs include both packaging materials and costs associated with equipment where semi or fully automatic lines must be set up to handle the production requirements.

Table V illustrates the packaging costs projected for a centralized food production system for a school district. Table I in Chapter 2 shows the annualized packaging costs for the existing system in operation in the district at the time of the study and the two central production alternatives studied.

E. *Projecting Costs for Facilities*

The facilities include the physical structures in which to produce the quantity of food identified as being required in the systems analysis, and the equipment with which to prepare it, store it, deliver it and serve it.

1. *Physical structure.* It may be necessary, in considering various alternatives, to either design completely new facilities or to expand or remodel facilities in use in an existing system. In the first instance, the cost will be dependent upon how productively the facility will be used when it is built and whether the production output will be increased at a given future time. Factors which have a direct bearing on facilities requirements and, therefore, directly affect their cost include: the number of meals to be produced per shift; the number of production days per year; the number of shifts of operation per day; whether there is to be separation of production from service in time or place; ancillary feeding requirements, etc.

In considering costs for the expansion of an existing system, every effort must be made to use equipment already available and perhaps, by physically rearranging the equipment, to minimize additional construction necessary. However, in the interest of planning a cost effective system, replacement of

TABLE III. Cost of Disposables Calculated for Three Alternative School Lunch Systems (1)

Item	Cost/Thousand ($)	Quantity Required Per Year	Cost/Year ($)		
			Present System	System A	System B
Trays	15.1836	1,598.040 3,409,740	24,263.04	51,772.26	51,772.26
Cutlery Packs	11.18	1,598.040 3,409,740	17,866.09	38,120.89	38,120.89
Napkins	0.739	3,623,400	2,677.69		
Straws	0.3592	4,566,635	1,640.34		
Total disposables (in 72–73)			46,447.16	89,893.15	89,893.15
Total disposables (in 74–75)[a]			51,091.87	98,882.46	98,882.46

[a] See Table II.

TABLE IV. *Cost of Cleaning Supplies for a School District (1)*

Item	Cost ($)
Garbage Can Liners	1,000.00
Detergent (pots & pans)	2,860.00
Detergent (dishwashing)	1,017.50
Dish Cloths & Mitts	1,000.00
Rinse Additive	3,535.00
Miscellaneous	2,500.00
Total Cleaning Supplies (in 72-73)	11,912.50
Total Cleaning Supplies (in 74-75)[a]	13,103.75

[a]*See Table II.*

existing equipment with more efficient equipment must always be considered.

The facility should be designed in such a way that most of the production equipment is mobile and can be moved to meet changing requirements as they occur. Finally, additional space required must be estimated and construction cost assessed. Obviously, in order to assess facility costs accurately, it is necessary to carry out the preliminary engineering layout and design work required to estimate construction and equipment costs with a degree of accuracy that will ensure that the facilities can, in fact, be built for the costs estimated in the study. Construction costs usually differ with the various functional areas of the production facility and often with the geographical location of the facility in question. Construction cost estimates should preferably be secured from construction companies operating in the area of the proposed construction site. In addition, the system designer should find out what comparable facilities were constructed within the same time frame and within a relatively close geographical location and check their construction costs to verify his estimates. Table VI shows the space requirements for various functional areas within a proposed central food preparation facility, while Table VII shows the construction costs estimated for this facility.

2. *Equipment Costs.* Production and packaging equipment re-

TABLE V. Cost of Packaging Supplies Projected for a
          District Level Centralized School Lunch
          Production Facility (1)

Item	Quantity Per 1 Menu Cycle @ 19.2M Meals/Day	Cost Per Meal ($)	Cost Per Cycle @ 19,200/day ($)
Bags for			
- Slabs	29,999		
- Pizza	600		
- Cookies	1,152		
- Salad	1,920		
- Rolls	16,130		
- Meats	2,944		
- Cakes	11,256		
Total	64,001	.094	6,016.09
Pans			
- 10" x 12"	1,362	.203	276.49
- 13" x 18"	11,256	.252	2,836.51
Dessert Cups	307,200	.015	4,608.00
Cartons	6,771	.260	1,760.30

Total Cost Per 6 Week Cycle $ 15,497.39

Cost Per Meal $ 0.026

Total Cost Per Year Based
   on 3,409,740 Annually $ 88,653.00

quirements can be estimated once a throughput analysis has
been completed. From the throughput analysis, types of e-
quipment and their numbers required can be determined and budget prices for these items can be secured from manufacturers,
local dealers or manufacturer's representatives. Equipment
should be sized for maximum utilization, minimum labor and

TABLE VI. *Square Footage of Various Functional Areas Within a Proposed School Food Service Central Food Preparation Facility Producing 32,000 Meals per Shift*

	Dimensions	Square Footage Per Area	Total
Ground Level			
Freezer Building	81.5' x 123.0'		10,024.5
Shipping Dock &	10.5' x 81.5'	855.75 sq.ft.	
Office	10.5' x 161.5'	1,695.75	
Receiving Docks	10.5' x 104.0'	1,092.00	
			3,643.5
Process Building	221.5' x 163.0'	36,104.5 sq.ft.	
	25.0' x 71.0'	1,775.0	
	25.0' x 12.'	300.0	
			38,179.5
Second Floor			
office, Labs,	107.5' x 43.0'	4,622.5 sq.ft	
Locker Rooms,	12.0' x 26.0'	312.0	
Toilets, etc.	25.0' x 71.0'	1,775.0	
			5,709.5
Total Area			58,557.0

TABLE VII. Estimated Construction Cost Projected for 1974-75 for School Food
Service Central Food Preparation Facility for 32,000 Meals Per Shift (1)

Area	Square Footage	Cost per Square Foot ($)	Total Cost ($)
Land (5 acres @ $ 15,000/acre)			75,000
Freezer Building,	10,024	35.00	350,840
Docks	3,644	25.00	91,100
Processing Building	38,180	50.00	1,909,000
Offices	6,710	35.00	234,850
			2,660,790[a]
Liquid Waste Treatment System			65,000
Processing Piping			36,000
Additional Wiring for Automatic Controls			30,000
Driveway, Parking, Landscaping			75,000
Fire Protection			22,000
Exterior Lighting			6,780
			234,780
Total Construction Cost			2,895,570

[a] Includes plumbing, heating and air conditioning, i.e., hot and cold water,
boilers, hot water heaters, electrical system.

TABLE VIII. Equipment Costs for a Proposed School Food Service Central Food Preparation Facility Producing 32,000 Meals per Shift (1)

Location Number [a]	Area	Approximate Total Cost ($)
I	Receiving Platform	3,500.00
II	Ready Dry Storage	28,950.00
III	Dairy Cooler	410.00
IV	Chilled Storage Area: Meat	820.00
V	Freezer Storage: Receiving	4,100.00
VI	Thawing Room	2,460.00
VII	Root Vegetable Storage	410.00
VIII	Vegetable Storage	410.00
IX	Vegetable Cleaning	44,694.00
X	Vegetable Preparation	6,474.00
XI	Meat Cutting & Preparation	49,017.00
XII	Ingredient Measuring	14,455.00
XIII	Warewashing	38,592.00
XIV	Staging Room	---
XV	Sandwich Preparation	31,790.00
XVI	Salad Preparation	12,812.00
XVII	Bakery	198,432.00
XVIII	Kitchen	264,155.00
XIX	Boning & Slicing	5,639.00
XX	Waste Disposal	12,100.00
XXI	Meal Assembly	353,850.00
XXII	Compressor & Maintenance	202,640.00
XXIII	Chilled Storage: Finished Products	2,500.00
XXIV	Storage Freezer: Finished Products	25,000.00
XXV	Frozen Food Staging	16,000.00
XXIX	Materials Handling	84,300.00
XXX	Miscellaneous Small Equipment	94,215.00
XXXI	Quality Control Laboratory	35,000.00
XXXII	Lunch Room	45,000.00
	Total Cost Estimated for 1972-1973	1,577,725.00
	Total Cost Estimated for 1974-1975 [b]	1,735,498.00

[a] See Figures 6 and 7, Chapter 14.

[b] See Table II.

minimal energy requirement. For central preparation systems
with service in satellite locations removed from the production facility, the number of meals to be served and the location of satellites will dictate the types and quantities of
serving equipment required and these must also be sourced and
priced.

Table VIII shows the equipment costs projected for the
school lunch facility described in Tables VI and VII. If e-
quipment already existing is to be used in one of the alternatives but not another, a monetary value for the equipment at
the time of the systems analysis must be also assessed.

F. *Projecting Labor Costs*

The labor requirements necessary to implement a proposed
food service system can be determined by carefully identifying
the work functions to be carried out at all levels of operations. Work functions can be identified by studying a similar
system existing elsewhere. Based on these findings, a staffing pattern and a level of staffing can be developed.

It is necessary, in projecting labor costs, to include all
those people *directly* involved in the food service system,i.e.
the production supervisor or kitchen manager, the food preparation workers, the pot and pan washers, the drivers who transport the food to serving sites, the food servers, etc. and
those *indirectly* involved, i.e. administrators, food service
directors, dietitians, office services personnel, maintenance
and repair crews, etc. In operations where food service is not
the only function, indirect labor must be allocated to food
service if persons in these indirect labor categories perform
other work functions non-food service related.

Within a specific job or wage category, it is convenient
to express labor as *full time equivalents* since the food service staff is usually made up to a large extent of part-time
workers. *Full time equivalents* allow meaningful comparisons
of systems to be made from a direct labor standpoint. Work
sampling studies may have to be conducted where job functions,
work schedules and worker utilization are not clearly documented.

Actual payroll data from records can be used as a basis
for converting labor requirements to cost figures. Such data
often show a number of workers performing identical job functions at different wage rates due to longevity increase. To
facilitate comparative cost analysis, a single experience level may be used. Uniform application of the wage rate for that
level will yield valid comparisons. Uniform application is
especially relevant when labor is expressed as full time e-
quivalents.

Labor costs calculations for a district level school lunch

program are shown in Tables IX, X, and XI. Table IX shows the staffing of the existing system and the projected staffing at school level for two modes of central food preparation. Table X shows the staffing of the central food preparation facility which would be required to support systems A or B, while Table XI shows the projected district level indirect labor costs (which would remain the same whether the present system were retained or one of the new systems were implemented). Table XII shows the *system effectiveness* of the three alternatives studied.

G. Determining Indirect Costs

In institutional operations, principal areas of indirect costs are utilities, insurance, employee benefits and management and administrative costs. In commercial profit making operations, there are, as already mentioned, the additional costs due to advertising, sales and marketing.

As in the case of labor costs, it may be necessary, to probe deeply to extract some of the indirect costs in institutional operations which are not normally allocated to specific operating areas. Thus, in hospitals, prisons and schools, the cost of utilities, would have to be prorated to the food service operation. The cost of food service-related procurement, travel, management and the cost of office supplies must also be taken into account. Other indirect administrative costs which might have to be prorated to the food service department can include: personnel administration, warehousing and data processing.

Indirect costs relating to capital outlay for construction tion of facilities and purchase of equipment must be included in the systems analysis. Capital outlay should be depreciated over a specific period of time consonant with government guidelines. The rate of depreciation is based on the expected useful life of the facility or equipment under consideration. Buildings are generally depreciated over a twenty-five to forty year period, while equipment may have a useful life of five to fifteen years and vehicles over about three to five years.

The cost of money (interest) should be included as an expense at the applicable rate. The repayment of principal should be included in the cash flow analysis for institutional projects where bonds have been floated to finance construction. In commercial operations, where available capital could be committed to a variety of investments, loss of interest on this capital must be charged to the project once the money is committed to it.

TABLE IX.   *School Level Staffing for Existing District School Lunch Program and Projected Requirements under Two Modes of Central Food Preparation (1)*

	Number of Personnel		
Category	Present System	System A	System B
Managers	16	38	16
Assistant Managers	7	-	-
SL Assistants I	11	-	-
SL Assistants II	184 3/4	67.5	75.5
Hourly Employee	14	56	80

III. COST COMPARISON OF FOOD SERVICE SYSTEMS

The results of the school food service systems analysis described in this chapter are shown in Table I, Chapter 2. It will be seen that when all costs were taken into consideration the alternative centralized food production systems ("A" and "B") were projected to increase meal costs to about $ 1.36 and $ 1.32 as compared to the projected cost of $ 0.92 if the present system were retained into the 1974-75 school year.

Scrutiny of the total cost of food, labor and supplies reveals that there is no savings to be achieved in going to central food preparation and that costs attributable to facilities and equipment required to implement the centralized systems would make their further consideration inadvisable. This case history therefore illustrates a situation in which judgments could be made at several points along the way in the systems study about the cost effectiveness of the system alternatives prior to the actual completion of the total systems analysis.

IV. REFERENCES

1. Res. & Dev. Staff, Project ANSER "Five County Management Improvement Project. Program Element 3 Facilities Alternative Planning" Project ANSER, Volusia County School District, Deland, Florida (1974).

TABLE X. Staffing and Labor Costs in Central Food Preparation Facility Producing 32,000 meals per Shift (1)

Area	Supervisors		Labor		Total
	No.	Cost ($)	No.	Cost ($)	Cost ($)
Direct Labor					
Ingred. Storage	1	4,900	1	2,838	
Ingred. Preparation	1	4,900			
Dry			2	5,676	
Vegetable			4	11,352	
Meat			2	5,676	
Main Preparation	1	4,900			
Kitchen			2	5,676	
Salad			8	22,704	
Bakery	1	4,900	8	22,704	
Assembly	1	4,900	12	34,056	
Freezing	1	4,900	1	2,838	
Packaging	1	4,900	6	17,028	
Storage & Shipping	1	4,900	5	14,190	
TOTAL 72-73	8	39,200	51	144,738	183,938
TOTAL DIRECT LABOR 74-75[a]					202,331
Indirect Labor					
Plant Manager	1	12,000			
Prod. Manager	1	10,000			
Account	1	6,500			
Secretary			1	5,000	
Clerk-Typist			1	4,200	
Maintenance	2	15,500	9	29,704	
Quality Control	1	9,000	1	6,000	
TOTAL 72-73		54,000		44,904	98,904
TOTAL INDIRECT LABOR 74-75[a]					108,794

[a] See Table II.

TABLE XI. District Level Staffing for an Existing School
Lunch Program and under Central Food Preparation Systems (1).

Personnel	Salary Allocation	Annual ($)	Amount ($)
Administative:			
Food Service Director	100 %		
Administrative Assistant	100 %		
Food Service Accountant	100 %		
Director Auxiliary Services	15 %		27,433.00
Field Service Assistant	100 %	10,000.00	10,000.00
Sub Total 72-73			37,433.00
74-75			41,176.00
Transportation :			
Driver	190/261 days	4,422.00	3,219.00
Helper	190/261 days	4,422.00	3,219.00
Sub Total 72-73			6,438.00
74-75			7,082.00
Maintenance (School Level):			
Equipment Repairman		8,500.00	8,500.00
Sub Total 72-73			8,500.00
74-75			9,350.00
Total 1972-73			52,371.00
Total 1974-75[a]			57,608.00

[a]See Table II.

TABLE XII. System Effectiveness of Three Alternatives School Lunch Systems (1)

System	Man-Days per Year			Productivity	
	Direct Labor	Indirect Labor	Total	Meals per Man-day	Meals per Man-hour
Present System	40,095	1,273	41,368	82.42	11.77
System A					
School Level	21,870		21,870		
CFPF	10,620	3,420	14,040		
Distribution	720		720		
District		1,273	1,273		
			37,903	89.95	12.85
System B					
School Level	20,583		20,583		
CFPF	10,620	3,420	14,040		
Distribution	720		720		
District		1,273	1,273		
			36,616	93.12	13.30

FOOD SELECTION AND MENU PLANNING

CHAPTER 4

FOOD FORMS FOR CONVENIENCE SYSTEMS

G. E. Livingston

I. INTRODUCTION

The last twenty years have witnessed a dramatic response on the part of the food processing industry to meet the changing needs of food service operators and, in particular, the need to reduce labor at preparation sites. What has resulted is an incredible and ever-growing array of *convenience foods* and *convenience recipe components,* to use the terms proposed by Dungan and Lacey (1). These authors defined a *convenience food* as "a menu item in a preserved state that, with objective finishing instructions, allows the serving of the menu item without need for skilled cook or baker to assure customer acceptance of that item". A *convenience recipe component* was defined as "an ingredient or a recipe subassembly in a preserved state that allows the user to proceed directly with the formulation of a menu item without the need for further preparation for the component". Today, the food service operator can indeed serve a full range of menu items "without need for skilled cook or baker to assure customer acceptance". All traditional and novel methods of processing foods are represented among these conveniences: freezing, refrigeration, dehydration, freeze drying, and the conventional as well as the newer methods of canning. The central question facing the food service systems designer is that of selecting the appropriate foods forms for a convenience system.

It has already been stated that the first step in developing a food service system based on convenience foods is to define the goals in terms of cost, logistical requirements, and consumer acceptance. To a large extent, these three factors are interrelated, in that the quality level that is feasible will be greatly influenced by cost and, at least in the case of centralized production systems, the cost will be influenced by the production volumes. Quality, therefore, must be defined, while bearing in mind realistically cost constraints. The

Copyright © 1979 by Academic Press, Inc.
All rights of reproduction in any form reserved
ISBN: 0-12-453150-4

quality levels of the products to be served should be described as accurately as possible. All decisions with respect to the
system, such as ingredients, preparation methods, serving procedures, and equipment must take into account the quality goal
that has been established. The level of built-in labor that is
desired must also be considered and defined. Obviously, all
products made in a centralized facility or manufactured commercially contain preparation labor that, therefore, reduces on-
site labor requirements. Although there are some convenience
foods available whose cost is at times lower than that of
freshly prepared foods, such as dehydrated mashed potatoes, convenience foods usually do cost more than the sum of the ingredients cost alone. Therefore, it is necessary to relate the
cost of convenience foods to the cost of food and labor, and
not to food cost alone. In planning systems utilizing convenience foods, the system designer should investigate the wide
range of options that are currently available in convenience
foods and recipes components. Today, literally everything from
soup to nuts is available in a convenience form. In addition,
however, the system designer has the responsibility of evaluating the feasibility and cost effectiveness of centrally preparing foods or food components in a captive food facility as
part of the convenience food system. Thus, a complete discussion of convenience foods and food components in the context of
food service systems should not restrict itself to foods that
are commercially available but include an evaluation of opportunities that exist for central preparation.

II. MARKET STUDY

A recent study by the Economic Research Service of the
United States Department of Agriculture (2) estimated the value
of convenience foods sold to the institutional market in 1973
to be over ten billion dollars. The study reported a survey of
152 food processors who had introduced a total of 6,357 convenience food items in the institutional market in the preceding
five years. Results of this survey are presented in Table I.
Fourteen categories of products were identified:hors d'oeuvres,
salads, entrees, side dishes, dinners, breads and rolls, cakes
and pastries, dessert pies, snacks, sauces and gravies condiments, bases and mixes, soups and "all other". The largest
number of items among the 6,357 total items or units introduced
between 1968 and 1973, were 2,573 entrees. Levels of prepared-
ness were categorized as follows: requires cooking, heat and
serve or mix and serve, table ready or thaw and serve. The
product forms in which these foods were available were freeze
dried, frozen, dry mix, dry-not mixed packaged, canned, and

TABLE I. *Number of Convenience Foods for the Food Service Market Introduced by Selected Food Processors, 1968 - 1973 (2)*

Food Category	Total Food items or units	Level of preparedness			Product form					
		Requires cooking	Heat'n Serve mix'n serve	Table ready thaw'n serve	Freeze dried	Frozen	Dry mix	Dry not mixed	Packaged: canned	Fresh
Hors d'oeuvres	228	51	158	19	0	216	0	0	9	3
Salads	77	5	0	72	0	5	0	5	37	30
Entrees	2573	1012	1550	11	5	2430	3	0	127	8
Side dishes	458	85	343	30	7	244	11	0	191	5
Dinners	271	60	156	55	0	266	0	0	0	5
Breads and rolls	169	31	64	74	0	112	27	0	0	30
Cakes & pastries	444	99	76	269	0	254	57	2	0	131
Dessert pies	231	103	53	75	0	142	37	0	8	44
Snacks	123	16	15	92	0	32	4	6	43	38
Sauces and gravies	202	53	127	22	2	39	103	14	38	6
Condiments	217	9	1	207	0	3	0	3	185	26
Bases and mixes	282	93	173	16	0	11	241	13	16	1
Soups	154	38	114	2	10	37	40	0	67	0
All other	928	355	365	208	13	544	130	70	89	82
Total	6357	2010	3195	1152	37	4335	653	113	810	409

fresh. By far the largest number of items 4,335 were frozen.
About 19 % of the products introduced were discontinued (Table
II). The largest rate of discontinuances, in proportion to in-
troductions, was in dinners and soups, where 34 % of the products introduced during the five year period were discontinued.
While the report does not provide an explanation for this relatively high failure rate, it might be related to the growing
inclination on the part of large food service operators to
venture into captive centralized production facilities in
preference to purchasing commercially packed, fully prepared,
convenience foods. Convenience components on the other hand,
are readily accepted as ingredients in the manufacturing of
these prepared foods. One fact that should not be overlooked
is the relative ease with which a food service operation can
centrally prepare chilled or frozen foods. It is far less
easy to venture into canning processes, not only because of
the capital investment involved, but because of the sophisticated food technology skills required. Thus, it is likely that
in the next decade, a growth in the number of commercially
canned entrees, at the expense of the growth of frozen entrees
which have been the preferred form in the United States thus
far, will be noticed.

II. TYPES OF CONVENIENCE FOODS

It is probably easiest to categorize convenience foods by
the position they occupy on a menu:

A. *Breakfast Foods*

1. *Juices.* The advent of single serving portions of fruit
juices and nectars in disposable plastic cups, has greatly facilitated the distribution of juices in mass feeding operations of all kinds,including hospitals,schools, and airlines,
where the use of bulk juice dispensers is neither feasible nor
desirable. Filling and sealing machines for preformed cups
are available for small to medium-sized institutions, while
larger units, which thermoform,fill and seal cups automatically, are adapted to the needs of larger institutions of centralized food production facilities. The latter can be used to
make, form and seal shallow containers of the same diameter as
the juice cups. These containers would be suitable for dessert
items such as puddings,gelatin desserts,or canned fruit. In addition to juices, beverage mixes which permit making a variety
of vitamin A and/or C fortified fruit beverages are also used
as breakfast drinks. Dehydrated fruit crystals have been in
existence for many years, as have the frozen mixes and concen-
trates.

TABLE II. *Number of Convenience Foods for the Food Service Market Discontinued by Selected Processors, 1968 – 1973 (2)*

Food Category	Total Food items or units	Level of preparedness			Product form					
		Requires cooking	Heat'n Serve mix'n serve	Table ready thaw'n serve	Freeze dried	Frozen	Dry mix	Dry not mixed	Packaged canned	Fresh
Hors d'oeuvres	34	9	25	0	0	32	0	0	2	0
Salads	10	5	0	5	0	5	0	0	5	0
Entrees	371	142	226	3	0	314	1	0	56	0
Side dishes	39	6	14	19	0	14	1	0	24	0
Dinners	92	3	89	0	0	92	0	0	0	0
Breads and rolls	52	0	34	18	0	46	0	0	0	6
Cakes and pastries	86	12	7	67	0	47	4	0	0	35
Dessert pies	55	11	15	29	0	33	1	0	0	21
Snacks	21	0	2	19	0	3	0	0	17	1
Sauces and gravies	30	17	13	0	0	2	17	5	6	0
Condiments	58	0	3	55	0	3	0	0	55	0
Bases and mixes	46	43	3	0	0	8	32	1	5	0
Soups	53	5	48	0	0	18	13	0	22	0
All other	277	208	26	43	8	205	1	27	30	6
Total	1224	461	505	258	8	822	70	33	222	69

2. Cereals and Hot Breads. Individually boxed servings of
dried cereal have long been standard, but the new packaging in
disposable plastic bowls provide an extra measure of labor
saving (Fig. 1).

Instant and mix-and-eat hot cereals eliminate the need to
cook hot cereals in institutions. Pancake and waffle mixes,
as well as frozen prepared versions on the market also, provide a measurable labor saving.

3. Eggs. Although quality frozen prepared egg products,
such as omelets are now commercially produced, this probably
remains one of the more difficult product areas. Frozen whole
egg in gallon containers, stabilized for steam table use, is
commercially available and offers a high degree of convenience
to the institutional operator. It is also feasible, in a captive central food preparation facility operating under highly
sanitary conditions, to prepare a frozen scrambled egg mix,
which is thawed on premise for the preparation of "fresh"
scrambled eggs. This approach has successfully been used in
some inflight first class passenger breakfast service.

In response to the needs of individuals seeking to adhere
to a "prudent diet", cholesterol free egg products have been
commercialized, permitting food service operators to feature
special breakfast menus for diet-conscious patrons. When cholesterol free eggs were first introduced, they were marketed to
the hospital trade, and dietitians feared that patients on a
low cholesterol diet would be misled if they were offered eggs
on their breakfast menus. Now that cholesterol free egg products are commonly available in most food stores, there is no
longer any cause for concern, and it is likely their usage in
food service will grow.

4. Meats. In the breakfast meat area, precooked sausage
links constitute an excellent convenience item suitable for
many types of food service operations. In systems where preplated meals are frozen, both the precooked sausage or
Canadian bacon have traditionally exhibited better storage
stability than ham. For the low cholesterol, low saturated
fat diets, the textured spun soy protein analogs provide a
reasonable imitation of the meat products.

5. Baked Goods. For rolls, dry mixes are probably the most
widely used. The other two forms available, chilled dough
products and frozen brown-and-serve or heat-and-serve, have
done less well. One reason for this is the relatively small
sizes of commercial frozen muffins, rolls, and sweet goods.
While these provide a reasonable unit cost, they tend to be
smaller than fresh on premise baked items, and therefore they
do not satisfy the requirements of many food service managers.

FIGURE 1. Individual servings of breakfast cereals in single service plastic bowls. (Courtesy Kellogg Company, Battle Creek, Michigan)

In a centralized food preparation facility, the production of baked goods made to satisfy the requirements of the end users, then shipped frozen and bagged for thawing or reheating on site, represents a practical solution, generally yielding high quality products.

6. *Condiments*. Unit portions of jams, jellies and syrups are commonplace and outside procurement is usually cost effective even for those systems having their own central production facilities. This is because of the high cost of the specialized packaging equipment required, and the huge volume of production required to operate it economically.

B. *Appetizers*

Prepared appetizers are generally frozen and are available in two types: prepared, thaw and serve canapes, and hot, oven-ready hors d'oeuvres, the latter generally consisting of raw puffed paste rolled around a filling such as a miniature frankfurter. Appetizers are not generally featured on institutional menus in the United States and are primarily for hotel, club and banquet use. In Western Europe, where cold hors d'oeuvres are traditional, even in school or in-plant feeding, canned prepared foods can be found which aim to fill this menu need. Such items include canned grated carrots or celery root vinaigrette. Frozen crepes with cheese or seafood fillings, miniature pizzas, or frozen quiche lorraine can make excellent hot hors d'oeuvres and have been used for that purpose for airline passengers.

C. *Soups*

In addition to the canned soups, soup bases, and dry soup mixes which have been available for many years, portion-packed instant soups, which require merely the addition of boiling water now provide an additional option for the food service operator. For example, in a hospital, this permits soup preparation in ward pantries with no more effort than that required to make a cup of instant coffee or tea. Combined with the use of built-in electric instant hot water makers, the use of these instant portion-packed soup mixes represents a very practical concept.

A recently introduced product for hospital use is the low sodium instant consomme concentrate in individual portion packs. Among the other potential sources of convenience soups, there are the aseptically packed, read-to-eat, soups in one liter thermoformed, polystyrene containers, commercially produced for the retail market in France. Although sterile, these products are sold chilled, to better preserve their organoleptic properties. This type of packaging goes one step beyond the technology of the gallon milk containers that have been used for soups in certain centralized food service operations in the United States. By using a closed filling system and a high degree of sanitary control, it is possible to pack soups that are virtually sterile, even with ordinary equipment, thereby attaining a very long storage life under refrigeration. While soups have been frozen in some centralized food service systems both in milk containers and polyester pouches, the far greater convenience of long life chilled soups or aseptically sterilized soups, along with the energy savings in processing, storage, and heating, would seem to make these approaches worthwhile.

D. Entrees

Since the entree is in calories, protein, and cost the most important part of the meal, it is not surprising that the greatest diversity of product forms is found in this menu area. For convenience, one can classify these products according to their preservation forms.

1. Frozen Products. In an evolutionary process–and the food service industry is in a period of rapid evolution–one may expect to find simultaneous evidence of the various transitional states. It is not surprising, therefore, that one can find raw products, portion-controlled raw products, ready-to-cook products and fully cooked and prepared frozen products all currently co-existing, with consumption gradually shifting from the former to the latter.

a. Raw meats, poultry, fish and eggs.

(1) Portion controlled cuts. The food service industry in the United States has all but abandoned the practice of in-house meat cutting in favor of the purchase of portion controlled meat, poultry and fish products. While these certainly eliminate some labor and provide a degree of cost and quality control, they are merely convenience components and not truly convenience foods. Yet it would be foolhardy to ignore their importance as raw materials in any food service system, whether preparation by on site or centralized.

While portion controlled meat and poultry products were first available in chilled form, they are increasingly being used in frozen form, which offers obvious advantages in convenience of distribution and storage. Frozen, portion con-

trolled, raw meat products include steaks of various types,
hamburgers, boneless roast, chops, and breaded veal patties.
The desire to achieve uniformity of portion size in steaks has
led to several interesting developments. In one process, meat
is placed in a press, while still partially frozen to yield a
uniform size piece from which steaks having identical external
dimensions can be cut. Thus, not only the weight, but also
the appearance of each steak will be exactly controlled merely
by slicing to a uniform thickness. Another process entails
the flaking of beef, using a specially designed cutting machine. The layers of thin flakes are reformed into steaks by
one of several alternative methods. In one, the meat is
formed into a log or loaf of the desired shape, which is compacted under high pressure, sliced and frozen (Fig. 2). In
another, the weight of meat desired of each steak is portioned
out and deposited in a steak shaped dye. When compacted under
pressure ranging to about 24,000 pounds per square inch,
the flakes are reconstituted into solid "steaks" which are
tender, yet have the appearance of natural cuts of meat, since
fibrous connective tissue, including cartilage and bone have
been severed. The process permits meats of varying fat content, or meat and rehydrated textured vegetable protein, to be
combined and uniformly mixed prior to reforming.

Poultry products include bone-in or boned chicken breast,
legs, thighs, and chicken or turkey rolls. Fish products are
generally sold as filets of steaks depending upon the species
involved. Breaded raw fish and shell fish products are widely
used, and, even when they are processed in a precooked form,
the flesh itself is generally raw.

The availability of scrambled eggs, stabilized with citric
acid to prevent discoloration on the steam table, has already
been mentioned in connection with breakfast foods but, of
course, central food preparation facilities requiring large
quantities of eggs for cooking or baking would use frozen
whole eggs, egg whites, or stabilized egg yolks in thirty
pound cans, or their dehydrated counterparts.

(2) Prepared, oven-ready products. One step up the ladder of sophistication and preparation from the products just
described, are the raw, oven ready types of products whose
primary appeal has been to the upper segments of the food service industry, such as clubs, hotels and airline caterers.
These products are different from those already discussed, in
that they involve the use of a recipe in the combination of
the basic meat, poultry or fish products, with sauces, stuff-
ings or garnishes that would normally have been added by a
chef on site. Veal Cordon Bleu, Chicken Kiev, Beef Kabobs,
Stuffed Sole, and many other products could be cited as examples of the oven ready category.

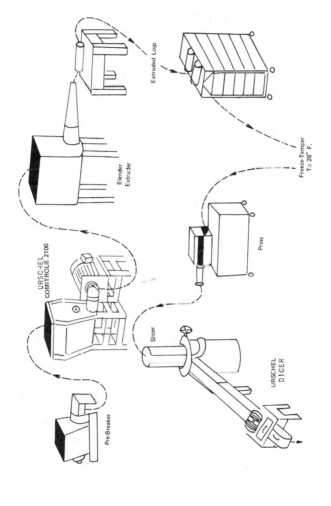

FIGURE 2. Flow diagram for the manufacture of formed, flaked, steaks. (Courtesy Urschel Laboratories Incorporated, Valparaiso, Indiana)

Pre-Breaker

URSC+EL
COMITROL® 2100

Blender
Extruder

Extruded Logs

Freeze-Temper
To 28° F.

Press

Slicer

URSCHEL
DICER

b. Precooked meat, poultry, fish or egg products.

(1) Dry products. Probably the widest range of frozen institutional convenience foods fall into the category of precooked products. For practical purposes they can be described as "dry" and "wet" products. Dry products are individual pieces of meat, poultry or seafood, generally bulk packed in cartons or in plastic bags within cartons, and include such foods as precooked hamburgers, meat loaf, meat balls, fish sticks, fried breaded chicken and fried shrimp. Precooked chicken and turkey roll, with variations of white and dark meat and containing a small amount of gelatin or soy protein as a binder, have also become of great importance to the food service operator. Along the same vein, but of better quality, are the boneless turkey roasts on which the skin is left, but whose natural shape and texture provide a cooked product closer to an oven roasted bird. Some packers inject into the raw roast, a self-basting solution containing turkey broth, salt, sodium phosphate and flavoring. Of interest to food service operations that have their own centralized food production facilities, is the in-house manufacturing of turkey rolls. This is a relatively simple operation in which the turkey is boned raw, and the raw meat stuffed into a casing in which the meat is cooked or roasted. Some operations use a single cook, others a double cook. If it is desired, dark and white meat can be packed separately, so as to permit the ratios of the two to be controlled in making up the finished turkey plates at the point of service.

Of growing importance too, are precooked beef roast which are commercially available, rare or medium rare (Fig. 3). A low temperature, long term cooking process is used to achieve the controlled cooking required for this product. In one method, roasts are vacuum sealed in heat resistant bags which are then immersed in water at $150°F$ ($65.6°C$) for about seven hours. current regulations require an internal temperature of $145°F$ ($63°F$) to be attained by the meat in order to destroy salmonella organisms which might be present (See Chapter 22). Cooked roasts are cooled and then frozen. The food service operator thaws the roast in a cooler and slices the product at about $38°F$ ($3.3°C$) before reheating. Juice released from thawing can be used to make an "au jus" gravy. Any available method of heating, such as oven, steam table, steam or microwave oven, can be used to bring the sliced roast beef to serving temperature. The preparation of a roast in this manner, should be of interest to food service systems designing their own centralized production facilities. While specialized equipment is required to maintain the time/temperature relationship needed, the process is not very complicated and does result in improved quality and yields in roast beef.

Super L: The Cook-In/Package-In System.

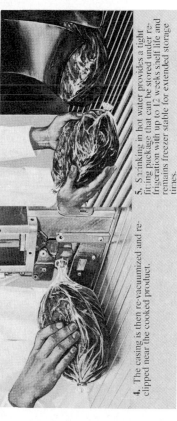

1. Seasoned meat is placed in casing, vacuumized and clipped. For "dry" roast an additional six inches is allowed in casing length.

2. The product is water cooked at controlled temperatures for the proper cooking time. Low heat cooking for longer periods produces greater yield of product

3. After meat is cooked to proper degree of doneness, the clip is removed from one end and juices are drained from the casing f "dry" roast is desired.

4. The casing is then re-vacuumized and re-clipped near the cooked product.

5. Shrinking in hot water provides a tight fitting package that can be stored under refrigeration with up to 12 weeks shelf life and remains freezer stable for extended storage times.

FIGURE 3. Cook-in package system for the manufacture of precooked roast beef. (Courtesy Cryovac Division, W. R. Grace & Co., Duncan, South Carolina)

A frozen precooked product which has been widely accepted,
is the   frozen, hard boiled, egg roll, which yields uniform
slices (Fig 4). To manufacture the roll, raw yolk is molded
to form an elongated body and coagulated, and the egg white is
molded to form a covering around the yolk, which is also coagulated. Commercially produced rolls weigh 17 ounces, and yield
approximately 75 slices, 5/32 inch thick, this being   approximately the equivalent of 17 medium sized eggs. Special egg
slicers are available which will cut an entire roll at one
time.

(2) Wet Products. Wet products are sauce-type products
which include the whole spectrum of main dishes from the every-
day beef stew to the fanciest lobster newburgh. While frozen
institutional entrees were first introduced in individual, portion-packed plastic boil-in-bag pouches, the preferred commercial form is now the aluminum size steam table pan, which holds
approximately five pounds and yields from 8 to 18 servings,de-
pending upon the product and the serving sizes. For centralized
food preparation facilities, the concept of the "slab pack",
which eliminates the relatively high cost of the aluminum tray,
is as valid today as it was twenty years ago when it was in
vogue in both the United Kingdom and the United States. Packaging equipment now available makes it feasible to produce slab
packs on form-fill-seal equipment, thus eliminating the relatively high labor costs formerly required by this packaging approach.

2. Refrigerated Products. Because of their inherent per-
ishability, refrigerated foods have not appeared as attractive,
as frozen foods, to the food service industry in the United
States. For this reason, their use seems to have largely been
confined to applications for which freezing, as a method of
preservation, was not suitable, such as in the case of salads,
gelatin desserts, and puddings. The food service system designer, however, in considering options for prepared foods, must
recognize the many advantages that are offered by a chilled
food system, namely lower energy requirements in production,
storage and reheating, fewer changes in product characteristics
(compared to freezing), no requirement for freeze-thaw stability, less capital tied up in inventory, etc. The principal
limitation of chilled systems, on the hand, has been the relatively short shelf life of their product. However, recent research has shown that cooked foods that are rapidly chilled
to near 32°F (0°C) in one hour or less and are then stored
below 36° F (2.2° C) can, for the most part, retain their organoleptic qualities for 4 to 6 days. The chilling must take
place rapidly however, preferably in 15-30 minutes and certainly in less than one hour. In many systems, the 4-6 day
storage life is long enough to permit the complete divorce of

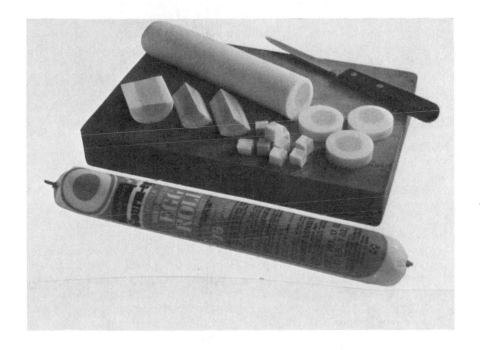

FIGURE 4. Twelve inch, frozen, hard-cooked egg roll product
equals approximately one dozen medium size eggs in weight and
provides 75 center-cut slices. (Courtesy Checkerboard Food-
service Division, Ralston Purina Company, St. Louis, Missouri)

the production operation from the serving operation even if the serving operation is serving three meals a day, seven days a week. It must be emphasized that quality retention can occur only if the system is equipped with blast chillers and storage refrigerators which permit the recommended times and temperatures to be observed.

Longer storage lives for chilled prepared foods have been obtained through the application of the principles involved in the Nacka System in its various forms, i.e. Delphin, Nacka, A.G.S., or Kap Cold. In these methods, foods are precooked and filled into plastic pouches, while still hot. They are evacuated, heat sealed, and pasteurized in a boiling water bath, after which the products are rapidly chilled and stored at refrigerator temperatures with a resulting storage life of 4 - 6 weeks. Although some operators have sought to apply these systems with the omission of the pasteurization step, this practice carries the risk that pathogens contaminating the food at the time of filling would not be destroyed prior to chill storage, and may proliferate if foods are held at improper temperatures at a later stage.

3. Dry Products. In addition to the dry egg products mentioned, which can be used in the preparation of egg-based entrees, there are dry sauce and gravy mixes intended for use in preparing main dishes. The application of freeze drying is generally limited to some entree ingredients, such as freeze-dried shrimp and crabmeat, which offer a high degree of convenience, and to complete casserole mixes, which include freeze-dried components and are more probably used in institutional operations. Of course, freeze-dried meal components have played an important role in certain military food requirements, such as long range patrol rations and the space program.

4. Canned Products. Canned foods represent one of the first types of modern institutional convenience foods since, they were associated with military food systems from the time of Nicolas Appert, the father of canning.

While conventionally canned entree products are available in the institutional size (No. 10) cans, the better quality canned main dishes on the market for the past two decades have been made by a process in which the products are presterilized under high temperature-short time conditions, and filled into cans while in a chamber in which the air pressure is maintained above one atmosphere (Fig. 5). Thus, a sterilizing temperature is maintained in the food during the filling process and after sealing, and any microorganisms present, in either the food or the container at the time of closure, are destroyed during the holding period that follows the sealing. This process has permitted the packing of many entrees into institutional size cans

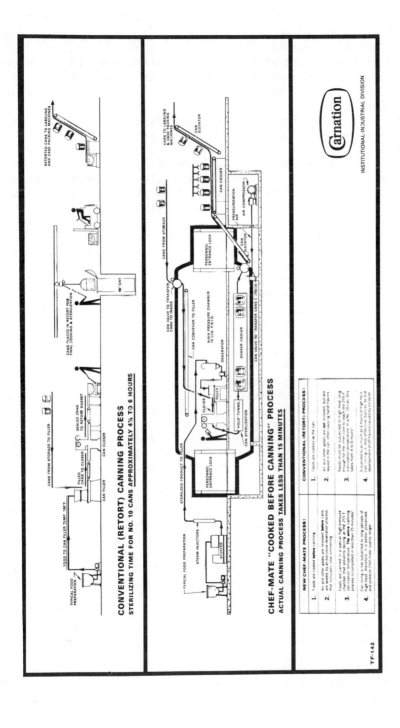

FIGURE 5. Comparison of conventional canning process and "cooked before canning" process, in which sterile product is filled into cans under elevated atmospheric pressure. (Courtesy Carnation Company, Los Angeles, California)

that would have undergone unacceptable quality deterioration if retorted after filling.

Of great interest at this time, is the advent of pouch packed and tray packed retorted entrees (See Chapter 6). It is likely that the retort pouch and small trays will find application only for special requirements where individual portion packs are useful, such as modified diet entrees for hospitals. The larger trays, such as the one third steam table size or the one half steam table size, already on the market, are highly appropriate to the needs of mass feeding operations. At the present time the material used in the trays is either aluminum or steel. The aluminum is plastic coated with a polyolefin or other plastic to provide desired heat sealability and barrier characteristics. Steel trays are either tin coated or plastic coated, but in either case, are sealed by conventional double seaming. Steel trays are somewhat more rigid than the aluminum trays of the same size, but are easily dented in comparison with conventional cylindrical steel cans. It is likely that present research will yield all plastic trays, thermoformed from coextruded compositions that will be less costly than either steel or aluminum, while providing greater rigidity and the capability of being used in microwave ovens. The obvious advantage of trays at the point of usage is the elimination of the need for a pan in which to reheat and serve the products from a steam table. Because of the very substantial reduction in the length of time required to sterilize foods in trays as compared to cylindrical cans of equivalent volumes, there is a significant improvement in quality retention which results in products that are closer in quality to that of frozen prepared foods than to that of conventionally canned foods. The feasibility of combining this type of packaging with high temperature-short time sterilization in agitating or rotary retorts, suggests that even greater improvements in quality retention can be anticipated. The type of processing involved in packing canned items, however, limit their production to the food processing industry, and it would be difficult to conceive of any but the largest food service operations installing such processing facilities, solely for their own usage.

It is worth noting that individual portion packed entrees in flat round cans have been used for several years in airline feeding. A newer form of this concept involves the use of single serving aluminum trays, heat sealed, with a plastic coated aluminum foil, and containing individual meal components packaged in a cardboard box with cut outs to accommodate the various components, i.e. appetizer, main dish, dessert, bread, and disposable flatware. Initial application of this type of packaging has been used in the manufacturing of shelf stable kosher or vegetarian meals.

E. *Fruits and Vegetable Products*

Canned fruits and vegetables, generally in No. 10 cans, have been available for so many years that one tends to forget that they are indeed convenience products or components. Frozen vegetables are widely used institutionally because of their excellent quality, and in recent years have been joined by heat and serve prepared frozen vegetables. Chilled fruit, such as citrus sections, and frozen fruit such as strawberries, peaches and blueberries are also staples as ingredients in food service systems.

A more recent development is the advent of salad greens with extended shelf lives. Since salads must be handled chilled, they have been a major problem in systems that were primarily based on frozen prepared foods. Cut lettuce with a 12 day shelf life can now be produced by vacuum packing washed and spin-dried shredded lettuce in special plastic bags that permit sufficient oxygen passage to prevent gassing, but not enough to cause browning.

F. *Desserts*

Desserts such as puddings, gelatin desserts, and canned or frozen fruit can be packed in individual cups for distribution in systems. Most baked desserts such as cakes, cookies and brownies can readily be frozen in order to permit centralized production and distribution to distant serving sites. Long shelf life and extended shelf life baked goods are now produced using the retort pouch or tray packs, and in-package infrared pasteurization respectively. The latter method can be used for cakes and crepes, as well as bread, and provides a shelf life of at least 90 days. Fruit pies are still best frozen raw and baked shortly before distribution, although prebaked frozen fruit pies are also manufactured in ready-to-eat, frozen form. The production of pies and cakes prepared in centralized facilities is a relatively simple operation and if frozen, packaged and stored properly,have a very long storage life.

III. OPTIONS FOR THE FOOD SERVICE SYSTEM DESIGNER

One can sum up the options available to the food service system designer in terms of the methods of preservation required to achieve various shelf lives (Table III).

Prepared food, packed in bulk, or as preplated meals, under ordinary conditions of chilled storage, has a shelf life of two to four days. Probably the widest usage for such meals is air-

TABLE III. *Types of Packaging and Treatments Used for Prepared Foods and Resulting Storage Lives*

Package	Treatment	Storage Temperature		Product Life
		(° F)	(° C)	
Covered Dish	None	35–45	2–7	2–4 Days
Covered Dish	Rapidly Chilled	32–36	0–2	4–6 Days
Pouch	Evacuated, Pasteurized, & Rapidly Chilled	32–36	0–2	30–45 Days
Plastic Container	HT-ST, Aseptically Filled	35–45	2–7	6 Months
Pouch or Tray	Quick Frozen	0	–18	½–1 Year
Can	HT-ST or Aseptically Filled	70	21	1–2 Years
Pouch or Tray	Retorted	70	21	1–2 Years

line feeding. If cooked food is panned while hot, and very rapidly brought to a chilled temperature using a blast chiller, it is feasible to hold many items in excellent condition for up to about six days. By filling the prepared food into hermetically sealed vacuumized containers, followed by pasteurization and rapid chilling, the microflora is further reduced and, since most psychrophiles are aerobic, the absence of oxygen precludes their development, and very good quality retention can be achieved for up to six weeks. Cooked products that are sterilized, aseptically filled in plastic containers, and held chilled, could be expected to have a shelf life of six months, this limitation being related to the container's poor gas barrier characteristics rather than to the presence of microorgan-

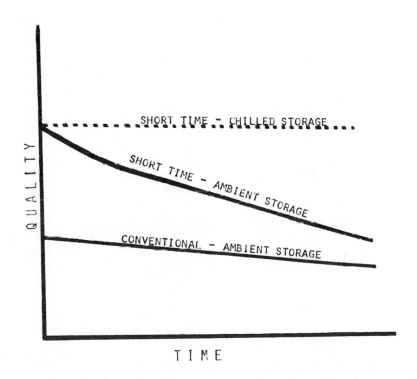

FIGURE 6. *Possible effects of storage time and temperatures on quality parameters in thermally processed foods, sterilized by conventional and high temperature-short time methods.*

isms. Depending upon the product, frozen foods, may have a
shelf life for as long as two years, but reasonable maximum
storage time in a system is six months to a year. Canned
foods, whether in cylindrical cans, pouches or trays, whether
conventionally processed, or processed by a high temperature-
short time or aseptic method will have shelf lives of two years
at room temperature. Thus the food service designer does indeed have a wide spectrum of choices, and decisions should be
based upon the system requirements, feasibility, and cost effectiveness of the alternate methods.

One final point might be made in terms of the newer generation of canned foods, namely that of pouches and tray packs.
It is known from work done on aseptically packed baby foods,
primarily vegetable products, that the initial superiority in
quality shown by these foods above conventionally processed
controls was lost over a period of months when stored at room
temperature, but was very well retained when stored under
chilled conditions (3). It is possible that for many pouch or
tray packed foods, particularly those containing vegetables, a
similar situation may be encountered. A graphic representation
of this hypothesis is shown in Figure 6. While there would undoubtedly be variations from product to product in terms of the
rate of change, it is possible for enough products to benefit
from being stored under chilled conditions if long term storage
is required to suggest that systems designers give serious consideration to chilled storage of such canned foods. A recent
review by Kramer (4) supports this contention.

IV. REFERENCES

1. Dungan, A. and Lacey, S. *Cornell Hotel & Rest.
    Admin. Quart. 10,* 6 (1969)
2. Linstrom, H. R., Seigle, N. and Morrissy, J. D. "The
    Institutional Convenience Food Market" *ERS-555,* U.S.D.A.,
    Washington, D. C. (1974).
3. Livingston, G. E., Esselen, W. B., Feliciotti, E.,
    Westcott, D. E. and Baldauf, M. P. *Food Technol. 11* (1)
    1 (1957)
4. Kramer, A. *Quick Frozen Foods, 41* (12) 24 (1979)

CHAPTER 5

ANALYSIS OF FOOD COSTS AND COST
ESTIMATION OF ALTERNATIVE FOODS

G. E. Livingston

I. INTRODUCTION

The analysis of food cost is a concern of management in
all sectors of the food service industry, whether commercial
or institutional, multi-unit or single unit. In commercial
food service, the objective, most frequently, has been to
maintain food costs as a percentage of the sales dollar. This
percentage ranges from the low 30's in the case of labor-in-
tensive white cloth restaurants, to 45 % for some cafeteria
operations, and as high as 50 % or 55 % in some subsidized
operations. In institutional nonprofit operations, the concern with food cost generally is to remain within the predetermined daily food allowance per customer, i.e. per student,
inmate, or patient.

For menu pricing purposes, the practice has been to determine the raw food cost for a particular dish by calculating
the number of portions obtainable from a given quantity (and
therefore a given cost) of raw materials. As one analyzes
food cost in a food service systems analysis, it is generally
necessary to use more refined approaches, especially if the
objective is to compare the cost effectiveness of alternative
food types. The shortcomings of the traditional methods can
be illustrated by the following examples:

(1) In a commercial operation, where the objective has
been set to maintain a given percentage food cost, one can
easily overlook the obvious fact that a higher percent food
cost could in fact be more profitable. For example, a menu i-
tem that might sell a la carte for $ 3.50 with a 30 % food
cost would yield a gross profit of $ 2.45. On the other hand,
an item on the same menu selling at $ 7.50 with a 50 % food
cost, would yield a gross profit of $ 3.75. Since this would
more than double the check average and increase the gross profit by 50 %, the fact that the food cost has been raised from

Copyright © 1979 by Academic Press, Inc.
All rights of reproduction in any form reserved
ISBN: 0-12-453150-4

30 to 50 % is quite irrelevant to the profitability of the
transaction. In fact, it should be management's goal under
these circumstances to sell as much of the higher priced item,
although the profit margin is lower, since presumably labor
and fixed costs remain the same.

(2) The fixation that the food service industry has had
with food costs has unfortunately reflected in an equivalent
degree of inattention to the equally important aspect of labor
cost. As the number of alternatives to be evaluated increases,
through the availability of commercially packed convenience
foods or through the possibility of central preparation, it
becomes crucially important to determine, with the highest degree of accuracy, the labor cost going into the preparation
of the different items on a menu. This, however, is not yet
the accepted practice in the food service industry. Even
those operators who might wish to determine the labor cost of
menu items on an individual item basis are not really structured to do it. Yet, without an accurate determination of the
combined food and labor cost of an item, it is not possible to
compare the cost of the item prepared on the premises with the
alternatives of outside procurement or central preparation.

(3) There has been a tendency in the industry to down-
grade the value of by-products when, in fact, a considerable
amount of on premise labor might be charged to them if it were
the practice for labor costs to be accurately allocated on
each menu item. For example, if one compares the alternatives
of buying whole chickens or chicken parts, it is immediately
apparent that, on a per pound basis, the whole chickens are
cheaper than the parts. The operator who buys whole chickens
to use certain parts for fried chicken and converts the rest
into chicken pot pies, and bases his menu prices strictly on
the raw chicken cost, is overlooking the fact that the preparation of the meat for the chicken pot pie (which involves
cooking, boning and dicing) makes the cooked chicken going
into this dish far more expensive than the cost of the raw
poultry. It might be more economical to procure the chicken
parts required for the fried chicken and eliminate the high
labor cost-low menu price pot pie or buy diced, precooked,
frozen chicken meat for this purpose.

The fact is that the notion that the kitchen labor is "already there anyway and might as well be put to good use" has
been a deterrent to the objective type of labor costing from
which the food service industry might greatly benefit.

II. FOOD COST ANALYSIS IN SYSTEMS STUDIES

The approach used in analyzing food cost is an application of conventional cost analysis methods. For the time frame set for the sampling period, i.e. one month, three months or a year, the total cost of food used is determined. This is readily computed from the value of the opening inventory plus the cost of all food items purchased during the period under study, minus the value of the closing inventory. While it would seem that every food service operation would have these data readily available, experience shows that in many institutions the available records do not readily permit computation of the total food cost. This is particularly true in those organizations which operate with a daily food cost budget allowance per person.

A. Food Cost per Meal

Assuming that one has determined the total food cost for the period, it is then necessary to compute it into a food cost per meal or daily food cost per person. In order to do this, it is necessary to secure an accurate count of the number of meals served. In this instance too, it has been observed that many institutions do not maintain a sufficient degree of accuracy in their records to permit precise meal count calculations. In many organizations a control exists to verify at meal times that persons eating in the dining hall are indeed authorized to do so but, except in well run commercial operations, proper records of free employee meals, special function meals, catered meals, management meals and guest meals are rarely encountered. It may, therefore, be necessary for the systems analyst to conduct a prospective survey rather than derive the required data from the available historical records. The problem with prospective studies, however, are that they tend to be short in duration and the particular period selected may not necessarily be representative of the whole year because of such factors as seasonal differences, weather and vacations.

B. Standard Meal Costs

In operations in which a menu cycle is used and standard recipes are employed, it is possible to calculate *standard food costs* for the reference period and compare these with the food costs actually achieved. Such a comparison will provide a measure of the efficiency of the system in achieving the meal cost targets. This approach parallels the type of cost analysis that is considered routine in food manufacturing and is rarely practiced in food service.

In setting food cost targets for food service operations, it is necessary to work with fairly complete product specifications for all major products purchased. Clearly, there can be no *standard food costs* unless there are *standard recipes* backed by product specifications for the raw materials used in preparing these recipes. Such factors as fat content, moisture content, drained weight, count and size are relevant to this issue.

C. Reducing Food Costs

Differences in yield achieved as a result of different cooking methods also interface with the question of food costs. Thus, in designing food service systems more is required than a mere standard recipe. What is needed is a *product manufacturing specification* which specifies the exact preparation procedure, equipment to be used and yields expected. One way to reduce food costs is to increase cooking yields. For example, reducing shrinkage in roast beef from 20 % to 10 % can reduce the cost of the cooked meat by about 10 %. If the meat is sold on a weighed portion basis, as in the case of take-out operations serving roast beef sandwiches, this is a very significant savings. Along the same lines, the addition of such ingredients as textured vegetable protein to increase the yield as well as to reduce the food cost per pound, is an effective way to reduce the cost of certain dishes.

One of the possible benefits of centralizing food preparation is the possible reduction in food cost achieved by reducing food waste. While it is difficult to find data on the magnitude of such savings it appears that food costs can be reduced from 5 to 10 % through the economies of scale that are achieved in centralized production. In addition to savings due to waste reduction, centralization of food production offers economies of scale due to the fact that indirect labor and overhead cost factors do not increase proportionately to the numbers of meals produced as do the direct raw materials and labor costs. Table I shows that meal costs in a projected central food preparation facility for school lunches could be reduced almost 22 % by increasing the annual output from 3.4 to 16 million meals.

Inherent in the design of a modern food service system, is the assumption that portion control will be effectively used in the procurement of all incoming materials, as well as in the preparation of the finished products. Another area that should be evaluated, initially and on a continuing basis, is the aspect of food waste. While measurements of plate waste are generally carried out for purposes of determining product

TABLE I. Estimated School Lunch Meal for Various Levels of Meal Production in a Central Food Preparation Facility (1)

Cost Components	Cost per Meal ($) at Various Annual Production Levels			
	3,409,740/year	5,760,000/year	8,000,000/year	16,000,000/year
Material Cost	0.5200	0.5198	0.5197	0.5194
Labor	0.0912	0.0588	0.0545	0.0524
Indirect Cost	0.3267	0.1936	0.1415	0.0762
Total Cost at CFPF	0.9379	0.7722	0.7157	0.6480
Delivery and Serving Costs	0.3807	0.3807	0.3807	0.3807
Total Cost Per Meal	1.3186	1.1529	1.0964	1.0287

acceptability, the information gained is useful for cost purposes as well. Plate waste is food waste and in many instances suggests that portion sizes may be too large and could be reduced or better controlled through preportioning.

III. MERCHANDISING

Experienced food service operators have learned to reduce food costs by proper menu planning. Since the most expensive part of the meal generally resides in the animal protein portion of the main dish it is relatively simple, in institutional feeding, to reduce food costs by reducing the portion sizes required in the expensive main dishes or by reducing the customer demand for them. This can be achieved in a manner which is entirely consonant with proper nutrition and good merchandising by offering customers an attractive array of foods preceding the main course. Such items as fresh hot rolls, mixed raw vegetables (e.g. celery, carrots, cucumber, tomatoes and olives) and hearty thick vegetable soups will effectively reduce the customer's desire to consume large portions of the main course item. Another device that can be used effectively is to tie in a favorite dessert, such as an ice cream sundae or strawberry shortcake, with a popular high priced meat item such as steak in operations where free access to seconds exists. Knowing that a favorite dessert is on the menu many a customer will skip a possible second helping of steak in favor of the dessert!

In some instances, site location of various food service units can be used as a means of controlling food costs. For example, workers in the Operations Research/Systems Analysis Office of the U.S. Army Natick Research and Development Command have shown that, in military installations, it is possible to provide free access to the more costly specialty or steak house operations without jeopardizing the daily food allowance, provided that the less costly fast food or short order type operations were located closer to the living or working quarters.

IV. ANALYSIS OF ALTERNATIVE FOODS

The systems designer is frequently concerned with the replacement of an existing food item or series of items by foods tha' are commercially manufactured or centrally prepared. To accurately determine the value of these alternatives one must cost each item out up to the point of service. This means

TABLE II. Cost Analysis of Breakfast Meal

1. Determination of direct labor cost in production

Operation	Times in Minutes		
	1st Cook	2nd Cook	Grill Cook
200 Breakfasts			
Casserole set-up	6		
Eggs – reconst.	25	30	
Ham – opg. & cutg.	30	40	
Ham & egg – cooking		16	
– assembly	16	30	
Pancake – reconst.			
– cooking	16	16	40
– assembly			
Hooding	17	17	17
Minutes	110	149	57
Hours	1.84	2.49	0.95
Hourly Wage	217 Kr.	192 Kr.	185 Kr.
Labor Cost	399.3 Kr.	478.1 Kr.	175.8 Kr.

Total Labor Cost: 1053.2 Kr.
Cost/meal: 5.27 Kr.
Meals/man hour: 37.9

TABLE II. Cost Analysis of Breakfast Meal (Cont.)

2. Determination of meal cost

Cost Component	Cost (Kr)
Food Cost	
Entree	
Scrambled eggs with ham	8.69
Pancakes	2.63
	11.32
Grapefruit Sections	3.86
Roll & Butter	4.69
Cupcake	3.95
Dry Goods	2.05
Syrup	2.96
	28.83
Labor	
Direct	
Food Preparation	7.89
Tray Cleanup & Assembly	3.19
	11.08
Indirect	11.04
Total labor	22.12
Overhead	8.56
Total Cost per Meal	59.51

TABLE III. Cost Analysis of Fish Meal

1. Determination of direct labor cost in production

Operation	1st Cook	2nd Cook	Grill Cook	Cat.Maid	Cat.Maid
			Time in Minutes		
120 Fish Cass.					
Casserole set-up	3				
Fish – pang. & stmg.	29	29			
– assembly	4	4			
Rice – prep.			29		
– assembly					10
Sauce – prep.			20		
– assembly			5		
Pimiento – slg.				2	
– assembly				5	
Potatoes – prep.		10			
– assembly	9	9			
Hooding	11			11	11
Minutes	56	52	54	18	21
Hours	0.933	0.866	0.9	0.3	0.35
Hourly Wage	217 Kr.	192 Kr.	185 Kr.	141 Kr.	141 Kr.
Labor Cost	203 Kr.	167 Kr.	167 Kr.	43 Kr.	50 Kr.
Total Labor Cost:	630 Kr.				
Cost/meal:	5.25 Kr.				
Meals/man hour:	35.8				

TABLE III. Cost Analysis of Fish Meal (Cont.)

2. Determination of meal cost

Cost Component	Cost (Kr)
Food Cost	
Hot Meal	
Fish	22.00
Curry Sauce	0.99
Corn	1.39
Pimiento	0.09
Mashed Potatoes	1.84
	26.31
Appetizer	16.31
Dessert	6.83
Roll & Butter	4.69
Cookie	3.05
Dry Goods	2.05
	59.24
Labor	
Direct	
Food Preparation	7.26
Tray Cleanup and Assembly	3.19
	10.45
Indirect	11.04
Total Labor	21.49
Overhead	8.56
Total Cost per Meal	89.29

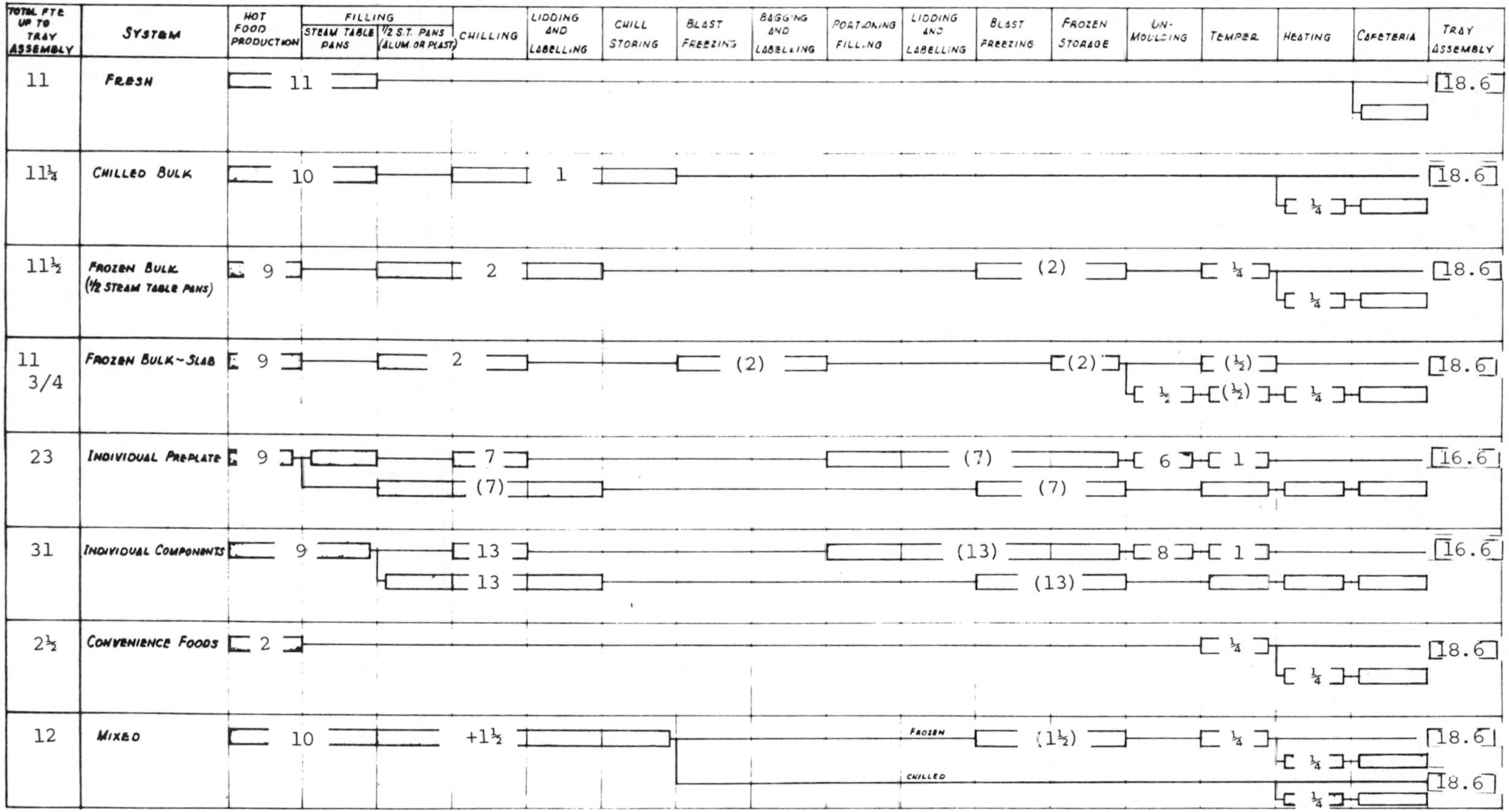

FIGURE 1. Staffing requirements for food production and meal assembly alternatives for a ready foods system for a 500 bed hospital. (Courtesy Food Science Associates, Inc., Dobbs Ferry, N.Y.)

that accurate measurements must be made of yields in preparation and the labor required. At least one complete preparation of the item must be observed, all labor inputs measured, and all raw material requirements and yields precisely determined. Tables II and III shows data collected on two airline meals prepared in a European catering kitchen. One meal is a breakfast, consisting of scrambled eggs with ham and pancakes and the other a fish dinner. While the food cost of the fish dinner (59.24 Kr) is more than double that of the food cost of the breakfast (28.83 Kr) the labor input into the breakfast (5.27 Kr) was greater than that required by the preparation of the fish meal (5.25 Kr). Had ingredient costs alone been used in this study, and an average percentage applied as is the usual practice in the industry, the true cost of the meals would not have been ascertained and management decisions on alternative meals could not have been made on the basis of valid data.

Figure 1 shows the staffing required for eight alternatives evaluated in connection with the design of a new food service system for a 500 bed hospital. It will be noted that the "ultimate convenience system", i.e. one based on the use of frozen individual preplated meals would have required more than twice as many workers (23 FTE) as the fresh system (11 FTE) up to tray assembly. (The "mixed system" was in fact recommended and successfully implemented by the hospital)

As more and more high quality convenience foods and options for central food preparation become available it will become all the more imperative for food service systems analysts to focus on the combined food and labor cost of each meal component rather than food cost alone.

IV. REFERENCES

1. Res. & Dev. Staff, Project ANSER "Five County Management Improvement Project. Program Element 3. Facilities Alternative Planning" Project ANSER, Volusia County School Dist., Deland, Florida (1974).

CHAPTER 6

NEW PACKAGING FOR FOOD SERVICE SYSTEMS

Rauno A. Lampi, Gerald L. Schulz, and Joseph W. Szczeblowski

Food Engineering Laboratory
US Army Natick Research & Development Command
Natick, Massachusetts

I. INTRODUCTION

Packaging for food service applications has traditionally been very similar to that used for retail food distribution. The main difference has been the size of the unit; the larger, so-called "institutional", sizes of containers and packages having been developed to lower the cost of packaging per serving. Examples include the No. 10 can; the one half and full steam table size aluminum pans with paperboard plug lids; polymeric bags for bulk, staple, or frozen products and for bulk blocks of frozen items; cylindrical, or square tins for such items as shortening and potato chips; and fiberboard shipping cases for frozen meat cuts. These concepts are still and will continue to be viable for many products and food service systems.

However, there are newer packaging methods that should be of utility in many modern food service systems. These developments have resulted from a variety of reasons, including:

(1) Recognition by the packaging industry that the food service industry will continue its dynamic growth and represents a distinct market for packaging

(2) The desire by food service operators to use prepared foods or components to an increasing greater degree

(3) Advances in packaging material technology and innovation in designs that make certain preservation methods feasible

(4) The recognition of packaging as a specific and well defined aspect of food service systems, and its role, in many cases, as an integral part of the marketing program

(5) The ubiquitous objective of lower packaging costs, the significance of which has been enhanced in recent years by

Copyright © 1979 by Academic Press, Inc.
All rights of reproduction in any form reserved
ISBN: 0-12-453150-4

energy conservation needs.

II. SHELF-STABLE FOODS

A. *Cylindrical Cans*

Packages for shelf-stable, high water activity foods (aw= 0.98) have been available for a long time in the form of the cylindrical No. 10 (603 x 700) 3-piece sanitary can. For low viscosity, or brine packed products, quality – in view of the heat absorption necessary for sterilization – has been acceptable. The use of such containers for conduction-heated foods is more limited. Innovations such as high rotational agitation (example: FMC Orbitort), high temperature/short time sterilization followed by filling under hyperbaric pressures and post-seaming cooling (examples: Flash 18, Super IT) have been utilized to speed heat transfer into, and minimize overcooking of, the contents. These latter concepts are independent of the container and have found their share of applications, because a high level quality in the processed products has been achieved.

A complete food service system for cafeterias has been built around a large 10 liter can (as compared to the conventional No. 10 can which hold slightly over 3 liters) by Finesko in West Germany (1). Sixty-four full course meals are currently available and six cans contain 100 meals. Rotational cooking is used for sterilization as well as for reheating prior to serving. Such rotational retorts are now finding their way into the U.S. canning industry.

B. *Flat Metal Container*

Szczeblowski (2) described preliminary feasibility trials using flat 30 or 50 mm deep, hermetically sealed trays sized to fit into a one half steam table opening to hold shelf-stable, ready-to-eat foods (Fig. 1). A flat shape is featured to reduce the total exposure time of the product to sterilization conditions (Table I). It has been reported that a 92 minute cook could be reduced to 35 minutes through the use of agitation employing a water cool with overriding air pressure.A lid, with or without the use of vacuum to reduced headspace air, is double seamed to the body of the conventional can would be, to form an adequately hermetic seal. The tray has a weight capacity of about 105 oz. This multifunctional container preserves product quality, permits storage without refrigeration,and acts as a reheating and serving container.

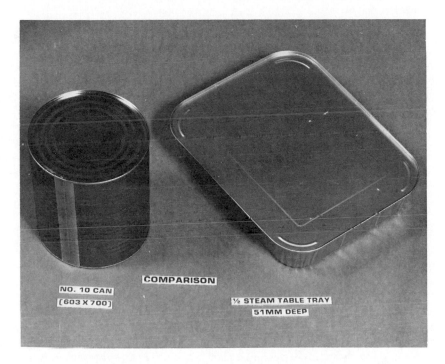

FIGURE 1.   Conventional No.10 can and the new steel ½ steam
table pan size tray.

TABLE I.   Content Weight, Volume, and Sterilization Time
           Differences Between ½ Size Steam Table Trays and
           Conventional No.10 Cans.

COMPARISON OF STERILIZATION TIMES FOR BEEF STEW

| CONTAINER | NET WEIGHT | | NO. OF 8 OZ | PROCESS AT 121.1°C |
	KG	LBS	SERVINGS	MINUTES
SHALLOW TRAY (31 MM)	1.7	3.7	8	45
DEEPER TRAY (51 MM)	2.8	6.1	12	93
#10 STANDARD CAN	3.1	6.7	14	215

There are two variations of steel plate traypacks currently available:

1. *The Central States Can Company* offers a tray fabricated of tin-free steel (Fig. 2). The flanged upper portion which holds the tray in the serving table well, is designed to permit closing by conventional can closing mechanisms and opening by means of standard can openers. No sharp edge is left after opening.

2. *The Kraft Company* has been test marketing "Tray-Pack" foods in a tray of its own design. In outer appearance (Fig.3) it is similar to that of the Central States container but differs in that #25 tin-plate (80 lb base weight steel) is used, the walls are smooth rather than dimpled, and the corner radii are sharper than those of the Central States tray.

C. Product Quality

Figure 4 shows typical products in traypacks. In feasibility tests, the first question that required an answer was that of product quality. It was felt that, if in the initial development, acceptance did not at least approach that of frozen control samples the concept could not be considered feasible. Figure 5 shows that quality and stability are satisfactory, even over a 26 month storage period at ambient temperatures. The illustration is for shallow pans since that particular container was the only one available at the time of the research study. Since then, preliminary storage tests with stew in deeper, i.e. 50 mm pans, have been started.

At the end of 12 months, the traypack was rated better than the frozen counterpart as shown in Figure 6. In addition, the container used for the studies shown in this figure was polymeric and apparently provided an adequate oxygen and water vapor barrier for beef stew.

D. Scope of Products

The scope of products compatible with the traypack concept has not yet been fully established. A cursory survey of the items currently offered to the food service field as preprepared or convenience frozen items reveals that 75 to 80 % of those currently offered could be tray packed. The United States Army Natick Research and Development Command has currently under evaluation Swiss Steak, Chicken Cacciatore, and Beef Burgundy with Vegetables and Rotini.

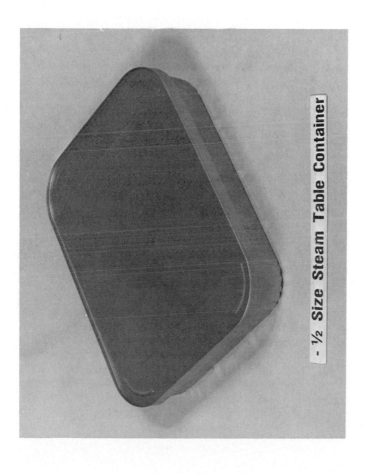

- ½ Size Steam Table Container

FIGURE 2. Steel One Half Size Steam Table Container Manufactured by the Central States Can Co

FIGURE 3. "Kraft Pan", Manufactured by Kraft, Inc. for its own Tray-Pack Products.

BEEF STEW

THERMAL PROCESS

CONTROL

FROZEN

6 MOS. AT 70°F

1/2 SIZE STEAM TABLE PAN

6 MOS. AT 0°F

FIGURE 4. Thermally Processed and Frozen Beef Stew Samples after Six Month Storage.

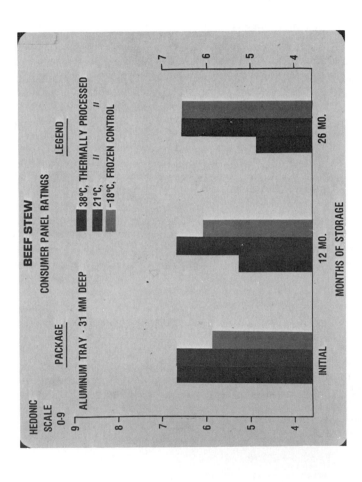

FIGURE 5. Consumer Panel Ratings of Thermally Processed and Frozen Beef Stew Stored for up to 26 Months. Thermally Processed Samples Were Stored at 21°C and 38°C.

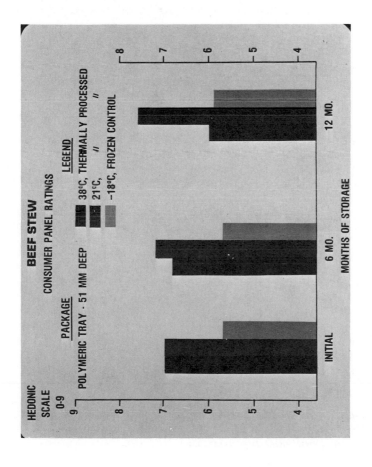

FIGURE 6. Consumer Panel Ratings of Thermally Processed Beef Stew Packed in Polymeric Trays and Frozen Controls Stored for up to 12 Months.

The Kraft Company is test marketing various items, including Beef Stew, Creamed Chicken, Chili with Beans, Ravioli with Meat and Macaroni and Cheese.

The Green Giant Company introduced its "Vacu-Pan" line of prepared foods to the food service industry in May 1978 (3). Products include Beef Stew, Lasagna with Meat Sauce, Stuffed Green Peppers with Beef and Creole Sauce, Stuffed Cabbage with Beef and Tomato Sauce, Salisbury Steaks with Beef Gravy and Cheese Ravioli in Tomato Sauce. Another packer, Bryan Foods, offers Chicken a la King, Beef Stew, Beef Stroganoff, Chicken and Noodles, Creamed,Wafer Sliced Beef, Lasagna with Meat Sauce and Chili with Beans. Blue Star Foods' tray-packed product line includes Beef Stew, Salisbury Steak, Chicken Breasts in Sauce, Chicken Cacciatore, Lasagna with Meat Sauce, Stuffed Cabbage with Meat Sauce and German Potato Salad.

Reheating times for ambient, chilled, and frozen samples of beef stew in a convection oven at $163^{\circ}C(325^{\circ}F)$ are shown in Table II.

A predecessor to the rigid tray pack is the semi rigid retortable container (Fig. 7). The semi rigid retortable container somewhat resembles the common drawn aluminum sardine can. It differs in that the aluminum walls are significantly thinner, $(100\mu$ vs $250\mu)$, the lid is sealed thermally to the body, and the container is marketed in a folding carton or similar outer protective means of packaging. The container can be opened using a knife, even a small plastic one, or by means of a tear tab. The inner protective and heat seal surface is either a polyolefin, such as polypropylene (40 to 75μ) laminated with an adhesive to the body, or a coating such as polyvinylchloride. The latter has been approved for test market purposes in the U.S.

Sizes cover a wide range – from 100 to 3000 gram net weights-the latter size configured to fit into steam table openings (1/3 steam table size).

The semi rigid container is applicable to a wide variety of products, but main dishes have dominated. The same rigid container does offer more physical protection for some types of products (such as canneloni) than a flexible package. It is also used in airline feeding where passengers can consume the food directly from the container.

E. *Production Equipment*

The production system is engineered specifically for the semi rigid application. Manufacturing starts with roll stock. Containers are formed on line, filled and sealed on the same system. Headspace air is avoided by flush filling and sealing under extremely high seal bar pressures. Retorting requires superimposed air pressure to prevent bursting. Speeds can be

TABLE II. *Reheating Times for Ambient, Chilled and Frozen Samples of Beef Stew in a Convection Oven at 163°C (325°F).*

EFFECT OF INITIAL PRODUCT TEMPERATURE ON REHEATING TIME (1)

PRODUCT (2)		OVEN	HEATING TIME (3)
DESCRIPTION	INITIAL TEMP °C	DESCRIPTION	MINUTES
BEEF STEW	24 ROOM		40
	2 CHILLED	FORCED CONVECTION GE MODEL CN 90A AT 163°C	46
	−29 FROZEN		90

(1) CONTAINER: TRAY 50 MM DEEP OF PP/SARAN/PP, LID OF PP/AL

(2) NET WEIGHT: 2.7 KG (12 SERVINGS)

(3) TEN (10) CONTAINERS PER LOAD

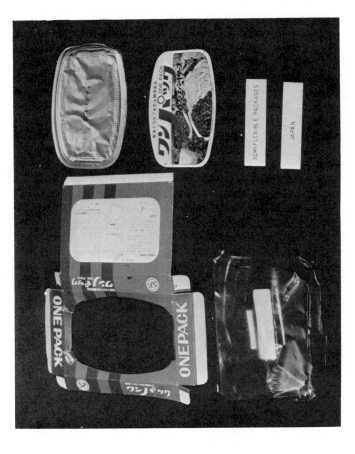

FIGURE 7. Examples of Semi Rigid Retortable Containers Used in Japan.

higher than currently possible for pouches because of the easier filling.

The semi rigid containers are very prone to denting, but very resistant to leaks. Present indications are that they can resist distribution system hazards satisfactorily. Test market studies should establish the significance of easy denting for the retail market. It is judged that the lack of rigidity should not deter institutional applicability.

F. Polymeric Containers

Formed polymeric container, with heat sealed foil laminate lids, can also be used for ready-to-eat, shelf stable foods. Concomitantly with the evaluation of the ½ steam table size tray packs made of steel plate, the U.S. Army Natick Research and Development Command has evaluated the same concept using thermoformed trays of coextruded high density polyethylene/polyvinylidene chloride/high density polyethylene and polypropylene/polyvinylidene chloride/polypropylene with heat sealed lids of foil laminate or the body material (Fig. 8). The stability data shown in Figure 6,was based on such a container. If adequate stability can be realized, as appears to be the case, such a container has the further advantage of heatability in microwave ovens. Table III shows the results of reheating trials.

Other drawn polymeric container constructions are compatible with hot fill systems for acid products, or aseptic techniques for low acid fluids, to avoid thermal stresses on the container. In these systems, the containers are thermoformed from sheet stock and filled, and foil laminate lids are sealed on in a totally enclosed system. Sterilization of the packaging body material and foil lids is usually by means of hydrogen peroxide aided by heat and sterile filtered air. Body materials include polystyrene, acrylonitrile butadiene styrene, and coextruded combinations with polyvinylidene chloride or polyethylene to achieve better barriers. Both single serving (fruit juice cups) and multiple serving sizes (soups) are feasible. For the larger sizes, a paperboard sleeve provides structural strength for the side walls. Coffee creamers, yogurt, and juices are commonly packaged in this type of container.

G. Flexible Packaging

Flexible packaging is feasible for shelf stable wet foods. The initial major research effort in this area has been that of the U.S. Army Natick Research and Development Command. Later Japanese, Italian, Danish, and several U.S. firms began developmental work. Commercialization began outside the United States. In 1976 in Japan, 600 million units a year were already

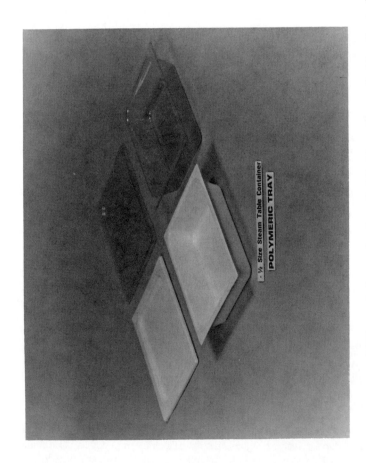

FIGURE 8. *Opaque and Clear Polymeric One Half Size Steam Table Containers.*

114

TABLE III. Comparison of Heating Times for One Half Size Steam Table Pans of Beef Stew in Polymeric Containers in Convection Oven and Microwave Oven.

HEATING TIME TO 74°C SERVING TEMPERATURE[1]

PRODUCT[2]	OVEN DESCRIPTION	HEATING TIME MINUTES
MEAT LOAF, SLICED W/GRAVY	FORCED-CONVECTION GE MODEL CN 90A AT 154°C	41
MEAT LOAF, SLICED W/GRAVY	MICROWAVE-AMANA RADARANGE, MODEL RR4 (14.5 AMP, 1600 WATTS)	25

(1) CONTAINER: POLYPROPYLENE, 1/2 STEAM TABLE SIZE, 50 MM DEEP TRAY; SARAN FILM LID.

(2) INITIAL TEMPERATURE: 24°C, NET WEIGHT: 3.1 KG (14 SERVINGS)

being sold, and in Europe 60 million per year. In Canada, Swan
Valley, Ltd. in British Columbia (Fig. 9), now a subsidiary of
Standard Brands Inc., progressed from test marketing to full
commercial distribution throughout the province by mid 1976. A
second Canadian firm, Magic Pantry is now marketing stuffed
cabbage rolls in retort pouches. In the U.S., ITT Continental
Baking began test marketing its "Flavor Seal" line of prepared
entrees in retort pouches in 1977 (3). The George A. Hormel
Co. is also now packing eleven meat-based products in pouches,
while Specialty Seafoods packs oysters and smoked salmon in
this fashion. In the U.S. also, the military have accepted
the packaging concept to replace the cans in operational rations and it is anticipated that $ 100 million worth of com-
mercially packed retort pouch products for military usage will
be procured in 1980 (3).

The retort pouch is a rectangular, 4-seal, flat package
made usually of a laminate of 0.5 mil Mylar/0.35 mil aluminum
foil/3.0 mil of modified, high density polyethylene or 3.0 mil
ethylene-propylene copolymers. Its usual measurements are
4-1/2" to 8" (11.5 cm to 17.7 cm) in width and 6" to 12" (15 cm
to 30 cm) in length, nominal thicknesses are 3/4" to 1"
(1.9 cm to 2.5 cm). With fluid products, such as stews or
chicken a la king it usually contains 120 to 300 gm of product.

Foil-free laminates, such as Nylon/polypropylene have been
used for vegetables, such as institutional and retail potatoes
where a 6 to 10 week shelf-life is adequate. Also, for relatively solid, moisture-free products, net weights can be as
high as 6.0 kg with accordingly larger pouches.

Except for some institutional packs, each pouch is enclosed
in an envelope-like folder or a folding carton. To meet the
military's performance requirements, the pouch is glued to the
folder or carton, but for commercial applications, gluing is
not necessary.

Food is first filled into the pouch, followed by air removal, closure sealing, and finally, retorting.

For the consumer market, several benefits of the retort
pouch package are quite evident:

Convenience	– *an easy-to-open, boil-in-bag product*
Quality	– *optimally sterilized product with minimum overcooking*
Energy Conservation	– *low energy usage for container fabrication; no refrigeration requirements; less clean-up*
Cost/Economics	– *currently speculative but competitive with conventional cans in the future, as line speeds increase and pouch packaging costs increase more slowly than can costs*

For its operational rations, the U. S. military are cur-

FIGURE 9. *Examples of Retort Pouch Packed Products Manufactured by Swan Valley in Canada.*

rently procuring 22 items including such products as chocolate nut cake, meatballs in barbecue sauce, ham slices, and frank-furters. The initial Canadian products included Chicken Stew, Potatoes in Butter Sauce, and Apple Slices.   ITT Continental Baking's initial line comprised Chinese Pepper Steak, Beef Bourguignon,Veal Scallopine and Chicken Cacciatore. In Europe, a large variety of prepared dishes have been marketed in addi-tion to sauces,vegetables and institutional potatoes. Japanese manufacturers have specialized in curry bases,soups and stews.

Potential applications for food service include:
(1) Therapeutic diet products for hospitals
(2) Portion-controlled entrees, such as stews, meat or poultry in sauce for normal diet and/or emergency use (Fig. 10)
(3) Sauces, such as cream sauces,spaghetti sauce or creole sauce to be served over or with other meal components (Fig. 11).
(4) Syrupless fruit for use in baked goods.
(5) Bulk packs of potatoes for hash browns, salad, or french fries.

For many products where a somewhat low temperature/longer time process is preferred for flavor development, the advant-age of the thin cross section of the pouch is the avoidance of peripheral overcooking. For other products, the pouch permits application of the high temperature/short time processing technique which limits physical and chemical degradation while providing bacteriological inactivation at temperatures in the area of $135^{\circ}C$ ($275^{\circ}F$). Japanese manufacturers have developed films capable of withstanding temperatures of $135^{\circ}C$ ($275^{\circ}F$) and even higher. This permits processing for short times of 3 to 9 minutes compared to 20 to 25 minutes at $121^{\circ}C$ ($250^{\circ}F$) or 35 to 40 minutes at $115^{\circ}C$ ($240^{\circ}F$).

One obvious advantage of high temperature/short time pro-cessing,using steam-air or water cook techniques,is the great-er production possible in the packing plant in view of the re-duced sterilization time required. However,increased producti-vity is only one benefit.Tests using lower and higher sterili-zation temperatures,have shown (Fig.12) that textural and also color, and overall appearance improvements are possible. Ja-panese researchers have backed their claims with analytical data. Table IV shows retention of quality indicators and nu-trients.

Aseptic techniques have been also applied to flexible packages but are currently limited to fluid products such as milk and juices. Sterilization of product is accomplished by high temperature-short time heat exchangers; sterilization of film is by alcohol, hydrogen peroxide, ultraviolet radiation, ethylene oxide gas, infrared heat or a combination of media. The packaging chamber atmosphere is kept sterile through the

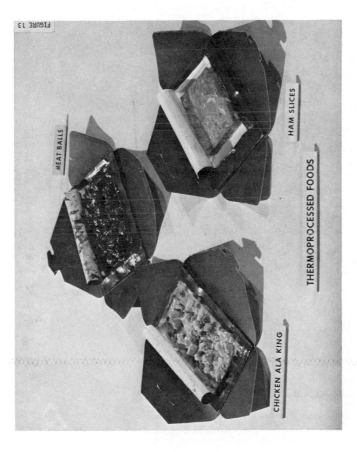

FIGURE 10. Examples of Retort Pouch Packed Foods for Military Ration Usage.

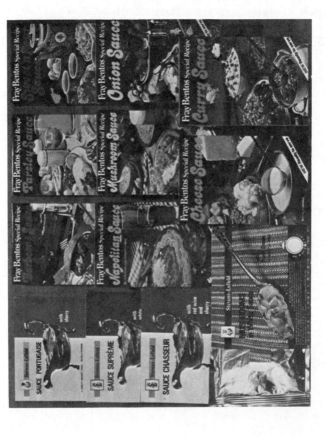

FIGURE 11. Examples of Sauces Packed in Retort Pouches. (Courtesy of DRG Flexible Packaging,Ltd)

FIGURE 12. Appearance of Retort Pouch Packed Foods Processed by High Temperature-Short Time Method and Conventional Sterilization. (Courtesy of Toyo Seikan Kaisha, Ltd)

TABLE IV. *Quality Retention in Retort Pouch Packed Foods Processed at Various Temperatures*[a]

Quality Parameter	Unsterilized Controls	Process Temperature (°C)				
		115	120	130	135	145
Thiamine Retention in Seasoned Eel (% Retention)	100	17.2	---	85.3		98.1
Texture Retention in Beef Steak (Hardness in cm/V)	15.2	8.4	9.6	13.8	13.4	15.1
Viscosity Retention in Cream Soup (Viscosity in cps)	14.8	24.0	20.0	17.7	17.3	15.0
Color Retention in Green Beans (Hue, a/b)	-98.4	-21.3	-32.4	-72.9	-76.6	-87.0

[a] process times for each temperature varied with product. All products were processed to F_o of 3.3 - 3.5.

use of heated and/or filtered air under positive pressure.

Packaging materials and designs run the gamut from polymeric laminate fin-seal bags of such construction as polyethylene/polyvinylidene chloride/polyethylene coextrusions holding from 0.2 to 1.2 liters of product (Thimonnier Twinpak System), to shaped polymer, foil, paperboard laminate materials and tetrahedral, brick shaped, and standard milk carton constructions, (Tetrapak, Purepac) which can be classed as either flexible or semi-rigid. Dispensing spouts for delivery of products such as salad dressing can be used with the milk carton designs.

III. SEMI-SHELF STABLE FOODS

The term semi-shelf stable would apply most appropriately to foods relying on low but not freezing temperatures and on mild heat treatment for their stability. The Nacka system developed in Sweden has received considerable attention (4). In this system, and its subsequent variations, a meal component for 1 to 6 servings is filled into a polymeric package, air is removed, the package is sealed, and the filled package is pasteurized in a hot water bath before being chilled by water or a cooling tunnel to $2^{\circ}C$ $(36^{\circ}F)$. Storage from time of packaging to consumption is at $3^{\circ}C$ $(38^{\circ}F)$ and shelf life is a reported maximum of three weeks. For reconstitution, the packages are placed in boiling water for 10 to 20 minutes.

The packaging need not be very sophisticated or costly. Most polymeric materials can withstand the maximum internal temperatures of $100^{\circ}C$ $(212^{\circ}F)$. The use of medium density polyethylene has been reported although eleven other candidate materials performed adequately. The design of the package can vary. Initially, tubular material sealed with metal clips was used. Variations since then include heat-sealed flat bags and drawn polymeric pouches. Where the last design is used, the polyethylene is supported by polyamide or polyester. The Cryovac "Kap-Cold System" represents the latest U.S. commercial adaptation of the Nacka process. Several U.S. manufacturers also offer films to tightly wrap meats for optimum, clean roasting to permit meats thus wrapped to be pre-roasted, stored, and finished off just prior to serving.

Schotte (5) has reported the use of wax-coated cellophane/polyethylene combination and lacquered polypropylene for packaging hot-air oven sterilized breads in Germany. Sterilization temperatures (product) range between 105 and $130^{\circ}C$ $(221-266^{\circ}F)$ and times from one to four hours depending on the type bread. By the use of heat-sealed, thermoformed packages similar to those used for luncheon meats, American Microfare (6) has extended sandwich shelf life. By excluding air from the package through proprietary means, a bread shelf-life of months is claimed.

IV. FROZEN FOODS

The aluminum tray with a paperboard plug lid is by far the most prevalent frozen food container for sizes from 4 oz. (100 g) to 120 oz. (3000 g). This supposition has been confirmed by surveys. The aluminum tray is relatively inexpensive, compatible with conventional oven reheating temperatures, and equipment for filling and lidding are readily available. There has been interest in tray style packages of other materials,mostly for the 4 oz. (100 g) to 8 oz. (200 g) sizes for individual servings to improve eye appeal, permit microwave heating, and be compatible with developmental vending systems.

Beyond the aluminum tray already shown, evaluations for cost, reheatability, and storage stability have included the following containers:

- Coated molded pulp with a heat-sealed polyester lid
- High density polyethylene or polypropylene coated paperboard tray with a heat-sealed lid of the same construction.
- High density polyethylene tray with a heat-sealed Mylar-polyethylene film lid
- Polypropylene tray with a heat-sealed Mylar-polypropylene film lid

A. Costs

Considering three cost factors, e.g. equipment, materials, and labor for the preparation of 2 million units per year, three materials were rated in the $ 0.037 to $ 0.093, or less than $ 0.10 unit range: molded coated paperboard, high density polyethylene, polypropylene. Three cost slightly higher,in the $ 0.125 to $ 0.138/unit range; they were aluminum, polypropylene coated paperboard and polyester. Polysulfone was a high $ 0.288/unit.

B. Reheating

All materials withstood microwave reheating, especially if metal shielding is used to optimize the heating effects. Only the polypropylene coated paperboard carton and aluminum tray withstood conventional and convection hot-air oven temperature of 375 to 400°F (191 to 204° C) when these latter two heating modes were required as back-up methods.

C. *Storage Stability*

The same basic containers were subjected to storage tests to determine their capabilities to store products for up to one year. Two products, chili, representing an acid food, and chicken a la king, a blander product, were used. After six months storage at $-20°$ F ($-29°$ C), results indicated no visual deterioration of package or product, staining, product-container reactions, or loss of heat seal (on lids). A trained taste panel evaluated the products for flavor, odor, texture and overall quality. Except for one package, no changes related to time or differences among the package constructions were detected. The exception, molded pulp tray, has apparently not protected the chicken a la king adequately; however, for chili, the pulp tray performance is still adequate.

Overall, if microwave heating with hot-air oven back-up of foods in their primary containers is desired and a shelf-life of 6 to 12 months is needed, the high density polyethylene or polypropylene coated paperboard trays seem most appropriate.

V. SELECTING PACKAGING SUB SYSTEMS

The packaging possibilities for any particular food service system or situation as noted, are many. Many concepts and approaches have been promoted by interests other than the groups responsible for their ultimate utilization. Some are deviations from existing systems to avoid proprietary conflicts. Others are spinoffs of related technology. Because of the obvious importance of packaging, a food packaging professional should be included in the design of any new food service system. A great deal of technology is available; the problem is to assure its proper use. A packaging professional will define the needs in terms of importance, establish criteria and levels of required performance, recognize constraints and select in an unbiased manner the best packaging method. Exact package burden and design will usually depend on:

Shelf Life

Length and Type of Distribution System

Degree of Control Exercised or Guaranteed Over ALL Operations and Storage Conditions

Desired Functions for Package; for example, to Act as a Reheating, Serving Vessel, and/or as Dinnerware

VI. REFERENCES

1. Anon. "I Can Cater to 500 People per Hour" *Brochure, Finesko,* Neuminster, West Germany (1975)
2. Szczeblowski, J.W. *Research and Development Associates Activities Rep. 25* (1) 77-84 (1973)
3. Bannaar, R. *Food Eng. 51* (4) 69 (1979)
4. Tandler, K. *Die Fleischwirtschaft 7,* 845 (1972)
5. Schotte, K. "Sterilized Sheets for Preserved Food" *Supplement to Verpackungs-Rundschau* (1974)
6. Anon. *Food Product Devel. 10* (1) 71 (1976)

CHAPTER 7

DETERMINING CONSUMER PREFERENCE
IN INSTITUTIONAL FOOD SERVICE

Herbert L. Meiselman

Behavioral Sciences Division
Food Sciences Laboratory
US Army Natick Research & Development Command
Natick, Massachusetts

Before dealing with the question of how to measure food
preferences, and including some examples of the type of data
available, it is important to place the issue of consumer food
preferences within the perspective of other measures of consumer and operator behavior that are of interest in the psy-
cological study of food service systems.

I. CONSUMER PREFERENCE SURVEYS

Opinion data can be collected from food service customers
on a large number of issues (Table I) through the use of
interviews or questionnaires. Information can be gathered
about the food itself, the service provided, and the physical
and social aspects of the eating environment. Obviously, in
certain food service operations, other questions become
relevant.

Over the past five years consumer opinion of military
food service systems has been measured in a variety of situations, including in dining halls and in the field, in virtually every climate imaginable, from below zero in Alaska and
the northern plains to 100 plus temperatures of the desert
and the humid heat of the southeast; in small, medium, and
large dining halls; and for all four military services with
their individual peculiarities. Nevertheless, the data
obtained have been limited in two ways. First, virtually all
of the data are from males, although it is planned to collect
substantial data from females too, in order to compare the

127

Copyright © 1979 by Academic Press, Inc.
All rights of reproduction in any form reserved
ISBN: 0-12-453150-4

TABLE I.   Factors in Consumer Opinion of Food
           Service Systems

Food	Food Service	Environment	Social
Quality	Personnel	Convenience	Eating companions
Quantity	Speed of service	Physical	Atmosphere
Variety	Hours of opera-tion	Decor	
	Expense	Monotony	

food habits of males and females. The second limitation is
that the data overrepresent the younger age groups, and
include very few opinions from people over age 50.

One of the surveys, which is administered in a group
setting, asks respondents to rate each of 14 food service
variables as a problem or an attraction. The variables are
then ranked according to the ratings, and the data from a
large number of test sites indicate that the variables associated with food consistently receive relatively high rank-
ings (Table II). This is especially true of food quality,
which is usually the most serious problem according to the
customers. The validity of this type of opinion data can
readily be established by examining certain other aspects of
the survey. One of the problems studied is that of standing
in line, one of the traditional complaints of military life.
When people are asked how serious they consider the problem
of standing in line to be, and how long they actually wait
in line, a clear relationship emerges (Table III). The
longer one waits in line, the more serious one rates the problem. This, and other examples of sensible relationships,
gives confidence in these types of data.

Another source of data, from Air Force personnel testing
an experimental cafeteria food system, confirms the relative
importance of food variables in general, and of food variety
in particular. When asked which factors determined their
food choices, the most common response was "liking for the
food," meaning that the person picked items he liked
(Table IV). Variety of food offered scored third, meaning
that people chose items based on their recent eating habits
to provide variety in their menus. Nutritional value and
caloric content ranked lowest in determining food choices.
This is consistent with observations of generally little

TABLE II.   The Ranking of Five Food Variables within a
            List of 14 Food Service Variables Tested at
            Eight Bases in the United States

Base	Rank[a]				
	Food quality	Food quantity	Weekday food variety	Weekend food variety	Short order food variety
Fort Lee	3	6	5	7.5	2
Fort Myer	1	5	3	2	4
Bolling AFB	1	7	3	2	5
Travis AFB	1	8	3	2	5
Minot AFB	1	4	5	3	7
Homestead AFB	1	4	3	2	7
Shaw AFB	7	6	9	10	8
Alameda NAS	3	8.5	5	4	1

[a]Low numbers refer to high rank.   Data only from personnel
receiving free food.

TABLE III.   The relation between Reported Delay in
             Serving Lines and the Stated Importance of
             Waiting in Line in Determining Dining Hall
             Attendance

Base	Delay at serving line (minutes)	Rank of 14 factors for attendance
Travis AFB	4.19	12
Loring AFB	4.73	9
Homestead AFB	5.45	7
Alameda NAS	5.74	8
Minot AFB	5.24	4.5
Shaw AFB	6.00	1
Fort Lee	8.23	1

TABLE IV. Rank of Eight Determinants of Food Choice in
Terms of their Importance[a]

| Food choice determinant | Rank based on soldiers' ration status | | | |
| | Monetary allowance instead of food | | Free food | |
	Pre	Post	Pre	Post
Liking for food	2	1	1	1
Food appearance	1	2	2.5	3
Food variety	3	3	2.5	2
Food cost	4	4.5	7	4
Familiarity of food	7	6	4	5.5
Compatibility	5	7	5	5.5
Nutritional value	6	4.5	6	7
Caloric content	8	8	8	8

[a]Before (pre) and after (post) conversion to cafeteria
system.

interest on the part of most military, and probably most
institutional customers, in these variables.

What does customer concern with food variety mean?
Without additional data, several hypotheses are possible:
people do not like what they are being served in general, not
enough choices are offered at each meal, not enough choices
are offered over a week or month's time. Other possibilities
do exist. In order to deal with any of these, however, one
must begin to understand people's attitudes toward food items
and how those attitudes are translated into actions and
habits.

The simple question of what foods people like or dislike
has been the focus of a great deal of research. The first
issue that must be addressed is how such attitudes are measured. Two different approaches to this question have been
used. One method is to measure how much a particular food is
liked (hedonic scales), and the other is to ask how frequently a food is desired (preferred frequency).

II. HEDONIC SCALES OF PREFERENCES

Hedonic scales seek to measure a degree of liking. A large number of different hedonic scales have been used in a variety of food service situations (Table V). Several studies have used small numbers of hedonic scale categories. Hall and Hall [3], for example, simply asked whether foods were disliked or were unfamiliar, and Abbot *et. al.* [4] used a two-point scale of acceptable and dislike (or "not tried").

TABLE V. Hedonic Scales of Food Preference Used by Various Investigators

Investigators	Number of scale points	Scale categories
Hall and Hall [3]	2	dislike, unfamiliar
Abbot et al. [4]	2	acceptable, dislike not tried
Einstein and Hornstein [5]	3	like a lot, like, dislike, do not know
Lamb et al. [6]	3	well-liked, indifferent, disliked, seldom or never eaten
Harper [7]	5	like very, like moderate, neutral, dislike moderate, dislike very
Kennedy [8,9]	5	very good, good, moderate, tolerate, dislike, never tried
Dove [10]	5	very good, good, moderately well, tolerate, dislike
Eppright [11]	5	very good, good, moderate, dislike, tolerate
Peryam et al.	9	like extremely, very much, moderately, slightly, neither like nor dislike, dislike slightly, moderately, very much, extremely

Einstein and Hornstein [5] used a three-point scale of like
a lot, like, and dislike (or "do not know") in their large
survey of college food service. None of these small scales
provided balanced categories above and below a neutral point.
The three-point scale used by Lamb *et al.* [6], well-liked,
indifferent, disliked (or "seldom or never eaten"), is more
balanced around neutral. This supports the assumption of
equal degrees of positive and negative effect as one moves
away from neutral. With small numbers of categories, the
generally observed tendency on the part of respondents to
avoid scale endpoints could seriously affect the data. This
avoidance of endpoints effectively reduces three-point scales
to single-point scales, five-point scales to three-point
scales, and so on.

Five-point scales (plus "not tried") have been used by
Harper [7] in work on vegetable preferences, by Kennedy [8,9],
by Dove [10], and by Eppright [11], who also used "never
tried" and "allergic" categories. In many of these scales
the naming of the categories makes the psychological distances
between scale points difficult to determine.

The nine-point hedonic scale (Table V) developed by the
Quartermaster Food and Container Institute has been subjected
to more research and use than any other food preference measure. A nine-point scale was chosen after determining that
increasing scale length did not significantly increase test
time or decrease test reliability, and did increase the
amount of information obtained [12]. The category labels of
the nine-point scale involve equivalent terms above and
below the neutral point (extremely, very, moderately, slightly)
that yield a scale symmetrical around its midpoint. Also,
use of the same verb with a different prefix (like and dislike)
keeps the scale simple to understand and produces opposites
equidistant from the center. Many of the other hedonic
scales have neither of these characteristics.

There are typically two criteria by which test designers
evaluate scales. Reliability, or reproducibility, is how
well repeated tests yield similar results. Validity is how
well the scale measures what the designer wants to measure.
Most hedonic scales have not been scientifically analyzed for
reliability and validity. Peryam *et al.* [13] studied the
reliability of the nine-point scale in surveys as many as
108 food items containing five repeat items. Correlations
for the repeat items exceeded 0.95.

In a more recent study of reliability of the hedonic
scale [14], 123 subjects were tested twice several months
apart, on a food preference survey composed of 416 items
judged on both hedonic and preferred frequency scales. Correlations of the hedonic scale data between the group's mean
food ratings were 0.92, and for individuals were 0.60. The

latter value was achieved by averaging across foods (instead of individuals) and taking the mean of the 123 correlations. In another study of food consumption, with a small sample of ten subjects [15], the correlation across all hedonic ratings of foods was 0.75 and across all subjects was 0.70.

Therefore, surveys of food names are quite repeatable in producing a similar ordering of items, e.g., hamburgers above tuna sandwich, above cheese sandwich. The repeatibility of any one person is somewhat lower and partly for this reason the food preferences of individuals are less predictable than those of populations.

In evaluating validity, one is generally interested in a criterion of actual eating behavior: how well will preference predict selection, intake, consumption, or waste of foods? Peryam et al. [13] studied two different measures of food behavior. The correlation between the percentage of men accepting each item, and the preference survey figures from a national survey of Army personnel was 0.59, whereas correlations of 0.74 and 0.77 were obtained between preference measures for the test population and serving proportion consumed, and percent accepting the item, respectively. In the study by Smutz et al. [15], the correlation between rated hedonic preference and actual selection by the same group of ten was 0.50.

Recently, preference for names on food surveys has been compared with preference for plastic food models to determine how the rating of a food name extends to a more realistic stimulus [16]. A correlation of 0.86 was obtained on the hedonic scale for 21 subjects rating 31 food names or models. Thus, subjects showed similar preferences to surveys and models. The correlation between these ratings and survey data was 0.66, confirming the finding by Peryam and his coworkers that preference data from the same population is advantageous in making predictions. Thus, the nine-point hedonic scale yields data that are highly reproducible and correlate well with ratings of stimuli other than names on a survey. The ability to predict actual food behavior is improved if food preference data is available from the target population.

Examples of Hedonic Data

A large variety of hedonic scale food preference data is available, ranging from small studies of specialized groups to large studies of military, college, and other populations. In some instances, the scale used to collect the data does not necessarily affect the ranking of the foods according to hedonic preference. For example, the food preferences of

college students who rated foods on the three-point hedonic
scale, and of military personnel who rated foods on the nine-
point hedonic scale, are similar in many cases. The comparison of the two surveys is shown for soup (Table VI). Since
the military survey contained more soups, it is not clear whether there would have been such close agreement if all soups
served to the military were compared with the same soups rated
by college students. Nevertheless, the agreement between surveys, with the exception of cream of mushroom soup, is quite
high. Both surveys yielded high preference for french fried
potatoes and low preference for sweet potatoes, high preference for green beans and green peas and low preference for
brussel sprouts, high preference for either whole kernel corn
or corn on the cob and low preference for baked squash. In
other words, despite differences in the scale used and in the
population studied, many patterns of food preferences emerged.

An extensive survey of food preferences in the U.S.
Armed Forces [17], utilizing a population of 4000 and 378
food items, permits many comparisons and conclusions to be
made. Interestingly, on the ninepoint scale, milk occupies
the least liked and most liked endpoints, with whole milk
being the most popular, and skimmed milk and buttermilk being
the two least popular beverages. Between these extremes,
different food classes show different distributions of preference scores. This is shown by ranking foods within quartiles

TABLE VI. *The Ranking[a] of Hedonic Scores of Seven Soups
by College Students and Military Personnel.*

College students [5]		Military Personnel [17]	
Rank	Variety	Rank	Variety
1	chicken noodle	1	chicken noodle
2	vegetable	2	vegetable
3	tomato	3	tomato
4	cream of mushroom	12	cream of mushroom
5	clam chowder	6	clam chowder
6	beef barley	8	beef barley
7	navy bean	9	bean soup

[a]The top-ranked soup has the highest mean hedonic score.

based on their hedonic scores, the first quartile containing
the best liked foods in the survey and the fourth quartile
containing the least like items (Figure 1). Entrees, salads,
and desserts contain many well-liked items; beverages and
starches show similar numbers of items within all quartiles;
soups, vegetables, and fruits all show many items within the
bottom-ranked items.

III. SCALES OF PREFERRED FREQUENCY

Preferred frequency scales have used either verbal categories of frequency or quantitative categories (Table VII).
Almost all preferred frequency scales of the former type have
had four or nine categories. These verbal scales have
depended heavily upon the temporal system of day, week, month.
Benson [20] used a four-category scale (once a day, week,
month, year), and Hartmuller [19], Peryam et al. [13], and

TABLE VII. *Preferred Frequency Scales of Food Preferences*

Termed Used	Reference					
	[18]	[19]	[13]	[20]	[21]	[22]
Often					X	X
Twice a day	X	X	X			
Once a day	X	X	X	X		
Every other day	X	X				
Several times/wk, 15 mo.			X			
Twice a week	X	X	X			
Once a week	X	X	X	X	X	X
Every other week	X	X	X			
Once a month	X	X	X	X		
Once every 3 mos.			X			
Once a year			X	X		
Never/unwilling to eat	X	X	X			X
Not familiar	X	X	X		X	X

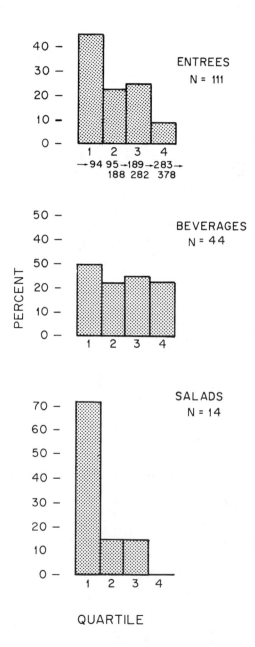

FIGURE 1. Quartile distribution of ranks for hedonic scores for entrees, beverages, and salads.

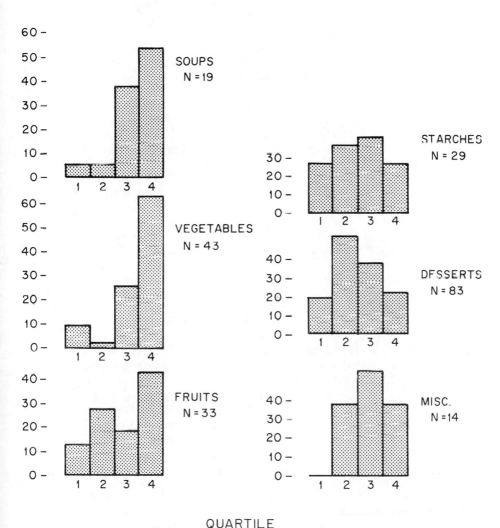

QUARTILE

FIGURE 1   (Continued).   Quartile distribution of ranks
for hedonic scores for soups, vegetables, fruits, starches,
desserts, and miscellaneous menu items.

Knickrehm *et al.* [18] used nine category scales (from twice
a day to once a month). Two other scales have added the
term "often" to temporal terms, Leverton [22] and Schuck [21],
although this addition appears difficult to define quantitatively. The scale used by the Army Quartermaster [13] was
occasionally extended to once every three months and to once
a year.

A basic question with these scales is the appropriate
temporal unit for making the preference judgments: should
people be asked their food preferences in terms of daily,
weekly, or monthly habits? The actual frequency corresponding to the verbal categories was provided by the Quartermaster survey. However, Knickrehm *et al.* [18] arbitrarily
assigned numerical ratings to the preferred frequency category
data to determine an arithmetic mean, a practice that appears
questionable.

Recently, two quantitative preferred frequency scales have
been developed at US Army Natick Research and Development
Command. In the first [14,23], the respondent indicates first
how many days per week he wants a particular food at each meal,
and then how many weeks per month. While this method directly
produces a quantitative estimate, it has several disadvantages.
It forces the respondent into a week-month system, assumes
repetition of a weekly pattern, and eliminates certain frequencies since it limits frequencies to 0 or 4-28 times per
month. The reliability of this scale is about the same as
the standard hedonic scale, with a correlation of 0.98 for
food means, and a correlation of 0.60 for individuals [14].

In the second survey format, the respondent could indicate
any preferred monthly frequency from 00 to 30 days. This
two-digit preferred frequency scale was included on the same
sheet with the hedonic scale. When hedonic scale and preferred frequency scale were used in the same survey but on
separate pages, the average correlation between the two
scores for the same foods was only 0.39 [23]; when the two
scales were paired on the same survey sheets higher correlations of 0.56 [17] and 0.68 [15] were achieved.

Preferred frequency scales of food preference appear to
show consistent appeal to food researchers. They do tap a
different aspect of food attitudes as shown by their moderate
to low correlations with hedonic data. Whether preferred
frequency, hedonic scales, or a combination of the two will
best predict actual behavior has not been resolved.

Examples of Preferred Frequency Data

Comparisons among the studies that have used preferred frequency scales are difficult because the data are reported in different ways. For example, Knickrehm *et al.* [18] report the percentage of the sample that would accept an item with a given frequency; Schuck [21] reports the food items that 10% or more of the students were willing to eat once a week, and so on. The Armed Forces data show that hedonic and frequency scales produce different distributions of items within some different food classes. Beverages, for example, show similar numbers within all quartiles of the distribution to all hedonic scores for all foods. However, preferred frequency scores place a large number of beverages in the upper quartile, because many beverages are consumed with relatively high frequencies. Conversely, entrees, which yielded many high scores for hedonic data, show many more moderate scores with preferred frequency scales, because few entrees are desired with high frequency. Most other classes do not show as dramatic a shift in distribution of scores from hedonic to frequency.

One consideration with preferred frequency data is whether the data can be used at face value, i.e., can consumers plan a menu by individually stating their desired food frequencies. The answer probably is no. However, it should be kept in mind that respondents were not asked to plan a menu, but to state their preferences item by item. The preferred frequencies of the highest ranking items do not lead one to suspect the problem. Milk is requested an average of 25 days out of 30, which is not unrealistic for such a popular item. Eggs cooked to order are preferred, 21 days; beer, coffee, and orange juice about 19 days out of 30, etc. Steak, cheeseburger, and fried chicken are the only dinner entrees in the top 50 items ranked by preferred frequency, and it is not unreasonable that these items might be desired more than ten times per month. When one moves from the highest preference foods to those with moderate and low preference, it becomes clear that the preferred frequency scores are too high. For example, corned beef, which ranks 339th out of all 378 foods, is still requested more than six times per month, and braised liver, which is 361st, is requested about six times per month. Furthermore, when all the item preferences are combined, it yields a total food preference vastly greater than one could accommodate in a three meal per day, 30 day menu. At the present time, it must be assumed that the order, or rank of the frequencies, is an accurate representation of preferences, but it is not known what corrections might be used on the frequency scores to yield realistic menus.

Another approach to preferred frequency has been to
determine the hedonic value of foods when served with different frequencies, which attempts to answer the menu planning
problem of serving cycles for individual foods. Benson [20]
asked respondents to give nine-point scale preference ratings
for foods if they were served 1, 4, 8, 15, or 30 times per
month. Unfortunately, the small list of food items, containing only 20 choices, does not permit many comparisons. More
recently, Rogozenski and Maskowitz [24] asked survey respondents to rate foods on the nine point hedonic scale when the
food was consumed three months ago, one month ago, two weeks
ago, one week ago, three days ago, and yesterday. The relationship of hedonic score to days since the last serving is
almost flat for some salads indicating high preferred frequency, and steep for certain entrees, indicating low preferred frequencies. While this approach to preferred
frequency scaling is potentially important, it has yet to be
validated or tested for reliability.

IV. COMBINED SCALES OF PREFERENCE

The scales discussed so far have been either hedonic or
preference frequency scales. Other scales have used both
hedonic and frequency categories within one scale. Schutz
[25] developed a unique approach to food preference measurement called the "Food Action Rating Scale" (FACT Scale), by
asking people to rank order 18 action statements representing
affective attitudes towards foods. Nine were selected to
give equal intervals: (1) eat every opportunity, (2) eat
very often, (3) frequently eat, (4) eat now and then, (5) eat
if available, (6) don't like, eat on occasion, (7) hardly
ever eat, (8) eat if no other choices, and (9) eat if
forced.

The standard deviation and mean difference of the FACT
scale and the nine point hedonic scale were very similar, and
correlated 0.97 for food means.

Van Riter [26] used a scale based on home use of foods,
specifically vegetables, including scale categories: "never
served at home," "one or more of my family disliked the
food," "prepared differently at home." These categories
point out important factors in food preference determination.
Whether they are good measures of actual preference is unclear
without comparison to other preference measures and actual
behavioral measures.

Another approach to the combining of scales has been the
use of both hedonic and preferred frequency scale data which

are collected together and then combined for decision-making purposes.

One way of dealing with both scales simultaneously has been to utilize visual presentation (Table VIII). Each scale was divided into high, moderate, and low groups, and then the two were combined. This yields a 3 × 3 matrix in which the nine possibilities include everything from foods of low hedonic value, which are desired with low frequency, to foods of high hedonic value, which are desired with high frequency. By comparing the preferred serving frequency to the actual serving frequency, one can determine whether foods are underserved or overserved. This results in the observation that some low hedonic foods are underserved and some hedonic foods are overserved (Table IX), perhaps as a result of the tendency on the part of menu planners to increase high hedonic foods and decrease low hedonic foods in menus.

Combined analysis of the two scales has also been used to objectively define high and low preference foods. Foods that are more than one standard deviation above or below a class mean or hedonic and frequency scales are labeled high or low-preference foods, respectively (Table X). The reference is to the class mean because it does not appear appropriate to compare a dessert to an entree or a vegetable. Thus, a food may have low scores but not be considered low preference if the entire class is low scoring. A food may have high scores but not be considered high preference if the entire class is popular.

Several observations and conclusions can be made from the list of high- and low-preference foods. Classes 02 through 07, the low-preference items, contain liquids, especially the soup, milk products, and fruit flavored juices and drinks. The high-preference items are the very familiar ones: chicken noodle soup, orange juice, grape juice, lemonade, and milk.

Interestingly, two "hot breads and doughnuts" (class 09) fall in the low-preference grouping. This does not mean that the items are not liked. It means that they are liked significantly less than their class average. Cold cereal and griddle cakes are high preference sources of breakfast starch.

Shrimp and lobster are high-preference seafoods, whereas fish items occupy the low places. There are more high-preference meats than low, and more high-reference short-order and sandwich items than low-preference items. The "stews and extended meats" class contains additional low-preference items. The low-preference items tend to be ethnic, combination items, such as casseroles, whereas the high-preference items tend to be either simpler items or Italian foods.

TABLE VIII. Relationship between Preference Scales for Evening Salads on the Hedonic Scale [23]

Frequency Scale	Low	Moderate	High
Low	Cabbage and sweet pepper salad Pineapple cheese salad Carrot salad Kidney bean salad Carrot, raisin, and celery salad Frijole salad Pickled green beans salad Pickled beet and onion salad		
Moderate	Waldorf salad Cucumber, onion, sweet pepper salad Cucumber and onion salad	Banana salad Assorted fruit salad Cottage cheese and fruit salad Mixed fruit salad Cole slaw Tossed cucumber and tomato salad Garden cottage cheese salad Vegetable slaw Potato salad Macaroni salad Chef's salad	
High		Lettuce salad Jellied fruit salad Lettuce and tomato salad Tossed vegetable salad	Tossed green salad

TABLE VIII (Continued). *Relationship between preference scales for Evening Fruits on the Hedonic Scale*

Frequency Scale	Low	Moderate	High
Low	Canned figs Canned prunes	Canned plums Canned apricots Canned grapefruit	
Moderate		Canned sweet cherries Fresh plums Honeydew melon Canned pineapple Canned apples Grapes Canned peaches Canned pears Cantaloupe Applesauce Fruit cocktail	Bananas Oranges Fresh apples Fresh pears Fresh peaches Tangerines
High			Watermelon

TABLE IX. *Underserving/Overserving of Evening Salads on the Hedonic Scale*

	Low	Moderate	High
Underserved	Cucumber and onion salad (1, 32%) Pickled beet with onion salad (1, 19%)	Lettuce and tomato salad (2, 449%) Jellied fruit salad (3, 65%)	Tossed green salad (4, 163%)
Overserved	Waldorf salad (2, 35%) Kidney bean salad (2, 57%) Cabbage and sweet pepper salad (2, 73%) Pineapple cheese salad (4, 74%)	Jellied banana salad (2, 10%) Tossed vegetable salad (7, 16%) Cole slaw (5, 30%) Chef's salad (6, 36%) Mixed fruit salad (5, 37%) Garden cottage cheese salad (2, 38%) Lettuce salad (13, 44%)	

TABLE IX (Continued). *Underserving/Overserving of Evening Soups on a Hedonic Scale*

	Low	Moderate	High
Underserved	Manhattan clam chowder (1, 9%)	Vegetable soup (1, 53%) Turkey noodle soup (1, 52%) Beef noodle soup (1, 39%)	
Overserved	Beef barley soup (2, 27%) Cnion soup (1, 42%)	Turkey rice soup (1, 7%) Beef rice soup (1, 21%) Minestrone (1, 31%)	

TABLE X.   Armed Forces High Preference and Low
           Preference Foods [17]

	Food Class	High	Low
01	Appetizers		
02	Soups	Tomato vegetable noodle soup Tomato soup Chicken noodle soup	Corn chowder Fish chowder Split pea soup Egg drop soup Onion soup Cerole soup
03	Fruit and vegetable juices	Orange juice Grape juice	Cranberry juice Prune juice
04	Fruit drink and iced tea	Lemonade Iced tea	Grape lemonade Lime flavored drink Cherry flavored drink
05	Hot beverages		Instant coffee Freeze dried coffee
06	Milk products	Milk Ice cream	Skimmed milk Buttermilk Fruit flavored yogurt
07	Carbonated beverages	Cola	Low calorie soda
09	Hot breads and dough-nuts	Doughnuts Sweet rolls	Plain muffins Coffee cake
10	Breakfast cereals	Cold cereal	
11	Griddle cakes	Griddle cakes	
12	Eggs		
13	Breakfast meats	Bacon Canadian bacon	Grilled bologna Scrapple
14	Fish and seafood	French fried shrimp Seafood platter Lobster	Baked fish Salmon Baked tuna and noodles

TABLE X (Continued).

	Food Class	High	Low
15	Meats	Roast beef Swiss steak Pot roast Grilled steak Grilled minute steak Barbecued spare- ribs Grilled ham Baked ham Italian sausage Fried chicken Baked chicken Hot turkey sandwich with gravy Hot roast beef sandwich with gravy	Grilled lamb chops Spareribs Corned beef Pork hocks Pickled pigs feet Sauerbraten
16	Stews and extended meats	Lasagna Pizza Spaghetti with meat sauce Spaghetti and meat balls Meatloaf Swedish meatballs Salisbury steak Beef stew	Chicken cacciatore Chili macaroni Ham loaf Vealburger Stuffed cabbage Corn beef hash Stuffed green peppers Pork chop suey Sweet and sour prok Sukyaki Baked tuna and noodles
17	Short order, sandwiches	Hamburger Cheeseburger Ham sandwich Bacon, lettuce, and tomato Grilled cheese Grilled ham and cheese Sloppy Joe Pizza	Frankfurter, cheese and bacon Salami sandwich Bologna sandwich Hot Reuben sandwich Hot pastrami Fishwich

TABLE X (Continued).

	Food Class	High	Low
18	Potato and potato sub- stitutes	French fried potato Baked potato Hashed brown potato Mashed potato Potato chips	Sweet potato Hot potato salad Boiled navy beans Fefried beans Rice pilaf Corn bread stuffing Savory bread stuffing Sausage stuffing
19	Green vegetables	Canned green beans Frozen green beans Canned peas Collard greens Buttered mixed vegetables	Frozen lima beans Canned lima beans Creamed frozen peas Fried cabbage Brussels sprouts Mustard greens Turnip greens Buttered zuchini squash
20	Yellow vegetables	Creamed style corn Corn on the cob Buttered whole kernel corn	Baked yellow squash French fried carrots
21	Other vegetables	French fried onion rings	Mashed rutabagas Fried parsnips
22	Fruit salads	Mixed fruit	Pineapple cheese salad
23	Vegetable salads	Cole slaw Celery and carrot sticks	Pickled beet and onion salad Carrot, raisin and celery Kidney bean salad
24	Tossed green salads		
25	Salad dress- ing	Thousand Island dressing French dressing	Sour cream dressing Blue cheese
26	Fresh fruit	Oranges Apples	Plums Honeydew melon Fruit cup

TABLE X (Continued).

	Food Class	High	Low
27	Canned fruits	Peaches Pears Applesauce Fruit cocktail	Plums Apricots Figs Stewed prunes
28	Cookies and brownies	Chocolate chip Peanut butter cookies Chocolate cookies Oatmeal cookies Brownies	Molasses cookies Coconut raisin Fruit bars Nut bars Butterscotch brownies
29	Cakes	Strawberry short- cake Pineapple, upside down Devil's food Banana cake	Spice cake White cake Peanut butter cake Yellow cake Cheesecake Gingerbread
30	Pies	Cherry pie Apple pie Pumpkin pie Strawberry chiffon pie Banana cream pie Lemon meringue pie	Raisin pie Pineapple pie Apricot pie Pineapple cream pie Sweet potato pie
31	Puddings and other desserts	Chocolate pudding Banana cream pudding Apple crisp	Bread pudding Rice pudding Fruit flavored yogurt
32	Ice cream and sherbet	Ice cream Milk shake	Butterscotch sundae Pineapple sundae

White potatoes tend to be high preference, whereas
potato substitutes tend to be low. Green beans, peas, mixed
vetables, and collard greens are high-preference items,
whereas lima beans, cabbage, brussel sprouts, and greens are
low-preference items. Corn is the only highly preferred
yellow vegetable. Unpopular salads are vegetable salads
(class 23). The absence of high-preference tossed green
salads does not mean that these items are unpopular; rather
they are uniformly popular, yielding no items more than one
standard deviation above or below the class mean. Plums,
apricots, figs, and prunes are among the low-preference fruits.
Popular desserts include many chocolate items, while unpopular
desserts include many with the unpopular fruits.

V.   CURRENT AND FUTURE RESEARCH

The current research program in food preference measurement at the US Army Natick Research and Development Command
centers on three areas. First, an effort has begun to break
down the overall population sample into subgroups that are
of interest for research reasons or for reasons of practical
interest. For example, analyses have been performed [27]
that separate the food preferences of black military personnel
and compare these with the preferences of whites. This represents one of the first objective analyses of so-called "soul
food." Further, food preferences of underweight and overweight personnel have been analyzed to investigate various
traditional assumptions of obesity theory and practice. For
example, overweight people do not state a preference for
desserts. In another analysis, the preference of each of the
military services has been compared to determine whether
individual service menu planning or centralized menu planning
is more appropriate [17]. More demographic studies are
planned in order to make the data useful for a wide variety of
situations and to bring these data into many interesting
research areas.
The second general area of research is the relationship
of these attitudinal data with behavioral data. The relationship between attitudinal measures of food habits and behavioral measures, such as food selections and food consumption
are being analyzed. The key here is the determination of
what predictive value there is to food preference measurement.
How will preference data predict actual selection and actual
consumption of an item? Another issue of behavior is related
to the effect of preferences and food habits on a person's
other performance. The question of whether a person's ability
to do a job is affected by food habits is largely unanswered [1].

Related to this is the third area of continuing research: the relationship of food preferences to menu planning. A variety of projects are underway or scheduled that will develop procedures for utilization of food preference data in menu planning. The purpose is to make available to the professional menu planner objective data from consumers on which to base decisions. Reliable and valid procedures that yield objective data will give consumers the voice in menu planning that they deserve.

REFERENCES

1. Jacobs, H. L., and Meiselman, H. L., Customer morale and behavioral effectiveness. Accomplishments and goals of psychological studies of food science systems. *Proc. Third Intern. Meeting, Food for the Armed Forces.* US Army Natick Res. & Develop. Command, Tech. Rep. 76-42-OTD (1976).

2. Siebold, J. R., Symington, L. E., Graeber, R. C., and MAAS, D. L., Consumer and worker evaluation of cash food systems: Loring AFB, Part 1: Short Term Findings. *U.S. Army Natick Research and Development Command Tech. Rep. 76-35-FSL* (1976).

3. Hall, I. S., and Hall, C. S., A study of disliked and unfamiliar foods, *J. Am. Dietetic Assn. 15*, 540-548 (1939).

4. Abbott, O. D., Townsend, R. O., and French, R. B., A survey of food preferences of Florida men, Bulletin 500, Agriculture Experimental Station, Gainesville, Florida (1952).

5. Einstein, M. A., and Hornstein, I., Food preference of college students and nutritional implications. *J. Food Sci. 35*, 429-437 (1970).

6. Lamb, M. A., Adams, V. J., and Godfrey, J., Food preferences of college women. *J. Am. Dietetic Assn. 30*, 1120-1125 (1954).

7. Harper, R., Some attitudes to vegetables and their implications. *Nature* 200, 14-18 (1963).

8. Kennedy, B. M., Food preferences of pre-army age California boys. *Food Technol. 3*, 93-97 (1952).

9. Kennedy, B. M., Food preference of women. *J. Am. Dietetic Assn. 34*, 501-506 (1958).

10. Dove, W. F., Appetite levels of food consumption. A technique for measuring foods in terms of psychological and nutritional values combined. *Human Biology 15* (3): 199-120 (1943).

11. Eppright, E. S., Food habits and preferences. A study
     of Iowa people of two age groups. Research bulletin
     No. 376, Agricultural Experiment Station, Iowa State
     College, Ames, Iowa (1950).
12. Jones, L. V., Peryam, D. R., and Thurstone, L. L.,
     Development of a scale for measuring soldiers' food
     preferences. *Food Res. 20,* 512-520 (1955).
13. Peryam, D. R., *et al.,* Food preferences of men in the
     Armed Forces. Quartermaster Food and Container Insti-
     tute for the Armed Forces (1960).
14. Waterman, D., Meiselman, H. L., Branch, L. G., and
     Taylor, M., The 1972 Westover Air Force Base preference
     survey and reliability study. U.S. Army Natick Labora-
     tories Tech. Rep. TR-75-22-FSL (1974).
15. Smutz, E. R., Jacobs, H. L., Waterman, D., and Caldwell,
     M., Small sample studies of food habits: (1) The
     relationship between food preference and choice. U.S.
     Army Natick Laboratories Tech. Rep. TR-75-52-FSL (1974).
16.

17. Meiselman, H. L., Waterman, D., and Symington, L.,
     Armed Forces Food Preferences. U.S. Army Natick Labora-
     tories Tech. Rep. TR-75-63-FSL (1974).
18. Knickrehm, M. E., Cotner, C., and Kendrick, J. G., A
     study of the frequency of acceptance of menu items by
     residence hall students of the University of Nebraska.
     Department of Food and Nutrition, Report No. 1,
     University of Nebraska (1967).
19. Hartmuller, V. W., Development of a separation rating of
     menu items for the Home Economics Food Service. Unpub-
     lished Master's Thesis, Purdue University (1971).
20. Benson, P. H., Relation of food frequency of serving.
     Final report of Project No. 7-84-15-007, Quartermaster
     Food and Container Institute (1958).
21. Schuck, C., Food preferences of South Dakota college
     students. *J. Am. Dietetic Assn. 39,* 595-597 (1961).
22. Leverton, R. M., Freshman food likes. *J. Home Econ. 36,*
     589-590 (1944).
23. Meiselman, H. L., Van Horne, W., Hasenzahl, B., and
     Wehrly, T., The 1971 Fort Lewis Food Preference Survey,
     U.S. Army Natick Laboratories Tech. Rep. TR-72-43-PR
     (1971).
24. Rogozenski, J. E. Jr., and Moskowitz, H. R., A system
     for the preference evaluation of cydic menus. U.S.
     Army Natick Laboratories Tech. Rep. 75-46-OR/SA (1975).
25. Schutz, H. G., A food action rating scale for measuring
     food acceptance. *J. Food Sci.* 30, 365-374 (1965).

26. Van Riter, I. G., The acceptance of twenty-six vegetables by college students. *J. Home Econ.* *48,* 771-773 (1956).
27. Meiselman, H. L., The role of sweetness in the food preference of young adults, *in* "Development of Sweet Preference" (J. M. Weiffenbach, ed.). USGPO, Washington, D.C. (1976).

CHAPTER 8

THE UTILIZATION OF COMPUTERS IN MENU PLANNING

J. L. Balintfy

School of Business Administration
University of Massachusetts
Amherst, Massachusetts

I. INTRODUCTION

Food management is concerned with the task of feeding a given population by converting raw or processed foods into edible products called menu items,and delivering meals that meet customer preferences, are nutritionally adequate, and can be produced with the facilities and budget available.

The essential interface between food management and customers is the menu. The menu from which the meals are selected defines,to a large extent, the acceptability, nutritional adequacy,and cost of the food service system. Furthermore, if the menu is nonselective, the food management has total control over these attributes.This is an important point because a very large and ever increasing number of the population, such as students, patients,military personnel, workers, and prison inmates, are regularly on diets served by such institutional feeding programs all over the world.

It is well known that menu planning always precedes, as well as determines, the process of preparation. Menu planning is, therefore, the primary decision making problem relative to which the procedures of food production are subordinate and well defined activities. Consequently, if the menu plan is optimal in some sense,all the steps involving the purchasing, production, and service of food can be organized to maintain the desired attributes of this optimum. Moreover, if the menu plan is prepared with the aid of a computer program and with access to all the data pertinent to food management,the information necessary for the operational control of food service will be available to food managers through the computers.

Copyright © 1979 by Academic Press, Inc.
All rights of reproduction in any form reserved
ISBN: 0-12-453150-4

For these reasons, over a decade ago, the author addressed himself to the problem of teaching a computer to plan menus. In so doing, a scientific methology evolved which formulated menu planning problems in mathematical terms, understandable by a computer (1). This was followed by the development of several fully computerized menu planning and food management information systems, one of which has been available since 1969 (2). Research is still in progress on many aspects of this problem, but definitive methods exist at this stage for planning non-selective and selective menus. The methodologies and examples of currently known computerized approaches to menu planning and related food management data processing systems are described in this chapter.

II. PLANNING PREFERENCE-MAXIMIZED MEALS BY COMPUTER

A. *Methodology*

The concept of optimal combination of menu items can be satisfactorily described as the maximally preferred combination of items. In this case, the total preference for the items is maximized while maintaining a given structure and maintaining desired levels of budget and nutritive value. Any level of food, budget, structural, and dietary constraints have a uniquely defined sequence of meals with preference as high as the constraints will allow. This preference maximum can be found by mathematical optimization techniques and by computer, and only after agreement on measurement and interpretation of data. Clearly food preference measures are quantitatively less tractable than food costs.

A major advance was made in this direction by recognizing that an individual's preference for a food is not an absolute number, but rather a function of time since last consumption (3). Studies have shown that the preference for an item gradually builds up over time, but drops as soon as one eats it. For example, no matter how much we might like turkey, eating turkey every day would cause our preference for this item to be diminished.

Figure 1 is an illustration of this phenomenon in more exact terms. The parameters of this function were estimated from responses to questionnaires (4). The graph shows the equal time intervals between service might be a good idea to avoid variations in the preference peaks. It also shows that the preference-time functions would effectively separate items in a sequence for optimal menus and that low preference items would not likely be included.

For the fixed time interval of a menu cycle, there is an

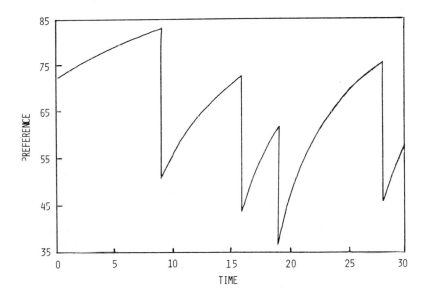

FIGURE 1.   The change of preference over time when the item is consumed on days 9, 16, 19, and 28, the item having been consumed 9 days prior to day 1. (The parameters of the preference-time function used for this plot are: a = 100, b = 40, c = 0.05 and r = 0.4.)

optimal frequency of the item. This is the frequency at which
the total preference (the sum of the peaks on Figure 1) is maximum. This observation leads to the notion of preference-frequency functions. Such functions can be estimated from standard
questionnaires. Figure 2 shows the method used in an inter-ac-
tive mode with a computer.

The use of preference-frequency functions for meal planning
is shown in Figure 3. The data (through the courtesy of NASA)
are taken from questionnaires filled out by an astronaut for a
set of Skylab menu items. For a particular item, such as filet
mignon, the corresponding row shows the increment in preference
as serving frequency per 28 day increases. It is seen that the
increments get smaller as additional servings contribute less
to the eating satisfaction of filet mignon. (Note that this astronaut apparently rated both beef items equally). For other
items, such as pork, saturation comes earlier. If there is a-
greement that there should be 28 dinner entrees planned for 28
days, which ones should occur on the menu and how frequently?

Relative to the one-course problem of Figure 3, the solution is easy to find. Items should be chosen in order of the
maximal incremental preferences until there is a collection of
28 items. The line in the data field shows the result of this
process. The optimum combination of entrees are uniquely defined and, as a by-product, one obtains a "threshold" preference, 8.84, i.e. the maximum rating that one serving of any new
item should have in order to be included in the menu. For the
sake of simplicity, this exercise considered preference alone
without regard to cost or nutritive value. It is possible to
interpret preferences as numerical quantities and to define
conditions of optimality in these terms. A more far-reaching
conclusion is that, with the aid of preference measures, choice
probabilities also can be defined, thus opening the way for
planning selective menus with scientific methodology.

B. *Computer Applications*

The computer technology of preference-maximized menu planning is still in its infancy. Thus far, only prototype models
have been built to demonstrate the feasibility of the approach
(5,6,7). One such model proved, with realistic data, that
school lunch menus could be planned directly from children's
preference questionnaires at about a 10 % saving in food cost
(7). The conceptual significance of this approach is that customers' preferences can be maintained at a desired level while
the foods served may follow the market price fluctuation at
minimum cost.

Figure 4 shows another type application. The problem was to
advise patients about which subset of items would be a good
"low calorie" choice. The average popularity of items was ob-

```
ENTER MENU ITEM NAME (UP TO 20 CHARACTERS)

? lamb

IMAGINE THAT YOU HAVE NOT EATEN LAMB
FOR A WHOLE MONTH.  HOW MUCH WOULD YOU LIKE TO EAT IT TODAY ?
(USE NUMBERS BETWEEN -4 and +4)

? 2

HOW OFTEN, PER MONTH, WOULD YOU LIKE TO EAT LAMB

? 4

ITEM NAME: LAMB
PREFERENCE AT 1 MONTH =  2     PREFERRED FREQUENCY =  4 TIMES/MONTH
```

YOUR CHANGING PREFERENCE IS DESCRIBED BY $2.29\ X - .29\ X^2$
WHERE X = FREQUENCY OF SERVING (TIMES/MONTH)

```
DO YOU WISH TO SEE THE GRAPH OF THE FUNCTIONS ?

? yes
```

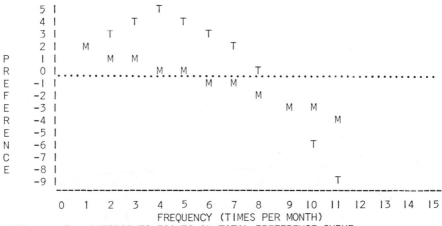

FIGURE 2. Total and marginal preference as they depend on serving frequency. (Source: COMCATER International, Inc.)

	FREQUENCY OPTIMUM	1	2	3	4	5	6	7	8	9	10
PRIME RIBS OF BEEF	8	89.64	60.28	48.64	42.03	35.68	28.88	21.67	14.18	6.51	-1.28
FILET MIGNON	8	89.64	60.28	48.64	42.03	35.68	28.88	21.67	14.18	6.51	-1.28
LOBSTER NEWBURG	3	35.60	16.93	10.46	3.68	-3.81	-11.67	-19.71	-27.84	-36.04	-44.26
CHICKEN W/GRAVY	1	16.41	5.48	-5.50	-16.47	-27.44	-38.42	-49.39	-60.36	-71.34	-82.31
TURKEY W/GRAVY	1	16.41	5.48	-5.50	-16.47	-27.44	-38.42	-49.39	-60.36	-71.34	-82.31
PORK LOIN W/DR,GR.	2	23.29	8.84	-8.21	-25.51	-42.87	-60.24	-77.63	-95.02	-112.41	-129.81
VEAL W/BBQ SAUCE	3	39.45	21.96	13.32	4.58	-4.53	-13.80	-23.17	-32.58	-42.01	-51.46
CHICKEN AND RICE	1	14.37	7.07	4.54	1.89	-1.04	-4.12	-7.26	-10.44	-13.65	-16.86
PORK W/SC. POT.	1	16.41	5.48	-5.50	-16.47	-27.44	-38.42	-49.39	-60.36	-71.34	-82.31

Total 28

THRESHOLD PREFERENCE LEVEL = 8.84

FIGURE 3. Table of incremental preferences of an astronaut for the Skylab menu items.

	PREFERENCE TOTAL	CALORIES KCAL	PROTEIN G	CALCIUM MG	IRON MG	VIT. A IU	THIAMIN MG	RIBBO MG	NIACIN MG	VIT. C MG
OPTIMUM MEAL PORK WITH GRAVY SAVOURY GREEN BEANS TOMATO AND LETTUCE SALAD FRENCH DRESSING WHOLE WHEAT BREAD BUTTER CHILLED FRUIT COCKTAIL COFFEE WITH SUGAR	18,49	686	39,1	123,5*	6,9	2060	1,36	,53*	9,7	37
OPTIMUM MEAL CONSTRAINED BY 40% RDA PORK WITH APPLESAUCE GREEN BEANS TOMATO AND LETTUCE SALAD FRENCH DRESSING WHOLE MILK	14,8	698	42,8	372	5,1	2111	1,39	,9	8,4	38
40% OF THE RDA FOR THE 19-50 years age male POPULATION			22,4	320	4,0	2000	,6	,72	8,0	18

* 40% RDA IS NOT SATISFIED

SOURCE: MARCH 6, 1974, MENU OF THE NAVAL MEDICAL CENTER

FIGURE 4. Display of preference-maximized dinner meals standardized for 700 calorie content.

tained from food management and used as preference measures.
Then a computer program determined the selections under two
conditions. First the items were selected on the basis of preference and caloric content alone. The preference-maximized
menu falls short of the 40 percent RDA allowance, in this case
for two micro-nutrients: calcium and riboflavin. Secondly, the
40 percent RDA allowance was enforced along with the previous
constraints. In this case, total preference dropped to 80 % of
the previous level, and the menu shows that too.

     This illustration demonstrates the inherent conflict be-
tween food preference and nutrition. One is tempted to observe
that the possibility of fortifying meals with added nutrients
might be the best course of action to permit planning high
preference menus meeting nutritional requirements.

III. DATA PROCESSING SYSTEMS

A. *Recipe Coding*

     Whether a menu is planned by hand or computer, it consti-
tutes a blueprint to be followed by food production and service. The menu, along with the demand for the various items, defines the product, i.e. the output of the food service system.
It provides information, not only to govern the conversion
process of raw foods into menu items, but also control other
aspects of food service. Relationship between the current food
prices and the raw food cost of meals; relationship between the
nutrient composition of ingredients and that of foods served;
and relationship between supplies on hand and those to be purchased are of crucial importance. Yet, food service directors
and dietitians know that without computers, these relations
cannot be readily expressed quantitatively because of the mass
of data and computational details involved. Computerization
means that tasks not manageable by manual methods will be performed by the computer, making new and more accurate information and control available to food management. This is made
possible by the standardization of recipes. Without standardized recipes there can be no computerized food management information system, and conversely, there are no truly standardized recipes without computerization.

     Figure 5 illustrates this premise. It is the computer image
of an institutional recipe for 100 portions. The original record on the recipe file contained little more than the name of
the ingredient and its measure.For the computer,each ingredient
was given a number that identified it within the food list. Also, each ingredient was given a nutrient code to correspond
with the list in which all the nutrients in one unit of the

RECIPE NAME VEAL SCALLOPINI

NO. OF PORTIONS 100

COLOR MULTI-COLOR   FLAVOR 100   MILD TEXTURE

MEAL CODE 4   COURSE CODE 3   SOFT TEMPERATURE

RECIPE CODE L103B

ESTIMATED PORTION SIZE 5.65 OZS

HOT ATTRIBUTES 0 0

YIELDS

INGR. NO.	INGREDIENT NAME	QUANTITY LBS.	OZS.	AMT.	UNIT MEASURE	PRE-PREP	PREP	COOK	E.P.	NUTR. CODE	S.FOOD GROUP	CD
L03-4055	FROZEN VEAL STEAKS	25.00	0.0	100.00	4OZ STEAK	1.00	1.00	0.66	1.00	23820	0	0
165-6867	HARD WHEAT FLOUR	1.00	2.0	4.50	CUPS	1.00	1.00	1.00	1.00	26500	0	0
262-8886	SALT	0.0	5.1	0.50	CUP	1.00	1.00	1.00	1.00	19630	0	0
L03-2730	PEPPER	0.0	0.2	1.00	TBSP	1.00	1.00	1.00	1.00	37410	0	0
L03-2670	LIQUID SHORTENING-FRYMAX	57.00	2.0	7.75	GALLONS	1.00	1.00	1.00	0.03	14017	0	0
L03-2670	LIQUID SHORTENING-FRYMAX	-55.00	-6.5	7.52	GALLONS	1.00	1.00	1.30	1.00	14017	0	0
823-7663	FRESH GARLIC, CHOPPED	0.0	1.0	7.00	CLOVES	0.88	1.00	1.00	1.00	10290	0	0
128-1179	DEHYDRATED CHOPPED ONIONS	0.0	4.0	0.50	CUP	1.00	1.00	1.00	1.00	14140	0	0
227-1387	DEHYDRATED GREEN PEPPERS	0.0	2.1	0.50	NO. 2½ CN	1.00	1.00	1.00	1.00	34560	0	0
616-81	SALAD OIL	0.0	3.9	0.50	CUP	1.00	1.00	1.00	1.00	14018	0	0
582-4060	CANNED TOMATOES, CRUSHED	12.00	12.0	1.67	NO.10CANS	1.00	1.00	1.00	1.00	22840	0	0
234-6217	BEEF GRAVY BASE	0.0	2.0	5.00	TBSP	1.00	1.00	1.00	1.00	30800	0	0
N00 8888	WATER	4.00	2.7	2.00	QUARTS	1.00	1.00	0.57	1.00	27010	0	0
262-8886	SALT	0.0	1.9	3.00	TBSP	1.00	1.00	.00	1.00	19630	0	0
127-8922	FRESH PARSLEY, MINCED	0.0	4.0	2.00	CUPS	1.00	1.00	1.00	1.00	14720	0	0
L03-2728	OREGANO	0.0	0.0	1.00	TSP	1.00	1.00	1.00	1.00	37340	0	0

PORTION YIELD IN OZS. 5.64   PERCENT DIFF. -0.12   PORTION COST $0.438

RECIPE YIELD IN LBS. 35.27   TOTAL RECIPE COST $43.82

PERCENT WASTE 0.02

NUTRIENT COMPOSITION/PORTION

CALORIE	PROTEIN	FAT	SFA	OLEIC ACID	LINOLEIC ACID	CHOLE-STEROL	CHO	CALC	IRON	SODIUM	POTAS-SIUM	VIT A	THIAMINE	RIBO-FLAVIN	NIACIN	VIT C
	GM	GM	GM	GM	GM	MG	GM	MG	MG	MG	MG	IU	MG	MG	MG	MG
287.	20.9	18.7	7.	6.	4.	74.	7.8	23.	3.0	1027.	522.	610.	0.10	0.22	4.6	16.

FIGURE 5. Computer image of an institutional recipe. (Source: National Naval Medical Center, Bethesda, Maryland)

given food were stored. Since the computer arithmetic requires
weight measures, the quantity of each ingredient was required
to be given in pounds and ounces, in addition to the units of
volume measures generally used. Finally, the conversion process
from "as purchased" to "edible portion" quantities was to be
noted by separately identifying the preparation, cooking, and
edible portion yield factors for each ingredient. Figure   5
shows the information extension, as well as the accuracy required in the proper coding of a recipe. It is clear that such
precision will considerably improve the standardization of the
product. It also allows for unprecedented accuracy in determining the quantities, food cost, and nutrients associated with
the input-output relations that are crucial for proper food
management and control. The coding procedures shown in Figure 5
were originally developed at Tulane University and are included
in the CAMP (i.e. Computer-Assisted Menu Planning) system and
its various derivatives.

B. Computer File Organization

As seen, food management involves the handling of a tremendous amount of data. The organization of this large volume of
data into well defined sets assists conceptual clarity and facilitates storage requirements. The systems evolved over the
years structure permanent data into three groups: food, nutrient, and recipe data. These data, once coded, may enter the
auxiliary disk files of the computer where they are instantly
available. Figure 6 shows the file organization of the CAMP
system.

The food file contains the name, unit of issue, the unit
price, and stock on hand of the food ingredients. The file is
updated whenever a transaction takes place. The nutrient file
contains the nutrient composition of foods. The data are obtained from tables such as the USDA food composition handbooks
or from food nutrient labeling information. As illustrated by
Figure 5, the recipe file contains information for each menu
item under consideration, including mono-ingredient items. This
file is heavily cross referenced with the food and nutrient
files when computations are taking place. The matrix file is an
extraction of data for mathematical optimization, and is used
for menu-planning purposes alone.

C. Food Management Information Systems

The operation of a computerized food management system is
based upon these permanently stored records, with the addition
of daily operational information. The process is described
through the examples shown in Figures 7-12 (8).
The system input is the designation of menu items by their

GENERAL DATA FLOW

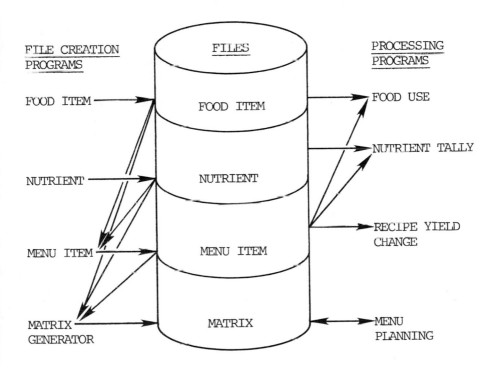

FIGURE 6. Computer file organization and use.

MENU FOR DAY 1   LUNCH

RECIPE CODE	NAME OF RECIPE	NUMBER OF PORTIONS TO BE PREPARED			PORTION COST	TOTAL RECIPE COST
		REGULAR *	SPECIAL KITCHEN *	TOTAL		
PO17D	TOMATO-RICE SOUP	340. *	60. *	400.	0.06	23.24
0013A	TARTAR SAUCE-CAFETERIA SERVICE	243. *	0. *	243.	0.02	5.86
0013C	TARTAR SAUCE-TRAY SERVICE	0. *	57. *	57.	0.02	1.22
NO01	BACON, LETTUCE AND TOMATO SANDWICH	0. *	125. *	125.	0.27	33.67
LO63C	GRILLED FRANKFURTER ON A ROLL	0. *	50. *	50.	0.10	5.07
LO96A	PARMESAN VEAL CUBES	378. *	22. *	400.	0.45	179.27
LC40D	STUFFED CABBAGE W/TOMATO SAUCE	170. *	22. *	192.	0.35	68.00
LO44D	BAKED CORN BEEF-APPLE SUGAR GLAZE	180. *	20. *	200.	0.48	95.68
QG22B	STEAMED CARROT COINS	200. *	100. *	300.	0.03	9.02
QG3PA	BUTTERED KALE	250. *	100. *	350.	0.05	17.29
MD47C	MIXED GREENS	0. *	162. *	162.	0.03	5.09
MD08C	CARAWAY COLESLAW	0. *	60. *	60.	0.05	3.20
GO09C	GERMAN CHOCOLATE CAKE	738. *	126. *	864.	0.27	232.20
JO12	ICE CREAM	0. *	110. *	110.	0.08	8.79

SYSTEM INPUTS

RECIPE CODES
PORTIONS TO
BE PREPARED

PRINTOUT SHOWS PORTION
COSTS AND TOTAL RECIPE
COSTS.

FIGURE 7. Confirmation of system input data by computer.

166

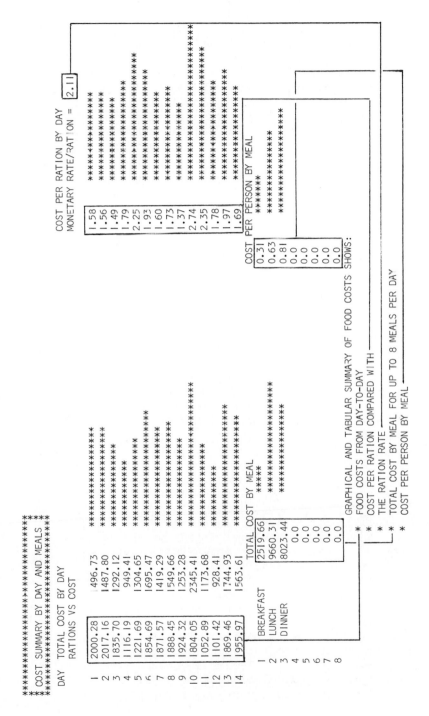

FIGURE 8. Food cost accounting report by computer.

NUTRITIONAL SUMMARY

NUTRIENT NAME	BREAKFAST	LUNCH	DINNER				
CALORIE	553.15	850.20	1011.25	0.0	0.0	0.0	0.0
PROTEIN-GM	17.86	36.71	50.64	0.0	0.0	0.0	0.0
FAT -GM	27.00	38.14	47.16	0.0	0.0	0.0	0.0
SFA -GM	7.90	10.28	12.97	0.0	0.0	0.0	0.0
OLEIC ACID	12.15	12.08	15.18	0.0	0.0	0.0	0.0
LINOL ACID	4.01	6.88	7.07	0.0	0.0	0.0	0.0
CHOLES -MG	103.27	140.80	164.81	0.0	0.0	0.0	0.0
CARBOHY-GM	60.01	91.84	95.84	0.0	0.0	0.0	0.0
CALCIUM-MG	137.72	167.31	246.25	0.0	0.0	0.0	0.0
IRON -MG	3.79	5.87	7.24	0.0	0.0	0.0	0.0
SODIUM -MG	1257.94	1994.57	2396.31	0.0	0.0	0.0	0.0
POTASSI-MG	577.64	1061.79	1248.08	0.0	0.0	0.0	0.0
VIT. A -IU	671.28	4740.13	3747.18	0.0	0.0	0.0	0.0
THIAMIN-MG	0.45	0.37	0.58	0.0	0.0	0.0	0.0
RIBOFLA-MG	0.33	0.58	0.71	0.0	0.0	0.0	0.0
NIACIN -MG	3.94	8.11	10.76	0.0	0.0	0.0	0.0
VIT. C -MG	29.14	26.78	33.28	0.0	0.0	0.0	0.0

FIGURE 9. Nutritional summary table. It shows the average level of each nutrient per person in each meal.

FOOD USAGE PREDICTIONS FOR WEEK 1

	PRICE/UNIT	STORE	W/TH	TH/F	F/SA	SA/S	SU/M	M/TU	TU/W	WEEKLY UNITS	USAGE VALUE	USAGE TO DATE UNITS	TO DATE VALUE
8905-00-LO3-4019 CRABMEAT, FRESH, CHILLED	3.50/LB	BB C	30.	0.	0.	0.	2.	0.	0.	32.	112.00	32.	112.00
8905-00-616- 50 FRANKFURTERS, FROZEN	0.74/LB	B8 F	5.	0.	5.	0.	5.	0.	50.	65.	48.10	65.	-48.10
8905-00-252-7669 HALIBUT, FROZEN, STEAKS, SKIN ON	1.15/LB	B8 F	0.	0.	0.	0.	0.	0.	50.	50.	57.50	50.	57.50
8905-00-410-4670 HAM, CANNED, WHOLE, PULLMAN-SHAPED	1.49/LB	B6 C	0.	0.	88.	8.	11.	0.	89.	196.	292.04	196.	292.04
8905-00-682-6643 HAM, COOKED, FROZEN, SMOKED, BONELESS	1.49	B8 F	0.	0.	0.	0.	60.	125.	0.	185.	275.65	185.	275.65
8905-00-LO3-4032 KNOCKWURST, FROZEN	1.15/LB	B8 F	0.	40.	0.	0.	0.	0.	0.	40.	46.00	40.	46.00
8905-00-926-1599 LAMB, ROAST, FROZEN, BONELESS LEG	1.81/LB	B8 F	0.	0.	0.	0.	140.	0.	0.	140.	253.40	140.	253.40
8905-00-LO3-4035 LAMBETTES, FROZEN, 25/4 OZ STUFFED BFST	10.31/BX	B8 F	0.	4.	0.	0.	0.	0.	0.	4.	41.24	4.	41.24
8905-00-L03-4-36 LASAGNA, FROZEN, 20 LB	25.00/CS	B8 F	0.	0.	0.	3.	0.	0.	0.	3.	75.00	3.	75.00
8905-00-126-4020 LUNCHEON MEAT, PORT OR PORK AND BEEF	6.15/CN	33A D	0.	0.	0.	6.	0.	0.	0.	6.	36.90	6.	36.90
8905-00-LO3-4039 MANICOTTI, FROZEN	10.06/CS	B8 F	0.	5.	0.	0.	0.	0.	0.	5.	50.30	5.	50.30
8905-00-LO3-4042 PASTRAMI, FROZEN	1.59/LB	B8 F	0.	80.	0.	0.	0.	0.	0.	80.	127.20	80.	127.20
8905-00-164- 485 PERCH, FROZEN, FILLETS	0.92/LB	B8 F	0.	70.	0.	0.	0.	0.	0.	70.	64.40	70.	64.40
8905-00-753-6503 PORK, DICED, FROZEN	1.29/LB	B8 F	0.	0.	0.	6.	0.	32.	0.	38.	49.02	38.	49.02
8905-00-LO3-4046 PORK SAUSAGE, FROZEN, LINK	1.02/LB	B8 F	57.	14.	0.	0.	0.	0.	0.	71.	72.42	71.	72.42
8905-00-753-6569 PORK, SLICES, FROZEN, LOIN, BONED, 5 OZ	1.36/LB	B8 F	135.	0.	0.	0.	0.	0.	0.	135.	183.60	135.	183.60
8905-00-126-8743 PORK, SPARERIBS, FROZEN	0.85/LB	B8 F	0.	0.	0.	218.	0.	0.	0.	218.	185.30	218.	185.30
8905-00-164-6874 SCALLOPS, FROZEN, SEA	2.50/LB	B8 F	0.	0.	0.	0.	2.	0.	0.	2.	5.00	2.	5.00
8905-00-L03-4-47 SCRAPPLE, FROZEN	0.61/LB	B8 F	0.	0.	0.	0.	13.	19.	0.	32.	19.52	32.	19.52
8905-00-582-4039 SHRIMP, FROZEN, RAW, PEELED, DEVEINED	3.65/LB	B8 F	0.	0.	30.	0.	6.	0.	0.	36.	131.40	36.	131.40
8905-00-LO3-4050 STUFFED CABBAGE, FROZEN, 48/CS	17.00/CS	B8 F	4.	0.	0.	0.	0.	0.	0.	4.	68.00	4.	68.00
8905-00-935-3161 TUNA, CANNED, SOLID PACK, WATER PACK	3.51/CN	33A D	0.	11.	0.	0.	3.	0.	0.	14.	49.14	14.	49.14
8905-00-582-4042 TURKEY, BONELESS, FROZEN, COOKED	1.08/LB	B8 F	0.	0.	0.	0.	0.	10.	9.	19.	20.52	19.	20.52
8905-00-262-7274 TURKEY, BONELESS, FROZEN, RAW	1.14/LB	B8 F	0.	0.	135.	0.	0.	34.	0.	169.	192.66	169.	192.66
8905-00-LO3-4053 VEAL, CHUCK, FROZEN, BONELESS, TIED	1.35/LB	B8 F	0.	0.	0.	0.	134.	0.	0.	134.	180.90	134.	180.90
8905-00-N00-1395 VEAL, DICED, FROZEN	1.35/LB	B8 F	124.	0.	0.	6.	0.	0.	0.	130.	175.50	130.	175.50
8910-00-656- 993 CHEESE, AMERICAN, PROCESSED, SLICED	1.01/LB	B4 C	0.	0.	0.	34.	0.	0.	9.	43.	43.43	43.	43.43

*DAILY USAGE PREDICTIONS

*TOTAL WEEKLY USAGE PREDICTIONS

*TO DATE USAGE PREDICTIONS

BREAKOUT OF INGREDIENTS ON DAY 8

8940-00-L03-4680
TOPPING, FROZEN, RICHS   ST.RM. CODE:B8   ST.RM TYPE:F   TOTAL ISSUE: 2. LB
MEAL: LUNCH   REC: J021G BUTTERSCOTCH PUDDING WITH TOPPING   WT: 2½ LBS   1¼ CAN

8945-00-L03-4763
MARGARINE, 72 RTS PATTIES PER LB   ST.RM. CODE:B4   ST.RM.   TYPE:C   TOTAL ISSUE: 25. LB
MEAL: BREAKFAST   REC: S094 MARGARINE   WT: 4¼ LBS   302-¼ PATTIES
MEAL: LUNCH   REC: S094 MARGARINE   WT:14¼ LBS   1024 PATTIES
MEAL: DINNER   REC: S094 MARGARINE   WT: 6 2/3LBS   482 2/3 PATTIES

8945-00-L03-4764
MARGARINE PRINTS, 1LB   ST.RM. CODE:B4   ST.RM.   TYPE:C   TOTAL ISSUE: 28.LB
MEAL: BREAKFAST   REC: E011A HOT BUTTERED GRITS   WT: 1   LBS   2   CUPS
MEAL: LUNCH   REC: S005B HAM AND SWISS CHEESE ON RYE   WT: 1 2/3LBS   0   QUART
MEAL: LUNCH   REC: L035D HAM CROQUETTES W/PINEAPPLE SAUCE

MEAL: LUNCH   REC: QG3VA BUTTERED LEAF SPINACH   WT: 2   LBS   4   CUPS
MEAL: DINNER   REC: L743A ROAST TURKEY   WT: 5½   LBS   11   CUPS
MEAL: DINNER   REC: 0021G SAGE DRESSING   WT: 2½   LBS   5   CUPS
MEAL: DINNER   REC: L027B GROUND BEEF STROGANOFF W/NOODLES   WT: 8   LBS   4   QUART
MEAL: DINNER   REC:E004B BUTTERED NOODLES   WT: 1   LBS   2   CUPS
                                              WT: 6   LBS   3   QUART

8945-00-616-81
SALAD OIL   ST.RM. CODE: 33A   ST.RM.   TYPE:D   TOTAL ISSUE: 4.CN
MEAL:BREAKFAST   REC: L042B CORNED BEEF HASH PATTIES   WT: 1½   LBS   1½   PINT
MEAL:BREAKFAST   REC: L078A GRILLED LUNCHEON MEAT   WT: 5   LBS   3   QUART
MEAL:BREAKFAST   REC: D065 CRISP GOLDEN WAFFLES   WT: 3   LBS   2   QUART
MEAL:BREAKFAST   REC: Q046B COTTAGE FRIED POTATOES   WT: 3   LBS   2   QUART
MEAL:BREAKFAST   REC: F013A SCRAMBLED EGGS   WT: 3¼   LBS   6   CUPS
MEAL:BREAKFAST   REC: F010A GRIDDLE FRIED EGGS   WT: 5¼   LBS   2 2/3QUART
MEAL:LUNCH   REC: L035G PORK AND VEAL LOAF   WT: 2   LBS   4   CUPS
MEAL:DINNER   REC: L027B GROUND BEEF STROGANOFF W/NOODLES   WT: 9 2/3OZS   1¼   CUPS
MEAL:DINNER   REC: L006B CHINESE PEPPER STEAK   WT: 3½   LBS   3 2/3PINT
MEAL:DINNER   REC: M049B CARDINAL VEGETABLE SALAD   WT: 8½   OZS   0 ½ PINT

8945-00-LO3-2670
SHORTENING, LIQUID, FRYMAX. SOYBEAN OIL   ST.RM. CODE:33A   ST.RM. TYPE:D   TOTAL ISSUE: 3.CN
MEAL: LUNCH   REC: L111D FISHWICH CN A BUN   WT:171 1/3LBS 23¼ GALLONS
MEAL: LUNCH   REC: L111D FISHWICH ON A BUN   WT 164 ½ LBS   22 GALLONS
MEAL: LUNCH   REC: L035D HAM CROQUETTES W/PINEAPPLE SAUCE   WT 114 1/4LBS 15¼ GALLONS
MEAL: LUNCH   REC: L035D HAM CROQUETTES W/PINEAPPLE SAUCE   WT 110 LBS   15½ GALLONS
MEAL: LUNCH   REC: Q045C FRENCH FRIED POTATOES   WT 428½ LBS   58¼ GALLONS
MEAL: LUNCH   REC: Q045C FRENCH FRIED POTATOES   WT 415 LBS   53 GALLONS
MEAL: DINNER   REC: L111E DEEP FRIED FILLET OF FLOUNDER   WT 77 LBS   10½ GALLONS
MEAL: DINNER   REC: L111E DEEP FRIED FILLET OF FLOUNDER   WT 74 LBS   10 GALLONS
MEAL: DINNER   REC: Q028A DEEP FRIED EGGPLANT   WT 85 2/3 LBS 11 2/3GALLONS
MEAL: DINNER   REC: Q028A DEEP FRIED EGGPLANT   WT 83 LBS   11 GALLONS

8950-00-127-9789
CATSUP, TOMATO, NO. 10   ST.RM. CODE:33A   ST.RM. TYPE:D   TOTAL ISSUE: 4.CN
MEAL: BREAKFAST REC: S024A CATSUP-CAFETERIA SERVICE   WT: 2½   2½LBS 0 1/3 NO. 10CAN
MEAL: LUNCH   REC: SC24A CATSUP-CAFETERIA SERVICE   WT: 19 1/3LBS 2 2/3 NO. 10CAN
MEAL: DINNER   REC: 0011A SEAFOOD COCKTAIL SAUCE-CAFETERIA SERVICE   WT: 7 ¼ LBS 1 NO. 10CAN
MEAL: DINNER   REC: S024A CATSUP-CAFETERIA SERVICE   WT: 4 LBS   0 2/3 NO. 10CAN

8950-00-616-5479
CATSUP, TOMATO, ½ OZ   ST.RM. CODE:B3   ST.RM. TYPE:C   TOTAL ISSUE: 1. HD
MEAL: BREAKFAST REC: S024B CATSUP-TRAY SERVICE   WT: 12½ OZ   25   PACKAGES
MEAL: LUNCH   REC: S024B CATSUP-TRAY SERVICE   WT: 2 2/3 LBS 83 1/3   PACKAGES
MEAL: DINNER   REC: SC24B CATSUP-TRAY SERVICE   WT: 1½ LBS   46   PACKAGES

8950-00-LO3-4834
HORSERADISH, FROZEN
MEAL: DINNER   REC: 0011A SEAFOOD COCKTAIL SAUCE-CAFETERIA WT: 1 LBS   1½ CUPS

FIGURE 11. Detailed breakout sheet indicating the total daily requirement of each food item and a recipe-by-recipe breakdown of the requirements of each item (negative quantities indicate reusable leftovers).

RECIPE YIELDS FOR DAY 1, LUNCH

RECIPE NAME   PARMESAN VEAL CUBES

YIELD 400

RECIPE CODE L096A

EACH PORTION 6.82 OZS.

#	Stock No.	Ingredient	Weight		Measure	
1	8905-00-N00-1395	VEAL, DICED, FROZEN	124	LBS	0	CUPS
2	8945-00-616- 81	SALAD OIL	3	LBS	6	CUPS
3	8915-00-128-1179	ONIONS, DEHYDRATED, CHOPPED, NO. 10	1	LBS	4	CUPS
4	8915-00-823-7663	GARLIC, DRY, TOPPED	0-$\frac{1}{2}$	OZS	4	CLOVE
5	8950-00-262-8886	SALT, TABLE, IODIZED	15-1/3	OZS	24	TBSP
6	9825-00-127-3074	SUGAR, REFINED, GRANULATED, 100 LB	14	OZS	2	CUPS
8	8950-00-L03-2730	PEPPER, WHITE, 1 LB	0	OZS	1	TSP
9	8950-00-L03-2711	CLOVES, GROUND, 1 LB	0-1/3	OZS	2	TBSP
10	8950-00-L03-2710	CINNAMON, GROUND, 1 LB	0	OZS	4	TBSP
11	8915-00-582-4060	TOMATOES, CANNED, WHOLE, NO. 10	51	LBS	6-2/3	NO. 10 CANS
12	0-00-N00-8888	WATER	50	LBS	6	GALLONS
13	0-00-N00-1040	SEPARABLE MEAT FAT	2-$\frac{1}{2}$	LBS	0	
14	8910-00-L03-4112	CHEESE, PARMESAN	3	LBS	13-2/3	CUPS

*QUANTITIES OF INGREDIENTS IN POUNDS AND OUNCES, AS WELL AS IN CONVENIENT MEASURING UNITS

COOKING PROCEDURE:

1. HEAT OIL, ADD VEAL AND BROWN WELL ON ALL SIDES. DRAIN OFF EXCESS FAT.
2. ADD ONIONS AND GARLIC TO VEAL, SAUTE UNTIL TENDER.
3. MIX SALT, SUGAR, CLOVES, CINNAMON, TOMATOES, AND WATER. ADD TO VEAL. BRING TO A BOIL. REDUCE HEAT. COVER AND SIMMER 2 HOURS OR UNTIL VEAL IS TENDER.
4. PLACE ABOUT 2$\frac{1}{4}$ GAL IN EACH PAN.
5. SPRINKLE 3/4 CUP CHEESE OVER VEAL MIXTURE IN EACH PAN.

*COOKING PROCEDURES

172

RECIPE NAME   STUFFED CABBAGE W/TOMATO SAUCE   RECIPE CODE L040D
YIELD 192   EACH PORTION 7.84 OZS.

1-8905-00-L03-4050   STUFFED CABBAGE, FROZEN, 48/CS   96   LBS   4   CASES

RECIPE NAME   BAKED CORN BEEF-APPLE SUGAR GLAZE   RECIPE CODE L044D
YIELD 200   EACH PORTION 6.25 OZS.

1-8905-00-L03-4007   BEEF, CORNED, FROZEN COOKED,
                      POUCH BAG   54   LBS   0
2-8915-00-584-1647   JUICE, APPLE, CANNED, SS, NO. 3   18-2/3 LBS   6   NO. 3 CYL CN
3-9825-00-127-3074   SUGAR, REFINED, GRANULATED, 100 LBS 10   LBS   5-2/3 QUARTS
5-8950-00-262-8886   SALT, TABLE, IODIZED   0-1/4   OZS   1   TSP
6-8920-00-160-6165   STARCH, CORN, EDIBLE   5   OZS   1   CUP

COOKING PROCEDURE: 1. ROAST IN PAN AT 360° F.
                      2. BRUSH WITH APPLE GLAZE.
                      3. SLICE THIN.

                      1. POUR APPLE JUICE IN SMALL STEAM KETTLE. ADD SUGAR, SALT, CORNSTARCH AND BRING TO A BOIL. LET STAND 5 MIN.
                      2. BASTE MEAT AND SERVE.

FIGURE 12. Scaled recipe printouts.

173

code numbers along with the sales estimate for a day, or a sequence of days. These data can be transmitted by cards or, more commonly, via terminal input. Figure 7 shows the confirmation of such an input by the computer. The system was designed for a hospital where special diets were prepared in a separate kitchen. Only the first day of the 14 day production plan is shown.

Figure 8 illustrates the resulting food cost accounting report. The ration cost is a fixed cost allowance that is compared with actual cost on a daily basis. The average nutrient composition of the meals for 14 days is shown in Figure 9. Both of these reports are computed from the data stored on the recipe file in conjunction with the input information shown partially in Figure 7.

Figure 10 is one of the most elaborate and useful reports for food production and issuing. The report indicates, on a daily, weekly, and cumulative basis, the food quantities (and their dollar values) needed for production. Such a report can be used for purposes of issuing and purchasing, and also for cost and price control before the menu is planned.

The report shown in Figure 11 is a breakdown of Figure 10 to the level of meal-by-meal preparation. The information displayed is ideal for the organization and control of ingredient preparation and the issue of supplies to the kitchen.

Figure 12 shows two scaled recipes with cooking procedure. This is the report issued by the computer directly to the cook. It is consistent with the previous ones; consequently, full operational control is established over the quality and of food service from purchase to service.

The major problem with this system lies with the art of forecasting sales. If the prediction is done for a short time only, or if the menu is nonselective, the reports will be accurate. Otherwise, the long-term reports have to be revised, or better forecasting techniques must be implemented. It should be noted that, in the case of nonselective menus planned by computer, the cost and nutrition reports become unnecessary, since these attributes are maintained by the program at the desired level.

V. CONCLUSIONS

Although it should be clear that computers can be used to plan menus and control food production, the fact remains that only a limited number of institutions are using such techniques and fewer still utilize them to their full potential. In the remaining institutions, there seem to be no explicitly stated objectives, constraints, measures, or rules in the traditional process of menu planning. Even if there were, the information-processing capacity of the human mind would obviate the use of accurate data.

Despite, or perhaps because of this situation, most food managers are satisfied with their menus (whether or not they maximize preferences), and tend to resist the idea of interference with their prerogatives. The suggestion of applying mathematics or computers to menu planning frequently stimulates a food manager's interest in using the computer as an information-processing tool. Since computerized information processing is an area in which operational needs of managers and the data needs of mathematical models overlap, it is best in this case to approach computerized menu planning in two stages. Computerization, as has been shown, does serve the manager's interest in facilitating the management function, but at the same time, contributes, through recipe coding, to the accuracy and accessibility of a data base on which models can be built for menu planning. The best approach, therefore, is to computerize data processing first. After that is accomplished, computerized menu planning will follow naturally.

VI. REFERENCES

1. Balintfy, J. L. *Communications of ACM* 7 (4), 255 (1967)
2. Balintfy, J. L. "System/360 Computer Assisted Menu Planning" *Contributed Library Program No. 360D - 15.2.013*, 286, IBM Corporation, Hawthorne, New York (1969)
3. Balintfy, J. L., Gelpi, M. J., Findorff, F. K. and Dennis, L. C. *J. Am. Diet. Assoc. 61*, 637 (1972)
4. Balintfy, L. J., Duffy, W. J. and Sinha, P. *Operations Research 22*, 711 (1974)
5. Balintfy, L. J. *Naval Research Reviews 27* (7), 1 (1974)
6. Sinha, P. "Preference Maximized Models of Menu Planning" *Ph.D. Dissertation*, Department of Industrial Engineering, University of Massachusetts, Amherst (1974)
7. O'Connor, A. "Preference Maximized School Lunch Menus" *Master's Thesis,* Department of Food Science and Nutrition, University of Massachusetts, Amherst (1975)
8. Armstrong, R. P., Balintfy, J. L. and O'Connor, M. A. *O.N.R. Technical Report No. 13,* Sept. (1973)

UTILIZING LABOR EFFECTIVELY

CHAPTER 9

TASK AND PRODUCTIVITY ANALYSIS IN FOOD SERVICE
OPERATIONS

Gary L. Hotchkin[1]

National Restaurant Association
Chicago, Illinois

I. INTRODUCTION

The National Restaurant Association (NRA) recently conducted a survey of employment (1). The questionnaire asked respondents: "Have you, or anyone who now lives at home ever worked, or work now, for any type of establishment that prepares
and serves food? (Including restaurants, drive-ins/take-outs,
coffee shops, family type, etc., as well as cafeterias or restaurants in hotels, schools, hospitals, factories, and offices,
sport arenas, etc). The work could be part-time, or full time,
and be in any position such as food preparation, service to
customers, maintenance, administration, management, ownership,
etc."

Respondents who answered affirmatively questions posed by
the survey regarding food service employment were asked to
write in the age and sex of the person and indicate if they
were currently employed or had worked in the position some time
in the past. Furthermore, they were asked to indicate if this
was a part-time or full-time job. As a check on the accuracy of
the response, a telephone survey was conducted with a sample of
100 households that indicated someone was presently employed in
the food service industry (FSI). The question was asked again,
and the title and job description of each worker obtained. The
telephone survey confirmed the fact that the questionnaire was
interpreted correctly by a significant portion of the respond-

[1]*Present address: Pipers Restaurant Division, Memphis, Tennessee*

Copyright © 1979 by Academic Press, Inc.
All rights of reproduction in any form reserved
ISBN: 0-12-453150-4

ents. Of the 100 households surveyed, 92 indicated they had answered the questionnaire correctly by their responses, while
the other eight had misread the questionnaire. It is not at all
unusual for respondents to misread or misinterpret questions on
self-administered surveys and this particular error rate does
not diminish the findings of this study to any appreciable extent. It is more than likely that a comparable offsetting error
exists for those who do in fact work in the food service industry and answered that they did not.

II. RESULTS OF FOOD SERVICE WORKER SURVEY

A. *Food Service Industry Worker Statistics*

1. *Current Employment* - Table I shows that 40 % of household show past or present food service employment. Of the 40 %,
11 % of households currently have someone working full-time or
part-time for the food service industry.
    Slightly less than half the households reporting a food
service industry employee noted that the position was a full-
time one, and slightly more than half noted that the position
was part-time.
    It can be seen in Table II that those households in which
there is a food service industry employee tend to follow the
same distribution in terms of household income as the population in general. However, household size tends to be larger
(26 % of food service industry households have five or more
members versus only 16 % for the total sample). As will be seen
later, the high incidence of young people working in the industry on a part time basis causes the FSI household to have a
higher proportion of households in which the head of the family
is between 35 and 54 years than U.S. households in general.
Whereas over half of FSI households (52 %) are headed by a wom-
an between 35 and 54. Of U.S. households only 38 % are in this
category.
    On a regional basis, it can be seen that the food service
industry is no less important in one region than it is in another. FSI households are distributed in the regions in the
same general ratio that all households are; however, it is
quite possible that New England has a slightly higher employment rate by the food service industry than others. The data
show that New England, overall, has five percent of the households, yet nine percent of the FSI households are concentrated
in this region.
    2. *Profile of Current FSI Workers* - As shown in Table III,
the FSI work force is relatively young. Workers 19 years or
younger make up one third of workers, and 24 years or younger,
one half of the work force. This low age factor derives in large

*Table I. Summary of 1975 Food Service Industry (FSI)
          Employment Statistics*

Estimated Number of U.S. Households	*70 million*
Percent of Households Presently Employed in FSI	*11 %*
Part-time	*6 %*
Full-time	*5 %*
Percent of Households With Previous FSI Employment	*29 %*
Percent of Households With Past or Present FSI Employment	*40 %*
Estimated Number of Household With Present FSI Employment	*7-8 million*
Average Number of FSI Employees in FSI Households	*1.2 people*
Estimated Number of People Presently Employed in FSI	*8 - 9 million*
Type of Employment	
Part-time	*52 %*
Full-time	*48 %*
Sex of Workers	
Male	*33 %*
Female	*67 %*
Age of Worker	
Under 25	*53 %*
25 - 44	*23 %*
45 and over	*24 %*

Table II.   Employment in the Food Service Industry by
            Household

	PERCENT OF HOUSEHOLDS REPORTING
Someone in household is presently employed in FSI	11
part-time	6
full-time	5
Someone in household was previously employed in FSI (but none currently)	29
No one in household ever employed in FSI	60
(Number of households)	(2,577)

measures from the high part-time employment rate, one of the
marks of the industry. One-third of FSI workers is male and two
thirds is female.

Table I shows that approximately half (48 %) of the FSI
workers are full-time employees. From Table IV it is evident
that 45 % of FSI workers are under 25 years, and that among
part-time employees six out of ten (59 %) are in the under 25
group.

The whole reason for the existence and the success of the
food service industry is people: people who enjoy the experience of eating out; people who want to get away from their day
to day routine; people who want a change of pace; even people
who simply want to avoid cooking and cleaning up for themselves. The food service industry has been successful because
it has met the needs of people. Yet, while people are the reason, the food service industry exists, people are also the
backbone of the industry. Mechanization has not and will not
take over and replace people because "people to people" contact
is an essential element which the food service industry must
continue to provide. It was speculated over ten years ago that
automated machinery would replace "people" from the deep frying
of French fries to the grilling of hamburgers. While the potential has existed for sometime, most French frying is still
"people controlled" today. Technological improvements, such as
automatic controls and microcomputers, reduce very significantly the human error, but people are still involved.

Table III. *Current Food Service Industry Workers by Age, Sex, and Work Status*

	PERCENT OF WORKERS REPORTING
Age	
14 - 19	*32*
20 - 24	*21*
25 - 34	*11*
35 - 44	*12*
45 - 54	*10*
55 and over	*14*
Sex	
Male	*33*
Female	*67*
Status	
Part-time	*50*
Full-time	*47*
No answer	*3*
(Number of workers)	*(333)*

III. CAREER LADDER STUDY

In April 1971, a three year study entitled the "Upward Progression of Hourly Workers in the Food Service Industry", began at NRA. The study focused on the elements of career laddering. While only some elements are discussed in this chapter, it should be noted that there are other key elements as well, including: organizational charting; promotional patterns; employee turnover and employee attitudes, which should be considered. While it is recognized that each of these elements contributes to morale and productivity of the employee, they are only secondarily related to task and productivity analysis.

In order to analyze the key element of career laddering the activity of task analysis it is necessary to define and analyze the task involved by FSI while in his job. The activity of task analysis required a definition of terms: (1) "task" is an isolated identifiable activity (example: "pour coffee in urn bag"), (2) "task conglomerate": a group of tasks forms a task conglomerate (example: making fresh coffee), (c) "job": several task conglomerate activities constitute a job (example: an eight hour activity for the title "Table Busser"):

Task ⟶ *Task Conglomerate* ⟶ *Job*

In the NRA study (2), each task involved in the food service operation was analyzed by 33 scales in the food service operation, evaluating relationships, including spatial and interpersonnal, according to a scheme adapted from the Gilpatrick study of Hospital Task Activities (3). Each task scales was assigned a numeric value. When all analyzed tasks were assigned number values they were programmed for a Hierarchical Clustering Scheme as defined by Johnson (4).

The resultant analysis produced both job relationships and training criteria by which tasks and jobs should be interrelated.

IV. EMPLOYEE PRODUCTIVITY

A. *Definition*

Employee productivity can be measured in a number of different ways. However, one of the most useful measurements show that:

$$Productivity = \frac{annual\ sales\ (\$)}{annual\ labor\ costs\ (\$)}$$

Productivity data are most useful when calculated by department, rather than for overall operations. Where it is possible to identify sales figures for individual departments, separate productivity measurements should be made. Productivity data for an organization are most useful when they can be compared to similar data for other organizations or industries, or to similar data for different time periods within the same organization. Little has been done to collect and disseminate productivity data in the food service industry, and thus it is difficult for a restaurateur to find data against which to compare his performance. However, some statistics do exist. For example, using the formula above to calculate productivity in terms of dollars, a study of restaurants in Michigan showed that productivity for cafeterias was $3.25 per employee and for table-service restaurants, $ 3.46 per employee. Selected data from that study are shown in Table VI.

In another study (6), using productive man hours per day as a measure of productivity, the U.S. Department of Agriculture found that overall productivity in commercial cafeterias in 1969 was 82.5 percent. Similarly, in 1971 (7), using the same measure of productivity, the Department of Agriculture found that the overall productivity for table service restaurants was 66.2 percent.

B. Causes for Low Productivity

There are many causes for low employee productivity. Among the most common are: obsolete equipment and/or physical facilities; lack of knowledge and skill; under utilization of employee skill; and low employee morale. Low productivity because of any or all of the last three suggests a need for a career development system.

TABLE VI. *Comparison of Productivity Figures for Different Types of Restaurant Operations*

Type of Operation	Employee Productivity ($ Sales Per $ Payroll)
Table Service	$3.46
Counter Service	$3.66
Drive In Service	$4.33
Cafeteria Service	$3.25
Other	$3.72

Annual Sales	Employee Productivity ($ Sales Per $ Payroll)
$200,000 or less	$3.85
$400,000	$3.77
$600,000	$3.68
$800,000	$3.60
$1,000,000	$3.53

C. Means to Increase Productivity

It is not hard to find advice on ways to increase productivity. The subject is a favorite with experts in the food service field.Kotschevar (8) has written extensively on productivity, and advises that the best way to achieve productivity is to plan work areas so that workers do not have to reach or move beyond certain limits. Avery, former head of the United States Navy Research Facility in Bayonne, New Jersey, advises that productivity can be improved by placing related pieces of equipment as close together as possible (9). The experts have advised better personnel management, including training, greater motivation, time and motion studies, and work simplification. Some consultants and equipment designers recommend bettor layout and modern food service equipment to reduce labor. Others predict that convenience foods will be the key to increased productivity. Companies which manufacture disposable tableware believe that they offer an equally important way of improving productivity. The manufacturers of vending machines make claims that their equipment can and will replace many food service workers. All these individuals are right when they say that their recommendations will increase productivity. However, none of their methods will increase productivity unless the food service operator first achieves full utilization!

D. Recommendations to Improve Productivity

Unfortunately, the restaurant industry's employees have a poor record of utilizing their time. The typical restaurant employee spends much time waiting, watching, or coasting. The need exists for carefully planned ways to utilize any time which is saved through improvements. One way to utilize available time is to provide alternative duties. The dishwasher, who can wash dishes in less time using a machine than he can by hand, can be assigned extra duties such as cleaning or receiving. Food service operators must make sure that equipment, devices, and products are being used to their full efficiency potential. A decision to buy equipment, devices, or products which are designed to increase efficiency should be based on the answer to the question, "How can the product be used to improve labor utilization?"

One of the problems is providing alternate duties or switching employees to different jobs in order to achieve greater utilization, is the natural resistance of employees to such practices. Specialization by establishing commissaries and hiring skilled, technically proficient individuals has often been proposed. While centralized production results in improvements in productivity, it can be costly to implement and savings through improved labor utilization can often be offset by costs generated by setting up the production facility.

Bishop (10) has shown productivity as high as 20 meals/labor hour on a sustained basis in state institutions in Texas. The national average in large hospitals is 11 meals/labor hour. School lunch productivity averages 12.5 meals/labor hour, with isolated examples as high as 20 meals/labor hour. Where productivity is attained and maintained, however, one finds new costs, such as transportation and packaging, which may offset savings attained through increased productivity.

Average figures for restaurants and hotels show a productivity of about 1.75 meals/labor hour (the lowest of any segment of the industry). The analysis of the jobs identify alternatives in job competition and make-up, and the productivity figures underline that there is still a tremendous distance to go before the goal of full labor utilization is achieved.

Productivity in food service operations receives less attention than it should because of the tempo established by the volume of business. However, it must be a measured concept of the future because of its direct impact on profits.

V. REFERENCES

1. Anon., "Survey of Food Service Industry Employees", *Natl. Rest. Assoc. News* (1975)
2. National Restaurant Assoc., "How to Invest in People", Natl. Rest. Assoc. Chicago, Illinois (1973)
3. Gilpatrick, E. "A Task Analysis of Jobs and Job Component Groups in Hospitals"
4. Johnson, S. C. *Psychometrika 32, 3* (1967)
5. Borsenik, F. D. "The Restaurant Industry in the State of Michigan: 1970", School of Hotel, Rest. and Instl. Mgt., Michigan State University, East Lansing, Michigan (1971)
6. Freshwater, J. "Productivity in Commercial Cafeterias", Agricultural Research Service, United States Department of Agriculture, Washington, D.C. (1969)
7. Freshwater, J. "Productivity in Table Service Restaurants", Agricultural Research Service, United States Department of Agriculture, Washington, D.C. (1971)
8. Kotschevar, L. H. and Terrell, M. E. "Food Service Planning", 2nd ed. Wiley, New York, New York (1977)
9. Avery, A. C. "Increasing Productivity in Food Service" Cahners, Boston, Massachusetts (1973)
10. Bishop, C. Personal Communication.

CHAPTER 10

OPTIMIZATION OF FOOD PREPARATION LABOR
THROUGH COMPUTER ASSISTED PRODUCTION PLANNING

Richard F. Bresnahan[1]

TRIMIS-ARMY
Walter Reed Army Medical Center
Washington, D.C.   20012

I. INTRODUCTION

The Tri-Service Medical Information System Agency (TRIMIS)
is a tri-service program for the application of automatic data
processing (ADP) to improve the effectiveness and economy of
health care delivery in the Army, Navy, and Air Force. The
TRIMIS effort encompasses development, evaluation, and installation of integrated and stand-alone medical automatic data
processing (ADP) projects assigned to meet joint service or
multi-agency medical systems requirements.

One of the systems being developed by TRIMIS is a computer
system to support the Hospital Food Service Division. The first
operational site for this system is the new Walter Reed Army
Medical Center.

Why have "systems" gained so much prominence lately in the
food service industry? To a great extent, it is due to the increasing cost of resources, such as food, labor, and energy,
that are consumed within a food service operation. Of these resources, food preparation labor is the most expensive single
resource consumed within most food service operations. In con-
fronting this situation, many food service directors have
turned to some sort of system in an attempt to optimize the u-
tilization of this resource.

Planning is an essential part of any system and a well
thought out plan will materially improve the performance of any

---

[1]*Present address: Analytic Services, Inc., Arlington, Virginia*

Copyright © 1979 by Academic Press, Inc.
All rights of reproduction in any form reserved
ISBN: 0-12-453150-4

food service system. Through good planning, it should be possible in the future to evaluate anticipated problems and   perhaps resolve them based upon the conditions defined by the
plans. Thus through the planning function, it will be possible
for the food service director to devote his or her time only
to those developments that were not planned.

II. USE OF COMPUTERS IN PRODUCTION PLANNING

The computer can be a valuable tool when placed at the disposal of the production planner. Various computer systems which
support the production planning function are presently in use.
One such system is the Army Medical Department's (AMEDD) ADP
System for Hospital Food Service, which is operational at seven
Army Medical Centers. Although this system provides support to
other food service functions as well as production planning,
and has objectives in addition to optimizing food preparation
labor, this chapter will only address computer support relating
to food production planning, and will focus on food preparation
labor.

A. *Files*

1. Menu File. The AMEDD ADP System for Hospital Food Service is designed around the hospital menu file. This automated
menu file is arranged by the day and meal. For each meal of the
hospital menu cycle, the file contains the recipe numbers for
each item on the menu. Production and service data, such as the
production area, start time, serving areas, and selection percentages associated with each item, are also contained in the
menu file. Since the menu is a cycle menu, once the menu is
established in the file, the user only has to review and update
the file to reflect menu changes and to incorporate operational
feedback from the production and service areas.

2. Census File. The system also contains a census file
which consists of projected census estimates. Daily, this file
is updated as required, and the computer calculates the number
of servings needed of each menu for the day. This calculation
is performed by multiplying the census forecast by the selection percentages contained in the menu file. For example, on
the hospital menu for a given day's dinner meal, there is a
choice between Beef Stroganoff or Baked Chicken. The selection
percentage is 70% for the Stroganoff and 30% for the Chicken.
If the census forecast is 1,000 then the number of servings
of the Stroganoff needed would be 700, and the number of serv-

ings of the Chicken needed would be 300.

3. Recipe File. Following the calulation of portions required, the computer accesses a file of standardized recipes and extends the needed recipes to the required number of servings. Based on this recipe extension process and the data contained in the menu file, the computer produces production reports that are used to guide the flow of goods, and organize the expenditure of labor resources during the food production activities.

B. Reports Provided

1. INGREDIENT SUMMARY - This document (Fig. 1) lists the ingredients and the quantities which are required for production on a given day and is used to withdraw ingredients out of inventory and into the Ingredient Room. The items on the document are listed in a predetermined sequence which simplifies the withdrawal activity and therefore helps to conserve labor resources.
2. FRESH FRUIT AND VEGETABLE PROCESSING WORKSHEET - This document (Fig. 2) lists the fresh fruit and vegetables which are required for food production on a given day. The document also contains the instructions for any pre-processing (e.g. "chip into 1/2 inch cubes") which may be required. A similar document is provided for meats.
3. INGREDIENT LABELS - These individual adhesive labels (Fig. 3) contain the name and quantity of each ingredient which is required by a recipe. Ingredients are weighed or measured and then packaged according to the label which is then attached to the package. This activity occurs in the Ingredient Room.
4. INGREDIENT ROOM DELIVERY SCHEDULE - This document (Fig 4) lists all the recipes which are to be produced on a given day and the times that the ingredients for those recipes are to be delivered to the food production areas.
5. PRODUCTION RECIPES - These documents (Fig. 5) are the actual recipes used by the food production personnel when producing the products. These recipes have been yield adjusted by the computer and they list all the ingredients required, the quantities, and the production instructions.
6. PRODUCTION WORKSHEET - This document (Fig. 6) summarizes all of the production activities taking place on a given day. It lists all of the items being produced, the quantities, the time production is to start, the production area, and the destination of the final product. This document is used by the production supervisor to monitor production activities.

INGREDIENT SUMMARY

FNSP23 UO-691   FOR 04 NOV 74

-LOC- ----------INGREDIENT---------- ---QUANTITY--- -COMMENT-

A-011 APRICOTS,WP-D   12.0 EACH
A-017 P/A SLICES,WP-D   8.0 EACH
A-018 PLUMS,WP-D   9.0 EACH
A-038 PEAS,DIET   6.0 EACH
A-041 TOMATO JUICE,DIET   0.2 EACH

A-060 MACARONI,ELBOW   13.6 LB
A-061 SPAGHETTI   56.0 LB
A-062 NOODLES,EGG   72.5 LB
A-064 RICE,WHITE   22.5 LB
A-071 DESS POWD W/GEL,RASPBERRY   0.4 LB

A-072 DESS POWD W/GEL,LIME   3.9 LB
A-076 DESS POWD W/GEL,CHERRY   2.6 LB
A-080 PIMENTO,DICED-C   2.5 QT
A-080 DESS POWD W/GEL, LIME   NA-CAL   0.1 OZ
A-082 PICKLES,SWEET,WHOLE-C   3.4 #10CN

A-083 PICKLES,SWEET,MIXED   1.1 #10CN
A-084 PICKLES,DILL,WHOLE-C   1.7 #10CN
A-100 MUSTARD,PREPARED   32.2 FL OZ
A-111 TOMATO PUREE   43.6 #10CN
A-131 KIDNEY BEANS-C   2.8 #10CN

A-169 CARROTS,SLICED-C   0.5 #10CN
A-170 OATMEAL   3.4 LB
A-209 BAKING POWDER,DIET   2.7 OZ
A-230 SOUP BASE,BEEF   0.2 LB
A-233 SOUP BASE,BEEF,SALT-FREE   9.7 OZ

A-312 BF CHICKEN   9.0 EACH
A-314 BF PORK   9.0 EACH
A-323 BF BANANAS   6.0 EACH
A-324 BF PEACHES   6.0 EACH
A-325 BF PEARS   6.0 EACH

A-326 BF BEETS   9.0 EACH
A-328 BF CARROTS   9.0 EACH
A-381 SALT   230.5 OZ
A-390 LEMON JUICE-C   9.9 FL OZ
A-391 BAKING POWDER   36.9 OZ

A-392 CORNSTARCH   1.2 LB
A-413 PUFFED RICE-I   95.0 EACH
A-422 GRITTS,HOMINY   25.1 LB
A-431 SUGAR,BROWN   15.6 LB
A-432 SUGAR,GRANULATED   6.8 LB

FIGURE 1. Typical Ingredient Summary

```
                               INGREDIENT ROOM WORKSHEET

FNSP24 00-723                  FRESH FRUIT AND VEGETABLE PROCESSING

INGREDIENT                 PRE-PREP   DEL-TIME    QUANTITY

APPLES,EATING-F              **NONE      1100     11 LBS 12 1/8 OZS
                                         1400     25 LBS  7 2/3 OZS
                         TOTAL **NONE              37 LBS  3 3/4 OZS
                    --------    ---------------------------------------------------

         TOTAL FOR DAY                            37 LBS  3 3/4 OZS

****************************************************************************

BANANAS-F                   **NONE      1000     23 LBS  5 3/4 OZS
                                        1100     27 LBS  8 1/3 OZS
                                        1200     32 LBS
                                        1400     29 LBS  2 OZS
                         TOTAL **NONE             112 LBS
                    ------------------------------------------------------

         TOTAL FOR DAY                            112 LBS

****************************************************************************

ORANGES-F                   **NONE      1100     11 LBS 12 1/8 OZS
                                        1400     25 LBS  7 2/3 OZS
                         TOTAL **NONE             37 LBS  3 3/4 OZS
                    ------------------------------------------------------

         TOTAL FOR DAY                            37 LBS  3 3/4 OZS

****************************************************************************

CABBAGE,WHITE-F           SHREDDED      0800     45 LBS  6 1/3 OZS
                       TOTAL SHREDDED            45 LBS  6 1/3 OZS
                    ------------------------------------------------------

CABBAGE,WHITE-F             WEDGES      0800      8 LBS  8 OZS
                        TOTAL WEDGES             8 LBS  8 OZS
                    ------------------------------------------------------

         TOTAL FOR DAY                            53 LBS 14 1/3 OZS

****************************************************************************

CABBAGE,RED-F             SHREDDED      1100     16 LBS  8 OZS
                                        1200     73 LBS
                       TOTAL SHREDDED            89 LBS  8 OZS
```

FIGURE 2. Typical fresh fruit and vegetable processing Ingredient Room Worksheet

DEL 0800 HRS ON TUE I OCT 74
            DINING HALL I
APRICOT HALVES CAL/R D.

APRICOTS,WP-D,#303 CN

   10 EACH

DEL 0800 HRS ON TUE I OCT 74
            DINING HALL I
PEAS NA-CAL/R D

PEAS,DIET,#303 CN

   4 EACH

DEL 0800 HRS ON TUE I OCT 74
            DINING HALL I
NOODLES NA/R BU

NOODLES,EGG

   3 LBS 9 2/3 OZ

DEL 0800 HRS ON TUE I OCT 74
            DINING HALL 2
RICE BUTTERED

RICE,WHITE

   10 LBS 6 1/3 OZ

DEL 0800 HRS ON TUE I OCT 74
            DINING HALL 2
RELISH TRAY #8

PICKLES,SWEET,WHOLE-C
  SLICES
   2 QTS 2 1/8 CUPS

DEL 0800 HRS ON TUE I OCT 74
            DINING HALL I
RELISH TRAY #8

PICKLES,SWEET,MIXED

   I QT 3 1/2 CUPS

DEL 0800 HRS ON TUE I OCT 74
            DINING HALL I
PLUMS CAL/R D.

PLUMS,WP-D,#303 CN

   9 EACH

DEL 0800 HRS ON TUE I OCT 74
            DINING HALL I
NOODLES NA-CAL/R

NOODLES,EGG

   I LB 3 1/4 OZ

DEL 0800 HRS ON TUE I OCT 74
            DINING HALL 2
NOODLES BUTTERED

NOODLES,EGG

   14 LBS 4 3/4 OZ

DEL 0800 HRS ON TUE I OCT 74
            DINING HALL I
RICE BUTTERED

RICE,WHITE

   II LBS 9 2/3 OZ

DEL 0800 HRS ON TUE I OCT 74
            DINING HALL I
RELISH TRAY #8

PICKLES,SWEET,WHOLE-C
  SLICES
   2 QTS 3 1/3 CUPS

DEL 0800 HRS ON TUE I OCT 74
            DINING HALL 2
RELISH TRAY #8

PICKLES,DILL,WHOLE-C

   2 QTS 2 1/8 CUPS

FIGURE 3. Typical ingredient labels

```
                                    DELIVERY SCHEDULE
         FNSP2I 00-688

         DINING HALL I                  SUN 29 SEP 74          DELIVER 0800 HOURS

         ---------RECIPE NAME--------- -RECIPE NUMBER- -PREP TIME- -DEL ST- --DAY MEAL---

         CREAM OF BEET SOUP            S-035-50-0I       0800        P      SUN DINNER

         CREAM OF BEET SOUP NA/R D.    S-035-70-0I       0800        P      SUN DINNER

         HAM AND CHEESE SANDWICH-GRL   M-II7-10-0I       0800        E      SUN SUPPER

         VEAL BABY FOOD SIR            M-I4I-90-0I       0800        P      SUN DINNER

         VEAL THINNED STRAINED         M-I4I-9I-0I       0800        P      SUN DINNER

         MINUTE STEAKS-GRL             M-234-10-0I       0800        P      SUN DINNER

         BREAKFAST STEAK               M-363-10-02       0800        G      SUN DINNER

         CHICKEN LIVERS ON TOAST       M-405-10-0I       0800        G      SUN DINNER

         CHITTERLINGS WOODYS           M-433-10-0I       0800        C      SUN DINNER

         CHICKEN GRAVY                 MA-072-10-0I      0800        G      SUN DINNER

         CHERRY SAUCE                  MA-075-10-0I      0800        C      SUN DINNER

         BAKED MACARONI WITH TOMATOES  MS-040-10-0I      0800        P      SUN DINNER

         MASHED POTATOES               P-020-10-02       0800        P      SUN DINNER

         MASHED POTATOES THINNED STRAIN P-020-9I-0I      0800        P      SUN DINNER

         OVEN BROWNED POTATOES CAL/R   P-025-20-0I       0800        P      SUN SUPPER

         OVEN BROWNED POTATOES NA/R    P-025-30-0I       0800        P      SUN SUPPER

         OVEN BROWNED POTATOES NA-CAL/R P-025-40-0I      0800        P      SUN SUPPER

         OVEN BROWNED POTATOES BL      P-025-50-0I       0800        P      SUN SUPPER

         RICE BUTTERED                 PS-00I-10-0I      0800        P      SUN SUPPER

         RICE BUTTERED                 PS-00I-10-0I      0800        C      SUN DINNER

         RICE CAL/R                    PS-00I-20-0I      0800        P      SUN DINNER

         RICE WA/R BU                  PS-00I-30-0I      0800        P      SUN DINNER

         RICE NA-CAL/R                 PS-00I-40-0I      0800        P      SUN DINNER

         MACARONI BUTTERED             PS-047-10-0I      0800        P      SUN DINNER
                                                                                PAGE I
```

FIGURE 4. Typical Ingredient Room Delivery Schedule

```
                          PRODUCTION RECIPE
FNSP20 UO-687                                          FOR SAT 26 JAN 74 DINNER

GS- 3-10- I ARABIAN PEACH SLD              DELIVER 0800 HRS FRI TO DINING HALL I STATION
                                           PREPARE 0800 HRS FRI     BATCH  I OF  I- 280 5
                                                            BATCH-VOLUME 7  PANS
            TOTAL-  280 SV 7  PANS         ---------PTS CODE LINE BREAKDOWN----------
    MAIN LINE     150 SV  3 3/4 PANS       IS - 130 SV
            PTS-  130 SV  3 1/4 PANS

------------------------------------------------------------------------------------
-------AMOUNT--------- --------INGREDIENTS--------- -PRE-PREP- --------INSTRUCTIONS----------
  7 =10 CNS   1/2 QT   PEACHES,SLICED-C                        I.  DRAIN AND SAVE LIQUID.
------------------------------------------------------------------------------------
    3 GALS    2/3 QT   FRUIT JUICE AND WATER                   2. COMBINE AND BRING TO A BOIL
    I GAL     1/4 QT   VINEGAR,WHITE                              ADD FRUIT.
   15 LBS  6 1/3 OZ    SUGAR,GRANULATED                          CONTINUE TO SIMMER ABOUT
    2 OZ    4 TBSPS    CLOVES,WHOLE                                 10 MINUTES.
    I LB      3/4 OZ   CINNAMON,STICK                              REMOVE FRUIT.
                                                                  STRAIN.
------------------------------------------------------------------------------------
   12 LBS  9 2/3 OZ    DESS POWD W/GEL,ORANGE                  3. DISSOLVE IN LIQUID.
------------------------------------------------------------------------------------
    4 GALS    3/4 QT   FRUIT JUICE AND WATER                   4. ADD.
                                                                 CHILL UNTIL SLIGHTLY
                                                                 THICKENED.
                                                                 FOLD IN FRUIT.
                                                                 POUR INTO PANS AND CHILL
                                                                 UNTIL FIRM.
                                                                 USE 12 x 20 x 2 INCH INSERT
                                                                 PANS.  I PAN PER 40
                                                                 SERVINGS.
                                                                 USE I GAL PER PAN.
------------------------------------------------------------------------------------
   II LBS  3 1/4 OZ    LETTUCE-F               LEAVES          5. SERVE ON LETTUCE UNDERLINER.
                                                                 PORTION SIZE INSTRUCTIONS.
                                                                 SMALL- CUT 5 X12.
                                                                 MEDIUM- CUT 5 X 8.
                                                                 LARGE- CUT 5 X 7.
```

FIGURE 5. Typical Production Recipe

II. APPLICATION TO A READY FOODS SYSTEM

Systems such as the one just described have proven to be of immense benefit to the production planner in a "conventional" food service environment.

However, the distinction becomes a little more apparent when one considers the requirements of a food service facility that incorporates the concept of "ready foods". In utilizing this concept an institution prepares, to whatever extent possible, menu items in large quantities, chills or freezes them for storage, and withdraws them at a later time for service as required. Within this environment one is able to separate, to a large extent, production planning from menu planning. In so doing, many of the constraints placed on the production sched-

```
BP26C UO-689                          FOOD PRODUCTION WORKSHEET

RECIPES FOR TODAY IN KITCHEN              SUN 29 SEP 74 - WEEK 2 DAY 6
DINNER
***************************************************************************************

M-100-10-  1 HAM-BKD SMOKED             DELIVERY AT 1400 HRS SAT TO STATION F
                                        PREPARE AT 0600 HRS SUN
TOTAL AMOUNT-   390 SV          PORTION SIZES
DISTRIBUTION                    SMALL- 60    GMS
   MAIN LINE- 230 SV            MED- 90    GMS
         PTS- 160 SV            LARGE-120   GMS
***************************************************************************************

M-363-10-  2 BREAKFAST STEAK            DELIVERY AT 0800 HRS SUN TO STATION G
                                        PREPARE AT 0800 HRS SUN
TOTAL AMOUNT- 320 SV            PORTION SIZES
DISTRIBUTION                    SMALL- 60    GMS
   MAIN LINE- 320 SV            MED- 90    GMS
                                LARGE-120   GMS
***************************************************************************************

M-405-10-  1 CHICKEN LIVERS ON TOAST   DELIVERY AT 0800 HRS SUN TO STATION G
                                        PREPARE AT 0800 HRS SUN
TOTAL AMOUNT- 180 SV            PORTION SIZES
DISTRIBUTION                    SMALL- 60    GMS
   MAIN LINE- 180 SV            MED- 90    GMS
                                LARGE-120   GMS
***************************************************************************************

M-433-10-  1 CHITTERLINGS WOODYS       DELIVERY AT 0800 HRS SUN TO STATION C
                                        PREPARE AT 0800 HRS SUN
TOTAL AMOUNT- 230 SV            PORTION SIZES
DISTRIBUTION                    SMALL-  2    OZ
   MAIN LINE- 230 SV            MED-   4    OZ
                                LARGE-  6    OZ
***************************************************************************************
```

FIGURE 6. Typical Food Production Worksheet

ule by the menu are removed. This allows the production planner
to concentrate on planning a production schedule which will optimize the utilization of food preparation labor.

The new Walter Reed Army Medical Center employs the concept
of ready foods. However, the computer system designed is also
capable of supporting a conventional food service operation.
Due to the increased importance and visibility being given to
production planning, labor utilization within conventional food
service operations using the computer system will also be improved.

The system designed for the new Walter Reed Army Medical
Center consists of a menu file that contains the same service
data that is contained in the menu file used in the prior system. In many cases however, an item is not to be produced and
served on the same day. In addition, an item can be produced on
one day in sufficient quantities to satisfy service require-

ments of more than one service day. Therefore, the production
data must be maintained in a separate file - the production
schedule file.

The link between these two files is an automated inventory
file. The inventory file contains a record for each ready
food item and maintains a perpetual inventory.

Service requirements can be computed in the same manner as
in the prior system, using census forecast and selection percentages. However, service requirements can be computed for
many days into the future. When these requirements have been
computed, the system enters the quantities into the inventory
file as projected debits to the "ready foods" inventory.

Two approaches to production planning were considered by
the design team. One approach was to establish an inventory re-
order level for each of the "ready foods" items. When the system determines, based on projected service requirements, that
the re-order level for an item has been reached, the system
would schedule that item for production. Based on scheduling
criteria, the system would select the production day and enter
the information into the production schedule file. The system
would then compute the production quantity based on projected
service requirements and inventory levels.

The other approach considered was to establish a production
schedule cycle similar to a menu cycle. Using this approach,
the production planner selects the production day for each item
and establishes the production schedule file as a cycle of production schedules. The computer system would calculate production quantities based again on projected service requirements
and inventory levels.

Each approach had its merits and limitations. Obviously,
the first approach requires more sophisticated computer support. However, with either approach, the key decision affecting production labor utilization is the selection of a production day. Whether it is the computer system or the production
planner that makes the decision, it is this decision and the
resulting production schedule which will determine to what extent food preparation labor will be utilized.

Can the computer make this decision? It is not an easy decision to make, in view of the constraints and variables which
must be considered. First, the menu has to be considered. The
menu items which are to be served and the quantities required
are of importance. Current and projected inventory levels have
to be taken into account. Then, of course, one has to consider
the amount and type of manpower associated with each production
task. How long, for example, does it take to produce 200 servings of sweet rolls? Does it take twice as long to produce 400
servings of the same sweet rolls? The effect that the production quantity has on the production time must be considered.

Another point to consider was "active" production time as opposed to "passive" production time. In the case of sweet rolls, the first thirty minutes of production might be an "active" production period. Then, while the dough is proofing, there may be a thirty minute "passive" production period during which there is no labor required. These periods of "active" and "passive" production times are what allows the production planner to assign an employee to produce more than one product during the same time period.

It is obvious that an enormous amount of data must be collected and many calculations performed to determine accurate labor requirements. Then, these labor requirements have to be matched against the available labor resources. As the production schedule evolves, it must continually be evaluated to determine if the available resources are being properly utilized. If they are not, the schedule may need revision.

This process is a monumental task to do effectively. The number of variables and constraints to be considered and the number of calculations which must be performed are probably beyond human capability to do accurately and in a timely manner. However, this is what planning is all about: collecting data, evaluating data, making decisions based on data, and analyzing the impact of the decisions. This planning must be done if the labor resource utilization is to be optimized. This is where the computer again can really be put to use.

Can the computer make these planning decisions? Can the computer evaluate the data and decide, in a ready foods environment, when items should be produced? With the proper set of application programs and files containing the necessary data, a computer can indeed make these decisions!

However, this does not mean that the food service director can then overlook the production planning function. The production schedule, and the data upon which it is based, must continually be monitored and analyzed to insure that current operating conditions are being reflected.

The computer system can be designed to provide various output reports, which provide the production planner the opportunity to evaluate the production schedule and the extent of labor utilization. A Labor Utilization Summary (Fig. 7), for example, shows the planner what items are being produced, where they are being produced, the production start time, and the "active" and "passive" production periods for each item. It allows the planner to pinpoint possible problem areas and periods during the day when the labor resources are not being utilized properly.

A report such as the Labor Utilization Summary can be provided and used with great effectiveness in both a ready foods, and a conventional food service operation. Regardless of whether the product planner, the menu planner, or the computer makes

the planning decisions, this report can be provided to evaluate
and analyze the impact of the decisions.

LABOR UTILIZATION SUMMARY (COOKS) APRIL 10

PRODUCT	QTY	6	7	8	9	10	11	12	1	2	3	4	5
BEEF BURGUNDY	800	AAAA	PPPP	PPPP	PPAA								
BAKED CHICKEN	1200	AAAA	AAPP	AAPP	PAAA								
VEAL PARMESAN	600	AAAA	AAAA	PPPP	PPPA	AA							
SWT SOUR PORK	400			AA	AAAA	APPA	A						
GRL LIVER	600			AAAA	AAAA	AAA							
VEG SOUP	1500						AA	APPP	PPPP	PPPA	A		
ENCHILADAS	800						AA	AAAA	AAAA	AAAA	PPPA		
CANDIED YAMS	600									A	PAAA	APPA	
TOTAL		3333	2222	3322	2235	3232	2111	1112	1223	2002			
AVAILABLE LABOR		3333	3333	3322	2333	3333	3111	1222	2233	1333			

FIGURE 7. *Typical Labor Utilization Summary report*

CHAPTER 11

REDUCING LABOR COSTS IN FOOD SERVICE OPERATIONS BY SCHEDULING

Robert S. Smith

US Army Natick Research & Development
Natick, Massachusetts

Richard J. Giglio

Department of Industrial Engineering
University of Massachusetts
Amherst, Massachusetts

I. INTRODUCTION

An effective means for decreasing labor costs is by more efficient scheduling of employees. However, food service managers experience problems in the scheduling of employees, which are complicated by the fact that food service operations experience highly variable manpower requirements throughout the workday. The workshift pattern is, of course, the single most important factor in determining an efficient employee schedule, and a technique for optimizing schedules to achieve minimal labor costs will therefore be described.

Personnel scheduling may be viewed as the process of converting labor requirements over definitive time intervals into precise worker assignments. A need exists in many types of organizations to devise an efficient system for scheduling personnel. This is especially true of service type operations in general, and food service operations in particular. For example, Lundberg and Armatus (1) stated that in restaurant operations as much as 33 per cent of the available labor is wasted through lack of proper scheduling.

Increasing the productivity of food service workers is of particular concern to the military services. Recent studies (2) of military food service systems show that labor costs amount to 50 per cent of the total meal cost. For example, in

201

Copyright © 1979 by Academic Press, Inc.
All rights of reproduction in any form reserved
ISBN: 0-12-453150-4

the dining facility selected by the authors for the application of the technique to be described, a total of 23 employees were required, with labor costs in excess of $ 288,000 annually. The significance of this expense is highlighted by the magnitude of the food service operations of the U.S. military services, for which the total annual operating cost is estimated to exceed four billion dollars. Clearly, even small improvements in worker productivity should yield labor cost savings of millions of dollars annually.

Techniques for determining more efficient employee schedules are, therefore, of great interest to military decision makers who are constantly searching for ways to reduce the operating cost of personnel associated with an all volunteer force. Consider for example the U.S. Army which currently operates nearly 1400 dining facilities worldwide. Work schedules for these facilities are currently determined manually by each dining hall manager. The efficiency of each schedule is, therefore, directly related to the ingenuity of the manager in dealing with the highly variable manpower requirements which exist throughout the workday.

II. SCHEDULING TECHNIQUES

A number of techniques for employee scheduling have been developed and can be used to solve various types of scheduling problems. These techniques include, but are not limited to, the following:linear, dynamic, integer, non-linear and stochastic programming; simulation and heuristics. Some of the more significant recent advances have been in the areas of scheduling toll collectors, bus drivers and telephone operators. In 1972, Tibrewala *et al* (3) developed an integer programming model for optimally scheduling employees having two consecutive days off when manpower requirements remained unchanged throughout a given work day. Tibrewala also developed a companion algorithm which allowed for manually computing solutions to this problem. Byrne and Potts (4) developed an eight phase integer programming algorithm for grouping candidate shift variables and then successively introducing integer constraints to match the demand histogram using a set of suitable fulltime and part-time shifts.

The application of the two phase algorithm to military food service is particularly interesting. Military food service demands extreme variability of manpower requirements throughout the work day. An hourly demand histogram for a dining facility under consideration is shown for week days in Figure 1. The requirements range from a low of 2, during the last period, to a high of 9, during the seventh period. Week end requirements

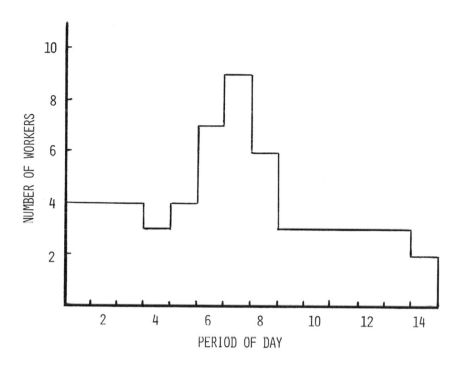

FIGURE 1. Minimum weekday manpower demand for cooks by the hour of the day.

are different from week day because of different operating hours and decreased customer attendance.

III. FORMULATING A MODEL

In preparing a model to schedule employees who are essentially interchangeable, the following constraints were adhered to: (1) schedules were provided for an "n" day period where manpower requirements change not only throughout the day, but also can change from day to day, for example,from week ends to week days, (2) days off need not occur simultaneously for all employees,but can be spread throughout the cycle with the proviso that each employee's days off will be consecutive.

The following terms will be used throughout the remainder of this chapter:

Work Shift Pattern - a pattern of work, rest, meal,and off duty periods for a work day. An example of three work shift patterns is provided in Table 1. On-duty periods are designated by "1" while off-duty periods are designated by "0".The ability to have staggered starting times and lunch breaks obviously enables more efficient schedules to be developed.

Employee Schedule - the assignment of employees to particular work shift patterns.

Workday - the total length of time the operation must function each day.

Full Time Shift - a shift of eight hours work.

Part Time Shift - a shift of less than eight hours of work.

Combination Schedule - a schedule in which some employees work full time shifts and other employees work part time shifts.

Split Shift Schedule - a shift consisting of eight hours of work with breaks in the middle of the work day. The total length of the work day depends upon the duration of the break.

The scheduling problem can be formulated as an integer program where the objective is to find an employee schedule which minimizes the total labor cost while satisfying the manpower requirements throughout the planning cycle. The appropriate mathematical equations are as follows:

$$\text{Minimize} \quad \sum_{j=1}^{p} \sum_{f=1}^{q} c_{jf} \, S_{jf} \qquad (1)$$

Subject to

$$\sum_{j=1}^{p} \sum_{f=1}^{q} \delta_{ikjf} \, S_{jf} \geq R_{ik} \quad \text{for } i = 1, \ldots, n \text{ (number of days in planning cycle)} \qquad (2)$$

and

$$k = 1, \ldots, m \text{ (number of periods in workday)} \qquad (3)$$

and

$$S_{jf} \geq 0 \text{ and integer}$$

where:

k = *index of period (e.g., hourly) during a work day*

C_{jf} = *the cost of each employee whose off day pattern is j and whose work shift pattern is f*

S_{jf} = *the number of employees who have off day pattern j and whose work shift pattern is f*

q = *number of work shift patterns*

p = *number of off-day patterns*

$\delta ikjf$ =   *1 if an employee with off day pattern j and work shift pattern f would be on duty*
       0 otherwise

R_{ik} = *minimum number of employees required on day i during period k*

Several points should be made in connection with the formulation presented by equations (1) through (3):

(1) The algorithm has to provide for the desired combinations of off days. One case commonly encountered is where all employees have two consecutive off days. In this instance there is a total of seven possible combinations.

(2) Other restrictions can easily be incorporated into this model. For example, if one of a certain set of work shift patterns is required to be in the solution (i.e. one may wish to insure that at least one full time worker is on duty at all times) this is easily accomplished by adding constraints.

(3) A single cycle problem ($p=1$, indices i and j not re-

TABLE I. Work Shift Patterns

Hour of Day	Work Shift Pattern		
	A	B	C
8 to 9 A M	1	0	0
9 to 10	1	1	0
10 to 11	1	1	1
11 to 12	1	1	1
12 to 1 P M	0	1	1
1 to 2	1	0	1
2 to 3	1	1	0
3 to 4	1	1	1
4 to 5	1	1	1
5 to 6	0	1	1
6 to 7	0	0	1

quired) is a particularly simple integer program.

(4) Provision can be made to account for both varying man-power requirements for each day of the planning interval and for each time period throughout the day. This can result in a large sized problem. For example, in a single period problem $(p=1)$, the maximum variables and constraints were 18 and 16, respectively. By comparison, when two day-to-day variations were introduced (weekday, weekend) the problem required 147 variables and 104 constraints for the same work shift patterns.

(5) The problem application that prompted this work has a period of $n=7$ days. Hourly employee requirements were constant through the 5 weekdays and were also the same on Saturday and Sunday.

Because a model which could be widely used in the field at installations with relatively small computers would be more useful, the size of the problem presented a significant obstacle. In the case of a scheduling problem involving over 100 variables and constraints, a sizeable computer system would be required which would greatly decrease the utility of the model. Therefore, a new approach was devised based on a two phase solution algorithm. The problem was regrouped into days which have the same hourly demands. Each subproblem could then be solved using a small integer program followed by an easy-to-use heuristic to obtain a final solution.

IV. TWO PHASE SOLUTION ALGORITHM

Tibrewala, *et al* (3) have developed a model for scheduling employees over an "*n*" day period where two consecutive days off were required during each period and daily manpower requirements were known. Their model has as its objective function the minimization of the total number of workers required over the planning cycle. However, it does not solve the general problem of employee scheduling in operations where the manpower requirements vary throughout the day.

The general mathematical formulation of their model is:

$$Minimize \quad \sum_{J=1}^{n} X_j$$

subject to

$$A_j \geq R_j \quad for \quad j = 1,\ldots\ldots, n \text{ (Number of days in planning cycle)}$$

$$X_j = 0 \text{ and integer}$$

where:

$$A_j = \left(\sum_{i=1}^{n} X_1 \right) - X_j - 1 - X_j = \text{(Number of employees working on day j)}$$

X_j = *Number of workers off for the pair of days j and J + 1, or n and 1 in the case of* X_n

R_j = *Minimum number of workers required on day j*

Although the model of Tibrewala *et al* (3) provides a means for optimal scheduling of employees over an "*n*" day period, it does not solve the problem of a composite planning cycle since it only applies when manpower requirements are constant through the workday. Therefore, a heuristic method for overcoming this obstacle was developed. The heuristic method requires an integer programming model as used for the single planning cycle problem, heuristics and an adaptation of Tibrewala's *et al* (3) model to arrive at the employee schedule.

A. Description

Phase I:

    A. Determine the employee schedules for both sets of man-power requirements: i.e., weekday and weekend, independently, using an integer programming formulation, or any other appro-priate method. Each set of manpower requirements which com-prises the planning cycle is treated separately and the size of the problem is manageable on even relatively small computer systems.

    B. Using the solutions in A above, define new composite workshifts by pairing up sets of work shifts from the solu-tions to the weekday and the weekend problems. Each composite workshift will specify the working hours for weekdays and weekends as well as the number of employees required. These hours will usually, though not always, be different.

    C. If policy requires that all employees work a full five day week, the pairing of work shifts in B above could affect the efficiency of the final schedule. It is, therefore, de-sirable to pair shifts in such a manner that the weekend shift does not have a manpower requirement which exceeds that of the weekday shift. For example, if a weekend shift having a man-power requirement for five employees is combined with a week-day shift which only requires three employees, the resulting schedule will have an excess of employees during weekdays be-cause of the difference in the duration of both components of the planning cycle. If all employees are to be given five days of work, then some of the weekend requirements (only two days) must be distributed throughout the weekday period which would require two less employees than during the weekend per-iod.

    D. It is desirable from employee morale and effective-ness standpoints to keep hours of work from weekdays to week-ends as similar, as practical, in each of the complete work-shifts. For example, it would be unadvisable to combine an 11 PM to 6 AM weekday shift with a 9 AM to 5 PM weekend shift since an employee assigned to this schedule would have only three hours off between Friday and Saturday.

Phase II:

A. *The problem is now regrouped into a number of independent problems, the number being determined by the number of composite workshifts defined in Phase IB. Each of these independent problems is then solved individually using the algorithm developed by Tibrewala, et al (3) to provide the off day patterns. In this instance, the solutions from Phase I provide the manpower requirements to be used in Tibrewala's model which yields the off day patterns. Once the day off patterns are known they can be directly translated into work schedules.*

B. *Each solution obtained in Phase IIA is then examined and compared against the daily manpower requirements. Any individuals in excess are identified for possible elimination. In cases where there are more than one candidate individual for elimination, the individual(s) are selected who would have three or more consecutive days off since this could improve employee morale and effectiveness. It is important to note that the manner in which shifts are paired up in Phase IB makes no difference in the efficiency of the schedule as long as it is not necessary to schedule all employees for five days work, thereby allowing for the elimination of any excess workers.*

B. *Example of the Two Phase Algorithm:*

Assume Phase I yielded the following solutions for the weekday and weekend schedules:

TABLE II. *Employee Work Schedule*

Work Tour	Work Hours	Number of Employees Required
	Weekdays	
A	8 – 4	4
B	9 – 5	2
C	11 – 7	3
	Weekends	
D	9 – 5	3
E	12 – 8	1
F	2 – 10	2

The heuristic of Phase IC is now applied to combine week-day and weekend requirements into composite shifts so that one can proceed to Phase II.

C. Composite Planning Cycle

TABLE III. Requirements of Composite Shifts

Composite Shift	Work Tour	Days of Week	Work Hours	Number of Employees Required
I	A	Mon – Fri	8 – 4	4
	D	Sat – Sun	9 – 5	3
II	B	Mon – Fri	9 – 5	2
	E	Sat – Sun	12 – 8	1
III	C	Mon – Fri	11 – 7	3
	F	Sat – Sun	2 – 10	2

Phase II is now begun where the problem is regrouped into three independent problems to be solved separately using the model of Tibrewala.

The problem structure for composite Shift 1, where requirements are R_1 thru R_5 = 4, R_6 and R_7 = 3, is shown below. In this problem X_1 has also been arbitrarily defined as Monday and Tuesday off. It should be noted that in a case where the number of work tours on weekdays and weekends is unequal, the tour left over after the composite shifts are defined is scheduled directly without the use of Tibrewala's model. In the case of weekday tours, all employees will have Saturday and Sunday off while, for weekend tours, off-days are arbitrarily assigned on weekdays.

D. Mathematical Formulation for Solving Problem of Shift I

$$\text{Minimize} \quad \sum_{j=1}^{7} X_j$$

subject to

$$X_2 + X_3 + X_4 + X_5 + X_6 \geq 4$$

$$X_3 + X_4 + X_5 + X_6 + X_7 \geq 4$$

$$X_1 + X_4 + X_5 + X_6 + X_7 \geq 4$$

$$X_1 + X_2 + X_5 + X_6 + X_7 \geq 4$$

$$X_1 + X_2 + X_3 + X_6 + X_7 \geq 4$$

$$X_1 + X_2 + X_3 + X_4 + X_7 \geq 3$$

$$X_1 + X_2 + X_3 + X_4 + X_5 \geq 3$$

and

$$X_j \geq 0 \text{ and integer}$$

The problem solution for composite shift I is:

$X_1 = 2$ (Two employees have Mon. and Tue. Off)

$X_3 = 1$ (One employee has Wed. and Thurs. Off)

$X_6 = 3$ (Three employees have Sat. and Sun. Off)

Translating the above solution into a schedule is straight-forward since the hours of work and off days are now known. It should be noted that even if an integer programming algorithm is not available, an approximate "hand" solution to the re-grouped problem can be employed in the overall algorithm.

This two phase algorithm is designed to be used for a seven-day cycle when there are two patterns of day-to-day variation i.e. weekends and weekdays. It is possible to extend the algorithm to cover the more general case of n day-to-day variation patterns, but no tests have been made regarding the efficiency of the general algorithm.

TABLE IV. Preliminary Schedule Derived From
          Application of Algorithm

Number of Employees	Mon	Tue	Wed	Thurs	Fri	Sat	Sun
1	off	off	8-4	8-4	8-4	9-5	9-5
2	off	off	8-4	8-4	8-4	9-5	9-5
3	8-4	8-4	off	off	8-4	9-5	9-5
4	8-4	8-4	8-4	8-4	8-4	off	off
5	8-4	8-4	8-4	8-4	8-4	off	off
6	8-4	8-4	8-4	8-4	8-4	off	off

The above schedule for Shift I is now examined and compared against the daily requirements. Excess manpower is identified and, if possible, eliminated. The final schedule for composite Shift I is shown in Table 5.

TABLE V. Final Schedule Derived From Application
          of Algorithm

Number of Employees	Mon	Tue	Wed	Thurs	Fri	Sat	Sun
1	off	off	off[a]	8-4	8-4	9-5	9-5
2	off	off	8-4	8-4	8-4	9-5	9-5
3	8-4	8-4	off	off	8-4	9-5	9-5
4	8-4	8-4	8-4	8-4	8-4	off	off
5	8-4	8-4	8-4	8-4	off[a]	off	off
6	8-4	8-4	8-4	off[a]	off[a]	off	off

[a]Indicates excess manpower which has been eliminated.

Following the same procedures, the schedules for composite shifts II and III would then be determined and added to the foregoing schedule to complete the problem.

E. Computer Running Times

Running times on a Control Data Corporation 3800 computer for the two phase solution algorithm, ranged from 0.6 to 2.5 seconds for Phase I for the problem described in the next section. The number of variables ranged from 14 to 16. By comparison, computer running times for Phase II ranged from 0.2 to 0.4 seconds for a problem having seven variables and seven contraints. It should be noted, however, that some portions of the solution algorithm were performed manually, i.e., the definition of the composite schedules and the interpretation of results of the integer programs. For long-term use subroutines could be developed to perform all operations on the computer.

The ability of the algorithm to generate near-optimal solutions has not been tested directly using a suitably large integer programming code. However, as previously noted, the solutions generated appear to be "good" and if implemented, hold the promise of saving significant amounts of manpower.

F. Effect of Work Shift Pattern on Efficiency

The single most significant factor affecting the efficiency[a] of the final schedule using the two phase algorithm is the work shift pattern. The results of a number of trial runs with a variety of work shift patterns are shown in Table VI. It can be seen that the weekly expenditure of labor ranged from a high of 488 man-hours for the eight hour shift to a low of 356 man-hours for the two hour part-time shift.

It is important to note here that if the work schedule matched the manpower demand graphs exactly for this application, a total of 346 man-hours would be expended weekly. By comparison, the results of the trial runs ranged from a low of 356 man-hours to a high of 488 man-hours weekly. Interestingly enough, for part-time shifts there is a direct correlation between the length of the shift and the schedule efficiency. Namely, as the length of shift increases, so does the total expenditure. This is attributed to the ability of the shorter duration shifts to better fill in the peaks and valleys of the manpower demand histogram.

A second important point which should also be made here concerns alternative optima. If the constraint for the allowable number of full time workers on the first and last shifts were varied, it would be possible to generate Phase I solutions which were equally good from the standpoint of the

[a]*Efficiency is defined as the total expenditure of labor man-hours over the planning cycle.*

TABLE VI. Results for Dining Facility Example

Shift Pattern	Number of Cooks	Increase (Decrease) in Number of Cooks[a] (1)	Weekly Labor Expenditure (Manhours)	% Differential[b]
8 hour	11		424	22.4
Combination:				
8 hr. & 2 hr.	26	14	356	3.2
8 hr. & 3 hr.	15	3	375	8.4
8 hr. & 4 hr.	12	0	384	10.9
8 hr. & 5 hr.	12	0	404	16.7
8 hr. & 6 hr.	12	0	418	21.4
Part Time:				
2 hour	39	27	356	3.2
3 hour	29	17	396	14.5
4 hour	20	8	384	10.9
Split Shift:				
8 hours	13	1	488	41.0
8 hr. & 2 hr.	33	21	374	8.0
8 hr. & 3 hr.	24	12	384	10.9
8 hr. & 4 hr.	20	8	392	13.3

[a] Compared to current staff of 12 full time cooks
[b] Percentage difference between the labor expenditure and minimum required staffing, 346 man-hours per week.

objective function value, but which resulted in different numbers of full-time and part-time personnel. This is a characteristic of combinatorial type problems and it provides a degree of flexibility which should be highly desirable from a
manager's viewpoint, since the units of full and part-time employees can be adjusted.

Extreme variability from one period to another is characteristic of food service which requires that a product in
preparation pass through a number of stages, each with differing work time requirements. Also, a finished meal frequently
consists of six or more components each with different processing requirements.

Workload variability is further increased in a military
dining facility since the kitchen is operational for up to 16
hours daily but customers are only served for three discrete
periods, usually totaling no more than six hours. In addition, daily customer attendance varies significantly from one
meal to another.

As a result, the efficient manual scheduling of employees
to compensate for the numberous peaks and valleys in the number of cooks required (while all employees are provided a
workday of specific duration and given two consecutive days
off) is a task which challenges even the most highly skilled
manager. For example, in the dining facility under consideration, the work schedule for cooks planned manually required
12 personnel working a total of 480 man-hours weekly. A two-
shift schedule was employed with the shifts overlapping for
two hours during the noon meal. By comparison, the absolute
minimum weekly manpower requirement based on the demand histogram was 346 man-hours. This meant that 134 man-hours (39 %)
were scheduled unnecessarily each week. Based on a 40 hour
week, this represented the equivalent of three and a fraction
man weeks which were scheduled when they actually were not required.

G. Personnel Savings

From Table VI it can be seen that there were significant
differences between the toal number of employees required compared to the old schedule which was prepared according to a
work shift pattern. For example, the eight hour shift pattern
was the only one which resulted in a savings of a full time
cook. However, it did not yield the most efficient schedule
of the shift patterns which were evaluated. By contrast, the
combination 8 hour full-time and 2 hour part-time shifts pattern yielded a schedule calling for 26 cooks (an increase of
14 as compared to the old schedule) while the weekly labor expenditure of 356 man-hours was the closest to the actual man-

power demand histogram. The important point to be made her is
that the most efficient schedule may not result in a decrease
in the number of employees when part-time shifts are allowed.
Therefore, the best schedule can only be determined after an
analysis of employee labor costs when both salary and fringe
benefits are considered.

H. Schedules, Productivity and Labor Cost

The best schedule, from a manager's viewpoint, is the one
which yields the greatest reduction in labor costs. A comparison of some of the more efficient schedules is made in
Table VII between the number of employees, the weekly labor
savings and the annual cost of labor.

It should be noted that the results shown in Table VII represent a composite for all workers in the dining facility
(cooks and food service attendants). The 8 hour shift pattern
resulted in a weekly savings of 112 man-hours as compared to
the old schedule, with an annual cost saving of $ 36,364. By
comparison, the combination of 8 hour full time and 4 part
time shifts yielded a more efficient schedule saving 160 man-
hours weekly while annual cost would be reduced by $ 51,760.
Interestingly, if all employees worked a 4 hour part time
shift, the weekly savings in man-hours would also be 160.
However, the annual cost savings would increase to $ 56,311.
The basic reasons for these differences in labor costs are
differences in the number of employees required and the Government's fringe benefit policy regarding part time employees.
These comparisons clearly show the importance of computing
total labor costs before a decision is made on any new employee schedules.

TABLE VII. Comparison of Schedule Efficiency and Labor Cost

Shift Pattern	Number of Employees	Weekly Labor Savings (Man-hours)	Annual Savings ($) [a]
8 hour	21	112	36,364
8 hour & 2 hour	50	186	52,640
8 hour & 3 hour	34	159	53,512
8 hour & 4 hour	28	150	51,760
8 hour & 5 hour	25	138	42,808
2 hour	78	206	47,198
3 hour	57	140	37,477
4 hour	40	160	56,311

[a] As compared to the current schedule which requires a staff of 23 full time employees at a total annual cost of $288,418.

V. REFERENCES

1. Lundberg, D. E. and Armatus, J. P., "The Management of People in Hotels, Restaurants and Clubs," Brown, Dubuque, Iowa (1971)
2. Smith, R. S., Byrne, R. J., Rogozenski, J., Bustead, R., Prifti, J. and Wolfson, J. "A Systems Evaluation of Army Garrison Feeding at Fort Lewis Washington," *Technical Report 72-37-OR/SA,* US Army Natick Laboratories, Natick, Massachusetts (1972)
3. Tibrewala, R., Browne, J. and Phillipe, D. "Optimal Scheduling of Two Consecutive Idle Periods," *Management Science, 19* (1), September, 1972
4. Byrne, J. L. and Potts, R. B. *Transport. Sci. 7,* (3) 224 (1973)

CHAPTER 12

DEVELOPMENT OF A COMPREHENSIVE MANAGEMENT TRAINING
PROGRAM FOR A FAST FOOD OPERATION

Robert A. Phinney

Sambo's Restaurants
Carpinteria, California

I. OBJECTIVES OF THE TRAINING PROGRAM

In developing a comprehensive management training program
for a multi-unit fast food operation one must consider four
elements of the operation which will impact on the training
  (1) The manager himself
  (2) The people he will manage
  (3) The machines which he must know
  (4) The systems which he must administer

II. STEPS IN MANPOWER DEVELOPMENT

There are three general steps in manpower development which
clearly apply to a fast food operation manager: hiring, training, and supervision.

Obviously the success of any managerial training program
will be closely linked to the hiring standards and policies.
How is the future manager to be recruited? How is he to be selected? How is he to be hired? How is he to be trained. How is
he to be supervised?

A comprehensive training program must concern itself with
all three of these steps of manpower development, not just the
training component alone. For who is recruited, as well as the
type of supervision this person will have on the job, will
definitely indicate how this person will have to be trained.
Among the other primary questions which must also be asked in
laying the ground work for a training program are:

Copyright © 1979 by Academic Press, Inc.
All rights of reproduction in any form reserved
ISBN: 0-12-453150-4

(1) How is the manager to be compensated? Will he be on a salary with a bonus? Will he have a salary plus an investment opportunity?

(2) What sort of background, education, and experience should this manager have? Will the type of recruit one is seeking like the job?

For example, will one be training a short order cook who will be paid under $800 per month, or will one be training a college educated businessman who has been earning over $15,000 a year and hopes to make much more in his new job? Quite obviously, the need for a comprehensive recruiting program must be recognized and developed if one does not already exist.

A. Hiring

If one is to develop a comprehensive recruiting program, one must determine:

(1) Who will do the recruiting? Should it be done by a trained recruiter or by the operations personnel? Should an outside recruiter be used?

(2) Who will do the selecting? Should it be the recruiter or should it be others within the company, such the operations management, who should do the selecting? What tools,if any,will be used to help in the selection process?

(3) Who will do the hiring? Will the person who recruits do the hiring or will the person who selects do the hiring? Should hiring be the responsibility of the personnel department or the training department?

(4) Who will have the accountability for the recruiting function?

The training staff must have some say in the recruiting, selecting, and hiring since they must deal with the results of the recruiting effort. For example, what if a 22 year old, long-haired, single bartender is recruited to manage a three quarter million dollar restaurant? Perhaps one might face a situation in which training is not possible!

B. Supervision

Before turning to the question of training one must define the nature of supervision. Some of the points which must be identified are:

(1) What is the style of supervision which is in effect in the organization?

(2) Will the supervisor act as the manager's superior or his consultant?

(3) Will supervision be constant and frequent or only as it appears to be required by the manager?

(4) Will the supervision be of the directive type or of the supportive type?

(5) What must the manager know that the supervisor might not know? This question is important because, when the manager trainee becomes a manager, his success as well as his on-the-job management training will be in the hands of his supervisor(s). In fact, the supervisors are an essential component of the continuing training which will take place after the completion of the informal traineeship. The training program must therefore address how the on-the-job supervision for the new manager must be implemented by the supervisors. A qualification process, for the new manager, with the qualification points provided by the operations department, must be established. The operations management, through the new manager's immediate supervisors, must track the new manager's record in achieving the qualification target which has been established. Thus it can be determined, with confidence, what the new manager has learned.

III. STRUCTURING THE TRAINING PROGRAM

Having thus discussed where training is positioned in manpower development, i.e. between recruiting and supervision, one can now examine the structure of the training program itself.

The trainer must, of course, set up some ground rules in order to get the operations personnel to define what they want in a new manager. The trainer should, therefore, determine: What *must* a manager know? What *should* a manager know? What *would it be useful* for a manager to know?

As he is obtaining answers to these questions, the trainer must also ascertain what is the manager supposed to know in the three areas previously identified, i.e. people, machines and systems.

A. *Knowledge Required about People*

What about people? One has to determine by consultation with the management of the operations department the answers to the following questions:

(1) Will the manager have to recruit?
(2) Will the manager have to select?
(3) Who will the manager hire?
(4) How will he train them?
(5) What training system is in use in a retail unit?
(6) Under what system will he supervise them?
(7) What must a manager know about people?
(8) What should a manager know about people?
(9) Finally, what would it be nice for a manager to know

about people?

B. *Knowledge Required about Machines*

Similarly the trainer must find out:
(1) What machines *must* a manager know?
(2) Specifically what is it about these machines that the manager must know?
(3) What machines *should* a manager know about?
(4) What is it about these machines a manager should know?
(5) What machines *would it be useful* for the manager to know about?
(6) What is it about these machines that a manager should know?

C. *Knowledge about Systems*

Finally, the trainer must establish:
(1) What systems *must* a manager know?
(2) What systems *should* a manager know?
(3) What systems *would it be nice* for a manager to know?
(4) Are there standardized operating procedures, recorded in a formal manual, or are they communicated informally?

D. *Level of Training*

As the trainer develops his program he must acquire first hand knowledge of the personnel at the levels for which the proposed programs are intended. For example, if he is going to train down to the retail unit level, he should meet with employees at the retail unit level. He then should work his way up the supervision ladder; if feasible, all the way up to the Director of Operations. The trainer should then prepare his material into an easily understood format and present it to the operations management.

At this point, the development of the contents of the new manager training program has been completed. One must note again the paramount importance of having the training staff and the operations management achieving a mutual agreement and understanding with regards to the contents of the training program. If this has not taken place, the manager will be jeopardized because the final training of the new manager will be in the hands of his supervisor. In the final analysis, the formal part of the training program only prepares the new manager for this key phase.

E. *Training Techniques*

How does one inject the "must know" and the "should know"

knowledge required by a new manager into the training program?
A four step approach can be used:
(1) Job knowledge
(2) Demonstration
(3) Practice
(4) Feedback and Critique
The total content of the program should be broken down into
modules of learning, and a priority order set up for the modules.

A question which arises at this point is: "what must the
trainee learn first: customer service or administrative procedures?" A good approach is to let the potential manager first
learn about people, by performing the tasks which the personnel
under him will perform when he becomes a manager. In a fast
food operation, it is a good idea to require potential managers
to achieve an actual, working knowledge of the various skill
positions involved in the restaurant. This experience makes it
feasible for future managers to train and supervise personnel
as well as to step in at any time to substitute for missing employees at any work station in the operation. Furthermore the
managers-to-be will gain first hand knowledge in these areas:
(1) What a cook must do and know
(2) How a cook should be trained
(3) How a cook's training program should be developed and
implemented
(4) What it is like to be a cook
It is best to concentrate on the trainee's learning in one
area (or employee skill) at a time, thus building the learner's
confidence that he is progressing satisfactorily. This strategy
permits the trainee to achieve a series of learning objectives
without feeling overwhelmed by the amount of subject matter to
be absorbed. This modulated approach, with a built-in qualification process, i.e. learner must acquire a predetermined a-
mount of knowledge with a predetermined level of success, is
much more thorough, and indeed faster, than an approach in
which all things are to be learned simultaneously.

As the learner proceeds through this stage, he is armed
with the written materials which focus his thinking toward what
the manager must know about what he, the learner, is currently
doing. At Sambo's Restaurants, once the manager trainee is
qualified in this initial skills segment (a period taking from
twelve to sixteen weeks) he attends a 24 day management class.
This class deals essentially with the job knowledge required of
a manager and views, from a management standpoint,the questions
relating to people, machines, and systems, and their interlock-
ing relationships. Having successfully demonstrated that he has
gained this required knowledge, the potential manager now moves
into his management internship. Here he actually practices and
applies what he has learned of management skills. As an intern

he goes through an individually paced qualification process, being checked off at each stage by the supervisor who will work with him as a new manager. Once the new manager is thus qualified, he is offered a permanent position, and he enters into his final development stage which is provided by his immediate supervisor.

In summary, a comprehensive management training program trains the right people to know the right things so that their supervisors can train them to get the results needed in order for each individual involved to meet his own and the company's objectives.

EQUIPMENT AND FACILITY PLANNING

CHAPTER 13

DEFINITION AND ANALYSIS OF EQUIPMENT REQUIREMENTS

Charlotte M. Chang

I. INTRODUCTION

Techniques exist which translate menu and meal requirements to actual production facilities and procedures. These
techniques allow estimates to be made for converting production guides into throughput of material through the system,
equipment required by size, type and number and production
flow patterns. The means by which one can arrive at throughput data and equipment requirements are discussed in this
chapter.

II. THROUGHPUT ANALYSIS

An input/output (I/O) matrix is a useful analytical tool
in helping to quantify systems requirements. I/O analysis is a
highly versatile forecasting method for examining complex relationships within a system. I/O analysis shows how an increase or a decrease in one segment of the system will affect
the other segments. I/O analysis traces through all inter-
systems relationships to provide information about the total
impact on all segments of the original increase or decrease in
any one segment.

I/O analysis has been used extensively to depict material
balance. Obviously, I/O matrices can be applied to food service systems to depict material balances and to show how increases or decreases in any one subsystem will affect all the
other functions. In food service systems, an I/O matrix is a
graphic presentation of quantitative data which relates to the
various system functions from the earliest point in time (procurement and storage of incoming ingredients), through meal
service to waste disposal and warewashing. The I/O matrix
identifies all the material flow which will take place within

227

Copyright © 1979 by Academic Press, Inc.
All rights of reproduction in any form reserved
ISBN: 0-12-453150-4

the system. From it will evolve quantitative data upon which facility planners can select equipment types, number of units and sizes or capacities, and make other decisions such as storage space allocations.

The following procedures illustrate the process by which one can prepare an I/O matrix:

(1) *Menu Planning.* Selecting the menu to be used should be the first step in the food service systems analysis. The menu has a direct impact on many subsystems including production. The information about the menu which is required for determining a throughput analysis includes:

(a) *Menu Items.* It is necessary to determine which foods meet the requirements of the system(s) of choice, whether or not there will be a menu selection, whether budgetary guidelines preclude use of certain foods or whether any food(s) introduce a new preparation procedure. Upon the menu rest the decisions on equipment types from a functional standpoint while production requirements dictate numbers and capacities of units of equipment as well as space and storage requirements. Some flexibility should be provided for menu changes, however, so that changes can be made at a later time without requiring equipment not previously specified.

(b) *Menu Cycle.* In institutional food service a menu cycle is frequently used. The length of the cycle can vary but the menu cycle nevertheless provides a good guide for production planning because in that one time period all possible menu items will have been produced. Where no cycle exists, a sufficiently long reference period must be defined and used for planning purposes. Thus, from the menu cycle or the reference period selected will evolve a basis for determining a production cycle.

(2) *Determining a Reference Period.* The base for data collection on material flow in a food service system should cover a time span long enough so that such considerations as seasonal variations and holidays do not result in erroneous conclusions regarding throughput on an average basis. Obviously, a reference period of one year is optimum, although not always practical.

(3) *Preparing Standardized Recipes and Production Guides.* Instructions for preparing the menu items to be in the system must be developed. Quantities of ingredients for multiple portions, yields, portion size, and preparation procedures must all be included. From these production guides, menu items can be scaled to the cycle requirements and production procedures (routing) be developed. A typical production guide for macaroni and cheese is shown in

Table I.

(4) *Summarizing Ingredient Quantities for the Entire Menu*. A tabulation of all the ingredient quantities for all the recipes in the production cycle must be made. This is best done by working on each menu category separately. For example, vegetables, entrees, starches, baked desserts, etc.

(5) *Scaling Up Production Guides to Production Cycles*. This step extends the quantities of each ingredient and menu item into totals required for the production cycle. Identical ingredients required in various recipes now become apparent as each recipe is analyzed for cycle frequency, portion size, total number of portions per day, and ingredient quantities per production cycle.

(6) *Preparing a Routing Schedule or Process Analysis*. Following a menu item through the preparation and production procedures it undergoes in going from stored ingredients to the final prepared food is called "routing" or "process analysis". Routing depicts stages of food handling from the earliest points (i.e. warehousing, commodity storage or receiving) through production, storage and distribution to the ultimate end, service.

(7) *Summarizing Unit Operations*. When the routing analysis for all menu items has been completed, one can derive totals for each production operation. In some instances, a unit operation may represent a single equipment type or a single piece of equipment or it may represent a functional equipment grouping or area.

A. Routing (Process) Analysis

A routing analysis for an entree item, macaroni and cheese is presented in Table II. The routing analysis takes into account all aspects of preparation relating to yield, including cooking losses due to evaporation or fat separation, the addition of water for cooking and the removal of water in draining the cooked macaroni. Operations required to prepare each recipe component are identified and the movement of ingredients from one unit operation to the next are shown. Ingredient quantities are projected for the entire production cycle. Thus to prepare macaroni and cheese, 1,200.00 lbs of dry macaroni must be moved from dry storage to dry ingredient scaling. After batching, the macaroni is placed in a pass through water cooker, where 9,600.00 lbs of water are added and the macaroni is cooked. After draining excess water, 5,640.00 lbs of cooked macaroni are obtained. In the meantime, salt, dry mustard, cheese, milk, flour and butter are scaled for subsequent sauce preparation. These ingredients are transported to a steam jacketed kettle where sauce preparation takes place. When

TABLE I. *Production Guide for Macaroni and Cheese for Type A School Lunch (1)*

MACARONI AND CHEESE

Main Dishes D-30

Protein-Rich Food

Ingredients	100 portions		For portions	Directions
	Weights	Measures		
Macaroni	3 lb 12 oz	3-1/2 qt		1. Cook macaroni (card B-4).
Boiling water		2-1/4 gal		
Salt	2 oz	1/4 cup		
Butter or margarine	6 oz	3/4 cup		2. Melt fat; blend in flour and salt. Stir into milk. Cook and stir constantly until thickened.
All-purpose flour	6 oz	1-1/2 cups		
Salt	2-3/4 oz	1/3 cup		
Hot milk		2 gal		
Dry mustard		2-2/3 Tbsp		3. Add mustard and cheese to sauce; stir until blended.
Cheese, shredded	6 lb 4 oz	1 gal 2-1/4 qt		4. Combine macaroni and cheese sauce.
				5. Pour into 3 greased baking pans (about 12 by 20 by 2 inches), about 10 lb 4 oz or 1-1/4 gal per pan.
				6. Bake at 350° F (moderate oven) 50 minutes or until brown.

PORTION: 1/2 cup—provides 1 ounce cheese.

Cost per portion _____

230

TABLE II. Routing Analysis for Production of Macaroni and Cheese in Central Food Preparation Facility Producing 32,000 Meals per Day (2)

Macaroni & Cheese	Wt./100 Portions	Wt.per 32,000 Portions	Wt.per 30 days	Raw Wt.	Dry Storage	Dry Ingred. Scale	Chill Storage Dairy	Cheese Shredder	Pass Thru Water Cooker	Steam Jackt'd Kettle	Cooked Wt.	Filling	Freezing	Frozen Storage
Salt	.29	94.72	94.72	94.72	94.72	94.72			40.00	54.72		12,984.30	12,984.30	12,984.30
Dry Mustard	.16	51.20	51.20	51.20	51.20	51.20				51.20				
Water	30.00	9,600.00	9,600.00	9,600.00					9,600.00					
Macaroni	3.75	1,200.00	1,200.00	1,200.00	1,200.00	1,200.00			1,200.00					
Cheese	6.25	2,000.00	2,000.00	2,000.00		2,000.00	2,000.00	2,000.00		2,000.00	5,640.00			
Milk	16.00	5,120.00	5,120.00	5,120.00	5,120.00	5,120.00				5,120.00				
Flour	.37	118.40	118.40	118.40	118.40	118.40				118.40				
Butter	.37	118.40	118.40	118.40		118.40	118.40			118.40				
					6,584.32	8,702.72	2,118.40	2,000.00	10,840.00	7,462.72	5,640.00	12,984.30	12,984.30	12,984.30

TO......

	1	2	3	4	5	6	7	8	9	10	11	12	13	14	15	16	17	18	19	20	21	22	23	24	25	26	27	28	29	30	31
1	**342.9**					342.9																									68.3
2		25.8				25.8																									
3			136.3				126.3																			9.0					
4				57.8																											
5					54.4								95.3																		
6						■						16.9			187.5											194.6					
7							■	50.8																							
8								■							50.8																
9									■						19.8																
10										■					8.9																
11											■				10.8																
12												■		16.9																	
13													■	95.3																	
14														■	99.5																
15															■	87.3	5.9	6.1	187.5	57.4	15.2	81.4	8.0	11.2	8.3						
16																■															79.2

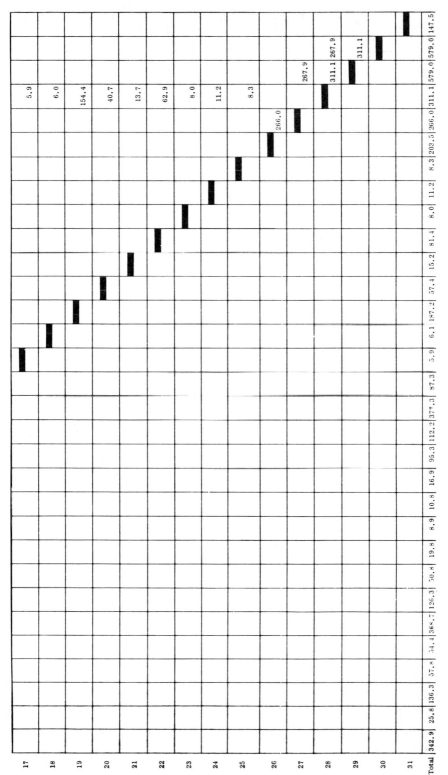

Fig. 1. See following page for legend and key.

FIGURE 1. Input–output material flow matrix for central food preparation facility producing 32,000 meals per day (2). Total pounds: 726.5 per 30-day cycle. All figures are in thousands of pounds.

Key to area designations:

1 – Incoming dry storage
2 – Incoming dairy storage
3 – Incoming frozen storage
4 – Incoming vegetable storage
5 – Incoming root vegetable storage
6 – Dry and dairy ingredient scaling
7 – Meat thawing
8 – Meat preparation – bagging and panning
9 – Meat preparation – mixing
10 – Meat preparation – meatball forming

11 – Meat preparation – patty forming
12 – Vegetable washing – leafy
13 – Vegetable washing – roots and tubers
14 – Vegetable preparation
15 – Ingredient staging (excluding bakery)
16 – Salad area
17 – Sandwich room
18 – Continuous braiser
19 – Steam jacketed kettles
20 – Convection oven

21 – Frying line
22 – Continuous water cooker
23 – Steamer
24 – Vertical mixer
25 – Boning and slicing room
26 – Bakery mixing
27 – Bakery oven
28 – Continuous chiller
29 – Continuous freezer
30 – Frozen storage
31 – Chilled storage

cooked, drained macaroni and prepared sauce are mixed, 12,984.30 lbs of product are available to be packaged, frozen and stored, in a freezer.

By summarizing the values obtained from the routing analysis on individual menu items to be produced in a cycle, one can determine the exact ingredient quantities, equipment and storage requirements for the production of the menu. Based on this information, equipment sizing and selection are not only simplified but made into an accurate process.

B. The I/O Matrix

From the routing analysis, one can then prepare the I/O matrix which is a summary of the unit operations shown in the routing analysis. A typical I/O matrix is shown in Figure 1. This matrix was prepared to show material flow in thousands of pounds through a central food preparation facility producing 32,000 meals per shift during a 30-day cycle (1). It will be noted that the two axes of the graph are identical. Their divisions represent the various unit operations within the processing facility from incoming ingredient storage to prepared food storage. Thus, Area 1 is "Incoming Dry Storage", while Area 31 is "Finished Product Chilled Storage". The matrix shows the movement of quantities of ingredients, or partially or fully prepared products, from one process area to another. The total quantities of all incoming ingredients, (including water) and of all outgoing products (plus liquid and solid waste and evaporation losses) must equal each other. The quantities shown in the I/O matrix provide the basis for planning the production facility required. Sizes of areas such as ingredient storage, or finished product storage, can readily be determined using the total quantities shown in the matrix and published information on density of various commodities. Similarly, equipment processing requirements shown in the matrix, serve as a solid basis for equipment sizing and selection.

From the I/O matrix one can also learn other important facts about the food service facility being planned:

(1) By preparing a material flow chart from the I/O matrix one can determine the areas of heavy traffic within the production facility.

(2) Water requirements for the production operation become readily apparent.

(3) Cooking losses can be traced.

(4) Unit operations can be summarized.

(5) Data compilation required to prepare the matrix provides a basis for a thorough menu analysis by food group or meal type and also facilitates nutritional auditing.

III. EQUIPMENT REQUIREMENTS

Equipment requirements exist at all levels of a food service system including production, distribution, holding, and
service. Equipment requirements can be evolved through an extension of the input-output matrix from information gathered
therein about material flow, unit operations and total quantity requirements. In a system in which food is prepared and
stored, one must address the important question of how much
food it is cost effective to produce and store. Several factors will influence this decision. While it is dangerous to
generalize about them, since each food service operation is u-
nique and may involve special considerations, the following
points might be considered:
    (1) If an operation is sufficiently large, the menu cycle
sufficiently long, and a certain menu item occurs more than
once within the cycle, it is generally reasonable to consider
producing and storing a sufficient quantity of that item for
one whole cycle in order to maximize production equipment u-
tilization.
    (2) In view of the high cost of energy required for freez-
ing and frozen storage it is necessary to compare reasonable
trade offs between efficient production and costly frozen
storage. In some instances it may be more cost effective to
prepare a menu item used in large quantities more than one
time per production cycle. Similarly the advantages derived
from the economies of scale resulting from large scale production must be weighed against the cost of monies tied up in
inventory.
    (3) For operations using small quantities of many differ-
ent menu items, a system utilizing a combination of two storage modes e.g. chilled and frozen, may prove more cost effective from the production and storage standpoints. By efficient production planning and inventory control such a system
can be made highly operable.
    (4) The number of locations to be served and their dis-
tance from the production facility may impose constraints on
the quantity of prepared food to be stored at any one time.
    In trying to quantify some of these cost related factors
by determining batch size for centralized frozen food preparation, Dorney *et al* (2), in their studies at the Catering Research Unit of the University of Leeds showed that an economic
zone does exist where total production and storage costs level
off and the economic batch size results in the lowest possible
per pound total cost. Large batch sizes reduce the per pound
set up and order costs but increase the storage costs. Smaller batch sizes increase the per pound set up and order costs
but decrease the storage costs.

A. *Production Equipment*

In the sense in which it will be used in this discussion, production equipment includes all of the storage areas and equipment which might be used in a food production facility. Included are the areas and equipment for ingredient storage, ingredient preparation, cooking, filling, portioning, packaging, prepared food holding, material handling, warewashing and waste disposal. Choice of equipment is generally made on the basis of its anticipated utilization level but there may be exceptions to this rule. It may be that a piece of equipment is necessary which might appear to be oversized but which in fact, because of its tremendous labor saving, is very valuable. A dicer-cutter, for example, which might sit idle most of the time can in a very short time produce all of the diced products for a particular production run. Such a procedure would be highly labor intensive if done manually or on a smaller unit.

Single shift operations are generally limited to four to six hours of actual food production time. The rest of the time is spent in ingredient preparation, finished products packing, equipment set-up, down-time, and breaks. This in turn affects the sequencing of the operations, i.e., filling, packaging, chilling or freezing and storing which all follow the production of the food. One way to achieve a smooth and efficient work flow is by means of split shifts, with the cooks commencing their work four hours before the filling line begins to operate.

Packaging line capacity may sometimes be the bottleneck in the production operation. Packaging lines for prepared foods are labor intensive and it may not be cost effective to set up extra lines at certain times to meet peak load requirements. Instead it may be necessary to use packaging line speeds as a means of determining production equipment requirements. This requires that one must single out the menu item to be produced in largest quantity during the production cycle and plan the production operation to produce this item at an hourly rate compatible with the packing operation.

B. *Distribution Equipment*

Prepared food can be distributed in at least four physical states, i.e. hot, chilled, frozen and ambient (thermally stable canned foods).

1. *Hot Food Transport.* Foods to be transported hot can be packaged in bulk or as preplated meals. Two means of transport are in common use: insulated containers or electrically heated hot holding cabinets. Among the questions to be con-

sidered for this system are (a) can the transporters be reused?
(b) can they be cleaned? (c) how much do they cost? In comparing costs, the following considerations must be borne in
mind: (a) insulated containers have a relatively finite number of reuse cycles, (b) holding cabinets which require a
larger initial capital outlay have a longer life, and can be
depreciated over their expected life, (c) rechargeable units
require a power source and a place to plug in the carts at
some central facility.

2. *Chilled Food Transport.* Hot chilled foods can also be
transported as bulk or preplated individual meals. However,
three transport modes present themselves for this purpose:
(a) insulated containers, (b) plug in chilled holding units,
and (c) refrigerated vehicle transport.
   Using refrigerated vehicles implies that (a) rapid chilling equipment and chill storage be available at the production
facility, (b) cartoning of the items takes place in the production facility, (c) refrigeration is available to store at
the serving site and (d) the serving site be equipped to heat
the hot portion of the meal.

3. *Frozen Food Transport.* Frozen food can also be preplated or frozen in bulk. A frozen food system generally implies that freezer storage space and reconstitution equipment
be available at the serving site. Storage costs at the serving site will be higher with the frozen system than with the
alternative systems but delivery costs may be reduced since
deliveries need be made less frequently. Proper refrigerated
vehicles must also be part of the system although, if the distance between production center and satellites is not excessive, insulated carriers may prove adequate. A frozen system
requires fairly elaborate filling, chilling, freezing, frozen
storage and cartoning equipment at the production facility.
In most frozen systems not all meal components can be handled
in the frozen state. One often has to devise a delivery
schedule to accommodate such foods as salads, milk, etc. in
the chilled state. Thus, a dual requirement for packaging
forms and transportation equipment may present itself.

C. *Defining Equipment Requirements*

   Table III illustrates the procedures to be followed in
preparing a menu item, spaghetti with meat sauce. There are
at least four preparation procedures which can be identified
for this menu item: (1) measuring the dry ingredients, (2)
cooking the spaghetti, (3) braising the ground beef and (4)
preparing the sauce.
   A routing analysis for spaghetti with meat sauce would

show that measuring of dry ingredients is a function of the
dry ingredient scaling area, cooking spaghetti is planned to
take place in a pasta cooker, meat searing would be done in a
steam jacketed kettle as would the preparation of the sauce.
In identifying choices of equipment for each of these preparation procedures one would find that (1) a floor scale is
the only piece of equipment with which to logically scale up
the dry ingredients for a production batch size, (2) to cook
the spaghetti one could use a kettle with a basket for
draining the finished cooked spaghetti or a continuous water
cooker. The choice of equipment would depend not only on the
quantity of food to be cooked for this particular recipe but
also how the quantity of this item relates to the quantities
of other items to be produced. For example, would the system
be large enough so that a continuous water cooker would be
used for other menu items as well? (3) Meat braising could be
done in at least four different pieces of equipment: a tilt-
ing fry pan, a steam jacketed kettle, an oven, or a continuous braiser. Here again, the evaluation of the continuous
braiser would take into consideration its application to
other menu items to be produced. On the other hand, it may
be that oven capacity is available for braising the ground
beef while all steam jacketed kettles would be fully utilized
in cooking sauce. In this case, it is clear that braising
must be carried out in the oven. (4) The sauce can be prepared by a batch process or by a continuous process. Continuous equipment to prepare sauces involves a rather costly and
elaborate system which would be appropriate only in a very
large production facility in which full utilization could be
made of this equipment.

D. *Analyzing Equipment Requirements*

The following assumptions will be made with reference to
the example selected, i.e. spaghetti and meat sauce: (1) The
facility will be required to produce 20,000 school lunches per
day. (2) Since no menu selection is offered and only one type
of meal is involved 20,000 portions of spaghetti and meat
sauce will be required each time this item appears on the
menu. (3) All the food to be served during the six week menu
cycle, will be produced in one shift per day, five days per
week. (4) Spaghetti with meat sauce is the menu item which
appears with the greatest frequency, as it is served three
times during the menu cycle.

The following assumptions will be made in defining the e-
quipment requirements for producing the spaghetti with meat
sauce:
(1) Portion weight will be 8 ounces.

(2) Each 8 ounce portion will consist of:

    4 oz cooked spaghetti
    2 oz cooked meat
    2 oz cooked sauce

(3) No evaporative losses of sauce will occur during cooking.

(4) Cooked spaghetti will go directly to the panning line from the pasta cooker. Sauce will be mechanically filled over it. Mixing of the sauce and spaghetti will take place at the serving site.

(5) Packaging will be in one-half size steam table pans holding 5 pounds each.

(6) Filling line speed will be six pans per minute.

(7) Packaging line utilization will be six hours per shift.

(8) The largest volume requirement in producing this menu item is that of the sauce.

(9) A continuous water cooker will be used to prepare the spaghetti and the meat will be braised in a steam jacketed kettle prior to adding the tomato sauce. The finished sauce will thus include the braised ground meat and the tomato sauce itself. It is this finished sauce upon which the volume requirement will be based.

(10) Meat shrinkage has been determined to be 33 1/3 %. Thus, one must start with 3 ounces of raw beef per portion to end up with the required 2 ounces cooked weight.

(11) A 250 % water absorption factor will be used for spaghetti in going from the dry to the cooked state.

Based on these assumptions one can calculate the following:

(1) The quantities of the three menu components for 60,000 portions of spaghetti with meat sauce would be:

    spaghetti, cooked - 15,000 lbs
    meat, cooked   - 7,500 lbs
    sauce, cooked   - 7,500 lbs

(2) Each half size pan would contain 2.5 lbs of cooked spaghetti and 2.5 lbs of meat sauce.

(3) 6,000 pans would be required to contain the 30,000 lbs of finished product required by the cycle.

(4) At a filling rate of six pans per minute, it would take 1,000 minutes or 16.6 hours to fill these 6,000 pans.

(5) Based on a six hours of packaging line time per shift, it would take 2.8 days to fill and package this one product.

Two alternatives present themselves for accomplishing the cooking, filling and packaging of this product:

(1) The necessary packaging lines can be set up to handle the product within a production shift.

(2) The product can be cooked on three different production days during the cycle.

For purposes of this example, one might assume the former
and work backward from the packaging line to the equipment
necessary to prepare the spaghetti with meat sauce so that it
could all be filled on one day.Since kettles have been chosen
as the production equipment of choice for sauce,one need only
then to determine kettle requirements to produce the sauce in
the given time period.

Assuming that one gallon weighs 8 pounds the meat sauce
requirement of 15,000 lbs represent 1,900 gallons. Several
factors influence kettle utilization in preparing the sauce:

(1) Each kettle can be utilized to no more than 3/4 of its
rated capacity.

(2) Kettle time must include time to load ingredients,
time to braise the meat, drain the fat, add the sauce ingredients, cook the sauce, cool the sauce if this is to be done
prior to filling, emptying the kettle, cleaning the kettle,
and making it ready for the next use.

For these reasons, one might prefer rather to speak in
terms of kettle hours. If one assumes that two hours of kettle time will be required for preparing the spaghetti sauce,
and a production shift with six hours of production time,
three two hour time periods are available in each production
day. For the example given this would translate to 1900 $\div$ 3 =
633.3 gallons being required to be produced in any 2 hour
time period. However, since kettle utilization is only 3/4 of
the volume the capacity required is 633.3 X $\frac{4}{3}$ = 844.5 gallon
per batch. In terms of kettle availability one would thus plan
on a kettle capacity of 900 gallons. Many combinations of kettles could be selected to meet these production requirements.
Some of these options are presented Table IV.

TABLE IV. *Kettle Combination Options for Production of*
           Spaghetti Sauce

	No. of Kettles				
Option No.	300 gal	250 gal	200 gal	150 gal	100 gal
1	3				
2	1	2			1
3	1		2	1	
4	1	1	1	1	

It is probably most advantageous to choose a series of kettles of different sizes rather than to opt for multiples of one kettle size. On the other hand, it does not necessarily make sense to choose one of each size since it may result in having an excessive number of kettles to operate to produce a single menu item. Thus, options 2 and 3 in Table IV would appear to be most desirable in the context of the example presented. These mixtures of kettle sizes also provide the capability and the flexibility for producing the other menu items required in the cycle.

Other factors which will influence the choice of kettles are such considerations as using the kettles as holding tanks. When a kettle is holding cooked product, it is not available for cooking another product. In this respect it may be better to use a separate tank to cool cooked products and to pump to the filling line. It is obvious that trying to circulate cold water through a kettle already reaching high temperatures during cooking, is less efficient than transferring the cooked product to a cooling kettle.

In the above example there is a possibility that the filling line, including this emptying of kettles, cooling and pumping to the line, will become the bottleneck; in this case, equipment requirements would have to be redefined in light of the new constraints imposed upon the system.

IV. REFERENCES

1. Anon. "Quantity Recipes for Type A School Lunches" *Publication No. PA-631,* United States Department of Agriculture, Washington, DC (1965)
2. Res. & Dev. Staff, Project ANSER "Five County Management Improvement Project. Program Element 3. Facilities Alternative Planning" Project ANSER, Volusia County School District, Deland, Florida (1974)

CHAPTER 14

DESIGNING CENTRALIZED FOOD PRODUCTION FACILITIES

G.E. Livingston

Food Science Associates, Inc.
Dobbs Ferry, New York

I. INTRODUCTION

At what level is it cost effective to build a central kitchen? That is a question which is frequently asked of food
service systems designers and facilities consultants. The fact
is that there is no single answer to this question since the
economics of each situation are entirely different.

It is necessary to cost out the facilities required to support any particular system alternative being considered, whether it be on-premise cooking, centralized cooking or a ready
foods program, in order to evaluate the cost effectiveness of
the alternative methods. Frequently, on-premise preparation
is the least expensive alternative because it eliminates packaging, distribution costs, and other costs associated with a
central food preparation facility. If the goal of the new system is to reduce the cost of preparation labor, this might in
fact be achieved by divorcing the preparation of the food from
its service without necessarily centralizing it. Generally,
when a centralized food facility is being considered, the goal
is to reduce labor costs, and clearly the labor cost reduction must be large enough to offset the added costs resulting
from packaging, distribution, storage, etc., if tangible benefits are to be obtained.

There are times, of course, when non-economic consider-
tions override the cost aspects. These might include instances
where there is a lack of skilled labor or of a dependable labor
supply. In other cases, the desire for a centralized facility
may be motivated by the goal of achieving a better degree of
control over quality than can be achieved with on premise preparation in a scattered number of sites in which it is not

Copyright © 1979 by Academic Press, Inc.
All rights of reproduction in any form reserved
ISBN: 0-12-453150-4

feasible or economical to provide skilled food preparation labor. At any rate, if the decision has been made to design a
centralized food production facility, or if it is required to
design such a facility in order to accurately cost out a central food preparation system as one of the alternatives in the
study, how does one go about doing it?

II. PLANNING THE MENU

It will be assumed that the preliminary investigation has
determined the preferred type of packaging required, i.e. bulk
pack or individual, pouch, tray or slab, etc. The next step is
to develop the menu, as a basis for planning the facility. This
menu may be a menu cycle or a restaurant type menu. In either
case one must develop an estimate of quantities of various
items to be produced in a given production cycle. If a menu
cycle is used, its length (and therefore that of the production
cycle) will be a function of customer requirements rather than
production considerations. Most menu cycles would be in the
order of eight to forty-two days in length. With a restaurant
type menu, a 2 - 4 week projection of requirements might
be used. (Because of the importance of the menu in the total
planning scheme, it is advisable to submit it to a nutritional
audit before formal adoption if it is the menu for an institutional food service system. If the audit indicates nutritional
shortcomings, the menu should be revised to correct them before
proceeding further.) The use of the menu cycle as the basic
point of departure in the planning of the facility should not
be construed, however, to mean that the facility can only produce this menu. If the menu is typical of the types of products demanded by the customer population, then the equipment
selected to supply this menu will be equally capable of supplying a different menu comprising the same mix of product types.
On the other hand, if products are added to the menu at a
later stage that were totally absent from the original menu,
the needed equipment might not be available for their production. For example, if the original menu cycle included no deep
fat fried items and no provision was made for this manner of
cooking, it would be clearly difficult to introduce deep fat
fried items, at a later stage.
Having defined the menu, the next step is securing the
standard recipes that will be used to implement the menu. The
production requirements should, of course, be known and management decisions must be made as to whether it is desired to operate one or two shifts per day and as to the number of days
per week and weeks per year. Of course, the greater the number
of shifts per year, the better the utilization of the facili-

ties and the lower the indirect costs on a per unit basis.
The estimated production requirements of the facility, and
the routing required in the preparation of each menu item, will
lead to the input-output matrix (Chap. 13) to be used to chart
the flow of product through the facility. In any well defined
facility, it is of course, essential to minimize cross traffic,
and a material flow chart derived from the input-output
matrix permits the designer to experiment on paper with a variety of configurations to determine the one which will achieve
the smoothest flow. If the facility is to be located in an existing building, it will be necessary to adapt to the constraints of the building. However, if the facility is to be
erected for the specific purpose of housing the central kitch-
en, it is then feasible to lay out the production areas and,
after having optimized them, enclose them in a suitable building shell. Frequently, the facility is to be built on a known
site. In this case the orientation of the building on the lot,
the access to the road, to parking areas, the availability of
turn-about space for trucks and the location of receiving and
shipping docks, all provide constraints which the designer must
bear in mind.

III. BLOCK DIAGRAM

At this point in the development of the facility, a "block
diagram" is prepared. This diagram shows the known areas of
the facility, attempts to size them somewhat in accordance with
their spatial needs and provides a graphical basis for an examination of adjacency factors and a review of product flow
through the facility. It is extremely useful at this point in
the design process, if it is feasible, to work with the individuals who will have the responsibility of managing the production operation once it has been designed. If it is possible
to have their input into the design process, they are far more
likely to be in accord with the final design of the facility
and will thereby have a built-in commitment to insure the success of the new operation. Somewhat along the same lines, a
forward thinking management which has hired a consultant to design the facility, would commit him in advance to provide
start-up training and technical assistance to insure the operational success of the facility.

IV. VISITING OTHER CENTRAL PRODUCTION FACILITIES

The importance of a series of visits by the management of

the future operation to several centralized food production
facilities in operation, at the earliest stages of the planning process. While no one wants to make mistakes, they inevitably do occur, and the more potential sources of error can
be identified early in the planning process, the more likely
it is that the new operation can be designed without such pit-
falls.

V. PRODUCTION FLOW

    The production flow within the central preparation facil-
ity will generally represent a compromise between the struc-
quirements of the raw materials. Separate refrigerated stor-
or site are involved, and the desired flow pattern based upon
the material flow chart. In most instances, a straight
through flow is preferred, with incoming materials being received at one end of the plant and finished product being
shipped out of the other end (Fig. 1a). If it is necessary to
have both the receiving and shipping docks side by side on one
end, a U shaped flow pattern should be considered (Fig. 1c).
In some instances an L shaped pattern is preferred (Fig. 1b).
Each configuration has its advantages and its draw backs. A
U shaped configuration for example, may offer the advantage of
being able to centralize both the raw ingredient and finished
product freezers and chillers in the same general area thereby
reducing the cost of the refrigeration facilities.

VI. FUNCTIONAL AREAS

A. *Storage*

    The functional areas in the facility will generally con-
sist of a receiving area, where fresh, chilled, frozen and ambient temperature raw materials are received. Separate storage areas are provided to meet the different temperature requirements of the raw materials. Separate refrigerated storage areas are usually provided for meats (35°F), dairy products (38°F), and vegetables (42°F). If roots and tubers are
received, they are generally stored separately as well (50°F).
The meat freezer (0°F) is generally located adjacent to the
meat chiller, which may in fact serve as a thawing area for
the frozen meat. An ambient temperature storage area is provided for canned goods, dried goods, bagged commodities such as
flour, sugar, etc., and nonfood supplies.

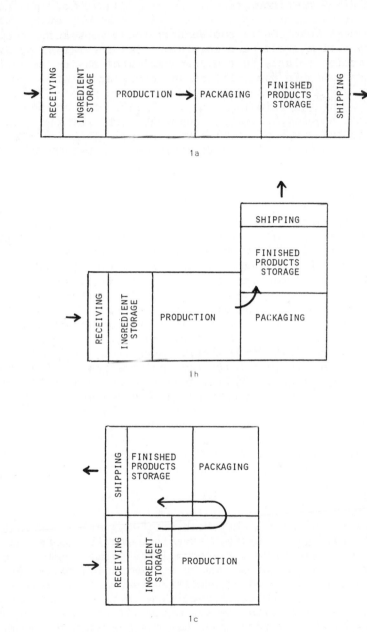

FIGURE 1. *Three possible configurations for a central food preparation facility: 1a - a straight through flow pattern; 1b - L-shaped flow pattern; 1c - U-shaped flow pattern. Site characteristics most frequently dictate flow pattern requirements.*

B. Ingredient Preparation

The next function in the central food preparation facility is that of ingredient preparation. The ingredient preparation function relates to the preparation of the raw materials in a form suitable for utilization in the production area. In the case of raw vegetables, this may mean peeling, slicing, dicing, washing, trimming, etc. In the case of meat, this may mean thawing, cutting, chopping, patty forming, dicing, etc. In the case of dry goods or canned goods it will mean opening containers and measuring either on a weight or volume basis.

C. Staging

The operation of a modern central preparation facility requires that ingredient preparation and staging be divorced from the food production operation in order to permit most efficient utilization of the cooks in the facility. To permit proper ingredient preparation and staging, it will be necessary to provide an ingredient weighing room within the dry ingredient storage area or adjacent to it. The function of this room will be to weigh and batch production sized lots of all the shelf stable ingredients. An area designated as the "ingredient staging room" will serve to receive ingredients from the various ingredient preparation areas and combine them as required for individual production batches. For example, all of the ingredients for a batch of beef stew including the diced meat, the cut vegetables and all the dry ingredients required would be premeasured, filled into suitable containers or bags, and grouped together on a cart in the staging area, ready for delivery to the production floor. Naturally, the staging area must be a chill room (45°F).

D. Cooking

Within the actual hot food kitchen, equipment must be provided for wet cooking, steaming, broiling, frying and baking. Wet cooking can be accomplished using steam jacketed kettles, but the use of automated or semi-automated equipment should be considered and carefully evaluated. For example, a continuous water cooker is available which can receive rice or dried pasta and, with the automatic addition of water and salt, cook it on a continuous basis after which it is automatically drained and rinsed (Fig. 2). Furthermore, because the unit involves a series of small buckets, it actually cooks in smaller quantities than a large steam jacketed kettle which, in the case of pasta or rice, is advantageous to quality and provides a greater degree of end product uniformity.

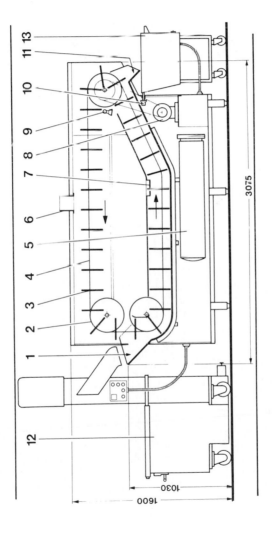

FIGURE 2. Automatic boiling water cocker: 1 – filling funnel; 2 – chain wheel; 3 – slats; 4 – transport chains; 5 – counter stream (calorifier) unit; 6 – vapor discharge ducts; 7 – overflow; 8 – drive motor; 9 – spray device; 10 – safety switch; 11 – discharge; 12 – automatic loading device/universal conveyor; 13 – heated standard distribution trolley. (Courtesy Crown–X, Inc., Cleveland, Ohio)

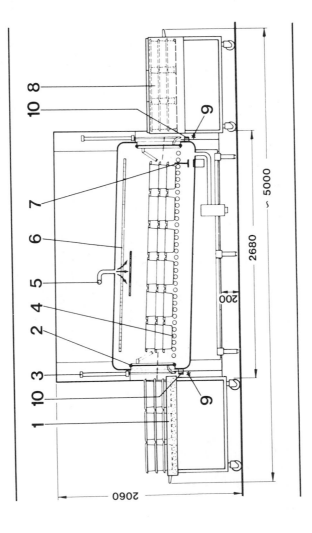

FIGURE 3. Automatic steam pressure cooker (15 PSI): 1 – loading trolley with cooking inserts; 2 – raisable door; 3 – door drive/hydraulics; 4 – roller conveyor; 5 – steam inlet; 6 – cold water spray system for rapid condensation of the steam after the cooking process; 7 – discharge block, which works electromagnetically to release the containers for discharge; 8 – heat insulated distribution trolley; 9 – instead of loading and distribution trolleys, roller conveyors can be inserted at this point; 10 – safety device. (Courtesy Crown-X, Inc., Cleveland, Ohio)

Along the same lines, steaming can be accomplished in batch type compartment steamers or in semi-continuous pass through steamers (Fig. 3). Broiling can be carried out in batch units or using one of many types of conveyorized tunnel broilers. Continuous frying lines, including battering and breading equipment, have long been used in the food manufacuring industry but in recent years continuous fryers and braising units, better suited to the needs of the central kitchen, have become available. Some of these units are versatile enough to be used for griddle work such as French toast or pork chops and, with an adjustment in oil level, to permit deep fat frying of chicken, fish or veal cutlets (Fig. 4).

Baking can be performed in a variety of ovens, including revolving tray ovens, roll-in rack convection ovens and in tunnel type ovens if the production volume warrants it.

To the maximum extent possible, it is highly desirable to keep as much equipment as possible on casters so that it can be moved. By judicious planning, overhead utilities will be made available to facilitate the relocation of equipment without requiring the installation of permanent connections each time.

E. Cold Food Production

The cold food production includes the make up of salads, sandwiches and desserts. Because the salad make up area draws heavily from the vegetable preparation room, it is most convenient if they are located adjacent to each other. In centralized facilities shipping salads to satellites, it is most useful if the salad greens and the dressing are shipped separately. Salad ingredients should be trimmed, washed, inspected, dipped in an antioxidant dip, centrifuged and bagged. Proper handling of the salad ingredients in the production plant will insure a shelf life of sufficient duration to satisfy the needs of the system. Salad dressings, either commercially procured or made in the central facility, would be combined with the greens at the serving sites because the salads would have a very limited shelf life if they were premixed centrally.

Sandwiches required in the system, would be made in a separate sandwich room containing primarily work tables, slicers and wrapping equipment for the prepared sandwiches. A few sandwiches can be frozen but it is generally preferred to handle sandwiches on a chilled basis. In some systems it has been preferred to prepare the sandwich fillings centrally and ship them in bulk to the sites for use there with fresh bread supplied to the units.

The make-up of cold desserts such as puddings and gelatin

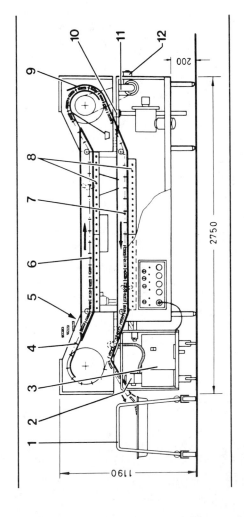

FIGURE 4. Automatic fryer: 1 – transport trolley with standard containers; 2 – recirculation pump; 3 – heatable oil reservoir cart; 4 – food carrier; 5 – loading zone; 6 – upper pan; 7 – lower pan; 8 – heating; 9 – turning zone with guide plate; 10 – lifting device; 11 –gearing motor; 12 – speed and frying regulator. (Courtesy Crown-X, Inc., Cleveland, Ohio)

desserts,requires steam jacketed kettles, cooling equipment, pumps and fillers (if single service portions of these desserts are to be packed).

F. Baked Goods

If baked goods are part of the system,a bake shop is generally provided. Because the bake shop will draw heavily upon the dry ingredient area, it is desirable to locate it as close as possible to the dry ingredient room. Similarly,because the bake shop generates a substantial volume of pans, it is desirable to have the pot washing area nearby.

The bake shop will be equipped to perform the functions that are required of it in the light of the menu cycle. If only sheet cakes, cookies, brownies and similar cake items are required, one or more mixers and ovens may be entirely sufficient. If sweet dough products such as Danish pastries are desired, suitable make up tables will be needed. Any yeast raised goods will, of course, require proofing cabinets, and the manufacture of doughnuts will also require the necessary extruders and deep fat fryers to be available. With few exceptions, most institutional systems do not find it worthwhile to bake their own bread.

G. Dry Mixers

In some instances, where systems are sufficiently large, it may be economical to prepare dry mixes for use in satellite facilities. Such mixes would include beverage mixes, dessert mixes, soup and gravy bases. This is a relatively simple operation requiring merely weighing, dry blending equipment such as a ribbon blender and appropriate packaging equipment.

H. Portioning and Packaging

The portioning and packaging equipment will be a function of the type of system selected and the volume of the operation. Automatic equipment is available for filling liquids and semi-solids such as stews and vegetables, but not yet for the placement of solid meat items in a tray or pouch. Therefore, entree or dinner assembly lines are in fact a combination of manual labor and automated equipment, the mix of the two depending upon the make up of the items. The line speed will also depend upon the tray size and complexity of the products being packed. Although high speed lines are used in the frozen food industry for the production of retail prepared dinners, the line speeds used for institutional production are usually considerably slower, i.e. in the order of 12 to 30 minutes. The line speed for bulk packed entrees is slower still in terms of trays per minute but not in portions per minute. The type of equipment used would, of course, depend upon whether one is filling and sealing aluminum trays or plastic packages which might be made on a form-fill-seal machine.

Following the filling and packaging operations, the product is generally chilled, frozen or, in some instances, canned. The product temperature at this point will depend upon whether it was prechilled before filling or filled hot. While prechilling offers the advantage of permitting a delay between the end of preparation and the beginning of filling, thus providing more flexibility in the operation of the plant, it may have the disadvantage of thickening the product in cooling and thereby damaging its texture or appearance during the pumping required for filling. Prechilling the food prior to filling, does reduce the load on the refrigerator or freezer and is, therefore, advantageous from that standpoint. It also eliminates steaming within the package and the resulting condensation which may occur.

Filling hot on the other hand, reduces the handling of the product, minimizes bacteriological risks (if it is properly done), and may have a beneficial effect upon product quality. On the other hand, it does increase the load on the refrigerator. One solution which has been proposed for frozen food facilities is to chill the product after filling in a blast chiller, after which it is transferred into a blast freezer for the freezing opeation. Interestingly enough, blast chillers are a new concept in the industry and have only recently become available as stock units for central kitchens operating chill systems. These blast chillers are roll-in or pass through roll-in type refrigerators operating with high velocity forced air movement. Some units combine mechanical cryogenic refrigeration to reduce cooling times (Fig. 5).

A variety of freezers are used in centralized food production facilities. These include plate freezer, blast freezers equipped for roll-in racks, blast freezer with spiral conveyor transport, tunnel type freezers and cryogenic freezers. A fairly new type of freezer is the stack freezer in which baskets of products are automatically loaded into stacks which travel automatically through the blast freezer (Fig. 6). Some highly automated central production facilities indeed use fully automated, computer controlled freezers.

With the advent of tray cans it is entirely probable that some food service systems, which can justify the high equipment cost and technical staff required, will opt to pack sterilized prepared foods in tray cans. The tray can filling equipment is comparable to that used in the filling of trays for freezing. However, the sealing equipment is different since it is designed to produce a hermetic seal on the tray by

*FIGURE 5. Two section model of Rapid Chill processing refrig-
erator, which quickly cools food from 140°F to 40°F, increasing the quality storage life of food products. (Courtesy Vic-
tory, Food Equipment Division, McGraw-Edison, Plymouth Meeting,
Pennsylvania)*

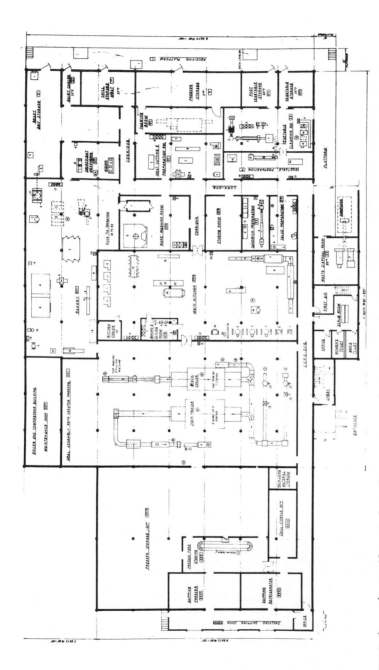

FIGURE 6. First floor plan for a central food preparation facility for a school lunch program based on the use of frozen bulk packs. The facility was designed to produce 32,000 meals per day, in five production days per week, one shift per day, 187 days per year, thus enabling output to be increased by adding to the number of shifts and/or production days. The facility, with a gross area of 58,557 square feet, includes storage space for a seven day requirement of incoming ingredients, and 30 days' output of finished products. See Table VIII in Chapter 3 for cost of equipment in the various areas of the facility (1).

heat or by double crimping. Tray cans eliminate the need for expensive refrigerated storage and reheating equipment (See Chapters 4 and 6).

The portioning and packaging area of the central production facility is a distinct separate area of production and should lie between the production and blast freezing and storage areas.

I. Finished Products Storage

Generally,both chilled and frozen type storage are required for the end products made in the facility. The size of these storage areas can be calculated by extension of the finished product data from the input-output matrix. Naturally, the packing of the products in those areas will be a function of the system. The packing might be in cartons, in plastic baskets or wire baskets.

A shipping assembly area will be necessary in which the outgoing shipments will be assembled and appropriately tagged for shipment. Awaiting loading on the trucks, these products will be stored under appropriate refrigeration.

J. Office and Personnel Facilities

The office facilities will, of course, depend upon the staffing level for facility management and clerical personnel. Food production supervisory personnel, receiving clerks, shipping clerks, should be located close to their areas of operation. The ingredient center or ingredient staging area should be under the control of an individual specifically responsible for that operation. A quality control laboratory, set up for the examination of incoming ingredients, the inspection of products being manufactured, and of the finished products, as well as for routine bacteriological testing, should be included in the plan. A test kitchen that can be used for the development of new recipes should also be provided.

Appropriate personnel facilities, such as locker rooms, toilets, lounges and lunchroom should be provided (Fig. 7). An important feature of a well designed central food production facility is limiting access to the production floor to authorized production personnel that have been properly gowned in clean uniforms and have washed and sanitized their hands. A practical means of insuring that no personnel will be admitted to the production floor without proper scrub down is to provide a scrub room as the means of access to the production floor from the employee facilities. This scrub room should be under the visual supervision of the production office.

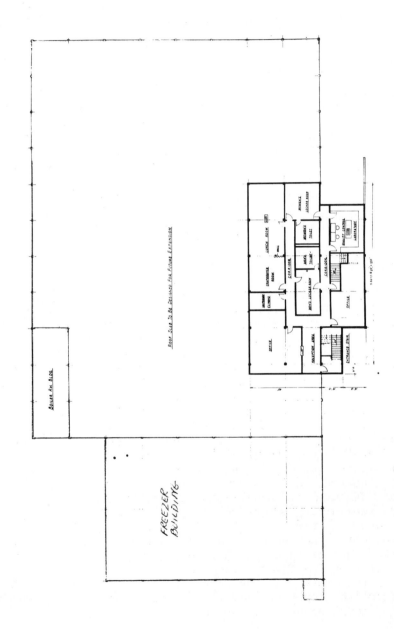

FIGURE 7. Second floor plan for the central food preparation facility shown in Figure 6 (1).

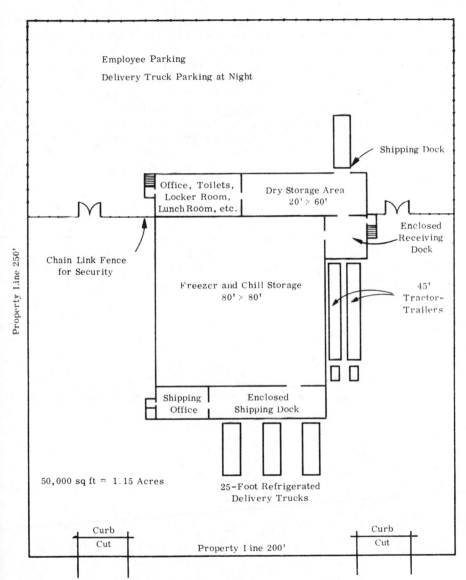

FIGURE 8. Block diagram for a distribution center for a regional school lunch food preparation facility based on the use of frozen bulk packs (1).

K. Waste Disposal

Proper facilities for the disposal of solid wastes should be provided. Generally, this involves the use of a number of trash and refuse collecting sites and the use of a dumpster outside the building. Using the input-output matrix, it is feasible to calculate the load of waste that will be generated in the operation. Based upon the type of processing involved it is also feasible to calculate the characteristics of the effluent from the facility and determing the need for a waste water treatment facility to reduce the BOD of the effluent before it is released into the municipal waste disposal system.

L. Distribution Centers

If the geographical area to be supplied by the central food preparation facility is large, or the facility is remote from some of the delivery points, the systems analysts should consider the possibility of including in the system one or more distribution centers to store and deliver products in their local areas (Fig. 8).

VII. REFERENCE

1. Res. & Dev. Staff, Project ANSER "Five County Management Improvement Project. Program Element 3. Facilities Alternative Planning" Project ANSER, Volusia County School District, Deland, Florida (1974)

CHAPTER 15

SITE LOCATION ANALYSIS FOR MULTI-UNIT OPERATIONS

John S. Thompson

John S. Thompson Company, Inc.
Los Altos, California

I. INTRODUCTION

Many attempts have been made in recent years to develop accurate computer-based models for use by retail chains in their site selection activities. While a few of these efforts have been undertaken by persons associated with universities or colleges, by far the greatest number of models has been developed by private corporations including companies in the fast food and supermarket sectors, using in-house market research expertise or outside consultants. As a result, most of these site location model building efforts have not been published.

This chapter describes the site selection model for a large, well known U.S. supermarket chain. Using an expanded data base from that initially utilized and a change in emphasis, from a micro to a macro methodology, resulted in the creation of a two-part model for screening potential sites for further, more detailed analysis. The methodology involved applies equally well to multiunit food service operations.

The model described is one of a group of site location models using the acronym "SPOT," which stands for "Site Prediction on Target".

This chapter will describe (1) the objective of the model building program, (2) the methodology, (3) the data base, (4) the model itself (disguised to protect the identity of the chain) (5) the testing procedure, and (6) the application of of the model.

Copyright © 1979 by Academic Press, Inc.
All rights of reproduction in any form reserved
ISBN: 0-12-453150-4

II. OBJECTIVE

Supermarket chains which expand very rapidly through a site acquisition and store building program (rather than by acquiring existing stores or chains) have long desired to have at their disposal a site selection model which would have the ability to distinguish among high volume, middle volume and low volume sites. Rather than to predict sales at a given site with a level of accuracy upon which real estate decisions could be made, the proposed model was to be used as a site pre-selector. If the model predicted a high volume site a more detailed follow up study would be made using other screening methods. Low volume predictions would result in discarding sites without further follow-up studies.

The model was to be inexpensive to apply so that reasonably quick baseline estimates could be made without necessary time-consuming field work.

III. METHODOLOGY

Using research developed in site selection and model building for non-food retailers, it was decided to develop a sales prediction model using a stepwise multiple regression procedure. The dependent variable (that which the model was to predict) was composed of two elements:

- number of transactions
- average ring-up

It was theorized that for supermarkets a one set of independent variables would influence the number of customers attracted to a store. Another set of factors would influence the average amount these customers spend. Thus it was thought better to break sales into its component parts, i.e. transactions and ring-ups.

IV. DATA BASE

The data base for the two models consisted of twenty-eight existing supermarkets operated by a major chain in a single geographical region. All stores in the model were supermarkets ranging from 20,000 square feet to 25,000 square feet in gross area. Although the chain also operates many larger combination food, drug and general merchandise stores none of these was included. Stores were all within 100 miles of one another and were all covered by a single advertising and promotion umbrella (although many newspapers and radio and television stations were used).

The independent variables consisted of a handful screened from an original group of over sixty. Most were demographic (from the U.S. Census of Population) but some were competitive variables. Some variables were judgmental but most were quantified "hard numbers".

Dependent variables (number of transactions and average ring-up) were provided by the supermarket chain for all twenty-eight stores.

V. MODEL DEVELOPMENT PROCEDURE

Customer source surveys were completed at twenty-two stores of the supermarket chain. From this initial research it became possible to delineate a standard trade area with a two-mile radius. Thus, the model predicts sales at new proposed sites considering demographic, geographic and competitive variables relating to a two-mile area.

Specifically, the mathematical model building steps for the site selection model were:

(1) *Define objectives in terms of desired accuracy and budget constraints.*

(2) *Determine variables to be considered for the model development phase.* Input from the chain's management was coupled with the authors' own model building experience to develop a list of sixty possible variables to be further tested.

(3) *Collect data for each of the variables.* This is an expensive and often tedious task but a very important one. Good data collection is absolutely essential for good model building.

(4) *Run initial correlations to examine relationships between variables.* Several variables proved to be highly related to supermarket transactions and ring-ups.

(5) *Perform stepwise regression to select a few of the most important variables.* The first of a long series of models was thus developed.

(6) *Correlate preliminary model errors with the remaining variables to select additional significant variables.* Only variables with a "T" statistically significant at the 95 % level or higher were allowed in the model.

(7) *Introduce substitutions and transformations of variables to improve the fit of the model and thus improve its accuracy.*

(8) Create variations of the model. About twenty variations were created with the final version presented in this chapter deemed to be the best.

Two types of site location models can be constructed:

(1) A micro model is one in which sales predictions are made for various sub-areas (usually census tracts) into which a trade area is divided. A micro model is used in conjunction with a separate model which predicts sales from beyond the area.

(2) A macro model, on the other hand, makes one prediction, using demographic and other variables which relate to the entire trade area. The supermarket site location model is a macro model. The weakness of the macro approach is that population or competition skewed to one side of a trade area may distort the prediction. Moreover, unusually good or bad access from one direction or another may affect the results. However, as a pre-selector or screening device, the macro approach seems to offer substantial advantages from a cost effectiveness standpoint over the micro methodology.

The supermarket model is a combination of two sub-models:

(1) A *Transaction Model* which estimates the number of expected transactions.
(2) An *Average Purchase Model* which estimates the average transaction size.

Previous supermarket research had disclosed that some variables affect the size of the purchase but not the number of purchases, and vice versa. By breaking sales into these two parts, it was possible to develop a better model. The final sales estimate is the product of the average purchase size estimate and the number of transactions estimate.

Sixty independent variables were examined to determine which, if any, effectively explained differences between the stores in terms of the two dependent variables. The variables selected for use in the models are shown in Table I.

The final model equation is shown in Table II.

The dictionary defines a model as a "miniature representation of something". Thus a supermarket model is a mathematical miniaturization of an entire chain of retail stores. If the control stores upon which the model is based are truly representative, the model will be better able to predict sales at the new sites. However, regardless of the size of the control store group or the degree to which control stores are truly representative, new sites frequently embody trade area or locational characteristics which are beyond the range of data encountered in the model building program. Consequently, site location mod-

TABLE I. Model Independent Variables

Variable Name	Description
Transaction Model -	
T1	Number of families (000's) with income of $7,000 to $15,000
T2	Total square feet of selling area of competitors (000's).
T3	Trade area access ("1" if good or very good; "0" if not).
T4	Trade area population (000's).
T5	Average family size.
T6	Free standing store ("1" if yes; "0" if no).
Average Purchase Model -	
A1	Residential land use (% of trade area).
A2	"Beyond access" rating ("1" if good or very good; "0" if not).
A3	Number of families (000's) with income of $7,000 to $15,000.
A4	Total square feet of selling area of competitors (000's).
A5	Average distance (miles) from competitive stores to site.
A6	Free standing store ("1" if yes; "0" if not).
A7	Same chain store within 3 miles ("1" if yes; "0" if no).
A8	Co-tenancy rating ("1" if poor or very poor; "0" if not).

TABLE II. Model Equations

Estimated Sales (000's for 2 weeks)	=	Estimated Number of Transactions (000's for 2 weeks) Estimated Average Purchase ($'s)
Estimated Number of Transactions (000's for 2 weeks)	=	$36.053 + 2.3021(T1) - 1.5584(T2) + 0.9181(T3) + 2.3034(T4) - 3.1002(T5) - 3.0926(T6)$
Estimated Average Purchase	=	$14.284 - .03(A1) + 1.825(A2) + 0.766(A3) - .2044(A4) + 2.108(A5) + 2.1057(A6) - 1.439(A7) - 2.997(A8)$

els are not always accurate. To ignore this fact may be disastrous, especially when a store opens and fails to live up to the expectations raised by unquestioned faith in the model!

In addition to those limitations of the SPOT macro model as pre-selector or screening model which have already cited, there are a few additional cautions which should be exercised in its application. The model is specific for the geographic area for which it was developed and should not be used in other areas until it has been tested against existing stores to be certain it predicts accurately. The image of the supermarket chain in a new area vis-a-vis competitive images may be an important variable to recalibrate.

Obviously the model can only be used at sites where the values of the variables are within the relevant range of those used in the model. Slight variations are acceptable, but if a trade area population is 50 % greater than any in the model, the final estimate should be viewed with caution.

Models become outdated as purchasing habits, competitive relationships and store images change. To insure that a model is always current, the model should include new stores as they come on stream. Also, it should be periodically updated for all stores in the model. Finally, any drastic change in advertising, pricing or merchandising by the supermarket chain, or the introduction of a new competitor with a radically new and highly acceptable merchandising strategy could render the model immediately obsolete.

A statistical summary of the model is shown in Table III.

VI. TESTING PROCEDURE

The SPOT macro model was validated against two groups of stores in independent tests. First, the model was tested against the stores on which it was based. Tables IV, V and VI report the estimated and actual results and the precentage error for the transaction model, the average purchase (ring-up) model, and the supermarket model (combined transaction and average purchase). Sales at twenty five of the twenty eight stores (89 %) were predicted within fifteen per cent.

A separate test of the model was made on seven randomly selected stores in the geographical area in which the model was developed. Of the seven stores two were smaller and considerably older than control stores in the model. The trade area of a third test store was separated from the site in such a way that roughly fifty percent of the population was channeled circuitously to the store directly in front of three very strong competitors. These kinds of store and trade area characteristics were well beyond the range of observed data in the

TABLE III. Model Statistics

Supermarket Model –	Absolute Mean Error	8%
	71% of the errors were within	+10%
	89% of the errors were within	+15%
	100% of the errors were within	+27%
	Standard deviation of errors	̄10.4
	95% Confidence Limits	+21%
	66% Confidence Limits	+10%
Transaction Model –	F Value	=40.1
	Standard Error of the Estimate	= 1.664
	Coefficient of Determination (R^2)	= .92
	Average Absolute Error	5.8%

Variable Name	Computed T Value	Average Relative Impact
T1	11.1	34%
T2	-14.9	35
T3	- 5.1	28
T4	- 2.9	1
T5	- 3.3	1
T6	- 3.1	1
		100%

Average Purchase Model –

	F Value	=19.8
	Standard Error of the Estimate	= .53
	Coefficient of Determination (R^2)	= .86
	Average Absolute Error	4.3%

Variable Name	Computed T Value	Average Relative Impact
A1	- 3.5	17%
A2	4.6	5
A3	- 4.0	16
A4	4.0	20
A5	- 4.0	29
A6	3.2	4
A7	- 3.9	3
A8	- 3.6	6
		100%

TABLE IV.   Transaction Model

Store No.	Estimated *Transactions (000's)	Actual *Transactions (000's)	Per Cent Error
1	21.812	22.709	- 4
2	9.078	9.777	- 7
3	25.788	24.695	4
4	30.822	31.229	- 1
5	15.586	13.244	18
6	13.897	11.499	21
7	13.945	17.973	-22
8	17.977	17.422	3
9	24.192	24.331	- 1
10	24.262	26.938	-10
11	22.829	23.230	- 2
12	21.997	21.536	2
13	13.774	13.635	10
14	17.166	17.867	- 4
15	22.225	22.111	1
16	21.757	23.094	- 6
17	21.062	17.582	20
18	23.842	24.842	- 4
19	15.926	15.866	0
20	23.081	22.797	1
21	21.599	21.687	0
22	29.607	28.306	5
23	20.128	19.663	2
24	24.178	25.459	- 5
25	25.398	24.794	2
26	16.271	15.481	5
27	21.866	22.220	- 2
28	23.372	23.450	0

*Average for 2 weeks ending 2/1/75

TABLE V.   Average Purchase Model

Store No.	Estimated Average Purchase* ($)	Actual Average Purchase* ($)	Per Cent Error
1	8.29	8.77	- 6
2	9.54	8.99	6
3	9.12	10.33	-12
4	8.57	8.39	2
5	8.90	8.22	8
6	9.63	9.64	0
7	8.08	8.06	0
8	8.60	8.61	0
9	10.08	10.09	0
10	8.45	8.58	- 2
11	10.90	11.10	- 2
12	8.24	8.10	2
13	9.60	9.67	- 1
14	10.11	9.76	4
15	9.05	9.71	- 7
16	8.25	8.12	2
17	10.46	10.99	- 5
18	10.32	10.14	2
19	8.07	7.66	5
20	8.67	9.37	- 7
21	8.53	9.19	- 7
22	9.47	9.03	5
23	9.18	8.63	6
24	8.11	8.11	0
25	9.82	8.95	10
26	5.86	5.76	2
27	10.71	11.62	- 8
28	10.19	9.25	10

*Average for 2 weeks ending 2/1/75

TABLE VI.   *Supermarket Model Development*

Store No.	Model Estimates			Actual *Sales ($)	Percent Error
	Average ($)	Number of Transactions	*Sales ($)		
1	8.29	21,812	180.8	199.2	− 9
2	9.54	9,078	86.6	87.9	− 1
3	9.12	25,788	235.2	255.1	− 8
4	8.57	30,822	264.1	261.9	+ 1
5	8.90	15,586	138.7	108.8	+27
6	9.63	13,897	133.8	110.8	+21
7	8.08	13,945	112.7	144.8	−22
8	8.60	17,977	154.6	150.0	+ 3
9	10.08	24,192	243.9	245.4	− 1
10	8.45	24,262	205.0	231.1	−11
11	10.90	22,829	248.8	257.8	− 3
12	8.24	21,997	181.3	174.5	+ 4
13	9.60	13,774	132.2	131.8	+ 0
14	10.11	17,166	173.5	174.3	− 0
15	9.05	22,225	201.1	214.6	− 6
16	8.25	21,757	179.5	187.5	− 4
17	10.46	21,062	220.3	193.3	+14
18	10.32	23,842	246.0	251.8	− 2
19	8.07	15,926	128.5	121.6	+ 6
20	8.67	23,081	200.1	213.7	− 6
21	8.53	21,599	184.2	199.4	− 8
22	9.47	29,607	280.4	255.6	+10
23	9.18	20,128	184.8	169.6	+ 9
24	8.11	24,178	196.1	206.5	− 5
25	9.82	25,398	249.4	221.8	+12
26	5.86	16,271	95.3	89.1	+ 7
27	10.71	21,866	234.2	258.3	− 9
28	10.19	23,372	238.2	216.9	+10

*Total for 2 weeks ending 2/1/75 (000's $)

model. Thus, in these three cases, the model predicted from 22 % to 39 % higher than actual sales. The other test stores were all predicted within 8 % of actual sales.

Table VII reports the results of the model test using stores outside the data base.

VII. APPLICATION

The model is applied to a proposed site by (1) completing a field survey and accumulating demographic and trade area data called for by the model, and (2) calculating sales by inserting the variable inputs into the model equation.

As in the model building phase, data collection in applying the model to a proposed site must be done accurately. A failure to count a competitor, for example, would increase (erroneously) the model estimate by a significant amount. It is equally important that the data collected for a proposed site be interpreted in a way similar to the interpretation utilized in the initial model building phase. Using the competitive example above, it is essential that the definition of a competitor for site evaluation purposes be the same in the application as in the developmental phase.

Table VIII shows the range, mean and standard deviation of the independent variables used in the model. These data offer guideline to the analyst in deciding whether field survey and demographic inputs are within the relevant range of the statistics upon which the model was based.

Experience has shown that in applying macro models similar to this supermarket model, but developed specifically for drug, department store, home improvement, apparel and fast food chains, adjustments must be made to make the model estimate most meaningful. An adjustment should also be made to account for a potential seasonal variation. Since the data used in the model were based on a very specific time period, e.g. the two weeks ending February 1, 1975, the output should be adjusted to reflect annualized sales.

If price increases have occurred between the two weeks ending February 1, 1975 and the time of the estimate, then the volume estimate should be adjusted accordingly. Prior price-elasticity-of-demand studies would be useful. If these kinds of data are not available an inelastic condition should be assumed. In other words, if prices have increased 5 % the estimate should be increased 5 %.

The supermarket model is a quantification of past experience. In some cases there has been either little or no experience about a variable to quantify. As a result, the model cannot determine the effects of that variable even though its ef-

TABLE VII. Supermarket Model Test for Stores Outside
the Data Base

Store No.	Model Estimates		Actual		Per Cent Error
	Average ($)	No. of Transactions	*Sales ($)	*Sales ($)	
101	9.67	21,854	211.4	202.0	+5
102	8.29	19,903	164.9	180.0	−8
103	12.58	20,211	254.3	238.0	+7
104	8.83	18,792	166.0	119.0	+39
105	10.94	20,924	229.0	188.0	+22
106	9.34	22,425	209.5	201.0	+4
107	8.18	25,562	209.0	165.0	+27

*Average for 2 weeks ending 2/1/75 (000's $)

TABLE VIII. Supermarket Model Variables

Variable Description	Name(s)	Range High	Range Low	Mean	Standard Deviation	Sub-Model Application Transaction	Average Purchase
No.of families (000's) with income of $7,000-$15,000	T1	12.6	2.2	5.946	2.644	X	
Total sq.ft. of competitors	T2,A4	23	8	15.820	3.959	X	X
Trade area access	T3	1	0	.620	.21	X	
Trade area population(000's)	T4	160	28	79.000	21.92	X	
Average family size	T5	3.9	2.7	3.500	.26	X	
Free standing store	T6,A6	1	0	.179	.39	X	X
Residential land use	A1	90	25	56.100	17.40		X
Beyond rating	A2	1	0	.357	.488		X
No. of families(000's) with income of $7,000-$15,000	A3	4.2	0.5	2.093	1.193		X
Avg. distance from competitive stores to site	A5	1.94	0.85	1.369	.301		X
Same chain store within 3 miles	A7	1	0	.21	.42		X
Co-tenancy rating	A8	1	0	.29	.46		X

fect may be determined logically. For example, inadequate parking is not a model variable; yet logic tells us it must have a
negative effect. Likewise, exceptionally good store management
can have a positive effect on sales beyond that estimated by
the model. Moreover, although "accessibility" is a variable in
the model its impact is moderate. Therefore, when looking at a
site which has very poor access the sales predicted by the model should be modified downward.

    As a screening or pre-selector tool this model appears to
have some merit. Only through use and recalibration can this
model become a viable means of evaluating sites. Under no circumstances should final real estate decisions be made using
this model. However, its use can result in lower analysis costs
if it allows chains to concentrate their analytical effort on
fewer sites, namely, those with known potential.

CHAPTER 16

ADVANCED EQUIPMENT FOR CONVENIENCE FOOD SYSTEMS

Robert V. Decareau

Food Systems Equipment Division
Food Engineering Laboratory
US Army Natick Research & Development Command
Natick, Massachusetts

I. INTRODUCTION

The tremendous growth of the eating-away-from home market
in the United States has brought with it a desperate need for
improved food service equipment and systems. Historically, the
equipment situation today is little different from the late
1700's when Benjamin Thompson, Count Rumford, invented the
roasting oven(1). Up until that time, meat roasting was carried out over an open fire. His experiments compared the quality and yield of meat roasted in his oven against open fire
cooking. In his own words, "to prevent all deception, the persons employed in roasting them were not informed of the principal design of the experiment. When these pieces of roasted
meat came from the fire they were carefully weighed; when it
appeared that the piece which had been roasted in the roaster
was heavier than the other by a difference which was equal to
six percent, or six pounds in a hundred. But this even is not
all; nor is it the most important result of the experiment.
These two legs of mutton were brought upon table at the same
time, and a large and perfectly unprejudiced company was assembled to eat them. They were both declared to be very good; but
a decided preference was unanimously given to that which had
been roasted in the roaster, it was much more juicy, and was
thought to be better tasted. They were both eaten up, and
nothing remaining of either of them that was eatable. Their
fragments, which had been carefully preserved, being now collected and placed in their separate dishes, it was a comparison
of these fragments which afforded the most striking proof of

Copyright © 1979 by Academic Press, Inc.
All rights of reproduction in any form reserved
ISBN: 0-12-453150-4

the relative merit of these two methods of roasting meat, in respect to the economy of the food. Of the leg of mutton which had been roasted in the roaster, hardly anything visible remained except the bare bone; while a considerable heap was formed of scraps not eatable which remained of that roasted on the spit."

It is interesting to note that, almost two hundred years ago, someone was concerned with not only the overall cooking yield, but also the yield of usable meat. Thompson was concerned also with efficiency and made precise calculations of the fuel requirements for cooking purposes as well as for heating living spaces. Since his invention of the roasting oven there has been relatively little change in oven design of real significance. Instead of coal, coke or wood, we now use electricity or gas. We do have thermostatic controls and the cosmetics are much nicer, but the cooking results are pretty much the same.

Today our interests have turned, to some extent, away from prime cooking to the use of precooked frozen foods and the equipment needed to reconstitute them. Co and Livingston (2) reviewed equipment available for reconstituting precooked frozen foods and listed chronologically some of the significant equipment developments. Only three years later, Livingston and Chang (3) felt compelled to discuss second generation equipment to emphasize that there was some development activity oriented toward the solution of food reconstitution problems. They also advanced some requirements for third generation equipment, noting that the needs for reconstitution equipment in the food service field were still not being met. Some of their comments about these needs are listed below because they are germane to the discussion of advanced equipment which is to follow:

(1) Automating reconstitution devices to minimize the personnel variables (making judgements, setting controls, etc.)

(2) Closer temperature control of ovens; i.e., more accurate thermostats.

(3) Conveyor type convection ovens, including automatic feed from freezer storage.

(4) High speed heating devices (3-minutes) for heating one or two steam table pans at a time.

(5) Temperature sensing devices for use in microwave ovens.

(6) Selective heating systems for heating meals on trays without heating other foods which should remain chilled or even frozen.

It is indeed impressive to realize today that many of these needs are either operational, in pilot test, or being studied. This will be more apparent from the discussion to follow. Recent development efforts have leaned toward more rapid heating equipment and improved efficiency of energy usage a greater degree of automation and more uniform heating results. In the context of more rapid heating and greater efficiency, it is appropriate to discuss a number of innovative approaches to food heating.

II. NEW APPROACHES TO FOOD HEATING

A. *The Chemetron Total Tray System*

This is an example of the extremes man will go in the solution of a problem. The problem is that in hospital food service if an item is removed from a patient's tray to be heated, there is an outside chance that it may not get back on the same tray. Such a mistake could have serious implications if the patient happens to be on a special diet.

A solution is found in U.S. Patents No. 3,854,021 (4) and 3,854,022 (5) which teach how to place the entire tray in a microwave oven and have it come out with the right foods heated and the others unaffected. The patents have been reduced to practice by Chemetron Corporation. (Figures 1 and 2).

The system thus developed consists of a rather special serving tray with a built-in sensing element, and a microwave oven which accepts only this tray, and only in one orientation. The foods which are to be heated must be placed in a specific area of the tray, and those which are not to be heated in another area. When the tray is inserted into the microwave oven, a metal cover located in the oven is lowered automatically into place over the cold foods to prevent them from being exposed to the microwave energy. Closing the oven door automatically cycles the microwave energy on. The special sensor built into the tray absorbs microwave energy at a rate proportional to the rate at which the food is being heated. When it reaches a certain temperature, the sensor affects a detector located below the oven floor and directly under the sensor in the tray causing a reed switch to open thereby turning off the microwave power. The tray can now be removed and delivered to the patient. If there should be any delay, the sensor will cool and the relationship between it and the detector will change resulting in the reed switch closing and the oven cycling back on. The oven will continue to cycle on and off to keep the food warm. A logic circuit built into the control system turns the oven off after ten such actions.

The Chemetron Total Tray system has been installed in two related hospitals in the St. Louis, Missouri area; 10 ovens in one and 17 ovens in the other. A third hospital system, the Metropolitan Medical Center and Hennepin General Hospital in Minneapolis is installing 44 ovens. In the latter complex, a central food preparation facility will furnish foods for the system.

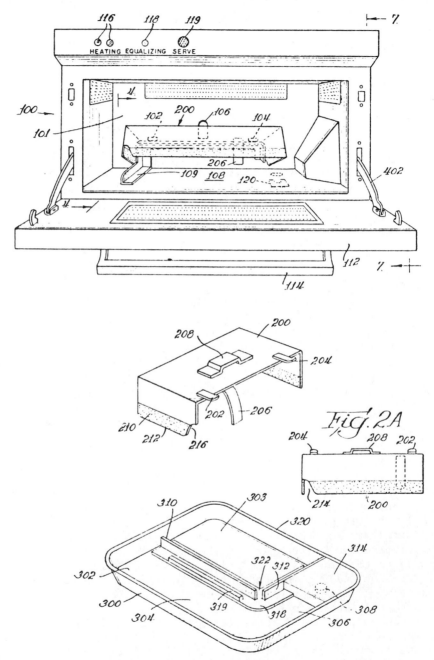

FIGURE 1. Chemetron Total Tray System. U.S.Patent No.
3,854,021 (Dec.10, 1974) drawing shows oven, shielding cover
(200) and special tray (320). The sensor (308) is positioned
by the tray guide (109) directly above the detector (120).

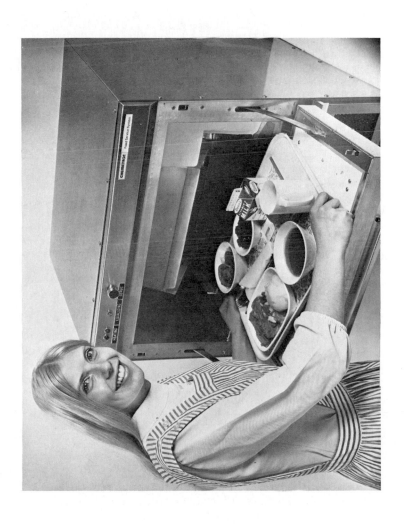

FIGURE 2. Chemetron Total Tray System. (Courtesy of Chemetron Corporation, Louisville, Kentucky)

B. THE TECKTON DIFFERENTIAL HEATING CONTAINER SYSTEM

Here is another example in the hospital food service area
of a problem in search of a solution. The problem is how to
heat an array of foods, a meal, in a microwave oven, so that
each food item is heated to its appropriate serving temperature. And to make it a real challenge, how can it be done from
the frozen state?

The solution is found in Patents No. 3,615,713 (6) and
3,547,661 (7). These patents teach that advantage can be taken
of the fact that microwave energy is reflected from metal.
Teckton, Inc., a Wellesley, Massachusetts firm, has designed a
metal holder which they call a Differential Heating Container,
for reasons which will become obvious, into which a frozen
multi-component dinner can be placed. The holder has openings
or apertures which permit microwave energy to pass in, the size
of the openings determining the amount of energy whick can
pass. The openings are oriented with respect to the frozen meal
components so that each receives the proper amount of microwave
wave energy to heat it to its correct temperature (Figure 3).

This system requires rather tight portion control to insure
consistent heating results and the food plate must be oriented
properly with respect to the Differential Heating Container. It
is possible with this system to heat a frozen dinner consisting
of an entree, mashed potatoes, a vegetable, a roll, and fruit
so that each item is properly heated, the roll is just warm and
the fruit is icy cold.

The system is being used at Mercy Hospital in Buffalo, New
York. It has also been tried in a school lunch feeding study
as well as in a program for feeding elderly citizens.

C. AN UNTENDED MEAL HEATING SYSTEM

This system is in the prototype stage at an advanced state
of fabrication. The problem it was designed to solve relates to
the need to provide, in certain cases, all the elements of conventional food service but without the staffing and equipment
of a full-scale kitchen operation.

The prototype is shown in schematic form in Figure 4 (8).
Individual meal components in microwave compatible packages are
stored in a freezer section of the device. A selector console
on the front identifies the meal components available. A total
of 12 selections are provided in this unit. A customer may select one item from each of the three columns, typically an entree, a vegetable, and a starch item. The selected items are
raised by an hydraulic system to a position where the top package in a stack can be moved by a collator above the stacks to a
position on an elevator platform. When all three selections are

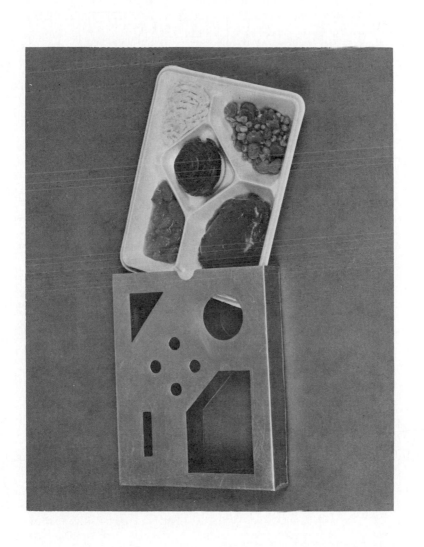

FIGURE 3. Differential Heating Container. (Courtesy of Teckton, Inc., Wellesley, Massachusetts)

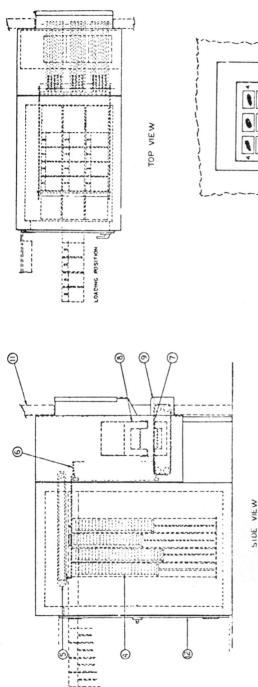

TOP VIEW

FRONT VIEW

SIDE VIEW

FIGURE 4. Schematic of Untended Meal Heating Device. Description of operation: (1) Photo display of food items, (2) Selection buttons, (3) Push to cook button initiates operation, (4) Freezer storage stack lifts selected portion into position for retrieval, (5) The collator collects one portion from each row, (6) Elevator lowers package to heating conveyor, (7) Heating conveyor advances into oven for reconstitution, (8) Oven consists of three parallel microwave ovens with directed hot air for surface crisping, as programmed by the select button, (9) Dispensing shelf, where heated products appear, (10) Select button indicates when next order can be entered, (11) Position of wall, if unit is installed to provide service through wall of dining area, and (12) Freezer door.

on the platform, it moves down to a second position where it
meshes with a belt that draws the items into side-by-side microwave ovens. The oven doors close automatically and the items
are exposed to programmed heating cycles developed for each
specific item. The heating cycles are typically two minutes or
less with few exceptions. After the cycle is completed the ov-
en door opens and the items move out to the delivery position.

A unique capability of the system is its ability to handle
crisp foods such as French fried potatoes and fried chicken.
These represent exceptions to the two minutes or less heating
cycles. Crisping is accomplished by directing hot air down onto the items during microwave exposure. Adequate crisping can
be accomplished in less than three minutes at air temperatures
of 400°F. An illustration of the directed hot air system concept is shown in drawings (Figure 5) from U.S. Patent Number
3,883,213 (9).

The packaging of products which must be crisped represents
a special challenge. Since the product must have adequate
freezer storage protection in distribution and in the storage
section, the package must be moisture vapor tight. Yet in order
to be exposed to the directed hot air for crisping, the package
must be opened. The solution in this case is to use a shrink
film overwrap. When the hot air hits the film it splits and
shrinks back out of the way almost instantly, thereby exposing
the product for crisping.

The above described crisping system is in commercial use
without the complementary microwaves for continuous baking of
frozen pizza. A pair of units at the student cafeteria at
Texas A & M University handle more than 1,000 pizza pies per
hour. The technique has also been used to heat prepared foods
in standard steam table pans. The heating time for five pound
quantities in half-size disposable aluminum steam table pans
is 16 to 18 minutes from 38°F, and the time is 36 minutes from
0°F to a final temperature of 160°F. Air temperature during
heating was 400°F. It is not too difficult to envision a progressive heating system for bulk packaged foods which could
provide trays of hot foods at a rate consistent with serving
line flow. Some work has been carried out on a system for tempering bulk containers of frozen prepared foods. The system
heats frozen food from 0°F to a tempered condition (26 - 28°F)
while maintaining food surface temperature below 30°F at all
times. A rack load of as many as 60 half-size steam table pans
has been tempered in three and one half to four hours. The system goes into an automatic hold once the tempered condition has
been reached. Foods at this temperature can be held for relatively long periods of time with no measurable deterioration.
They can also be heated to serving temperature with only a
slight penalty in heating time over foods at 38°F. Coupling automatic feeding of tempered foods into a conveyorized directed

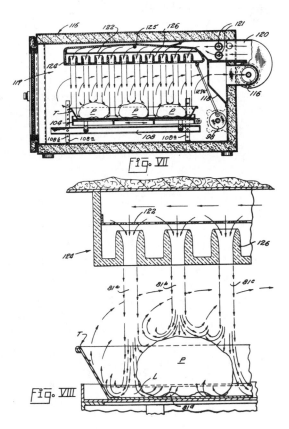

FIGURE 5. *Illustrations from U.S. Patent No. 3,884,213 indi-*
cate how hot air is directed down onto products to improve heat
transfer.

hot-air crisping system described above can provide foods for
the serving line as they are needed. When compared to batch-
type convection ovens,   in which all of the pans of food are
ready at one time, but cannot be used at once, the last tray
being held warm with the nutrients deteriorating all the time,
it is seen that the progressive heating system has considerable merit. Although there is no complete system available on
the market, the elements are available.

D. *High-Speed Meat Roasting Equipment Systems*

The problem to be solved is how to optimize the meat roasting process in terms of time, yield and quality. The approach
used was to analyze the heat transfer factors of specific food

materials to determine the maximum rates at which heat could be applied to obtain the desired results. Energy sources such as forced convection, radiant and microwave alone or in combination, were investigated. A mathematical model of the roasting process was derived for conventional roasting and later expanded to include the use of microwave energy. Important to the solution of the mathematical model was information of the evaporative cooling rate and data on the dielectric properties of meat. The dielectric data measurements were made at the Massachusetts Institute of Technology's Nutrition and Food Science Department at three different microwave frequencies (300, 915 and 2450 MHz) and over the temperature range of $-40°C$ to $120°C$. Data are shown in Figure 6 for the two higher frequencies, where it can be seen that the penetration of microwave energy at 2450 MHz is relatively constant over the entire temperature range, while penetration at 915 MHz decreases with increasing temperature.

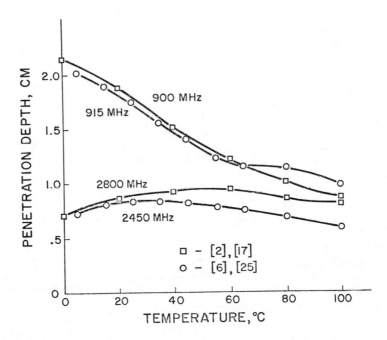

FIGURE 6. *Penetration of microwave energy as a function of frequency and temperature.*

With the refined math model equations, it was possible to obtain computer printouts of temperature profiles in meat roasts under a variety of conditions. All work was carried out using a cylindrical roast configuration to simplify the prob-

lem.   Figure 7 illustrates the initial temperature condition
along the centerline of the roast.   Figure 8 shows the temperature pattern for conventional roasting after 90 minutes,   and
Figure 9 after 168 minutes when the roast had a center temperature of 140°F (60°C). Figure 10 shows the results obtained in
90 minutes at 2450 MHz at a power level of 300 watts.   The pattern is typical of the results obtained in a microwave oven
where the ambient temperature condition is about room temperature.   Evaporative cooling is responsible for lower surface
temperatures. The temperatures are highest at the ends because
of the greater surface area and hence the greater heat load in
these areas.

The next series of figures represent computer generated results at 915 MHz,   the lower of the two frequencies.   In Figure
11,   the effect of the greater penetration at this frequency is
quite evident. As the roast cooks, and the temperature near the
surface increases,   penetration begins to decrease and the center peak begins to diminish (see Figures 12 and 13). The slight
penetration advantage does result in a significant decrease in
roasting time, 60 minutes compared to 90 for 2450 MHz. The temperature patterns   at completion of roasting are almost identical.

To further illustrate the kind of control possible with a
microwave system,   the   next series of figures illustrates the
effect of reducing the heating rate at the ends of the roast by
the use of metal foil shielding for a portion of the cooking
period.   Aluminum foil was applied to the ends of the roast to
cover about three centimeters   at each end.   The   temperature
patterns shown in Figures 14 and 15 show how effective this is.
The foil is removed about 15 minutes before completion to allow
the ends to cook,   and the final result is shown in   Figure 16.

Equipment with which to carry out meat roasting and other
cooking studies is shown in   Figure 17.   The oven has   variable
microwave power   at both 915 MHz and 2450 MHz   to about 2 kilo-
watts; controlled oven temperature in the 200 to 550°F   range;
controlled steam pressure at   5, 10, and 15 psig;   and an   IBM
card reader to permit programs to be run in an   automatic mode.
Although much confirmatory work remains to be carried out,   a
number   of   general conclusions can be drawn from   roasting results to date:

(1) A power level of 300 watts   appears   to give the most
uniform results and the best yield for   roasts of the   configuration used. Yields of 85% and better have been obtained.

(2) 915 MHz   appears to be the better   microwave frequency
of the two for meat roasting.

(3) The results   appear to be in general agreement with the
computer generated data.

The next step is to develop an equipment design,   one   in
which the personnel variable is minimized; i.e. one   in which

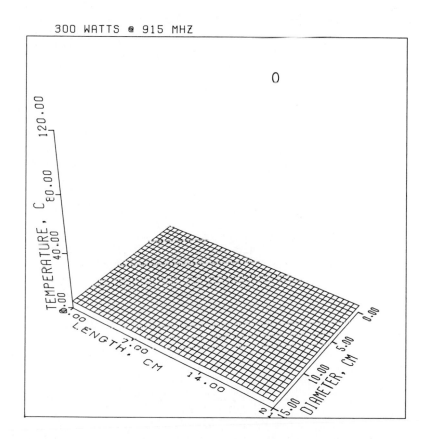

FIGURE 7.   Computer printout of initial temperature conditions
in cylindrical roast of beef.

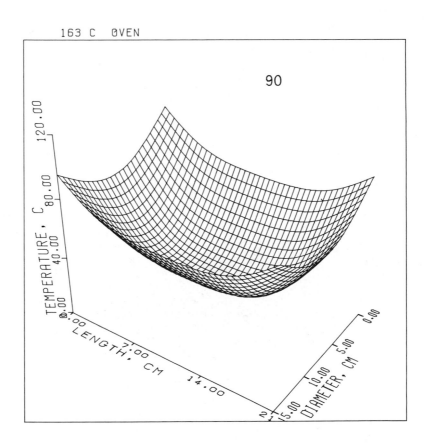

FIGURE 8.   Computer printout of temperature profile in roast of
beef after 90 minutes   in a 163°C (325°F) oven.

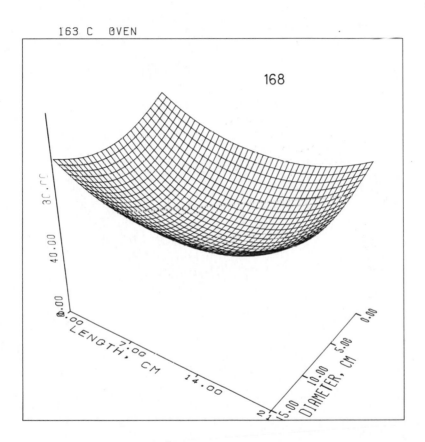

FIGURE 9. *Computer printout of temperature profile in roast of beef after 168 minutes in a 163°C (325°F) oven.*

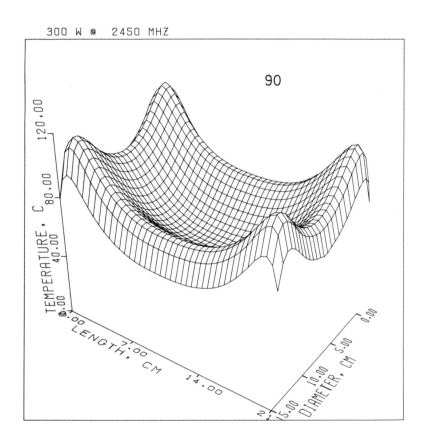

FIGURE 10. Computer printout of temperature profile in roast
of beef after 90 minutes in a 300-Watt microwave oven operating at 2450 MHz.

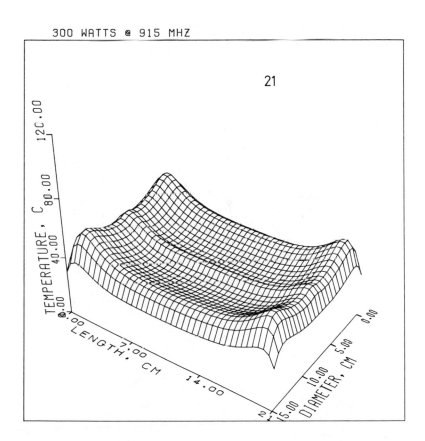

FIGURE 11.   Computer printout of temperature profile in roast
of beef after 21 minutes in a 300-Watt microwave oven operating at 915 MHz.

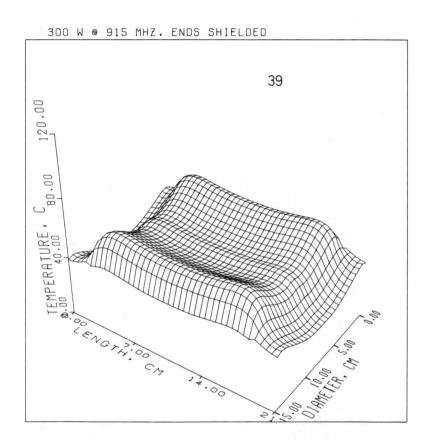

FIGURE 12. Computer printout of temperature profile in roast of beef after 39 minutes in a 300-Watt microwave oven operating at 915 MHz.

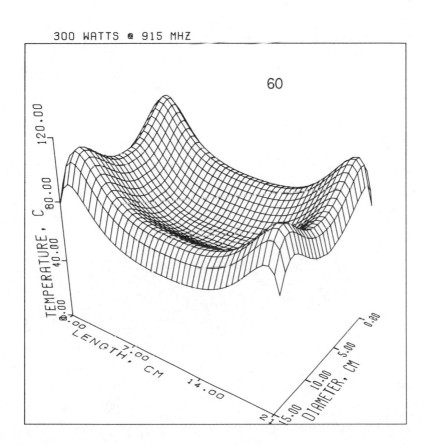

FIGURE 13. Computer printout of temperature profile in roast of beef after 60 minutes in a 300-Watt microwave oven operating at 915 MHz.

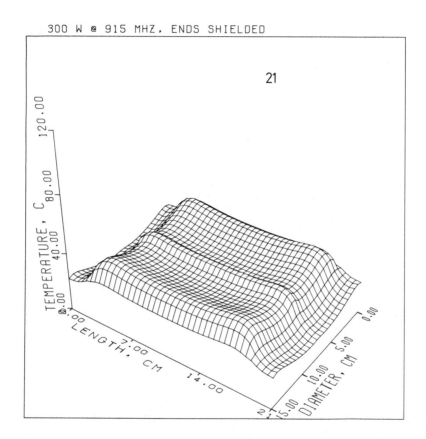

FIGURE 14. Computer printout of temperature profile in roast of beef with the ends shielded with aluminum foil after 21 minutes in a 300-Watt microwave oven operating at 915 MHz.

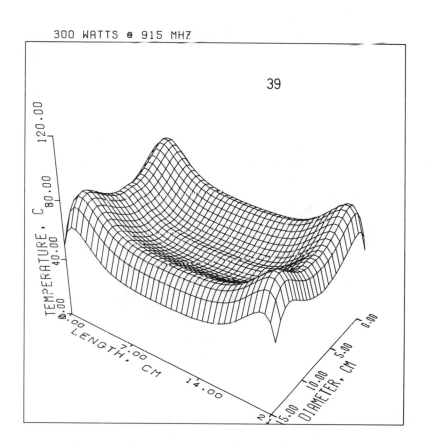

FIGURE 15.   Computer printout of temperature profile in roast of beef with the ends shielded with aluminum foil after 39 minutes   in a 300-Watt microwave oven operating at 915 MHz.

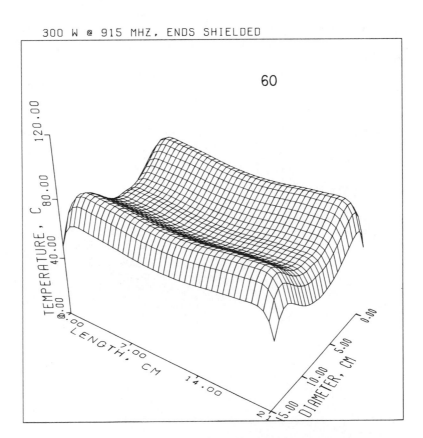

FIGURE 16. Computer printout of temperature profile in roast of beef with the aluminum foil shielding removed after 60 minutes in a 300-Watt microwave oven operating at 915 MHz.

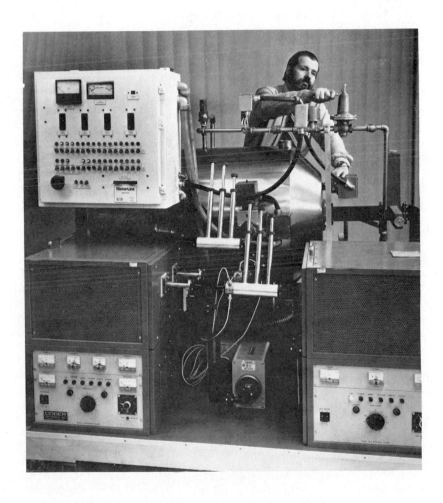

FIGURE 17. Research oven used for beef roasting studies.
(Courtesy of Raytheon Company, Waltham, Massachusetts)

few, if any, judgements are required on the part of the cook.
Since microwave energy can be precisely controlled, a programmed oven is envisioned, which requires little more than loading
the oven and pressing a start button. It should not be necessary to set a thermostat, and the oven should turn itself off
at the end of the cooking process so that overcooking and low
yields would be a thing of the past.

III. FUTURE DEVELOPMENTS

Of the six needs for reconstitution equipment, identified
by Livingston and Chang (3), no comment has been made thus far
on closer temperature control of ovens, high speed heating devices and temperature sensing devices for use in microwave
ovens.

It is clear that a need does exist for better oven temperature control. The technology is there, but the cost is the
main deterrent to adoption.

A high-speed heating device to heat one or two steam table
pans of food at a time in three minutes may be beyond the state
of the art. Calculations indicate that the power required to
do the job for one pan, based on 10 pounds of product per pan
at an initial temperature of $0^{\circ}F$ is approximately 12.6 KW of
microwave power at 100 % efficiency. To generate this much microwave power would require about 25 KW of line power. The cost
of such equipment today might be $2,000 per kilowatt of micro-
wave power. It is unlikely that the total cost of such a device
could be justified for the small benefit gained. The more logical approach would be to keep a supply of product at tempered
conditions and heat from that state. However, this would only
reduce the power required by 50 % and the equipment cost would
still be excessive. If one considers increasing the time to
6 minutes, then the power required drops to 3 KW for a full-
size pan and 1.5 KW for a half-size steam table pan. At these
levels there is equipment available without the need for a new
engineering design effort.

There is considerable work being done today on temperature
sensing devices for microwave ovens. Bimetallic thermometers
can be used in roasts and other large food masses in microwave
ovens, and a number of manufacturers offer them for this purpose. Some interesting work employing fiber optics and liquid
crystals also is being done, though mostly in the biological
area, over rather limited temperature ranges. However, the
technology appears to be expendable to the temperature range of
interest for food thawing, heating and cooking.

It is clear, from the equipment and equipment concepts discussed, that the technology being used today was unavailable

during Benjamin Thompson's time and indeed even up to the
1940's. Microwave technology certainly represents a significant
advance over conventional equipment, and it is evident that one
is just now becoming aware of the potential of this form of energy, either alone or in conjunction with other heat forms. The
possibilities of microwave and steam pressure, or infrared are
largely unknown and need to be investigated. Perhaps the answer
to a 3-minute heating cycle for steam table pans lies in the
application of steam pressure and microwave energy, assuming
that acceptable costs are attainable.

IV. REFERENCES

1. Brown, S.C., ed. "The Collected Works of Count Rumford",
   Vol. III, Harvard Univ. Press, Cambridge, Massachusetts
   (1969)
2. Co, D.Y.C.L. and Livingston, G. E. *Food Technol. 23*, (12),72
   (1969)
3. Livingston, G.E. and Chang, C. M. *Cornell H & RA Quarterly
   13*, (1) 57 (1972)
4. Moore, D.G. "Electromagnetic Heating System which Includes
   an Automatic Shielding Mechanism and Method for its Operation", U.S. Patent No. 3,854,021 (1974)
5. Moore, D.G. "Electromagnetic Oven System for Automatically
   Heating Variable Numbers and Sizes of Food Items or the
   Like", U.S. Patent No. 3,854,022 (1974)
6. Stevenson, P.N. "Selective Cooking Apparatus", U.S. Patent
   No. 3,615,713 (1971)
7. Stevenson, P.N., "Container and Food Heating Method", U.S.
   Patent No. 3,547,661 (1979)
8. Smith, D.P. and Harris, H. H. "Factors in Design and Construction of a Device for Heating and Dispensing Food Components" *Technical Report 75-41-FL*, U.S. Army Natick R & D
   Command, Natick, Massachusetts (1974)
9. Smith, D.P. "Cooking Apparatus", U.S. Patent No. 3,884,213
   (1975)
10. Nykvist, W.E. and Decareau, R.V. *J. of Microwave Power 11*,
    (1) 3 (1976)

CHAPTER 17

THE ROLE OF HUMAN ENGINEERING
IN FOOD SERVICE SYSTEMS DESIGN

Lawrence E. Symington

Behavioral Sciences Division
Food Sciences Laboratory
US Army Natick Research and Development Command
Natick, Massachusetts

The field of human factors engineering is concerned with
two major human system components: those who are involved
in operating the system and those who are recipients of the
system's output. In food service systems, the main focus of
concern is the food service worker with secondary attention
being paid to the customer. The human engineer is typically
a psychologist and/or an engineer who applies psychological,
engineering, and other principles to characterize the role of
the human in the system. The human engineer is specifically
concerned with those aspects in the design that will ensure
the system conforms to the capabilities of the human who is
expected to be part of it. Environmental conditions (e.g.,
optimum temperature and noise levels), workspace layout
(e.g., enough space for workers not to interfere with each
other), the design of specific pieces of equipment (e.g.,
height of work surface or clarity of display gauges), safety,
and training are all considered in terms of fitting the human
and nonhuman parts of a given system together.

Table I presents a human factors checklist that was used
to compare three alternative military field feeding concepts.
The list was used by a human factors specialist in an operational evalution of field kitchens at a military camp. Note
that all the areas of coverage cited above appear in this
checklist, with the exception of training, which is implicit
in many of the checkpoints. While this particular checklist
concerns itself with many problems that are specific to
military field feeding, it is not difficult to draw similar
guidelines for human factors evaluation of nonmilitary,

301

Copyright © 1979 by Academic Press, Inc.
All rights of reproduction in any form reserved
ISBN: 0-12-453150-4

TABLE I. *Human Factors Checklist for Three Military Field Kitchens*

Human factors/safety checkpoints

---

1. Environmental conditions
   a. Lighting
   b. Temperature
   c. Humidity
   d. Noise
   e. Effects of rain, snow, or wind

2. Workspace dimensions/layout (to accommodate 5th to 95th percentile of users)
   a. Arm reach
   b. Height of equipment
   c. Clearances for whole body, head, limbs, etc.
      1) In equipment operation
      2) In entry and exit
      3) In moving around kitchen
      4) In relation to other operators
   d. Visual functions
   e. Work flow (e.g., workspace elements arranged in anticipated sequence of operation, etc.)
   f. Customer flow

3. Physiological factors
   a. Poor postural control in operations
   b. Fatigue inducing activity

4. Specific equipment design (ranges, burners, grills, coffee makers, etc.)
   a. Displays (gauges, indicators, etc.)
   b. Controls
   c. Ease of operation
   d. Safety

5. Storage space
   a. Organization of storage area (ease of storage and removal
   b. Reach distance to storage area
   c. Lighting
   d. Safety

---

institutional or commercial food service operations. The
following examples should serve to illustrate the potential
of the human factors engineering for contribution to food
service system design in both the military and the civilian
sectors.

I. ENVIRONMENTAL CONSIDERATIONS

Two environmental factors that can affect food service
operation are lighting (illumination) and temperature.
Unless illumination reaches certain minimum levels, performance in tasks will deteriorate. Some tasks require more
illumination than others. Slicing vegetables, for example
requires less illumination than reading the small numerals on
a meat thermometer. Table II provides illumination figures
for general types of tasks. Note that 2 figures are given:
a recommended level and a minimum level. The most efficient
work performance is possible at the recommended levels, while
serious performance decreases can occur below the minimum.

*TABLE II. Representative Illumination Requirements for
Specific Tasks*

| *Type of task or work area* | *Footcandles[1] (lux)* | |
	Recommended	*Minimum*
Corridors or halls	*20 (215)*	*10 (110)*
Stairways	*20 (215)*	*10 (110)*
Rough bench or table work	*50 (540)*	*30 (325)*
Reading small print	*70 (755)*	*50 (540)*

[1]*As measured at the task object or 30 inches (760 mm)
above the floor.*

The main environmental problem in food service is the high temperature generally encountered in food preparation areas. It can be a particulary acute problem in military field feeding, since cooling systems are not available. As it concerns work efficiency, temperature means more than just the reading obtained by using an ordinary thermometer, which measures only dry bulb temperature. Anyone who has experienced both dry and humid, hot climates knows that the same dry bulb temperature feels hotter in a wet climate, and kitchens tend to have a wet climate environment because of the moisture that results from food preparation. For this reason, human factors specialists use an index called effective temperature which combines the total effects of temperature, humidity, and air movement with the heat or cold a human feels into a single value. This effective temperature (ET) is measured by obtaining dry bulb and wet bulb temperatures (the latter with a moist wick surrounding a thermometer bulb), and represents the numerical value of still, saturated air that would produce the same feeling. Table III illustrates how ET changes at a given dry bulb temperature as wet bulb temperatures change. The rule of thumb for extended periods of work is that the ET be maintained at, or below, 85°F (29°C).

In practice, particularly in military field feeding, temperatures may exceed this limit. When they do, not only worker performance, but worker health is also threatened. At 90°ET, for example, workers should limit their exposure to 4 hours, at 95°ET to 2 hours, at 100°ET to 1 hour, and at 103°ET to 1/2 hour.

TABLE III. *Approximate Effective Temperatures at Selected Dry and Wet Bulb Readings*[1]

Wet bulb temperature (°F)	Dry bulb temperature (°F)			
	70	80	90	100
60	66.5	71.5	75.5	79
70	70	75	79	82.5
80	–	80	84	86.5
90	–	–	90	92.5

[1]*Temperatures are of air velocities from 0-30 ft/min.*

II. WORKSPACE

The design of the workspace itself (i.e., where the oven should be in relation to the deep fat fryer or the sink) is an extremely critical factor in terms of the effect on system performance as well as on human efficiency and safety. Several questions should be considered when designing a work area such as a kitchen.

A. What must an operator (a cook in this instance) be able to see, other than his own equipment, to perform his task efficiently and safely? This might include other food service personnel, equipment such as clocks or order slips.

B. What must the cook hear? Does he need to communicate with any specific fellow workers, or hear customer orders either from the customer or waiter?

C. What does the cook need to reach or manipulate other than at his work station (i.e., stored pots or pans, ingredients)?

D. How much clearance should there be for the body, head, and arms in moving around the kitchen, or in relationship with other food service workers? (Are two cooks so close together that they interfere with each other? Is there adequate space for one worker to pass by another if such passage is required?)

E. How should work stations and individual pieces or groups of equipment be arranged to provide a logical work sequence for an individual operator (i.e., the vegetable cutting board next to the sink)? How can one provide the minimal amount of interference among workers? For example, if workers A and B work together 50% of the time, and worker C always by himself, worker C's position should not be between A and B.

Clearly, there are going to be some physical situations that constrain the designer's ability to place equipment optimally from the worker's point of view. The galley in a submarine, for example, out of necessity is going to be far smaller than the kitchen in a base dining hall or a commercial restaurant. Furthermore, the smaller the overall space, the more critical it becomes that interworker interference be minimal, and work sequences well thought out. Incidentally, the cost of too much space can be almost as high as too little. Consider the time wasted in walking 200 feet to a vegetable refrigerator or sink instead of 25 feet!

There are several design tools available to assist the
human factors engineer in recommending workspace arrangements.
Certainly, consideration of the architect's drawings or blue-
prints is helpful. More helpful are reduced scale models,
reduced scale mockups, or even full scale mockups [1]. A
full scale mockup constructed of scrap wood and cardboard can
be very effective in revealing potential clearance hazards as
well as awkward operating positions or reach problems. Sometimes a mockup of only the most complex section of the work
area will be sufficient. A final tool, link analysis, delin-
eates all connections between man and man, or man and machine
in the system and leads to a diagram where the number of
"crossings" of such links are minimized for the most effective and orderly operation.

In the discussion of workspace arrangement, integral factor is that of the size and shape of the human operator.
Antropometry is the science which deals with the measurement
of physical features of both the static and dynamic body. It
provides information about such factors as height, weight,
and arm reach, which are useful in workspace design and in
operator-equipment dynamics, aspects which will be discussed
below. Current anthropometric tables are published in many
handbooks [2,3].

A common error of system developers is designing for the
average (50th percentile) operator. Suppose, for example,
clearance is designed between two stoves to accommodate this
theoretical average man, and the actual cooks happen to have
a breadth which approaches the 90th percentile. Obviously,
the potential for a congestion problem becomes quite high,
not to mention the potential burn hazard! The solution to
this problem is to design for the 5th to the 95th percentile
operators using the relevant extreme in any particular case.
For example, the height of the top shelf in a storage space
should be just within the reach of the 5th percentile operator, and the ceiling height in a kitchen should be high
enough for the 95th percentile operator to have sufficient
head clearance. A design error that is often made in this
respect is making a ceiling just high enough for clearance,
and then placing a light fixture that drops down 2 or 3
inches from the ceiling, directly above the main traffic
lane.

III.   OPERATOR-EQUIPMENT DYNAMICS

The relationship between the operator and his equipment
has many facets ranging from ideal heights and reach distances to the number of operations on the equipment the operator can adequately handle in a given time span. A few
examples will serve to illustrate human factors considerations
for equipment in a food service operation.

Much of the work performed by a food service employee is
carried out on some sort of flat surface with the operator in
a standing position. Since the operator is likely to be
standing for relatively long periods of time at such a work
surface, it is extremely important that it be the ideal
height (36" plus or minus 0.5"). This allows for appropriate
precision of work and induces minimal postural fatigue.

A piece of equipment may be at perfect height and reach
distance and lead to still other problems. An example is a
self-service milk dispenser that is bolted to the floor, with
one inch of space under the body of the machine. The potential for spillage is high, but sanitary cleaning under such a
device is hardly convenient. Designing the unit to be moved
easily or allowing 4-6 inches of space beneath it for mop
access would facilitate adequate sanitation.

Pot wash sinks present some unique problems in terms of
working height. The lip of the sink must be low enough to
allow the worker to work comfortably, but high enough so that
the water level, where the washing actually takes place is
high enough to allow effective washing operations and to prevent water spillage. The current military field feeding
system has an even more serious problem in this respect since
the "sink" is a 32 gallon can with an immersion heater occu-
pying some of the workspace.

IV.   SAFETY

Safety is an area that cuts across all aspects of human
factors since optimal design is synonymous with safe design.
An excessively high environmental temperature is unsafe, as
is a low hanging ceiling light fixture, and a cooking range
that is too high for the operator to reach with ease.

A few scattered examples can illustrate some safety
problems in food service operations which are of concern to a
human engineer.

Many older ranges were designed with controls located on a raised section mounted at the rear of the cooking surface. To light or adjust the burners, a cook had to reach across the burners--a particularly hazardous maneuver with a gas range. Newer designs place controls on the operator side of the range.

Tripping can be reasonbly common, particularly where a worker carries large cooking pots or sheet pans that interfere with the ability to see the floor. Rubber floor mats placed in a traffic area should be ramped at either end to prevent this kind of hazard, and care should be taken to keep cords and other floor level impediments away from traffic areas. Any change in the floor level in a work area necessitates stairs or a ramp, and should be avoided if possible. If dual levels are necessary, care should be taken to make the ramp or stairs as safe as possible. In developing a military field kitchen trailer, for example, great attention was paid to the tread depth and riser height of the stairs leading to the ground level from the trailer. The top stair, however, was approximately 2/3 as high as the other three, and cooks and customers descending from the trailer made several dangerous missteps because of this height change.

The potential burn hazard from a griddle or grill is another example of a safety hazard. Most are therefore equipped with spatter guards to protect the cooks, and the customers also, if the grill is on a serving line. Another potential hazard for the cook is the heat from the griddle itself, heat which is directed mainly toward the cook's groin area. In one experimental field griddle, recently tested in the military, groin level temperatures reached as high as 165°F. Relatively simple additions of a heat shield and side vent pipes reduced these temperatures to a far more comfortable, and safer, maximum of 93°F.

V. TRAINING AND JOB SATISFACTION

Two areas which human engineers also consider in the evaluation of systems are training and job satisfaction. A well trained worker theoretically increases the efficiency of a system. In the food service area, how much training should be classroom type and how much should be "hands on"? What performance measures are used to assess the effects of training? Does training in a laboratory with small scale cooking equipment transfer to equipment used in large quantity feeding operations? All of these questions are relevant to food service training, and are within the domain of the human factors engineer in evaluating a food service system. Needless to say, a satisfied, motivated food service worker is as important to the success of a food service system as raw food quality, modern equipment, and an environmentally ideal designed facility [4].

VI. THE CUSTOMER

The second group of humans involved in food service systems is the customer. Much of what has been stated concerning environment, layout, interaction with equipment, including tables and chairs, and safety, is relevant to the design of the customer side of a food service facility. As a matter of fact, a human factors design related problem, speed or service or waiting in line for meals, was rated either as the worst or the second worst problem for customers in various military food service facilities studied [5,6]. Decor, another part of the customer environment, has been shown to play a large role in customer acceptance of dining facilities.

VII. METHODS

Beyond the specific methodological tools for human engineers already mentioned, the typical *modus operandi* of the human factors engineer is the careful study of plans and/ or the observation of existing systems, and the application of human factors handbooks [2,3]. In addition, a tool that has been extremely successful is the use of surveys and interviews of both customers and food service workers [7,8]. This technique has proved very useful in channeling more traditional human factors in environmental design efforts.

REFERENCES

1. Seminara, J. L. and Tevis, J. M., Mockups: Plain and
    fancy. Machine Design, 20, June, 1973.
2. Van Cott, H. P. and Kinkade, R. G., eds. "Human
    engineering guide to equipment design" (revised edition).
    U.S. Government Printing Office, Washington, D.C., 1972.
3. Anonymous, U.S. Army Missile Command. "Military stan-
    dard: Human engineering design criterial for military
    systems, equipment and facilities." MIL-STD-1472B,
    1974.
4. Symington, L. E. and Meiselman, H. L. "The food service
    worker and the Travis Air Force Base experimental food
    system: Worker opinion and job satisfaction." United
    States Army Natick Development Center Technical Report
    75-94-FSL, Natick, Mass., 1975.
5. Branch, L. G., Symington, L. E., and Meiselman, H. L.
    "The consumer's opinions of the food service system:
    The 1973 Minot Air Force Base survey." United States
    Army Natick Laboratories Technical Report 74-7-PR,
    Natick, Mass., 1973.
6. Branch, L. G., Waterman, D., Symington, L. E., and
    Meiselman, H. L. "The consumer's opinions of the food
    service system: The 1973 Fort Lee Survey." United
    States Army Natick Laboratories Technical Report 74-49-
    PR, Natick, Mass., 1974.
7. Symington, L. E. and Meiselman, H. L., "Human factors and
    environmental design in military food service facilities:
    A survey approach." Proceedings of the Eighteenth Annual
    Meeting of the Human Factors Society, Human Factors
    Society, Santa Monica, California, pp. 135-137, October,
    1974.
8. Meiselman, H. L., Symington, L. E., Smutz, E. R.,
    Moskowitz, H. R., Nichols, T. L., and Eggemeier, T.,
    "Field feeding: Behavioral sciences studies." United
    States Army Natick Development Center Technical Report
    76-3-FSL, Natick, Mass., 1975.

CHAPTER 18

ANALYSIS OF ALTERNATIVES IN USING DISPOSABLES VERSUS
REUSABLES

Frank D. Borsenik

College of Hotel Administration
University of Nevada, Las Vegas
Las Vegas, Nevada

I. INTRODUCTION

Warewashing has been treated as a necessary evil in the food service industry. It is something that must be done. This assumption does little to encourage study in this area. In fact, most food service establishments do not know how much it costs them to accomplish this fundamental task.

When one considers the magnitude of the basic task of warewashing, the figures are staggering. For example, in 1976, using a conservative estimate, about 20,500 persons made their living each day throughout the year in warewashing and its related activities. Thus, 164,000 man hours of work each day of the year were spent in this apparently menial task. Yet, with all of the scientific tools and methods of analysis available, very little research has been devoted to this labor intensive task. One hears from management that the cost for this task is high. Management is oblivious to the plight of the food service worker for whom this task continues every hour of the day for 365 days each year. Based on an hourly wage of $ 3.00 (since increased), and taking into account the other related costs involved in warewashing, one has a very conservative 1979 estimate of $ 1,000,000 per day for this task. Yet the industry continues to operate as it has in the past, with little relief in sight.

Copyright © 1979 by Academic Press, Inc.
All rights of reproduction in any form reserved
ISBN: 0-12-453150-4

II. DESIGNING A COST MODEL

The purpose of this chapter is to establish a model, or format, that can be used to analyze the cost of investing. Once the manager or consultant can establish how much this task is costing now, he can move forward to a system that could provide a lower cost and increase the profitability of the unit.

Food service subsystems for warewashing and disposables can be illustrated by diagrams. Figure 1 shows a cyclic system for warewashing. Figure 2 shows an alternative system for disposable eating utensils. The basic systems involved are very simple. Fundamentally, Figures 1 and 2 are accurate for a general situation but, to compound the problem, there are different types of food service. Each of these different types of food service will generate a new system, or subsystem that makes the problem more complex. Some examples of the complex issue posed by differing types of food service are shown in Figure 3.

Using Figures 1 and 2 as references, one can see from Figure 3 that at least one alternative could be eliminated at this point. No operator would yet consider the use of disposables for intensive table service (French service). It simply would not be appropriate. On the other hand, many operators would not consider the use of dishes for fast food service. They frequently assume that only disposables can be used. Many operators, however, are already using combinations of disposables and washable eating utensils. They believe that they are saving money, but rarely base their decision on a serious analysis.

Additional subsystems are generated when one reviews the table cleaning function. Figure 4 lists a number of typical methods used for table clearing. The systems become more complex as one reviews the warewashing function, as various alternatives are available for this task (Fig. 5). Finally, the storage of clean utensils present additional alternatives, including a manual system, the use of dish carts, or conveyor systems.

Based on the number of alternatives identified, the analyst is now faced with a minimum of 189 alternative subsystems available for each type of food service unit. Needless to say,

$$Purchase \longrightarrow Storage \longrightarrow Use$$
$$\downarrow \qquad\qquad \downarrow$$
$$Disposal \longleftarrow Warewashing \longleftarrow Cleaning\ Tables$$

FIGURE 1.   Warewashing System

it becomes a nearly impossible task to consider all alternatives in a reasonable period of time. The problem could be
handled by a computer, if all the required input data were
known and available. Compounding the 189 alternatives are the
costs of each of the subsystems, which will vary with different
manufacturers of system components, utility rates, availability
of utilities and maintenance and repair policies, and these represent only a small sampling of variables.

Purchase ⟶ *Storage* ⟶ *Use*

Disposal ⟵ *Clearing Tables*

FIGURE 2. *Disposable System*

Table Service

1) *Intensive*

2) *Moderate*

3) *Minimal*

Cafeteria

Fast Food

FIGURE 3. *Examples of Types of Service*

Manual
Small Trays
Large Trays
Bus Pans
Bus Carts
Conveyors
Self Bussing

FIGURE 4. *Current Techniques Available For Clearing Tables*

Manual
Warewashing Machines
        Door
        Conveyor - Two Tank
        Conveyor - Three Tank
        Flight
        Carousel I*
        Carousel II*
        Carousel III*
        Ultrasonic

  *Types I, II and III have different rack capacities
  per hour

FIGURE 5.   Current Available Alternatives For Warewashing.

III. ANALYZING ALTERNATIVES

Figure 6 indicates a possible system based on the use of disposables, while Figure 7 shows general examples of alternatives for the warewashing cycle. It should be noted that even the disposable system will involve some type of warewashing system because of cooking pots and pans, which are not generally disposable at this time. Also, the serving trays used in many units require washing.

The selection of the best alternative is often based on the cost of the system. However, cost is not the only variable. Some others are frequently evaluated and it may be desirable to optimize one or more of them. Some other factors of importance are: convenience; sanitation; uniform products; ease of storage; storage life; employee training; ease of waste disposal. Optimizing one or more of these factors could lead to the selection of different alternatives. Regardless of the variable to be optimized, cost is frequently a critical factor in selecting one system over another. Because cost is such an important factor, and often the only factor that is considered, the remainder of this chapter is devoted to its analysis.

Purchase   Store At   Products   Self
Paper & ──→ Point of ──→ Packaged ──→ Bussing─→ Disposal
Plastic   Use

FIGURE 6.   Disposable System

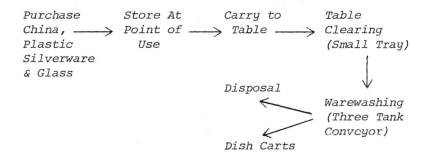

FIGURE 7. Warewashing System

IV. ANALYSIS OF A COST MODEL

A. Cost Graphs

Prior to the actual development and analysis of a cost model, several simple, yet revealing, total system cost graphs should be reviewed. These graphs will reflect some basic economic principles that one should not overlook when analyzing systems.

Figure 8, which relates income to costs in a total disposable system, indicates a low cost investment with a high variable cost, as one would expect to find in the case of a system based on disposable ware.

Figure 9, which relates income to costs in warewashing systems, indicates that there are three major points of interest. Point a_2 (Fig. 9) is much farther to the right than Point a_1 (Fig. 8), indicating that Warewashing System A should be considered when there is a sufficient volume (i.e. number covers). When the volume is between a_1 and a_2 the disposable alternative is more worthwhile than Warewashing System A. As one proceeds to the right of the graph, with more covers, there comes a point when Warewashing System A becomes less costly than the disposable alternatives. Warewashing System A should only be considered when the number of covers is to the right of point b, but only up to point c, where the total cost curves of warewashing systems A and B cross. Point c represents the economic breakeven point between alternatives A and B. This graph illustrates the fact that it becomes very difficult to look at limited amounts of data and analyze what should be done. Future activities must be investigated and one must look at the long range picture.

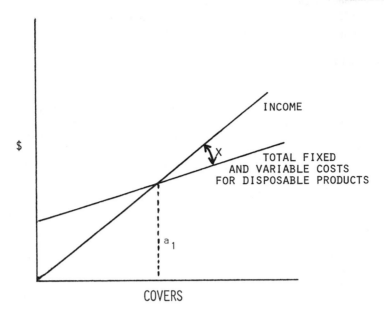

FIGURE 8. Total disposable system costs versus income. Point a_1 shows that at a relatively low number of covers the system becomes economical. The x area indicates the relative profitable area when using this system.

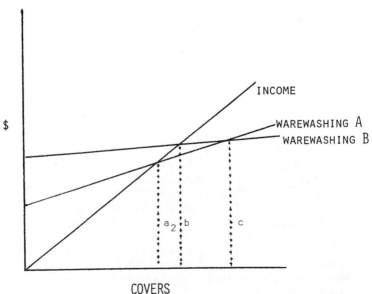

FIGURE 9. Total warewashing costs for two alternatives A and B.

B. *Variable Costs*

Generally, as fixed costs increase, variable costs decrease. In each of the cases described above, a high fixed cost was associated with a low variable cost. While the use of disposable products results in a very low fixed cost, the variable cost associated with each cover is usually very high. The same may apply to warewashing systems where the variable cost is frequently lower when one invests more money for more efficient equipment. Some concrete examples will be given to illustrate this relationship.

C. *Identifying and Quantitating Cost Factors*

The various cost factors which must be included, in analyzing alternatives are: purchasing products (flatware, cups, silverware, etc.); clearing tables; warewashing; disposal; storing clean tableware.

1. *Product Costs.* The purchasing of products include various items such as the cost of placing the order and receiving the goods, the cost of the products prorated over the life of the products, taxes, such as property taxes, insurance costs, interest on investment, space charges for storaging the products. These may be shown as:

$$PC = PP/EL + T_p + I_{1p} + I_{2p} + S_p$$

Where:
PC = *product cost*
PP = *purchase price, including the cost of placing orders and receiving the products*
T_p = *taxes on the products*
EL = *estimated life*
I_{1p} = *insurance cost for the products*
I_{2p} = *interest on the investment in the products*
S_p = *space charge, or rental charge for floor space*

a. *Purchase costs.* Naturally product cost varies with the type of service and the atmosphere one wishes to create in the unit. The cost per setting for reusable products could vary from $ 5 to $ 80. The cost for disposable papers and plastics could vary from $ 0.05 to $ 0.50, depending on the type of facility, quality of disposables, and the number of disposables used in serving or packaging the items.

b. Product life. The estimated life for disposables is one, i.e. a life of one use. The average life of reusable products varies from 2 to 5 years.

c. Taxes, insurance and interest. Taxes, insurance, and interest are all functions of the purchase price or market value of the products. Taxes may vary from two to ten per cent of the market value. Insurance will usually cost one or two per cent of the market value. Interest could vary from six to twelve per cent. Some analysts will use the average interest method to determine interest cost. This method is shown below:

$$I_{2p} = r \ (PP + S)/2$$

Where:

I_{2p} = *interest on investment*

r = *rate of return/or current interest rate*

PP = *purchase price*

S = *salvage value*

d. Space charge. The space charge is usually considered as the cost of renting comparable space in the local area. The current rental rates are between $ 5 and $ 15 per square foot per year.

2. Cost of Clearing Tables. The second cost factor is the cost of clearing tables. Included in this cost is the labor cost for clearing tables, labor cost for clearing tables, labor supervision costs, equipment and supply cost, and floor space costs. These are shown as:

$$TC = L + LS + ES + S_p$$

Where:

TC = *table clearing costs*

L = *labor costs*

LS = *labor supervision cost*

ES = equipment and supply costs

S_p = space charge

a. *Space charge.* The space charge varies as indicated a-
bove and may appear to be a duplication of the above costs
(purchase cost). If in fact it is, it should be counted as zero.

b. *Labor equipment and supply costs.* Labor, equipment and
supply costs are shown in Table T. Labor supervision costs
would include the cost of supervision, fringe benefits, and
employee training. Supervision and fringe benefits could be
assumed at 25 per cent of the labor cost in the food service
industry. The cost of training has been estimated at $ 500 per
employee. Some studies have shown that employee turnover could
be very high in this area, as much as 1,200 per cent per year
(i.e. one employee hired each month for each available position). Payroll records would indicate how significant this
factor is in any particular operation.

3. *Warewashing Costs.* The most complex cost factor is the
warewashing cost. Some typical cost considerations in warewashing include: labor, fringe benefits, supervision, and employee
turnover; equipment cost, including initial cost and installation; taxes, repairs maintenance and insurance; operating cost,
including water, heat and detergents; floor space charges;
breakage; rejections. These can be shown by the following relationship:

$$WC = L + LS + E/EL + E_m + OP + S_w + B + R$$

Where:

WC = warewashing costs

L = labor costs

LS = labor supervision costs

E = equipment, initial and installation costs

EL = expected life of equipment

E_m = equipment costs of taxes, insurance, repairs
        and maintenance

TABLE I. Man-Hours and Equipment Costs Per 1,000
          Washable Pieces for Table Clearing Tasks (1)

		Type of Service		
Equipment	Intensive	Moderate	Minimal	Cafeteria
Small Trays (Conveyor Rack, Flight & Door)				
Man-Hours	2.14	1.65	1.22	1.56
Equipment	$ 0.01	$ 0.01	$ 0.01	$ 0.01
Small Trays (Carousel)				
Man-Hours	2.02	1.53	1.11	1.45
Equipment	$ 0.02	$ 0.02	$ 0.02	$ 0.02
Large Trays				
Man-Hours	1.63	1.19	0.99	-
Equipment	$ 0.02	$ 0.02	$ 0.02	-
Bus Pans				
Man-Hours	2.27	1.58	1.06	1.15
Equipment	$ 0.06	$ 0.06	$ 0.06	$ 0.06
Bus Carts				
Man-Hours	1.74	1.21	1.01	1.07
Equipment	$ 0.30	$ 0.30	$ 0.30	$ 0.30
Self Bussing				
Man-Hours	-	-	-	0.06
Equipment	-	-	-	$ 0.17

> OP = operating costs of equipment including water, heat, and detergents
>
> S_w = space charge for warewashing
>
> B = breakage of dishes
>
> R = rejection rates of washed items

a. *Labor, equipment and operating costs.* Standard labor times for mechanical warewashing systems are Shown in Table II. Labor supervision costs are the same as those indicated above. The equipment cost per year is the difference of the initial and salvage values divided by the estimated life, which is usually estimated to be 10 years for mechanical warewashing equipment. The taxes and insurance would follow the same percentages as those given above, while repairs and maintenance could vary between 10 and 25 per cent of the initial cost per year. The operating cost can be taken from manufacturers' data. Some typical data are shown in Table II for various types of equipment. Space charges would be as indicated above. Typical breakage costs vary from five to twenty per cent of the inventory of dishes. Typical rejection rates are: flatware—three per cent; cups—two per cent; glasses—six per cent; silverware—nine per cent. An average of five percent could be assumed for most operations.

b. *Disposal costs.* Disposal costs vary greatly from one region to another. These costs usually include a sewage charge, if a garbage disposal is used; incineration costs if applicable, and garbage collection costs. These costs have not generally been quantified. Very limited data indicates that these costs can vary from one quarter to two per cent of the gross sales of the unit. The higher percentage is for units with complete disposables for food service.

c. *Clean tableware storage costs.* The final cost factors are those associated with storing clean tableware. In a unit with disposable table service this cost would be minimal. In other units the total costs will be a function of labor, supervision, equipment and floor space. The total cost is:

$$SCT = L + LS + E + S_p$$

TABLE II. *Man-Hours and Equipment Operating Costs Per 1,000 Washable Pieces for Warewashing (1)*

Warewashing	Service*	Man-Hours	Equipment Operating Costs
Conveyor-Rack	R	1.02	$ 0.47
(2 Tank)	C	1.20	0.47
Conveyor-Rack	R	0.96	0.51
(3 Tank)	C	1.13	0.51
Flight	R	0.88	0.42
	C	1.06	0.42
Door	R	1.41	0.52
	C	1.81	0.52
Carousel I	R	0.85	0.55
	C	0.98	0.55
Carousel II	R	0.85	0.55
	C	0.98	0.55
Carousel III	R	0.85	0.55
	C	0.98	0.55

*R = restaurant table service/counter service
C = cafeteria service

where:

SCT   = *cost for storing clean tableware*

L   = *labor costs*

LS   = *labor supervision costs*

E   = *equipment cost*

S_p = *space charge*

Once again the space charge may be a duplication of previous charges and, if in fact it is, its cost in this relationship would be zero. The standard man hours are indicated in Table III. Labor supervision costs are the same as those indicated above. The equipment cost would be similar to those discussed above.

4. Complete Cost Model. The complete cost model may be represented as:

Total cost = *PC + TC + WC + D + SCT*

where:

PC   = *product cost*

TC   = *table clearing cost*

WC   = *warewashing cost*

D   = *disposal cost*

SCT   = *storing clean tableware cost*

Two examples will be shown, which should indicate the use of the above model. One example will use disposable products and the second complete reusable tableware, including linens for the table. Tray service customer bussing will be assumed, as the only fair comparison between disposables and reusable flatware would probably be for a cafeteria type service. Other data will be indicated in the examples.

(1) Food Service Data:

    Annual sales: *$ 500,000*
    Average check   *$ 2.00*
    Annual covers: *250,000*

TABLE III. Man-Hours and Equipment Costs Per 1,000
Washable Pieces for Storing Clean
Tableware (1)

	Dish Carts	Manual
Man-Hours	0.16	0.48
Equipment	$ 0.95	$ 0.30

Covers per day: 685
Service: cafeteria (self bussing)
Small trays will be used for bussing by both the
  customers and employees
There are 10 units of flatware, silverware, cups,
  glasses, etc, per cover

A door type dishwasher will be used with disposable
  products and a flight type dishwasher will be used
  with reusable dishes.

(2) Dish data:

$ 15.00 per place setting
Life of dishes: 2½ years
Dish inventory: 2½ times number of seats
Space requirements for dishes: 40 square feet

(3) Disposable data:

$ 0.20 per cover
two week inventory required
Space requirement: 40 square feet
Tray cost: $ 2.00 per tray, 3 year life

(4) Taxes: 5 % of market value for dishes and disposables

(5) Interest: 9 %

(6) Insurance: 1 %

(7) Space Charge: $ 10.00 per square foot per year

(8) Salvage value of dishes: $ 0

(9) Labor cost: $ 2.50 per hour

(10) Fringe benefits and supervision: 25 % of labor cost

(11) Labor turnover: $ 500   per   employee   with   an   employee
turnover rate of 200 % (two employees are hired   for
each position per year.)
If the   employee is   paid for 2,000   hours per year,
the   annual wage is $ 5,000   and labor turnover   is
$ 1,000 per year, hence,   labor turnover is 20 %   of
labor   costs   per   year ($ 1,000/ $ 5,000).   Total
labor overhead is: 25 % + 20 % = 45 %

(12) Equipment costs:

(a) Door type dishwasher: $ 3,000*
(b) Flight type dishwasher: $ 10,000*
*includes installation costs
(c) 20 % salvage value
(d) Expected life: 10 years
(e) Taxes: 2 % of initial cost
(f) Insurance: 1 %
(g) Repairs and maintenance: 15 % of initial cost
(h) Space requirements:
Door machine: 150 square feet
Flight machine: 400 square feet
Breakage: 10 % of dish inventory per year
Rejection rate: 5 % of items washed per cycle

(13) Disposable costs:

With disposables: 1 % of gross sales
With dishes: ¼ % of gross sales

(14) Linen costs:

(a) Commercial laundry: $ 0.08 per pound
(b) Napkins:
¼ pound each
1 per cover
Life: 100 washes
(c) Table covers:
2 pounds each
Changed each day
Life: 250 washes
(d) Napkin cost: $ 0.50
(e) Table cover cost: $ 5.00

(15) Seats in food service unit: 100

(16) Disposable Systems costs:

    (a) Product cost
       (i) Purchase price of 2 week inventory
          685 covers X 14 days X $ 0.20 = $ 1,918
          Total product cost per year:
          250,000 covers X $ 0.20 = $ 50,000
     (ii) Estimated life: one use or cover
    (iii) Taxes: (there is an average of 7 days in
         inventory)
         $ 1,918/2 X 0.05 = $ 48
    (iv) Insurance: (there is an average of 7 days in
         inventory)
         $ 1,918/2 X 0.01 = $ 10
      (v) Interest on investment
         0.09 X ($ 1,918 + $ 0)/2 = $ 86
     (vi) Space charge
         $ 10 (per square foot) X 40 (square feet = $ 400
    (vii) Total product cost: $ 50,544

    (b) Cost of clearing tables
       (i) Labor cost: (refer to Table I)
         0.06 man hours per 1000 units
         Units per day: 10 (per cover) X 685
           (covers per day) = 6850
         0.06/1,000 X 6850 X 365 (days per year)
           = 150 man hours per year
         150 X $ 2.50 = $ 375
     (ii) Supervision:
         $ 375 X 0.45 = $ 169
    (iii) Equipment and supply cost (see Table I)
         $ 0.17/1,000 X 250,000 = $ 43
    (iv) Space charges: ($ 0 as this has been taken
         into account with the previous computation)
      (v) Total costs: $ 587

    (c) Warewashing cost
      Only trays must be washed.   Pots and pans cost
      would be similar for both operations.
        685 trays are washed each day
      (i) Labor cost (see Table II)
         1.81 man hours per 1000 items
         1.81/1,000 X 685 X 365 = 453 man hours per
          year
         453 X $ 2.50 = $1,133 per year
     (ii) Supervision
         $ 1,133 X 0.45 = $510

(c) *Warewashing cost (continued)*
  (iii) *Equipment annual cost*
         ($ 3,000 - 0.2 X $ 3,000)/10 = $ 240
  (iv) *Equipment costs (taxes, insurance, etc)*
         a. *Taxes:* 0.02 X $ 3,000 = $ 60
         b. *Insurance:* 0.01 X $3,000 = $ 30
         c. *Repairs and maintenance:* 0.15 X $ 3,000
            = $ 450
         d. *Total:* $ 540
  (v) *Operating costs (see Table II)*
         $ 0.52/1,000 X 685 X 365 = $ 130
  (vi) *Space charge*
         150 (square feet) X $ 10 (per square foot)
            = $ 1,500
  (vii) *Breakage*
         10 % of tray inventory
         250 trays in inventory
         Cost of inventory: $ 2 X 250 = $ 500
         Cost: 0.10 X $ 500 = $ 50
  (viii) *Rejection cost*
         This implies that 5 % more items will be
         washed which in effect increases the vari-
         able cost of warewashing by 5 %
         0.05 X $(1,133 + 510 + 130 + 50) = $ 91
  (ix) *Total Costs:* $ 4,194

(d) *Disposal costs*
   0.01 X $ 500,000 = $ 5,000

(e) *Storing clean tableware (trays only)*
   (i) *Labor (see Table III)*
         0.48/1,000 X 685 X 365 = 120 man hours for
            the manual operation
         120 X $ 2.50 = $ 300
   (ii) *Supervision*
         0.45 X $ 300 = $ 135
   (iii) *Equipment cost ($ 0)*
   (iv) *Space charge ($ 0)*
   (v) *Total:* $ 435

(f) *Total costs:*
      $ 60,760 per year or $ 0.24 per cover

(17) *Warewashing system cost with dishes:*

(a) *Product cost*
      (i) *Purchase price of 250 sets of place settings*
         250 X $ 15 = $ 3,750

(a) Product cost (continued)
      (ii) Estimated life
          2½ years
          Cost: $ 3,750/2.5 = $1,500 per year
    (iii) Taxes
          0.05 X $ 3,750 = $ 188
     (iv) Insurance
          0.01 X $ 3,750 = $ 38
      (v) Interest
          0.09 X ($ 3,750 + $ 0)/2 = $ 169
     (vi) Space charge
          $ 10 X 40 = $ 400
    (vii) Total cost: $ 2,295

(b) Cost of clearing tables
     (i) Labor cost (see Table I)
          0.06/1,000 X 6,850 X 365 = 150 man hours
          150 X $ 2.50 = $ 375
     (ii) Supervision
          0.45 X $ 375 = $ 169
    (iii) Equipment and supply costs (see Table I)
          $ 0.17/1,000 X 250,000 = $ 43
     (iv) Space charge ($ 0 as it has been taken into
          account in previous computations)
      (v) Total cost: $ 587

(c) Warewashing costs
    6,850 items per day
     (i) Labor (see Table II)
          1.06/1,000 X 6,850 X 365 = 2,650 man hours
          2,650 X 2.50 = $ 6,625
     (ii) Supervision
          0.45 X $ 6,625 = $ 2,981
    (iii) Equipment annual cost
          ($ 10,000 - 0.2 X $ 10,000)/10 = $ 800
     (iv) Equipment costs (taxes, insurance, etc)
          (aa) Taxes: 0.02 X $ 10,000 = $ 200
          (bb) Insurance: 0.01 X $ 10,000 = $ 100
          (cc) Repairs and maintenance: 0.15 X
             $ 10,000 = $ 1,500
          (dd) Total: $ 2,600
      (v) Operating costs (see Table II)
          $ 0.42/1,000 X 6,850 X 365 = $ 1,050
     (vi) Space Charge
          400 X $ 10 = $ 4,000
    (vii) Breakage
          10 % of inventory
          0.10 X $ 3,750 = $ 375

(c) *Warewashing costs (continued)*
    (viii) *Rejection*
        0.05 X $(6,625 + 2,981 + 1,050 + 375 =
        $ 552
    (ix) *Total costs:* $ 18,983

(d) *Disposal cost*
    0.0025 X $ 500,000 = $ 1,250

(e) *Storing clean tableware*
    (i) *Labor (see Table III) Using dish carts*
        0.16/1,000 X 6,850 X 365 = 400 man hours
        400 X $ 2.50 = $ 1,000
    (ii) *Supervision*
        0.45 X $ 1,000 = $ 450
    (iii) *Equipment (see Fig. 12)*
        $ 0.95/1,000 X 6,850 = $ 7
    (iv) *Space charge ($ 0)*
    (v) *Total costs:* $ 1,457

(f) *Linen costs*
    (i) *Laundry charges for napkins*
        ¼ *(pound)* X $ 0.08 *(laundry rate)* X 685
        (covers) X 365 *(days)* = $ 5,000
    (ii) 2 *(pounds)* X $ 0.08 *(laundry rate)* X 100
        (tables) X 365 *(days)* = $ 5,840
    (iii) *Napkin replacement cost per year*
        685 *(covers)* X $ 0.50 *(cost each)* X
        365/100 *(replacement factor based on*
        100 use life) = $1,250
    (iv) *Table cover replacement cost per year*
        100 *(tables)* X $ 5.00 *(cost each)* X
        365/250 *(replacement factor based on*
        250 use life) = $ 730
    (v) *Total costs:* $ 12,820

(g) *Total costs:*
    $ 37,392 or $ 0.15 per cover

As the number of covers in the examples increases, the selection of the correct alternative should not present a difficult decision. It should be noted that the fixed and variable cost of each of the systems are:

Disposable system:
    Fixed cost: $ 2,867 *per year*
    Variable cost: $ 0.23 *per cover*

Warewashing system:
> *Fixed cost:*   *$ 8,945 per year*
> *Variable cost:*   *$ 0.11 per cover*

As indicated earlier in this chapter, the system with the highest fixed cost has a lower variable cost. This implies that at some specified point, about 139 covers per day, the warewashing and disposable systems have the same cost. Above 139 covers per day, the warewashing system is more feasible, whereas, below 139 covers per day, the disposable system is more feasible.

V. REFERENCES

1. Freshwater, John F. and Daniel Steckter, *"Evaluation of Dishwashing Systems in Food Service Establishments"*, *Marketing Research Report No. 1003,*Agricultural Research Service, United States Department of Agriculture, Washington, DC (1973)
2. Borsenik, Frank D. Unpublished data.

CHAPTER 19

COST OPTIMIZATION IN DISTRIBUTION SYSTEMS

Robert W. Jailer

Planning Research Corporation
Systems Sciences Company
Englewood Cliffs, New Jersey

I. INTRODUCTION

Based on its dictionary definition, "optimize" appears to
be a very simple concept: "to make as effective, perfect, or
useful as possible." In a discussion of cost optimization,
it might appear that relatively straightforward objectives
should be considered, i.e., the design of the best distribution system possible from the cost viewpoint, or the redesign
of an existing system for the best operation from the same
viewpoint.

As soon as the meaning of the term "best" is examined in
the context of a given system or class of systems, it is
found that the problem can rapidly become complex. First,
the best cost picture must be determined from the standpoint
of the system operator. Some food distribution systems are
run by commercial organizations that sell their products to
customers operating business enterprises separate from the
distribution system. In such a case, the best cost structure
for the operation of the distribution system is the one which
maximizes the system operator's profit in the long run. Other
distribution systems, such as restaurant chains, provide
their products to customers who really belong to the same
business entity as the system itself. There are some situations under which the individual users of such a system's
products can be treated as customers in the same sense as in
the first group. In other cases, however, this may not be
possible, and the distribution system must be optimized from
the viewpoint of cost in an overall analysis that also considers the cost factors in the customer operations. Finally,

Copyright © 1979 by Academic Press, Inc.
All rights of reproduction in any form reserved
ISBN: 0-12-453150-4

there are large-scale food distribution systems that are not
operated with the profit motive of the commercial business
firms, i.e., the institutional food systems run by both private and governmental agencies. Optimization from the viewpoint of cost here does not include a profit factor, and
consequently must be treated in a somewhat different manner.

There is a further complexity in defining the best cost
picture for a given distribution system that must also be
considered at the outset, especially when dealing with food.
A food distribution system does not deliver a product, or
series of products, to the customer that can be defined with
a relatively simple set of standards. It is unlike a system
delivering steel bars of specific metallurgical and dimen-
sional specifications to a manufacturer. The concept of
quality, or at least of minimum acceptable quality, in the
products delivered is a very important factor in optimizing
the cost of a food distribution system. Cost can be measured
in relatively simple numbers, dollars. Food quality, however,
is measured by a complex set of standards, some of which are
subject to quantitative definition, while others are wholly
qualitative or subjective. Thus, before beginning to optimize
a food distribution system on the basis of cost, a decision
must be made to limit the decisions on cost reductions by the
consideration of quality.

While quality is one of the prime limiting factors or
side considerations that complicate the systems analysis and
operations research problem in the cost optimization of distribution systems, it is by no means the only one. Others may
include time factors related to both responsiveness and frequency of service, geographic factors requiring decisions on
whether service is to be provided to customers that are difficult to reach from the distribution center or centers, configurations of existing road networks, legal constraints of a
wide variety that limit choices, including building and zoning
codes, vehicular restrictions in transportation, limits on the
number of hours a truck driver can work in a day, union rules,
and many others.

In optimizing the operation cost of a distribution system,
identification of all of the factors involved is needed.
Establishment of a means of evaluating those that cannot be
treated quantitatively in terms of cost or other measures, and
the relationship between all the various cost factors, as
limited by the various side considerations in a modeling
process that will eventually lead to an optimum system design
from the cost viewpoint must be made.

II. SYSTEM DEFINITION

One of the first problems in attacking the cost optimization of a food distribution system is to define the actual
system to be optimized. This is not always obvious. The
magnitude of the problem that must be attacked, and the possibility of arriving at a usable solution in a reasonable length
of time, and at a cost for the analysis that will not be
totally out of line with the benefits to be derived, depend
upon the boundaries selected for the analysis at the outset.
Some food distribution systems are relatively straightforward.
A food manufacturer with a limited number of individual products may have a warehouse at his manufacturing plant from
which he ships to the warehouses of distributors who are
separate business enterprises. The boundaries of his cost
optimization problem in food distribution can be limited to
packaging, order picking, vehicle loading, and transportation.
This makes for a relatively simple cost optimization process,
although some of the problems in optimizing transportation
networks, especially if there are many points of destination
for less-than-truckload shipments and a complex road network,
have never really been optimized.

The situation becomes more complex when attempting to
extend the operations to be optimized to such related areas
as the manufacturer's warehouse inventory control and his
order processing system. The optimization process must then
consider inventory control risk situations, the processing of
information involved in translating the customers' orders to
cases of food to be loaded on trucks, minimum order size, and
maximum time lapse between receipt of order and delivery of
merchandise.

As the boundaries of the distribution system to be optimized become broader, the situation becomes more complex. If
the customer to whom the manufacturer ships is part of the
same system, as in the case of a manufacturer with many geographically dispersed warehouses served from one or more
production plants, then there is a two-stage order-pick/
shipping/transportation/receiving/storage/order-pick/ ship-
ping/transportation problem to be optimized. Further, if the
customer is a user of the food rather than just a trans-
shipper, a further set of dimensions is introduced into the
system boundaries.

In any event, the system to be optimized must be examined
carefully from a cost viewpoint at the outset of the analysis,
and a definitive set of boundaries selected within which the
analysis will proceed.

III. APPROACH TO THE PROBLEM

    To illustrate the approach to cost optimization in a sys-
tem, a selected model of moderate complexity might be examined. The core of the system is a number of warehouses that
serve a relatively large number of customers geographically
scattered. The warehouses, in turn, receive their inventory
from a number of manufacturing plants, each of which produces
a specific product line. There are a series of initial questions that must be answered in the development of a distribution system plan that will be optimized for cost, within the
types of constraints already discussed, before beginning to
develop the optimization model.
    Over what period of time is the system expected to run in
the optimum mode? At this point, one of the real problems in
system optimization, that being nothing is static, is faced.
Over the years, the conditions under which the system must
operate, the cost factors, technology, product mixes, and
many other factors change. If it is to be useful, system
optimization must attack the problem in a flexible way, and
must plan for a foreseeable number of years. Intermediate
range planning, for one to five years, for the distribution
system optimum cost configuration is probably desirable.
    In developing the first step of the plan, a number of
objectives must be established in terms of what the analysis
is expected to provide. For the example being discussed, an
analysis that looks at either a new distribution system or a
modification to the existing distribution system is indicated.
The objectives of the model should respond to the following
questions

    A.   How many distribution warehouses are needed?
    B.   Where should they be located?
    C.   How large should each warehouse be?
    D.   Which customers should be served from which ware--
houses?
    E.   To which warehouse and customer should each plant's
production be allocated for each product produced?
    F.   How should the transportation system be organized for
the flow of products through the entire distribution system,
from plant output to customer receipt?
    G.   In the case of modifications of existing systems on a
cost-optimization basis, how do the cost savings and customer
service levels of the optimum distribution design compare with
a projection of the current system operating through the
intermediate range period?

If an analysis of these questions is made, it becomes evident that an attempt is not being made to optimize every individual factor in the system operation. The basis for the optimization is the number, location, size, and function of each warehouse, and an evaluation of the transportation problem, although not only on the basis of truck schedules. It should be noted that the processing of orders from customers, inventory control in warehouses, materials handling, product packaging, transportation routings and dispatching, and other operational considerations have not been made part of the primary set of questions.

This should not be interpreted to mean that these factors will not require detailed analysis in the optimization process. In the initial planning, however, extreme complexity can be avoided by assuming that these functions are performed as economically as possible within the constraints of the desired level of service. Their costs are considered, in conjunction with the individual costs of the optimization model, as a series of suboptimization steps. Suboptimization in this context refers to the isolation of a specific operation, and its individual study as a separate subsystem, in relation to the total system operation, in order to determine the optimal method of organizing it from a cost standpoint.

IV. MODELING

At this point it is possible to develop the initial cost model. A cost model is a representation of the operation of a system, much as an architect builds a small-scale model of a building in the process of planning a structure. The model is a representation of how the system operates. The model is usually idealized, in the sense that it is somewhat less complicated than in reality, and consequently easier to use for analytical purposes. The simplification achieved in models, compared with the realities of the system, lies in the fact that only the relative properties of reality are selected to represent the model.

There are a number of types of models, but only two will be discussed here. An iconic model and a symbolic model will be discussed.

An iconic model is a large-scale or small-scale representation of a system that looks like what it represents; an example is a map. In food distribution systems, however, what is required is a flowchart that shows the movement of the food commodities from their manufacturing sources through the warehouses, to the ultimate consumers. Such a flowchart

provides the initial understanding of the distribution system
and a framework for the development of a symbolic model.
Ideally, the symbolic model will be a series of mathematical
relationships, based primarily on cost, between the various
factors being considered in the cost optimization of the system. It is important to recognize that these mathematical
equations must be constructed to answer all the questions
previously outlined simultaneously, rather than piecemeal,
since each cost element must be considered in relation to its
impact on all other costs.

In its initial stages, a flowchart will show the production plants, the distribution network from these plants to the
warehouses, and the distribution networks from the warehouses
to the customers. Information is added on the specific
product lines that can be produced in each plant, handled in
each warehouse, and distributed to each customer. Then all
costs involved must be identified. In the example selected,
these include,

A. production cost of each product at each plant,
B. transportation costs from the plants to the
warehouses,
C. warehousing and inventory costs at each warehouse
for each product,
D. transportation costs from the warehouses to the
customers,
E. costs (and savings) of constructing new warehouses,
expanding existing warehouses, or closing down warehouses
that may not be needed in the new system, and
F. income from sales, if the consideration in the optimization process are broad enough to affect the size or service
level of the existing market.

The transition from the flowchart model to a mathematical
model, that will permit analysis of cost and adjustment of the
individual factors to allow determination of the optimum cost
structure, must be made within the context of a series of
specifically defined restrictions, including

A. the actual production capacities of each plant for
each product (recalling that an attempt is not being made to
optimize the entire production and distribution systems, but
only the distribution portion),
B. individual warehouse size limitations,
C. a customer-warehouse relationship such that
    (1) all foreseeable customer demands can be
    satisfied (assuming that undesirable customer demands
    are eliminated from the system),

(2) a warehouse-customer service relationship established on the basis of economical delivery in accordance with the desired level of service to the customer, and

(3) a general rule that each customer is assigned to a specific warehouse for service, unless unusual circumstances require exceptions,

D. Other constraints on system configuration imposed by law, company policy, customer demand for service, etc. These may include such factors as minimum and maximum number of warehouses to be considered for the system, and specific locations desired for one or more warehouses for reasons other than system cost optimization.

The cost optimization problem is one of minimizing the set of costs enumerated, subject to the restrictions discussed. It is a difficult problem to solve in a system of this complexity. In many cases, it will be necessary to develop a computerized model to (1) allow exploration of the effect of changes in the restrictive parameters on system cost optimization, (2) to permit complex relationships between costs of various portions of the system operation to be explored, and (3) to obtain a sufficient number of runs through the model to give the analyst confidence that he is approaching the optimum in system design.

The model developed for distribution system optimization will be a collection of precise mathematical statements and assumptions about the system, sufficiently comprehensive in detail to permit answering the initial set of questions about the optimum systems configuration. It must be realized, however, that the design of a usable model for manual or computer manipulation will always be a compromise between the degree of detail desired and the cost of the use of the model. It is essential that the real system be reflected in the model in enough detail to assure that the mathematical manipulation will yield valid outputs that will be accepted by the system management. It is also necessary to keep the amount of detail to a level that will not be so great that the input data requirements will be unreasonable, or that computational techniques will require excessive time or computer usage. Thus, both oversimplification and excessive detail must be avoided.

The key system features that make for realism in distribution system cost optimization modeling include,

A. A representation of the complete product line to be handled, including package size and products that require different environmental considerations. Definition of a single composite product to simplify the modeling process indicates

a lack of realism in the system analysis. On the other hand,
incorporation of representations of every individual product
and product package size make for excessive complexity. Some
compromise is necessary, representing both environmental
handling requirements and package size.

B. Representation of each stage of distribution, i.e.,
plant to warehouse and warehouse to customer. Design of a
system model that represents the flow from plant to customer
without considering the intermediate warehousing fails to
represent the system adequately for cost analysis purposes.

C. Reality in designating plant capacity and warehouse
capacity limits. If necessary, this must be done by product
or product group. It is necessary for the model to handle
warehouse size, usually in terms of throughput volume. Minimum and maximum warehouse size limitations can be built into
the model to keep the throughput of the warehouse within the
bounds of practical capacity for an existing facility, or to
specify a minimum size limit related to operating efficiency
for a warehouse to be built. Consideration of variation of
warehouse size in exercising the model is necessary, however,
since warehouse economies of scale must also be considered.

D. Economies of scale and fixed costs in warehousing.
The warehousing cost curve as a function of throughput must
be examined to ensure that it is free of step functions that
would distort the applications of the estimated fixed warehousing charges in the analysis. If the analytical treatment
of warehousing cost variations with throughput and warehousing
fixed charges are such that the step functions cannot be
avoided, it usually means that the size constraints selected
are not adequate.

E. Customer assignment to warehouses. Most systems generally assign the customer to a single warehouse for service,
since in practical application this is generally the most
economical means of operation. Exceptions may be necessary,
however, in cases in which customer demand is sufficiently
large for a given product or mix of products to permit minimum transportation cost shipments directly from a plant to the
customer, usually in truckload or car lot. If such cases are
possible, the model must include consideration of the choice
between serving the customer directly from the plant or from
an intermediate distribution center.

F. Other configuration constraints. These are generally
characteristics of the individual system and generalization
is difficult. It is necessary to make a deliberate effort to
identify all such constraints at the start of the modeling,
and to incorporate those in the model that can be shown
analytically to have major effects on the outcome of the
analysis.

The initial model may not contain specific factors for such things as alternative modes of transportation, differing unit transportation costs for shipments of varying weights and products, and plant location factors. Such variables are generally considered in the cost optimization study by varying the input data for successive model evaluation runs to explore the effect of changes on the cost structure. While it is possible to build these and other factors into the cost model, the increasing complexity of data input, and requirements for excessive computation time generally make such a model impractical for analytical use.

V. COMPUTATION

The computational requirement is the key factor in cost optimization modeling that must be kept in the forefront as the work proceeds. A cost optimization model is usable only if it can be applied in a realistic manner, at reasonable cost, and with sufficient flexibility to permit exploration of all possible system configurations and subsystem rearrangements necessary to convince the system manager that the final solution has considered all possible variations. The point to be kept in mind during development of the model is that some computational method must be used to obtain a solution to the optimization problem. The computational method must be reasonably efficient, if the cost of optimization is to be kept within bounds, and must be sufficiently explainable and convincing to system management if the conclusions of the cost optimization study are to be accepted and implemented.

In general, there are major criteria that the model's computational method must meet. First, it should optimize. This is not as obvious a statement as it seems on the surface. In using the model to compute the optimum system characteristics, it is necessary to specify the tolerance on the error within which the model output will approximate the true mathematical optimum. If such tolerances cannot be specified in advance, and demonstrated to be real, the computational method, or the model, will not really optimize.

In producing an optimum solution to the system design problem, the model should handle all of the essential decision variables simultaneously. If the model dissects the problem and deals with each subsystem separately, or if it considers only a limited range of possible decisional alternatives, it will not produce a mathematically justifiable optimum solution.

The degree of optimization that can be achieved through the model is almost always relative. No matter how much detail is built into a model, it still involves an approximation to reality and simplification of the actual system operation. Further, in real world cases, the input data for the computations are not always precise. In the design of new systems, it is frequently necessary to calculate or approximate costs on the basis of projections, estimates, assumed inflation rates, etc. The degree of tolerance of error specified for the operation of the model must be selected within the context of the uncertainties of the input data.

Thus, while we must take the attitude that our cost optimization model really will optimize, we must accept the fact that no model is an exact replica of reality, and that some tolerance for error in the output, due to uncertainties in the input and assumptions in modeling, will always exist.

Second, the computation method must be selected on the basis of practicality in terms of time and cost. Whether the model is designed for manual or computer computation, it must be run more than once in any practical situation. Usually, the early model runs are directed toward input data validation, refinement of computational methods, and getting a feel of the way the model performs.

Once the inputs have been validated and the model adjusted to the point at which the systems analysts have confidence in its operation, a single optimization run is rarely adequate for the solution of the problem. Generally, many subsequent secondary optimization solutions are required to address specific questions and to explore the effects of adjustment on the system.

Third, multiple optimization runs should be relatively fast, reliable, and readily performed. Secondary evaluations of the model will invariably be required to determine the sensitivity of the analysis, to run tradeoffs between cost and such factors as energy consumption, operating cost reductions, capital expenditures, and the quality of customer services. It will probably also be necessary to run secondary evaluations of the model to answer the "what if" type of question which invariably arises when interim results are presented to system management. Such questions frequently involve the effects of retaining or closing marginally effective facilities, altering facility service areas, and eliminating certain types of customers. Other secondary runs are usually required in planning the implementation of the new system. There are also other types of secondary runs that may be necessary to answer the questions addressed in a distribution system planning study, to ensure that the full benefits inherent in a

distribution model are being achieved, and to build up sufficient credibility so that system management will be willing
to accept and implement the major findings of the study.

   In planning for a cost optimization project, it is generally necessary not only to plan for the development of the
model and the required input data, but also for a relatively
large number of computational evaluations. It is difficult to
specify the number of evaluations that will be required without knowing the specific problem to be attacked. However,
planning for the project should be conservative in this
respect and might assume that between 15 and 25 computer runs
may be needed.

VI.   COST OF OPTIMIZATION STUDIES

   As is obvious from the discussion to this point, cost
optimization in its true sense, is a complex, costly under-
taking that usually requires professional systems analysts
and operations research practitioners, and generally the use
of a computer. It is also a time-consuming process. There
is no way to specify the actual cost of performing the cost
optimization analysis without first knowing the system to be
optimized. A preliminary estimation factor, based on experience with computerized modeling of large scale systems,
suggests that the usual cost will run between 3 and 10% of the
annual value of the throughput of the system for an operation
with a moderate number of different products. However, this
factor must be used with great caution. Cost optimization in
a high-value throughput system may be a much less expensive
operation if the product line is simple, the number of customers is relatively small, and the number of facilities to be
considered is, or can be, limited. On the other hand, cost
optimization for a relatively low-value throughput system may
be much more expensive if a large number of diverse product
lines are involved, if there are many customers, and if it is
not possible to limit the number and location of system facilities that must be analyzed.

VII. ALTERNATIVES

   Is there an alternative? If insistance on true mathematical optimization is made, the answer is probably "no".
There are techniques, however, that can be useful in reducing
system costs and approaching optimization. One of these is

suboptimization. In such an analysis it is possible to
literally "take the system apart" and look at its various
subsystems individually, and then as units of the whole. The
usual technique is to examine all subsystems, and determine
which of these interacts most significantly, from a cost and
operational effectiveness viewpoint, with all of the other
subsystems. In the case of food distribution systems, it is
usually the warehousing and transportaion portion of the
system. The procedure, then, is to examine the range of
possibilities for the warehousing and transportation systems,
establish models for significant or representative points in
the range, and suboptimize this system first.

Each of the remaining subsystems is then examined individually from the viewpoint of its operation and cost inter-
actions with the warehousing and transportation systems. Each
is modeled to the extent required to suboptimize its operational structure from a cost viewpoint, considering the inter-
actions with the warehousing and transportation systems and
other subsystems. Adjustments are made between subsystem
operational details until, in the judgment of the analyst, no
further improvements can be made.

It must be stressed, however, that this is not really an
optimization process, as it cannot be established that the
final output is, in fact, cost optimized, at least not in a
mathematical sense. However, when the level of accuracy of
the data available for most cost optimization projects is
considered, and when the problems of replication of the real
world system in a workable mathematical model are evaluated,
it is generally found that affordable cost optimizations have
a considerable amount of uncertainty associated with their
final output. Since the results of a suboptimization study,
and the procedures used in its analyses, are usually easier
to explain to management than the more sophisticated mathematical and computer techniques used in true cost optimization, the suboptimization route is frequently more prudent and
more practical.

CHAPTER 20

MANAGEMENT INFORMATION SYSTEMS FOR FOOD SERVICE OPERATIONS

H. C. Gibbons, Jr.[1]

TransTech, Incorporated
Atlanta, Georgia

I. INTRODUCTION

It will come as no surprise to those who work in an advisory capacity to the food service management field that no particular effort has been made to establish formal management information systems until the last few years, and that, on the whole, there is as yet little desire to implement such systems on the part of many managers. Food service operations have traditionally been operated on the basis of intuition, educated guesswork, and the repetition of prior experience. Management has generally been based on reactions to recent events, and planning consisted of a review of what was done on the same day of the production cycle the last time around. This habit may have evolved over the long years when raw materials from which the finished products were prepared were highly variable, and the ability to adjust to the variations of chance was an absolute requisite. Indeed, this ability to be flexible may have the principal basis for the expertise which many managers felt they possessed, and helped to develop a definite mystique for them.

II. THE DEVELOPMENT OF MANAGEMENT INFORMATIONS SYSTEMS

The studies initiated by Dr. Joseph Balintfy and his asso-

---

[1]*Present address: Dennis-Weingarten Associates, Inc., Prairie Village, Kansas*

Copyright © 1979 by Academic Press, Inc.
All rights of reproduction in any form reserved
ISBN: 0-12-453150-4

343

ciates at Tulane, (see Chapter 8), opened the door to the development and application of management information systems.
These established a format for management, tested its validity,
provided for its adjustment, then locked in a pre-determined
course of action. By using the computer to collect, correlate,
analyze and produce data relevant to the making of management
decisions, the Balintfy team laid the base for a radical change
in the management of food service operations.

A food service production facility is a factory which requires all of the elements of management needed in any factory,
regardless of the product it manufactures. Indeed, it has a
greater need than most to base its management on scientifically
processed data, because, in every production day, it deals with
a large spectrum of widely differing products. The kitchen
must develop a plan for action for both the short and the long
range; determine the quantities of product to manufacture; procure, store, inventory, and issue the raw materials; manufacture to very precise tolerances; distribute to a highly critical
and knowledgeable clientele under extreme pressures of sales-
manship; account for the costs of production and, in many
cases, the levels of nutrients; and constantly relate these
actions to possible revisions in the basic plan under which it
operates. In factory-type central kitchens, which are becoming
increasingly popular, cost controls as demanding as those existing in any commercial factory must be developed and rigidly
met.

The introduction of the computer-based management information system provides a scheduled flow of information, based on
required input at pre-determined times, which is processed according to a predetermined pattern, and provided to the manager
at the interval he has selected. The information is used by
the manager to make decisions. In food service, as in any manufacturing operation, computer-assisted management information
systems can reduce costs, improve the utilization of management
time, and increase product consistency.

Computer-assisted management information systems enable
managers to make decisions whose accuracy and effectiveness can
also be assessed by the system. In an operation where the manager is a symbol and the cook is in fact running the show, or
in a kitchen which is coasting along on its own, a management
information system would produce nothing except an added expense. The facilities in which the most dramatic results are
obtained with such systems, are not the ones in which poor operations existed, but rather the ones in which the supervision
was superior, costs were below average, high quality products
were produced, and top management was very well satisfied. The
fact is that, in such cases, management was truly managing before the arrival of the computer, and was able to use the collected information effectively in decision making. While a

management information system will make a good manager into a superior one, the elements of personal industry and ability on the part of managers remain essential.

III. EXAMPLE OF A HOSPITAL FOOD SERVICE MANAGEMENT INFORMATION SYSTEM

Applying tested factory systems to the development of management information systems for a hospital food production facility, a format was developed around the six major management areas:

PLAN	–	what needs to be produced on a daily basis and over a long range period, based on analysis of the recipes and the menus
PURCHASE	–	only the raw materials necessary to produce the finished product in the planned quantities
INVENTORY	–	the purchased raw materials, including receipt, storage and issue to production in accordance with the production schedule
PRODUCE	–	the product according to the forecasted quantities, using the blueprint, i.e. the recipe
DISTRIBUTE	–	within a rigid time frame pattern and in measured quantities
ACCOUNT	–	for what has been done, to provide information needed to modify plans for the future

To effectively manage change and establish procedures in these areas, a data base had to be assembled. This data base in essence was a reflection of the minds of the people who would be using the system. Its elements had to include a recipe file containing not only the recipes in current use, but a sufficient quantity of acceptable recipes which fill specific criteria with different ingredient combinations to enable changing the menu to respond to cost of ingredient availability fluctuations.

A second element of the data base was the menu file itself. In health care institutions, the menu is broken into many menus to reflect modifications in consistency, level of nutrients, or production methodology. The menu file had many satellites, all relating to the primary file.

The third element was an ingredient file, which was generated by analysis of all potential ingredients in all recipes available for use under any menu combination, but organized to limit purchase to ingredients actually occurring in recipes being used.

The fourth element was the nutrient file, which should be virtually identical for all institutions, since it is derived from the very limited source material available, primarily U.S. Department of Agriculture food composition data for nutrient levels found in commercially prepared products, and the material provided by convenience food manufacturers relative to their own products.

The final element varied in form, and was essentially a file which controlled the sequence of application of the various functions available from the system.

In the operation of a management information system, the fixed information contained in the files is applied in relation to variable information to produce data which can be directly applied to management action.

A. *Planning*

Planning means recipes, menus, and careful, thorough, preproduction analysis. It also means the establishment of an organized budget plan, the development of information which will be used in the other management activities. The result levels attained in the entire operation are based upon the recipe and menu combinations; consequently, the relationship between the computer and the menu is critical. While the computer can, of course, be used to assist in menu planning (See Chapter 8), it is feasible also to use the computer simply to analyze a conventionally developed menu to see how closely it meets the criteria which have been set for the operation. Analytical routines can produce:

  (1) Cost for each menu item, and combination totals for the day
  (2) Cost diagnostics for each day of a cycle of any length, and for each course appearing in the menu pattern
  (3) Recipe usage reports which rank each recipe by frequency of appearance
  (4) Nutritional analysis of levels in various combinations for each day of the cycle
  (5) Dominant flavor appearance listings
  (6) Attributes diagnostics, which reveal how often particular classes of food are served, such as casseroles, cakes, pies

The modification of the original menu on the basis of these factors can provide a menu which meets all criteria at a probable cost level (Fig. 1).

M E N U
FOR DAY 19

TRANSTECH INCORPORATED   11/21/71 3.07 PM
COST   RFC NO   NAME

BREAKFAST (CATEGORIES 1-5)
1	2.10	1107	*HALF BANANA
	6.75	1314	ORANGE JUICE
2	8.84	3406	*OATMEAL
	5.00	3502	BRANFLAKES 40 PERCENT
3	2.98	5802	*SOFT COOKED EGG
4	7.44	5501	*BACON
5	1.66	3101	*BISCUIT HOT

LUNCH (CATEGORIES 6-11)
6	2.89	4156	*CREAM OF POTATO SOUP
	7.53	1316	PEACH NECTAR
7	21.03	5132	*SWEDISH MEAT BALLS
	35.44	5202	ROAST LEG OF LAMB AU JUS
8	1.31	3310	*NOODLES BUTTERED
9	2.96	2179	*FROSTED BUTTERED SUCCOTASH
	4.54	2171	FROZEN SPINACH WITH VINEGAR
10	3.08	1433	*SUNSET SALAD
11	1.59	7211	*CHOCOLATE CUPCAKE
	4.50	7116	CUSTARD PIE

DINNER (CATEGORIES 12-17)
12	4.44	1326	*APPLE JUICE CND
13	14.84	5129	*TUNA FISH SOUFFLE
	18.50	5116	BRAISED BEEF LIVER
14	2.09	3321	*POTATOES LYONNAISE
15	3.56	2112	*BUTTERED SLICED BEETS
	7.54	2116	AU GRATIN BROCCOLI
16	2.88	2338	*TOMATO SLICE WR PEPPER RING SALAD
17	3.71	7613	*LEMON CUPS
	4.43	1148	GREEN GAGE PLUMS

MENU ANALYSIS

	COST	CAL	PROT(G)	FAT(G)	SFA(G)	OLC(G)	LNOL(G)	CHOL(G)	FIBR(G)	CHO(G)
AVG DAILY $	0.98	1745.	73.3	69.5	20.0	29.2	8.3	206.	3.1	443.
* ONLY	0.78	1749.	63.6	80.3	23.4	36.3	9.9	196.	3.0	464.
BR & BEV	0.45	680.	16.0	29.0	15.0	10.0	0.	90.	0.1	83.

	CALC(MG)	PHOS(MG)	IRON(MG)	NA(MG)	K (MG)	VT A(IU)	THIA(MG)	RIBO(MG)	NIAC(MG)	VT C(MG)
AVG DAILY	379.	1228.	14.5	2810.	2142.	26953.	1.3	2.3	31.9	119.6
* ONLY	378.	1072.	12.0	3098.	1703.	3611.	1.2	1.1	29.5	64.5
BR & BEV	400.	350.	3.2	600.	550.	1000.	0.3	0.6	4.0	3.5

FIGURE 1. Typical computer printed menu for one day in the menu cycle. Note the cost and nutrient analyses shown on the menu. (Courtesy TransTech, Incorporated, Atlanta, Georgia)

B. Purchasing

Purchasing reconciles menu items and recipes with production forecasts to assure that all of the components necessary to produce the finished product will be on hand when needed. Purchasing must extend every ingredient in every recipe in the menu by the meal count forecast, check inventory levels, and then purchase the needed ingredients. However, a food service operation offers a unique purchasing problem because the products produced change frequently. The computer's speed and ability to remember each standardized recipe's data provides the solution to this problem.

The computer can provide pricing information, assist in maintaining par stock inventories and print out a purchase list for any forecasted period. It should have the ability to receive newest purchase prices and produce a report which shows the percentage of change since the last purchase (Fig. 2). It should permit identification of budget-threatening ingredients and find their recipe occurrence.

C. Inventory

Inventory control means maximization of return on investment by avoiding the expense of maintaining excess quantities, the failure to provide needed ingredients, and the development of obsolescent stock. A system should provide a form for taking inventory, based upon stock location; the extension of physical inventory data to show usage by item, collective usage by food and product group, and stockbook listings showing activity by item (Fig. 3).

D. Production

Production control is the area in which most substantial cost reductions are made. Initially, a forecasting system produces a production work schedule for each day. On the basis of experience, management forecasts the number of portions to be produced and served. Using this forecast figure, the computer generates three important collections of information:

(1) A Production Recipe for each production item, calculated by comparing the master recipe in the data base to the forecast figure, then printing a single-use recipe which will produce the exact number of portions forecasted (Fig. 4).

(2) A Storeroom Issue Requisition, which combines all foods needed for the day's production into a single listing for each food, even if that food appears as an ingredient in several recipes.

(3) A Grocery List, showing the foods to buy; this list

```
                          P R I C E   U P D A T E
                     FOR PERIOD OF 12/29/73 TO 01/25/74

        TRANSTECH INCORPORATED                              02/11/74      11.38 PM
```

INV NO	INVENTORY ITEM NAME	OLD BPRICE	BUY UNIT	NEW BPRICE	PERCENT CHANGE
21215	GRAPES WHITE SDLS 24 LB LUG	10.42	LUG	11.25	7.0
21220	GRAPEFRUIT FR 40 LB BOX	5.19	BOX	5.34	2.0
21300	LEMON FR 37 LB BOX	8.75	BOX	8.84	1.0
21325	MELON HONEYDEW FR 14 LB CTN	17.10	CARTON	17.80	4.0
21375	ORANGES FR 40 LB BOX	6.53	BOX	6.40	-1.0
24510	CHICKEN ALA KING FL 18 SW 6/10	25.70	CASE	25.96	1.0
26030	MEATLOAF W GRAVY (IND) SB 4/5 LB	15.75	CASE	16.22	2.0
26375	SWISS STEAK SB 6/3.5 LB	58.10	CASE	56.34	-3.0
26435	BEEF STROGANOFF ST 4/70 OZ	49.10	CASE	48.60	-1.0
26560	MACARONI AND CHEESE SB 4/5 LB	9.50	CASE	9.70	2.0
26590	SPAGHETTI W MEATBALLS SB 4/5 LB	11.90	CASE	12.38	4.0
26610	ALASKA KING CRAB NEWBRG ST 4/72 OZ	65.70	CASE	64.40	-1.0
26805	BAKED BREAST OF CHIX ST 4/66 OZ	37.99	CASE	37.60	-1.0
30060	BEANS GREEN CUT FZ 12/2.5 LB	9.50	CASE	9.69	1.0
30150	BEANS LIMA BABY FZ 12/2.5 LB	10.80	CASE	11.34	4.0
30160	BEANS WAX FZ 12/2.5 LB	8.40	CASE	8.65	2.0
30210	BROCCOLI SPEARS FZ 12/2.5 LB	8.75	CASE	9.54	9.0
30240	CARROTS DICED FZ 12/2 LB	6.40	CASE	6.21	-2.0
30250	CARROTS SLICED FZ 12/2 LB	4.80	CASE	4.90	2.0
30360	CORN WHOLE KERNEL FZ 12/2.5 LB	5.73	CASE	5.79	1.0
30470	ONIONS CHOPPED FZ 10/2 LB	8.85	CASE	8.94	1.0
30600	PEAS GREEN FZ 12/2.5 LB	5.30	CASE	5.67	6.0
30630	POTATOES FRENCH FR FZ 12/2.5 LB	7.45	CASE	7.23	-2.0
30660	POTATOES HASHBROWN FZ 6/2.5 LB	4.92	CASE	5.02	1.0
30720	SPINACH LEAF FZ 12/3 LB	8.83	CASE	8.92	1.0
30800	SQUASH YELLOW WINTER FZ 12/4 LB	6.12	CASE	6.30	2.0
30940	VEGETABLE MIXED FZ 12/2.5 LB	5.90	CASE	5.78	-2.0

FIGURE 2. Typical computer price update. Based on most recent invoices, this report provides timely information about current price changes. (Courtesy TransTech, Incorporated, Atlanta, Georgia)

PHYSICAL   INVENTORY   RECORDING   FORM

	TRANSTECH INCORPORATED						02/10/74	9.19 PM	PAGE 44	
LOC (COLUMNS)	INV NO – – – – – ON HAND – – – – – 1 – 7 8– 12		BUNIT	13–16	IUNIT	INVENTORY ITEM NAME	DATE 17 – 22	CLIENT 76–78	CC 79–80
031	36255	.....	CASE	....	CAN	POTATOES INSTANT MASHED 6/10	......	0	07
035	36305	.....	CASE	....	BAG	POTATOES SLICED DEHY 6/2	......	0	07
041	36310	.....	CASE	....	BAG	POTATO CHIPS 30 INDV/CASE	......	0	07
043	36315	.....	BOX	....	LB	POTATO CHIPS BULK 3 LB/BOX	......	0	07
045	36510	.....	BOX	....	LB	DATES PITTED 35 LB BOX	......	0	07
045	36600	.....	BOX	....	LB	PRUNES 30 LB BOX	......	0	07
045	36750	.....	BOX	....	LB	RAISINS 30 LB BOX	......	0	07
061	76015	.....	CASE			ALUMINUM PIE PANS 10 IN 500/CASE	......	0	07
062	80015	.....	GAL			AMMONIA	......	0	07
062	81000	.....	CASE	....	LB	APEX DISHWASHER COMPOUND 125 LB	......	0	07
067	73005	.....	ROLL			ALUMINUM FOIL 18 IN HEAVY 25 LB	......	0	07
E11	38000	.....	CASE	....	CAN	ASPARAGUS LS 24/303	......	0	07
E11	38005	.....	CASE	....	CAN	BEANS WAX LS 24/303	......	0	07
E21	34045	.....	CASE	....	CAN	APPLE RING SPICED 6/10	......	0	07
E21	38015	.....	CASE	....	CAN	BEETS SLICED LS 24/303	......	0	07
E22	38020	.....	CASE	....	CAN	CORN WHOLE KERNEL LS 24/303	......	0	07
E23	38025	.....	CASE	....	CAN	BEANS GREEN LS 24/303	......	0	07
F14	1000	.....	LB			BEEF BRISKET CORNED	......	0	07
F14	1050	.....	LB			BEEF GROUND BULK	......	0	07
F14	1075	.....	LB	....	PATTY	BEEF PATTIES 4 OZ	......	0	07

FIGURE 3. Typical physical inventory recording form. The order in which items are printed matches the organization in the storerooms. The proper use of the information on this report not only increases inventory accuracy but also saves as much as two-thirds of inventory-taking time. (Courtesy TransTech, Incorporated, Atlanta, Georgia)

```
        TRANSTECH INCORPORATED          PRODUCTION RECIPE          02/10/74      9.18 PM

3300  HAMBURGER CASSEROLE              COOKING TEMP-    350        SERVING PAN-  4 IN FULL
                                       COOKING TIME-    30M        SERVING UTENSIL- SPATULA
FOR 342 SERVINGS, 9.9 OZ. EACH         PORTIONS/PAN-    24         SERVING TEMP- HOT
                                       PREPARATION TIME-           ST TBL SETTING-

ING CODE          QUANTITY                    INGREDIENTS

  1050            82 LB        1 OZ     BEEF GROUND
 20610             6 LB       13 OZ     ONIONS FR FINELY CHOPPED
 20050             6 LB       13 OZ     CELERY FR FINELY CHOPPED
 20705                                  GREEN PEPPER FR CHOPPED FINE
 33785   AP 6 CAN  5 LB        5 OZ     TOMATOES CRUSHED CND
 43740             3 TBS   1-1/2 TSP    PEPPER BLACK
 43875             1 LB        1 OZ     SALT
 41795            27 LB        6 OZ     MACARONI
 43875         13-3/4 OZ                SALT (FOR MACARONI)
     0            13 GAL   2-3/4 QT     WATER BOILING
 14010   AP 6 LB             13 OZ     CHEESE AMERICAN SHREDDED

                  INSTRUCTIONS
1. BROWN BEEF IN ITS OWN FAT WITH ONIONS.
   DRAIN EXCESS FAT.
2. ADD CELERY, PEPPERS, TOMATOES, PEPPER AND SALT TO MEAT MIXTURE.
   COVER AND SIMMER UNTIL VEGETABLES ARE TENDER.
3. ADD MACARONI GRADUALLY TO SALTED WATER. BRING TO A BOIL STIRRING
   OCCASIONALLY. BOIL FOR 15 MINUTES. DRAIN.
4. COMBINE MEAT SAUCE AND MACARONI. MIX WELL.
5. POUR 1 3/4 GAL MIXTURE INTO EACH 12X20X4 INCH COUNTER PAN.
   SPRINKLE WITH SHREDDED CHEESE.
6. BAKE AT 350 DEGREES 30 MINUTES.
7. CUT 24 PIECES (6 X 4) PER PAN.

                          3300   HAMBURGER CASSEROLE
```

FIGURE 4. Typical computer production recipe. This report shows a recipe for Hamburger Casserole, based on 100 portions, sized to the forecasted 342 portions. This recipe would first go to the ingredient assembly area as assembly directions. It would then accompany all the ingredients to the preparation area as a production guide for the cooks. (Courtesy TransTech, Inc., Atlanta, GA)

should be collected by product group and sequenced by
the purveyor from whom it is most often purchased.
     The production section will eliminate all calculations by
cooks and storeroom clerks and take the padding and guesswork
out of purchase and issue. Institutions report a reduction in
food cost as high as 18 % in the first year of use of the computer to control production.

E. Cost Accounting

     Cost Accounting should provide complete data on each peri-
od's performance so that one can identify any performance factors that need corrective action. It should show the relationship between planning and actual performance and indicate the
area in which deviation is occurring so that corrective action
can be taken.   Calculation of selling prices required to operate profitably at current production costs should be developed,
and summary accounting should reveal such factors as performance standard variation and cost center accounting allocations
(Fig. 5).

F. Nutrient Accounting

     Nutrient Accounting as used in health care institutions
should include the ability to analyze any menu combination to
indicate precise levels of nutrients planned, and also permit
re-analysis on the basis of quantities of food actually consumed (Fig. 6). Some colleges and in-plant feeding operations are
using this feature to calculate caloric and saturated fat levels which, when posted on menu boards, assist diet-conscious
customers in adhering to their diets. One college reported
that posting a list of calories contained in the serving portion of the various menu items resulted in a significant reduction in food consumption in a girls' dining room.

IV. BENEFITS

     The introduction of a computer-based management information
system has benefits and problems not directly related to the
system.   Initially, it is resisted by chefs who feel it is an
infringement on their historic role as creative artists. The
fact is that, with the standardization of raw ingredients and
recipes, creativity is not only not needed but can actually be
detrimental.   If the recipe is developed to meet the standards
of the institution, it should be prepared the same way each
time. The computer system will virtually assure this if it is
used properly.   After a period of time, cooks become the

MENU ITEM INDEX AND SERVING COSTS

TRANSTECH INCORPORATED   12/17/74   7.09 PM

| | | | | SERVING | | | SUGGESTED PRICE AT P/C FOOD COST |
REC NO	RECIPE NAME			AREA	WEIGHT	COST	30 P/C	40 P/C
2447	*LS TOMATO RICE SOUP		MU	A	4.0 OZ	.033	.13	.10
2450	*SCOTCH BROTH		MU	A	4.0 OZ	.031	.10	.08
2452	*LS SCOTCH BROTH		MU	A	4.0 OZ	.034	.11	.09
2455	*MOCK TURTLE SOUP		MU	A	4.0 OZ	.055	.18	.14
2457	*LS MOCK TURTLE SOUP		MU	A	4.0 OZ	.058	.19	.15
2460	*VEGETABLE SOUP		AFP7	A	4.0 OZ	.029	.10	.07
2462	*LS VEGETABLE SOUP		A=P7	A	4.0 OZ	.030	.10	.08
2600	*KNICKERBOCKER SOUP	AFO18		A	4.0 OZ	.031	.10	.08
2602	*LS KNICKERBOCKER SOUP	AFP18		A	4.0 OZ	.029	.10	.07
2610	*MINESTRONE SOUP	AFP19(1)		A	4.0 OZ	.029	.10	.07
2612	*LS MINESTRONE SOUP	AFP19(1)		A	4.0 OZ	.031	.10	.08
2620	*MULLIGATAWNY SOUP		AFP20	A	4.0 OZ	.021	.07	.05
2622	*LS MULLIGATAWNY SOUP		AFP20	A	4.0 OZ	.025	.08	.06
2630	*NAVY BEAN SOUP		MU	A	4.0 OZ	.031	.10	.08
2632	*LS NAVY BEAN SOUP		MU	A	4.0 OZ	.031	.10	.08
2650	*SPLIT PEA SOUP	AFP23(1)		A	4.0 OZ	.030	.10	.08
2652	*LS SPLIT PEA SOUP	AFP23(1)		A	4.0 OZ	.014	.05	.04
2700	*BACON LETTUCE TOMATO SANDWICH	AFN1		A	5.6 OZ	.214	.71	.54
2701	*PIMIENTO CHEESE SANDWICH			A	3.4 OZ	.133	.44	.33
2705	*BACON CHEESE TOMATO SANDWICH AFN1(5)	AFN4		A	5.9 OZ	.252	.84	.63
2710	*SLICED BEEF SANDWICH	AFN4		A	4.6 OZ	.276	.92	.69
2712	*LS SLICED BEEF SANDWICH	AFN4		A	4.3 OZ	.293	.98	.73
2715	*SLICED CORNED BEEF SANDWICH	A=N9		A	4.4 OZ	.258	.86	.65
2720	*CHICKEN SALAD SANDWICHES	AFN18		A	4.7 OZ	.265	.88	.66
2722	*LS CHICKEN SALAD SANDWICHES	AFN18		A	4.1 OZ	.277	.92	.69
2725	*EGG SALAD SANDWICHES	AFN10		A	4.7 OZ	.114	.38	.29
2727	*LS EGG SALAD SANDWICHES	AFN10		A	4.3 OZ	.128	.43	.32
2730	*HAM SALAD SANDWICHES	AFN13		A	4.8 OZ	.250	.83	.63
2735	*TUNA SALAD SANDWICH	AFN15		A	4.8 OZ	.225	.75	.56
2737	*LS TUNA SALAD SANDWICH	AFN15		A	4.6 OZ	.187	.62	.47
2740	*BAKED HAM SANDWICHES	AFN11		A	4.6 OZ	.267	.89	.67
2745	*CHEESE AND BOLOGNA SANDWICH	AFN5		A	5.2 OZ	.172	.57	.43
2750	*PEANUT BUTTER/JELLY SANDWICH	AFN14		A	5.3 OZ	.131	.44	.33
2752	*LS PEANUT BUTTER/JELLY SANDWICH AFN			A	5.0 OZ	.164	.55	.41
2755	*BOLOGNA OR SALAMI SANDWICH		MU	A	4.3 OZ	.159	.53	.40
2760	*LUNCHEON MEAT SANDWICH		MU	A	4.3 OZ	.186	.62	.47
2765	*AMERICAN CHEESE SANDWICH		MU	A	3.3 OZ	.111	.37	.28

* INDICATES RECIPES WITH PREPARATION INSTRUCTIONS.

FIGURE 5. Typical computer menu item index and serving cost report. For each menu item, this report lists each recipe along with its serving weight (or volume) and food cost. It also shows suggested prices at 30 % and 40 % food cost. This report is helpful in setting consumer prices and/or analyzing per meal expenditures. (Courtesy of TransTech, Incorporated, Atlanta, Georgia)

R E C I P E   N U T R I E N T S   P E R   S E R V I N G

TRANSTECH INCORPORATED   02/12/74   12.20 PM

REC NO   RECIPE NAME

3010 SUKIYAKI   AFL6(1)

WT(OZ)	CAL	PROT(G)	FAT(G)	SFA(G)	OLC(G)	LNOL(G)	CHO(G)	FBR(G)	CHL(MG)
6.60	233	22.7	11.9	0	0	0	7.8	.8	93

CALC(MG)	PHOS(MG)	IRON(MG)	NA(MG)	K(MG)	VT A(MG)	THIA(MG)	RIBO(MG)	NIAC(MG)	VT C(MG)
43	224	3.47	848	486	448	.11	.24	7.8	19

3030 SIMMERED CORNED BEEF   AFL44

WT(OZ)	CAL	PROT(G)	FAT(G)	SFA(G)	OLC(G)	LNOL(G)	CHO(G)	FBR(G)	CHL(MG)
2.20	233	14.1	18.7	9	8	1	1.2	.0	83

CALC(MG)	PHOS(MG)	IRON(MG)	NA(MG)	K(MG)	VT A(MG)	THIA(MG)	RIBO(MG)	NIAC(MG)	VT C(MG)
7	57	1.78	1343	93	2363	.01	.10	.9	0

3035 NEW ENGLAND BOILED DINNER   AFL43

WT(OZ)	CAL	PROT(G)	FAT(G)	SFA(G)	OLC(G)	LNOL(G)	CHO(G)	FBR(G)	CHL(MG)
8.30	301	16.4	18.7	9	8	1	16.2	1.2	83

CALC(MG)	PHOS(MG)	IRON(MG)	NA(MG)	K(MG)	VT A(MG)	THIA(MG)	RIBO(MG)	NIAC(MG)	VT C(MG)
55	113	2.50	1085	469	2363	.11	.17	2.5	36

3037 LS. NEW ENGLAND BOILED DINNER   AFL43

WT(OZ)	CAL	PROT(G)	FAT(G)	SFA(G)	OLC(G)	LNOL(G)	CHO(G)	FBR(G)	CHL(MG)
7.60	226	19.6	9.4	0	0	0	14.7	1.0	80

CALC(MG)	PHOS(MG)	IRON(MG)	NA(MG)	K(MG)	VT A(MG)	THIA(MG)	RIBO(MG)	NIAC(MG)	VT C(MG)
50	203	2.75	47	558	209	.14	.19	7.6	35

3050 MEAT LOAF   AFL35(2)

WT(OZ)	CAL	PROT(G)	FAT(G)	SFA(G)	OLC(G)	LNOL(G)	CHO(G)	FBR(G)	CHL(MG)
4.70	284	29.3	13.1	0	1	1	9.8	.1	125

CALC(MG)	PHOS(MG)	IRON(MG)	NA(MG)	K(MG)	VT A(MG)	THIA(MG)	RIBO(MG)	NIAC(MG)	VT C(MG)
37	258	4.07	810	591	104	.13	.28	14.2	3

FIGURE 6. Typical computer nutrient accounting report. This report provides information on 19 nutrients present and presents the data in terms of quantity of each of these nutrients per serving of each recipe. This information is especially useful to therapeutic dietitians in developing special diets. (Courtesy of TransTech, Incorporated, Atlanta, Georgia)

strongest supporters of the system. They find that quantities forecast are accurate; the problem of running out which creates so much consternation in conventional systems is minimized; leftovers which must be worked into subsequent menus are reduced, and the working climate in the kitchen is improved.

Customers are more satisfied, because they realize that they can rely on the consistent high quality of the food, its availability when they want it, and the standard sizes of the portions being served.

Management is pleased because budgets are met, and any deviation from plan can be readily identified and explained by the reports generated by the system.

Clinical dietitians in the health care institutions using food service management information system have the assurance, possibly for the first time in their professional lives, that the diet which they have prescribed will be accurately produced and served to their patients.

The food service manager, of course, carries the burden of controlling the system which controls his department and exposes his mistakes. Notwithstanding this risk, it is already apparent that food service managers who leave institutions which were equipped with computer-based management information systems will rarely accept new positions in operations that do not have or plan to acquire such systems.

INSURING FOOD QUALITY AND WHOLESOMENESS

CHAPTER 21

NUTRITIONAL CONSIDERATIONS IN MENU AND
SYSTEMS DESIGN OF FOOD SERVICE OPERATIONS

Catharina Y. W. Ang[1]

Food Science Associates, Inc.
Dobbs Ferry, New York

I. INTRODUCTION

The food service industry has been growing very rapidly
over the past two decades and the growth is expected to continue at a more rapid rate in the next decade. It has been predicted (1) that the frequency of meals eaten out will increase
from the present average of one out of three to about one out
of two by 1980 - 1985. Clearly, the nutritional quality of
meals eaten outside of home is of great importance to one's nutrient intake. The significance of adequate nutritional planning is particularly great in institutional systems, such as
school breakfast and lunch programs, or in college, hospital,
nursing home or military feeding.

Frequently, especially in areas other than school, hospital or military feeding, food service management and indeed
most customers are not aware of the nutritional importance of
the meals served, since it is generally taken for granted that
the American diet is adequate in most nutrients. However, surveys conducted by the U.S. Department of Agriculture showed
that many individuals are not getting enough of certain vitamins and minerals, especially vitamin C, vitamin A, calcium and
iron (2). Even schools and colleges are not always providing
the students with nutritionally balanced meals. Murphy *et al*
(3) reported that the Type A lunches in some schools supplied
substantially less of some nutrients than is indicated by the
1/3 RDA for children of that age group. Vitamin B_6, vitamin A,
vitamin D and thiamine were most often short of standards.

[1]*Present address: USDA-SEA, Athens, Georgia*

Copyright © 1979 by Academic Press, Inc.
All rights of reproduction in any form reserved
ISBN: 0-12-453150-4

Walker and Page (4,5) found that in 50 U.S. colleges, one
third of the meals served fell below the RDA for vitamin D,
3/5 of thiamine and 3/4 short in folacin and vitamin B_6. An
average of 42.3 % of total calories was attributable to fat.
No college served meals containing less than 35 % of calories
from fat.

Poorly planned menus may supply too much protein and too
many calories and too little of some micronutrients. A nutritional sound food service system starts with a sound and balanced menu, but also requires the system to be designed so
that it can produce meals with maximum nutrient retention.

In designing food service systems, the entire emphasis is
most often placed on costs, convenience, labor productivity,
etc., without considering the nutritional implications of the
system. Sometimes, even when the designer wishes to consider
the nutritional aspects of proposed systems or subsystems, only limited information is available. Recent reviews on the
effects of food service handling on nutrients have been published by Livingston *et al* (6) and Lachance (7).

II. MENU DESIGN

A. *Development of Nutrient Standard Menus*

In an effort to provide school children with nutritionally
adequate meals, the Food and Nutrition Service of the United
States Department of Agriculture has proposed a set of "Nutrient Standards" for different age groups. School lunch menu
planners can plan their menus based on these "standards". A
similar approach has been pursued by the U.S. Department of
Health, Education and Welfare for the Nutrition Program for
the Elderly, where the 1/3 RDA standards for the meals were
required. Menu planning based on a nutrient standard is also,
of course, used for patients on modified or restricted diets.

The computer-assisted menu planning system as described by
Gelpi *et al* (8) and Balintfy (9) can be ideally applied to nutrient standard menu planning. But this system requires a
large number of precoded recipes and, more importantly, a
large capacity computer and a complex programming design.

Harper *et al* (10) developed a simplified method to carry
out the nutrient composition calculations required in planning
nutrient standard menus by means of an abacus-like device
which sums up the nutrients in each menu item by "bead units".
A row of beads corresponds to each nutrient in the standard.
Each bead unit represents 10 % of the meal standard for that
nutrient. In planning a menu, the corresponding units of

beads for each nutrient of a specific item are moved from one
side to the other. When 10 beads are moved to the opposite
side, the standard for that nutrient is met. Harper *et al* (10)
proposed that four additional beads per nutrient be allowed to
accumulate toward the next day's menu. The information on the
number of bead units for each nutrient in a particular item is
precalculated and supplied in a simple form to the menu planner. The abacus method has been tested in 60 schools in three
U.S.D.A. regions (10). The precalculations of nutrient composition of approximately 625 items were accomplished by a computer, using Agriculture Handbook No.8 data (11).

B. Computer-Assisted Nutritional Auditing

A simple computer programming method has been developed to
audit product formulations or special recipes from a nutritional standpoint. A complete nutritional profile of the recipes,
meals or products can be obtained in a short time. Handbook
No.8 (11) data are stored in magnetic tapes for ready access.
One sample page of such a computer print-out is shown in Table
1.

A typical example of a project requiring computer-assisted
nutritional auditing involved a study of school lunch systems
in several Florida school districts. The existing school menus
were processed using the computer, and the audit showed that
the Type A lunches served in the schools were adequate in protein and riboflavin, but were frequently low in vitamin A, thiamine, niacin, calcium and iron when compared with the 1/3 RDAs
for 10 - 12 year old children. Based on the initial print-out,
menu adjustments were made and the revised menu was processed
again. As a result of the auditing, a revised menu cycle that
would supply nutritionally adequate and balanced meals, was
recommended to the schools. This process may involve several
computer runs, but the speed and accuracy are far beyond any
manual calculation.

Computer data processing was also used by Miskimin *et al*
(12) in calculating the nutrient content of 156 frozen preplated school meals made by several nationally known companies. It
was determined that nutrients such as vitamin C, phosphorus,
vitamin A, calcium, thiamine, iron and calories were sometimes
at levels below the 1/3 RDA standards. Based on these calculations, and due to the fact that menu alternatives are often not
economical and/or not highly acceptable, Miskimin *et al* strong-
ly recommended nutrient fortification to achieve the required
standard in these school lunches.

C. Nutritional Data Sources

Presently, most nutritional calculations are based on the

TABLE I. Example of a Computerized Nutritional Audit of a Meal in an Hospital Menu Cycle

INGREDIENT	SODIUM MG	WATER GM	FOOD ENERGY CALORIES	PROTEIN GM	FAT GM	CARBO-HYDRATES GM	CALCIUM MG	IRON MG	VITAMIN A IU	THIAMINE MG	RIBO-FLAVIN MG	NIACIN MG	ASCORBIC ACID MG
367 HAMBURGER 2.26 OZ	41.13	43.03	113.27	13.09	6.32	0.00	7.59	1.96	12.65	0.05	0.11	3.16	0.00
1871 RICE 30.00 GM	1.50	3.59	108.89	2.00	0.11	24.11	7.19	0.86	0.00	0.13	0.00	1.04	0.00
2089 MUSHROOM, CREAM OF. 2.30 OZ	256.31	57.31	36.06	0.64	2.57	2.70	10.94	0.12	19.31	0.00	0.03	0.19	0.00
2064 BEEF BROTH, BOUILLON, A 0.53 OZ	96.75	13.65	3.85	0.62	0.00	0.32	0.00	0.05	0.00	0.00	0.00	0.14	0.00
475 BREAD CRUMBS, DRY, GRATED 4.50 GM	33.12	0.26	17.63	0.56	0.20	3.30	5.48	0.16	0.00	0.00	0.01	0.15	0.00
1317-3MARGARINE 4.50 GM	44.41	0.67	32.40	0.02	3.59	0.01	0.89	0.00	148.49	0.00	0.00	0.00	0.00
857 CORN, SWEET 50.00 GM	0.50	38.50	39.50	1.50	0.25	9.39	1.50	0.39	175.00	0.04	0.02	0.75	2.50
2282 TOMATOES, RIPE. 50.00 GM	1.50	46.50	11.00	0.54	0.09	2.34	6.50	0.25	449.99	0.02	0.01	0.34	11.50
459 WHITE BREAD 28.00 GM	141.96	9.79	75.31	2.43	0.89	14.11	19.59	0.67	0.00	0.07	0.04	0.64	0.00
1317-3MARGARINE 4.50 GM	44.41	0.67	32.40	0.02	3.59	0.01	0.89	0.00	148.49	0.00	0.00	0.00	0.00
1963 SALT 0.30 GM	116.27	0.00	0.00	0.00	0.00	0.00	0.75	0.00	0.00	0.00	0.00	0.00	0.00
2715 FRENCH CHEESE CAKE 1.50 OZ	68.46	18.90	131.04	2.09	8.52	12.01	25.19	0.46	136.92	0.01	0.05	0.08	0.16
GRAND TOTAL	846.34	232.91	601.39	23.58	26.20	68.36	86.59	4.96	1090.89	0.36	0.31	6.54	14.16
MINIMUM LEVEL STANDARD				16.00				2.20	520.00	0.20	0.20	3.40	
MEET MINIMUM LEVEL				YES				YES	YES	YES	YES	YES	
CALORIC DENSITY		38.72	100.00	3.92	4.35	11.36	14.39	0.82	181.39	0.06	0.06	1.08	2.35
CALORIC DENSITY STANDARD				4.60				0.62	150.00	0.05	0.05	0.99	
MEET CALORIC DENSITY				NO				YES	YES	YES	NO	YES	
RDA - USRDA-1			2500.0	45.0			1000.0	18.0	5000.0	1.5	1.7	20.0	60.0
PERCENT OF RDA			24.05	52.40			8.65	27.58	21.81	24.47	18.79	32.70	23.61

data found in U.S.D.A. Handbook No.8, published in 1963 (11).
However, there are limitations to the use of food composition
tables in the Handbook. An updated version, produced in loose
leaf form, is currently being prepared. Another useful source
of data is the U.S.D.A. Handbook No.456 (13), *Nutritive Value
of American Foods in Common Units* (13). Since this book tabu-
lates food composition in household measures and market units,
it is primarily intended for nutritional calculations involving
conventional menus, where the quantity of ingredients is often
expressed in common measures. A machine readable form of this
handbook will be available also.

D. *Meals with Limited Menu Selections*

As more sectors of the population eat in fast food restaurants, the nutritional adequacy of these meals is of great concern. Appledorf (14) analyzed some typical fast food meals.
One such meal, including a hamburger, french fries and a vanil-
la shake, was found to be low in iron content, unless the a-
mount ingested was increased to supply about one half of the
RDA for calories. Vitamin content was not analyzed. Consumer
Reports (15) pointed out that nearly all meals, including pizza, and fish and chips, were too heavy in calories. Several of
the meals analyzed provided almost one half of the daily requirements of the typical adult male. Six nutrients, namely
biotin, folacin, pantothenic acid, vitamin A, iron and copper
were most commonly found to be in short supply. According to
Consumer Reports (14), people on low sodium diets encounter a
problem with most fast food operations.

To overcome the nutritional problems of meals when a limited selection is offered, several approaches can be pursued:
(1) nutrification, (2) addition of menu items, or (3) providing
nutritional labeling information. Nutrification, that is fortification with nutrients, may not be the most desirable method
of overcoming the nutritional deficiencies of a limited menu
diet. The addition of new menu items selected to supply the
lacking ingredients could very well be the best approach. The
use of salad bars in fast food operations, and the serving of
raw vegetables such as carrot sticks, cherry tomatoes and cole
slaw in inflight snack meals, are among the recent developments
that suggest a growing awareness among non-institutional operators of their responsibility to supply balanced meals. Supplying nutritional information about fast food items to customers would call attention to the adequacy or deficiency of the
meals eaten, and allow the selection of other foods to supply
the lacking nutrients.

III. SYSTEM DESIGN

A. Selection of Raw Materials

With the advances in food technology, the spectrum of food materials available in both the retail and institutional markets has been greatly expanded. There are in addition to raw, fresh ingredients, many kinds of semiprocessed or completely processed products. For example, there are frozen, canned and frozen prepared vegetables; frozen portion-controlled meat items; prebreaded, prefried fish and poultry products; enriched or fortified breads and cereals, and new convenience products, including various food analogs, such as the soy-based "meat" products. Almost every item is available in several forms or types. A food service system designer, in deciding what types of products to choose, should consider if there are differences in their nutrient contents. Generally, one can use U.S.D.A. Handbook No. 8 (11) as a guide. Fennema (16) compiled data from this source to show the differences in vitamin losses from vegetables during canning and freezing. For vitamin A, the average losses were 10 % in canned and 12 % in frozen products. For thiamine, riboflavin, niacin and vitamin C the average losses in frozen vegetables were 20-26 %, whereas the losses in canned products were 42-67 % as compared to freshly cooked products.

Another example of differences in nutritive quality is the vitamin content of mashed potatoes prepared from fresh potatoes and dehydrated potato flakes or granules. The data drawn from Handbook No.8 (11), as shown in Table II, indicates that, while the riboflavin content reported is reasonably constant, the thiamine and ascorbic acid content of mashed potatoes made from the dehydrated products are about half of the levels reported for mashed potatoes made from fresh potatoes. It is important therefore to take into consideration the vitamin-fortified convenience products now available to the institutional trade.

TABLE II.   Thiamine, Riboflavin, and Ascorbic Acid Content
of Mashed Potatoes Made from Different Forms (11)

Potato Form	Vitamin content in mg/100g on a wet basis		
	Thiamine	Riboflavin	Ascorbic acid
Fresh	.08	.05	9
Dehydrated flakes	.04	.04	5
Dehydrated granules	.04	.05	3

Data in Handbook No.8 can serve only as a guide, of course. Many users find that the information on specific items of interest is not listed in the Handbook or that values in the Handbook are different from actual analytical results. For example, Handbook No.8 shows data for canned versus fresh or frozen products, but does not specify can sizes. Some studies have indicated that the No.10 cans, commonly used in institutional food service, retained lower amounts of vitamins as compared to the same products packed in smaller sized cans(17,18, 19). For example, in corned beef, the thiamine retention is reduced from 80 % in No.2 cans to 38 % in No.10 cans, while riboflavin retention is reduced from 103 to 97 %. In luncheon meat, niacin retention in 6 lb. cans is 21 % less than in No.2 cans.

With increasing numbers of new products and processing techniques, the data in Handbook No.8, which was published in 1963 are no longer adequate. Fortunately, since the advent of nutritional labeling regulations by the U.S. Food and Drug Administration in 1974, many food manufacturers have been including nutrition information on labels, or supply the information upon request in the case of institutional products. Food service system designers should secure nutrition information from food suppliers before making decisions on the selection of product forms.

B. *Ingredient Handling*

Following procurement of raw or processed ingredients, many preparation steps take place before the actual cooking and serving of foods. The methods of handling may have significant effects on nutrient retention. Certain aspects require particular attention: storage time and temperatures of raw materials, especially with frozen,chilled, and canned foods, thawing methods used in readying frozen meat, poultry, and fish for cooking and preparation procedures for raw fruits and vegetables.

C. *Storage Time and Temperature*

In an institutional food service operation, whether in an on-premise or central preparation system, raw materials are generally procured in sizeable quantities and stored. Furthermore, in a number of countries, donated or surplus commodities have, at times, been extensively used in feeding programs. These donated products may be subject to prolonged storage prior to their use.

Canned or other shelf-stable food products do undergo chemical reactions at room temperature, the extent of change being dependent on the time and temperature of storage, the packaging system, and the product characteristics. Studies have shown,

for example, that canned peas retained 81 % ascorbic acid, 70 %
thiamine, and 90 % carotene during storage at 80°F for twenty
four months (20). Under the same conditions of storage, orange
juice retained only 50 % ascorbic acid. It is thus relevant to
stress that cool storage (65°F or below) and short storage time
are desirable practices when planning storage facilities and
procedures for a food service system.

In many establishments, meats, poultry, and fish are procured chilled or frozen. In general, the losses of nutrients
during freezing and subsequent frozen storage of meat products
are low, provided storage temperatures are sufficiently low and
adequate protective packaging materials are used. Prolonged
storage, however, will undoubtedly result in some loss of B vitamins, especially thiamine (21).

D. Thawing Methods

Presently, many conventional food service operations purchase beef and other meats in a fabricated form. These meats
are usually packed in unit cartons weighing up to 50 lbs and
the various cuts of meat within these cartons may or may not be
separately wrapped. Packages of this type are generally thawed
whole in large operations. The possibility of nutrient losses
in this type of thawing is very real, since a long time is required to thaw the products.

When meat is thawed directly in water, leaching is an important mechanism of nutrient loss. Losses of B vitamins from
unpackaged beef steak have been shown to be greater when water
thawing is used than with air thawing at various temperatures.
Thawing meat in a refrigerator generally results in lesser or
equal losses of B vitamins than thawing in air or in water(16).

The use of microwave energy for the thawing of frozen foods
as explored in recent years, would have the obvious advantage
of a more rapid rate of thawing and therefore has the potential
of retaining more nutrients in thawed foods. Bezanson et al
(22) compared the quality and sanitary aspects of microwave
with typical water defrosting procedures for frozen shrimp. The
results indicated that microwave thawing retained about 2.6 %
more protein than did water thawing. This represented a 13.9 %
greater retention in protein. The moisture to protein ratio
was also smaller during microwave defrosting. Fat and ash content were similar for the two methods.

Microwave thawing tunnels for tempering bulk food from frozen storage to a chilled condition are in use by food processors and are being recommended for use in large institutional
food service operations.

E. Preparation Procedures for Raw Fruits and Vegetables

Food products which readily undergo browning in the presence of air (e.g. peeled white potatoes, cabbage, and salad greens) are sometimes held in plain or salt water, or water containing a reducing agent such as sulfite to inhibit the oxidative reactions until the foods are to be used in cooking. These conditions may result in leaching out the water soluble nutrients and may destroy thiamine, riboflavin, and niacin to some extent (23). For example, peeled potatoes, soaked for 28 hours in water, lost 14 % ascorbic acid, 8 % thiamine, 6 % riboflavin, and 14.2 % niacin.

In view of all the losses of nutrients that can occur in the handling of raw materials in institutional food preparation it behooves food service management to integrate inventory control, production planning, logistics, and quality control to maximize the quality attributes of the prepared food, sensory, nutritional, and microbiological.

F. Cooking Methods

1. *Batch Size Selection.* One of the significant aspects of food service, as compared to the home preparation of food, is the quantity of food cooked at a given time. In large institutional kitchens, one may use steam jacketed kettles in various sizes for cooking main dishes or vegetables. The use of large cooking batches requires extended time for filling, mixing, heating, cooling, and transferring. Unfortunately, there is virtually no published data available on batch size in relation to nutrient retention.

In cooking individual pieces of meat, poultry, or fish items, in roasting, baking, broiling, or frying, the differences between domestic and institutional cooking are not as serious as in the cooking of bulk materials. Continuous cooking equipment (water cooking, steam cooking, frying, roasting) is now available. Generally, this type of equipment, although intended for large operations, cooks foods in small batches, and is likely to be advantageous from the standpoint of nutrient retention (24).

2. *Selection of Equipment and Techniques.* There are many alternative ways to cook foods. For instance, vegetables may be cooked in boiling water, by high or low pressure steam, by stir-frying, or by microwave. There are now also many types of new or improved equipment developed for institutional usage such as the automated and/or continuous cooking equipment. What kind of equipment should one choose and what would be the differences in nutritional effects? There is a paucity of data in this area. Lachance (25) has reviewed the available informa-

tion on nutritional losses when common cooking methods are used. Wagner (24) studied vitamin C losses in vegetables cook- ed in a continuous steamer and reported that these losses were 13 to 30 % lower than those encountered when the same vegeta- bles were cooked by open kettle boiling. A bulletin from one equipment supplier compared vitamin C retention in the hot holding of vegetables following boiling in water, with cooking in a pass-through pressure steamer followed by a short holding time. The retention of vitamin C in brussel sprouts and pota- toes cooked in the continuous pressure cooker was much greater than that achieved when boiling water was used. It is encour- aging that at least some equipment manufacturers now provide nutritional data on foods prepared with their equipment.

The use of microwave ovens in food service operations is not new. Since microwave energy cooks foods at a very rapid rate, and since the cooking of vegetables in microwave ovens requires little or no water, this method has a potential bene- fit in retaining more heat-sensitive and water-soluble nutri- ents. Data on the comparison on conventional cooking with mi- crowaves have been published by a number of investigators.

Some of the recent data, such as reported by Baldwin and Tattambel (26) indicated that total cooking losses, including evaporation and drip losses, were greater in microwave heated frozen rib-eye steaks than in those gas oven heated. However, the microwave cooked steaks contained more nitrogen than the conventionally cooked steaks.

Bowers et al (27), Wing and Alexander (28) and Engler and Bowers (29) compared the vitamin B_6 content of meat items cook- ed by a conventional method with the microwave method. Results on a dry weight basis indicated that a slightly higher vitamin B_6 content was found in pork muscles cooked conventionally, but a significantly lower amount of vitamin B_6 was found in chicken breast samples cooked by the conventional methods as compared to microwave cooking. In the case of reheated of precooked turkey roast, only slight differences were observed between the two methods.

One can conclude, from the published information, that mi- crowave heating is equal to or better than many conventional cooking methods in preserving nutrients in most food items.

G. Service of Prepared Foods

Institutionally prepared food is generally held for a peri- od of time prior to, or during, service. For instance, in a self-service operation, such as a cafeteria, hot food may be held in a steam table during the serving period. Cold food may be held in the chill section of the self-service counter. In conventional restaurants or hotels, a bain marie or a dry food warmer may be used for holding hot foods. In some feeding systems, a central kitchen is responsible for food production and prepared food may be held hot or cold in insulated containers and delivered to the serving sites. In other instances, the prepared hot food is held chilled or frozen for later use on the same premises, or for delivery to other serving sites, followed by reconstitution to the serving temperatures. Some systems use commercially available frozen prepared foods.

   1. *Hot Holding for Delayed Service and Transporting.* Temperatures for hot holding are normally in the range of $140°$ to $212°F$ (60-100°C). The time period from preparation to service may be up to three or more hours. This kind of practice is common in cafeteria-type restaurants, schools, hospitals and airline operations, and much of the heat labile nutrients may be lost during the holding period. Data (30) indicate that, for example, cabbage held on a steam table lost 25 % of its initial ascorbic acid content after 15 minutes, 40 % after 30 minutes, 50 % after 45 minutes, 60 % after 60 minutes, 70 % after 75 minutes, and 75 % after 90 minutes. A delayed service method, to brown top round beef roasts at $425°F$ ($218°C$) followed by holding at $140°F$ ($60°C$) for 24 hours was reported to retain more thiamine but less riboflavin than roasting at $300°F$ ($148.9°C$) without further holding (31).
   In systems where hot cooked foods are placed in insulated food carriers for transportation one might expect that nutrient losses would be lower than those occurring when steam table temperatures are used. However, Wagner (24) reported that significant vitamin A and vitamin C losses can occur when foods are held in insulated containers. Table III shows the vitamin losses in several food products.

   TABLE III.   *Vitamin A and C Losses in Foods Held Hot in*
                Insulated Container after Cooking(24)

Food product	Vitamin	% Loss after		
		1 Hour	2 Hours	3 Hours
Fried egg	A	6.0	7.5	15.5
Liver	A	12.6	16.8	22.0
Mashed potatoes	A	16.0	28.1	44.0
Cabbage	C	61.0	71.9	80.0
Spinach	C	53.8	68.1	75.3

Head (32) determined the losses of nutrients occurring during transportation of foods in insulated carts from a central commissary to satellite schools. Results showed 19 % loss of ascorbic acid and 20 % of iron from hot foods. Riboflavin, thiamine, and calcium showed no change.

A recent advertisement from a cart manufacturer claimed that there was no nutritional loss in meals held in their specially designed hot holding carts(140-160°F;2 hours). Nutrients studied were thiamine, niacin, available lysine, and vitamin A. Vitamin C, which is very unstable to heat and oxidation, was not included. Furthermore, data shown were expressed per 100 g wet weight basis instead of on a dry basis or per serving basis. The moisture loss that was evident during the holding would compensate for nutrient losses in the heat labile nutrients. This, unfortunately, is an example of how nutritional data can be misinterpreted and used to reach invalid conclusions.

2. Chill-Holding for Delayed Service and Transporting. Salads, desserts, and beverages are usually held chilled in food service operations. Harris and Von Loesecke (33), reviewing published data from a variety of sources, indicated that chilled items gradually lose their vitamin content, especially vitamin C during the chill-holding. For example, 53 % of ascorbic acid in cole slaw was lost in two hours when vinegar was used on cole slaw. Cucumbers lost 33-35 % ascorbic acid after standing for one hour, and 41-49 % after three. Cantaloupe slices lost 35 % ascorbic acid during 24 hours of refrigerated storage. Orange juice held at 48°F (9°C) lost 17 % thiamine in 24 hours.

Head (32) reported that losses of ascorbic acid, thiamine, and iron were significant in cold foods held in insulated containers for 60-100 minutes during transportation from a central commissary to schools, but no information was given as to the actual holding temperature or the type of cart.

It is relevant to stress that to preserve their nutrient content, cold foods should be properly packaged and stored or displayed at a sufficiently low temperature (below 40°F) for a minimum period of time.

3. Chill-Holding and Reconstitution. The trend of modern food service systems is to separate the production from the service of food, both in time and in place. Hot food can either be chilled or frozen and then reheated at the time or place of serving. A variety of packaging materials and techniques, chilled or frozen holding equipment, delivery and transportation means, and thermal reconstitution methods are available to the system designer.

Some areas of concern are the different types of distribution and forms of packing used, such as individual portioning, preplating, or bulk packing, and where, when, and how this handling should take place for optimal nutrient retention. Unfortunately nutritional information of this type is scant. Only fragments of systems have been evaluated in most studies.

Chill-holding of prepared foods, followed by reheating at serving time appears to be nutritionally superior to hot holding of freshly prepared foods for three hours, which is a common practice in conventional food service operations. Wagner (24) reported that vitamin A and vitamin C losses in a number of food items chilled after cooking and held for 24, 48, or 72 hours prior to reheating to 158°F (70°C) were considerably lower than losses in foods held hot for three hours.

In some food service operations, beef or turkey roasts may be precooked, sliced, held chilled, and reheated to serving temperature when needed. Boyle and Funk (34) compared thiamine retention in beef roast, sliced hot at 140°F (60°C), with beef that was chilled for 24 hours, then sliced and reheated to the same temperature. The chilled, sliced, and reheated beef showed 68 % thiamine retention compared to 79 % for beef held hot for 90 minutes and then sliced.

Various types of heating equipment are available for the thermal reconstitution of chilled or frozen prepared foods. These include forced air convection ovens, hot water immersion heaters, conventional electric or gas ovens, low or high pressure steamers, and infrared or microwave ovens. Comparison of these different heating methods on nutrient retention is obviously important.

Bowers and Fryer (27) studied the retention of thiamine and riboflavin in cooked, cooked and reheated, and cooked, frozen, and reheated turkey muscles, using gas and microwave ovens. Their results on a moisture free, fat free, basis showed no significant difference in thiamine retention between the two types of ovens used, but a higher riboflavin content was found in muscles heated by gas ovens. Different treatments using the same oven had no significant difference on the retention of thiamine and riboflavin.

A supplier of food service equipment, who offers a system that involves rapid chilling of cooked foods to below 3°C and chill-holding at 3°C or below for up to 5 days before reconstitution in a specially designed infrared oven, reported on nutrient losses in this system. Losses were significant for vitamin C but not for vitamins A, B_1 and B_2 and pantothenic acid, except for the vitamin A in fish and vitamin B_2 in green vegetables in which the reductions were significant. The nutritional data being reported on a per 100 g wet basis makes it difficult, however, to evaluate the results.

4. Frozen Holding and Reconstitution. Erheart (35) studied
ascorbic acid retention in broccoli that was freshly cooked and
compared it with retention observed when broccoli was frozen
and cooked in a covered pan, or frozen and reheated in a "boil-
in-bag". On a dry basis, the ascorbic acid content of the raw
samples averaged 998 mg/100 g; of the freshly cooked samples,
548 mg/100 g; of the frozen conventionally heated samples, 553
mg/100 g, and of the boil-in-bag samples, 635 mg/100 g. Thus,
the latter method proved helpful in retaining more ascorbic acid than is retained in fresh cooking or in freezing followed by
conventional heating.

The staff of the Catering Research Unit at the University
of Leeds (36) compared ascorbic acid, thiamine, riboflavin, and
lysine contents of prepared foods, frozen in bulk, and reheated
using convection ovens (i.e. "cook/freeze" system) with conventionally prepared hospital foods. Their data (Table IV) show
that the cook/freeze system resulted in a significantly higher
ascorbic acid retention than the conventional system, but differences in thiamine and riboflavin content between the two
systems were not significant. Improved lysine retention (i.e.
less damage to protein quality) was also observed with the frozen system.

Kahn and Livingston (37) reported that selected, frozen
prepared, individually packaged main dishes, such as beef stew,
chicken a la king, shrimp newburg, and peas in cream sauce, retained an average of 93.5, 90 and 86 % of thiamine after reheating in microwave, infrared and hot water immersion, respectively. The same products, freshly prepared and held on a
steam table for one, two or three hours, retained only 78 %, 74
%, and 67 % thiamine respectively.

Lachance *et al* (7) compared the thiamine retention of commercial frozen chicken pot pies that were baked in a convection
oven,infrared oven or conventional electric oven to an internal
temperature of 180°F. They also determined the effect of steam
table pan holding of uncovered products. Their results showed
that chicken pot pies retained thiamine rather well during reheating, except in the electric oven, where a longer time was
required. Subsequent holding on the steam table resulted in
additional losses.

Ang *et al* (37) compated vitamin retention in six bulk-packed products, prepared freshly by conventional methods, and held
hot for up to three hours, with frozen prepared products reheated in microwave, infrared or convection ovens, or in a high
pressure steamer.The six products studied were:mashed potatoes,
peas with onions, diced carrots, beans with frankfurters, pot
roast with gravy, and fried fish portions. They found that the
microwave, or infrared, heating or reheating of frozen foods
(4-5 lb packs) resulted in: (1) similar effect in most cases,
(2) equal or greater retention of thiamine and riboflavin as

TABLE IV. *Nutrient Content of Conventionally Prepared Foods and Precooked Frozen Foods Reheated in Convection Ovens (36)*

Food	Ascorbic Acid		Thiamine		Riboflavin		Lysine	
	Conventional (mg)	Cook/Freeze (mg)	Conventional (mg)	Cook/Freeze (mg)	Conventional (mg)	Cook/Freeze (mg)	Conventional (mg)	Cook/Freeze (mg)
Potatoes	11.3[a]	28.4	–	–	–	–	–	–
Cabbage	5.2	11.7	–	–	–	–	–	–
Peas	4.0	12.0	.15	.26	–	–	–	–
Pork roast	–	–	.92	.11	.24	.20	–	–
Roast lamb	–	–	.22	.22	.19	.18	6.22[b]	7.21
Fried cod	–	–	.12	.10	.04	.06	–	–
Minced beef	–	–	–	–	–	–	6.80	6.74

[a] mg vitamin/100 g edible portion
[b] available lysine in g/16 g N

compared to fresh preparation followed by 1½ hour hot holding, and (3) retention comparable to, or better than, those encountered after convection heating. The average retention values are shown in Table V. To heat single layered fish portions (2 lbs/pack), the convection oven was found to be slightly more favorable than the microwave or the infrared ovens, with respect to thiamine retention. High pressure steaming, in most instances, resulted in substantially lower amounts of thiamine and riboflavin than the other reconstitution methods, but was superior to three hour hot holding after preparation.

Ang et al (39) further reported that the infrared reheating of char-broiled frozen beef patties retained significantly lower amounts of thiamine and riboflavin as compared to other heating methods, and infrared heating was also relatively unfavorable to thiamine retention in frozen fried chicken parts. In all cases the hot holding practice for three hours was greatly detrimental to thiamine content.

Five of the bulk-packed products studied by Ang et al (38) were freeze dried and evaluated for protein quality by Bodwell and Womack who reported that the conventional or convenience food handling procedures did not seriously damage the nutritive value of the protein (40).

IV. SUMMARY AND CONCLUSIONS

To insure everyone an adequate and balanced nutrient intake when eating away from home, food service operators have a responsibility to provide nutritionally sound menus, using well-designed systems that maintain the maximum levels of nutrients present in the raw food.

A good menu is the most essential element of the system. Personnel in charge of the menu development should have knowledge about the nutritional composition of foods. Computer assisted auditing can be easily used to handle the calculations. Meals offering limited menu selection, such as in fast food restaurants, should be supplemented with other items, such as fresh fruits and vegetables to make deficiencies in micronutrients. Nutritional information labeling would be helpful in educating consumers in making proper food choices.

Following menu planning, a food service system should be designed with constant consideration of its nutritional implications. Meals produced using a poor system may be of low nutritional quality, even if the menu has been planned properly. The system designer should first select the raw ingredient forms that are of best quality and most suitable to his menu and anticipated system. Next, decisions must be made concerning ingredient storage and handling methods, cooking procedures,

TABLE V. Riboflavin and Thiamine Retention in Freshly Prepared and Bulk Packed Frozen Foods Subjected to Various Heating Treatments (38)

Treatment	Percent Retention	
	Riboflavin	*Thiamine*
Freshly Prepared Foods:		
No holding	95.20	97.79
Held ½ hour	94.25	94.23
Held 1-½ hour	93.18	89.77
Held 3 hours	91.50	83.68
Frozen Prepared Foods:		
Thawed	95.77	98.57
Reheated in convection oven and held ½ hour	94.72	89.84
Reheated in infrared oven and held ½ hour	94.44	91.77
Reheated in pressure steamer and held ½ hour	90.41	85.42
Reheated in microwave oven and held ½ hour	94.34	91.41

[a] *average of 4 to 5 products*

equipment selection, hot, chilled or frozen holding of prepared food, packaging, transporting, reheating, and serving of meals. The impact of the proposed alternatives on nutrient retention should be one of the major factors in making these decisions.

The stability of nutrients is also affected by light, air, temperature, and holding storage time. Nutrient losses are also associated with physical separations, such as occur in trimming, leaching, and dripping. Nutrient preservation can be enhanced by minimizing unfavorable conditions. Different methods of food preparation and handling affect nutrient retention differently, and this must always be taken into account.

It is unfortunate that there is only limited information available on nutritional studies conducted under well controlled research conditions and utilizing a proper design so as to be able to compare alternative systems. It is difficult to directly compare the results reported by various investigators since sample collection, food handling procedures, and data presentations vary significantly.

In reviewing the literature, however, one may conclude that certain nutrients, for example thiamine and ascorbic acid, are very unstable to high temperature and air and the hot holding of prepared foods for a long period of time is detrimental to these nutrients. Chilled or frozen holding of cooked items and later reheating, at the time and site of serving, may be advantageous in a nutritional sense. However, the time lag between the end of preparation and packing for chilling or freezing, the rate of cooling, the packaging materials, the temperature and length of time in holding, the reheating methods and other handling details all influence the final nutritional quality of meals. The food service sytem designer should always analyze the extent of exposure of foods to the nutritional factors in a proposed system, and search for data to assist in making sound decisions. Last but not least, research is definitely needed to generate quantitative nutritional information to guide the developments in the food service industry.

V. REFERENCES

1. Livingston, G. E. *Cereal Foods World, 20,* 534 (1975).
2. Anon. "Dietary Levels of Household in the United States, Spring 1965", Agric. Res. Serv., U.S.D.A. (1968)
3. Murphy, E. W., Koons, P. C. and Page L. *J. Am. Diet. Assoc. 55,* 372 (1969)
4. Walker, M. A. and Page, L. *J. Am. Diet. Assoc. 66,* 146 (1975)
5. Walker, M. A. and Page, L. *J. Am. Diet. Assoc. 68,* 34 (1976)

6. Livingston, G. E., Ang, C. Y. W. and Chang, C. M. *Food Technol. 27,* 28 (1973)
7. Lachance, P. A., Ranadive, A. S. and Mates, J. *Food Technol. 27,* 36 (1973)
8. Gelpi, M. J., Balintfy, J. L., Dennis II, L. C. and Findorff, I. K. *J. Am. Diet. Assoc. 61,* 637 (1972)
9. Balintfy, J. See Chapter 8
10. Frey, A. L., Harper, J. M., Jansen, G. R., Crews, R. H., Sighetomi, C. T. and Lough, J. B. *J. Am. Diet. Assoc. 66,* 242 (1975)
11. Watt, B. K. and Merrill, A. L. "Composition of Foods: Raw, Processed, Prepared" *Handbook No.8,* U.S.D.A., Washington, DC (1963)
12. Miskimin, D., Bowers, J. and Lachance, P.A. *Food Technol. 28,* 52 (1974)
13. Adams, C. F. "Nutritive Value of American Foods in Common Units" *Agriculture Handbook No. 456,* U.S.D.A., Washington, DC (1975)
14. Appledorf, H. *Food Technol. 28,* 50 (1974)
15. Anon. *Consumer Reports 40 (5),* 278 (1975)
16. Fennema, O. *in* "Nutritional Evaluation of Food Processing" (Harris, R. S. and Karmas, E., eds.) p. 244, 2nd ed. Avi, Westport, Connecticut (1975)
17. Feaster, J. F., Tompkins, M. D. and Ives, M. *Food Ind. 20,* 82 (1948)
18. Greenwood, D. A., Kraybill, H. R., Feaster, J. F. and Jackson, J. M. *Ind. Eng. Chem. 36,* 922 (1944)
19. Cain, R. F. *Food Technol. 21,* 998 (1967)
20. Feaster, J. F. *in* "Nutritional Evaluation of Food Processing" (Harris, R. S. and Von Loesecke, H., eds.) p. 337, Wiley, New York (1960)
21. Schweigert, B. S. and Lushbough, C. H. *in* "Nutritional Evaluation of Food Processing" (Harris, R. S. and Von Loesecke, H., eds.) p. 376, Wiley, New York (1960)
22. Bezanson, A., Learson, R. and Teich, W. *Microwave Energy Applic. Newsltr. 6,* 3 (1973)
23. Feaster, J. F. *in* "Nutritional Evaluation of Food Processing" (Harris, R. S. and Von Loesecke, H., eds.) p. 109, Wiley, New York (1960)
24. Wagner, K. H. "On the Question of Vitamin Preservation in Food which has been Treated According to the Multimet-Multi-Serv Procedure, as Compared to the Preservation in Orthodox Thermo-Containers (Thermophores)" *Bulletin CX-167,* Crown-X, Cleveland (1971)
25. Lachance, P.A. *in* "Nutritional Evaluation of Food Processing" (Harris, R. S. and Karmas, E., eds.) p. 463, 2nd ed. Avi, Westport, Connecticut (1975)
26. Baldwin, R. E. and Tettambel, J. E. *Microwave Energy Applic. Newsltr. 8,* 3 (1974)

27. Bowers, J. A. and Fryer, B. *J. Am. Diet. Assoc. 60,* 399
     (1972)
28. Wing, R. W. and Alexander, J. C. *J. Am. Diet. Assoc. 61,*
     661 (1972)
29. Engler, P. P. and Bowers, J. A. *J. Food Sci. 40,* 615
     (1975)
30. Harris, R. S. *in* "Nutritional Evaluation of Food Proces-
     sing" (Harris, R. S. and Von Loesecke, H. eds.) p. 418,
     Wiley, New York (1960)
31. Gaines, M. K., Perry, M. K. and Van Duyne, F. O. *J. Am.
     Diet. Assoc. 48,* 204 (1966)
32. Head, M. K., *J. Am. Diet. Assoc. 65,* 423 (1974)
33. Harris, R. S. and Von Loesecke, H. "Nutritional Evaluation
     of Food Processing", Wiley, New York (1960)
34. Boyle, M. A. and Funk, K. *J. Am. Diet. Assoc. 60,* 398
     (1972)
35. Erheart, M. S., *Food Technol. 23,* 238 (1969)
36. Staff, Catering Research Unit, "An Experiment in Hospital
     Catering Using the Cook/Freeze System" University of
     Leeds, Leeds, United Kingdom (1970)
37. Kahn, L. N. and Livingston, G. E., *J. Food Sci. 35,* 349,
     (1970)
38. Ang, C. Y. W., Chang, C. M., Frey, A. E. and Livingston,
     G. E., *J. Food Sci. 40,* 997 (1975)
39. Ang, C. Y. W., Basilio, L. A., Cato, B. A. and Livingston,
     G. E., *J. Food Sci. 43,* 1024 (1978)
40. Bodwell, C. E. and Womack, M. "Effects of Heating Methods
     on Protein Nutritional Value of Five Fresh or Frozen Food
     Products", presented at Inst. Food Technol. Meeting, New
     Orleans, Louisiana, May 1974

CHAPTER 22

ESTABLISHING AND MAINTAINING MICROBIOLOGICAL
STANDARDS IN FOOD SERVICE SYSTEMS

Gerald J. Silverman

Food Sciences Laboratory
US Army Natick Research & Development Command
Natick, Massachusetts

I. INTRODUCTION

The main objectives for monitoring food service operations are to produce safe and wholesome products and to minimize microbiological and chemical deterioration during processing and storage. The terms "safety" and "wholesomeness" are often legally defined, while the techniques involved in effectively monitoring these systems can, in fact, vary greatly, reflecting the diversity and complexity of individual production operations, products, and methods of delivery. The surveillance system must also be cost effective. These objectives, however, are readily attainable because the causative microorganisms involved in food intoxication, infection, and spoilage generally behave in biologically predictable ways. Their control requires the exercise of principles well established in food microbiology. Nevertheless, problems occur continuously.

Foodborne disease incidents have occurred with varying frequency in every type of feeding system. When individual facilities are examined, some appear to be a higher risk to the consumer than others. It is estimated that 600,000 food establishments in the United States serve approximately 150,000,000 meals daily and the ability of regulatory agencies to monitor them effectively is limited. The main responsibility therefore lies within a facility (1). While the number of cases reported each year is a small fraction of those actually suspected of occurring, recent data (2) indicate that during the years 1968-1972, 43 % of reported foodborne disease outbreaks were due to mishandling in food service facilities or processing plants.

Copyright © 1979 by Academic Press, Inc.
All rights of reproduction in any form reserved
ISBN: 0-12-453150-4

II. HAZARDOUS MICROORGANISM

Hazard represents the number and nature of the organisms
present, including the probability of whether they or their
metabolites will be able to infect a consumer.   The definition
of the safety of any food item is really probabilistic.   Hazard analysis is a term generally employed for assessing a production or feeding system in order to determine those areas or
operations in which microorganisms can be introduced into the
system or can proliferate.   These latter points or operations
are known as "critical control points."

The fact that hazardous organisms are present does not
mean that a foodborne illness is a certainty (3). Bryan identified the most significant factors responsible for outbreaks,
including failure to refrigerate foods, inadequate heating of
foods, infected food handlers, preparing food too far in advance, adding raw ingredients to cooked foods not receiving any
further processing, holding food at a temperature at which bacteria can multiply or are not destroyed, improper heating of
foods, and contamination of cooked foods by raw foods and poor
sanitation.   Even though the number of microorganisms that are
of potential concern are numerous, in reality, those of greatest concern are far fewer (Table I).   The four gram-positive
organisms produce specific enterotoxins, and three also produce
heat-resistant spores. While the toxin of *Clostridium botulinum*
is extremely potent and the presence of any viable cells is
therefore considered significant, small concentrations of the
other three gram-positive organisms are generally tolerated,
although not their toxins.   In certain cases, especially that
of *Staphylococcus aureus*, low numbers of relatively heat-labile
cells are not a good guarantee of the absence of enterotoxin.

*TABLE I.   Microorganisms Capable of Causing Foodborne
Intoxication and/or Infections*

Organism	Gram	Spore	Enterotoxigenic	Infective
Clostridium botulinum	+	+	+	
Clostridium perfringens	+	+	+	
Bacillus cereus	+	+	+	
Staphylococcus aureus	+		+	
Escherichia coli	−		+	+
Salmonella	−		+	+
Shigella	−		?	+
Klebsiella			?	+
Vibrio parahaemolyticus	−			+

The gram-negative organisms are considered to be infective rather than enterotoxigenic but, in fact, recent studies (4,5) of Enterobacteriaceae indicate that enterotoxins are also involved. Organisms such *Pseudomonas aeruginosa* (6) are mainly opportunistic pathogens and are of concern in specific situations. Some of these microorganisms are also capable of contributing to spoilage.

To control these organisms, Morrison (7) recently stated that "(1) if they are not in the food, prevent their entrance; (2) if they are naturally in the food or get in from contact with the environment destroy them; (3) if they cannot be destroyed, prevent their growth." This is a sensible guide that should be followed by those in food service.

The organisms listed in Table I are capable of being isolated directly by specific media and identified by confirmatory tests that, in many instances, are time consuming. Nevertheless, the trend is for regulatory agencies to incorporate specific organisms into their regulatory constraints.

A traditional method for evaluating the microbiological quality of foods is by utilizing indices that are capable of being readily quantitated (Table II). Indices are presumed to be an indirect measure of the presence of food poisoning, infectious, or excessive numbers of spoilage organisms. They do indicate inadequate processing or postprocessing contamination, and are useful if employed on selected products and processes (6,8). Obvious advantages of using indices are that they are rapid, simple, and economical. They can be extremely useful for imposing internal constraints (i.e. standards). An example of their use in a military feeding system is given in Table III. These cooked items were considered as being nonconforming by having one or more of the indices exceed their constraint. Other data had demonstrated that foods properly processed and served at the proper temperature (140°F;60°C or 55°F 13°C) easily conformed to the externally imposed constraints. Most of the items that exceeded some constraint were also served at an improper temperature.

TABLE II. Microbial Indices

Aerobic plate count	Fecal streptococci
Anaerobic plate count	Halophilic organisms
Psychrophilic plate count	Osmophilic organisms
Thermophilic plate count	Spore count
Coliforms	Direct microscopic
Fecal coliforms	Dye reduction

TABLE III. Cooked Items That Exceeded the Internal
Microbial Constraints[a,b]

	Serving temperature		Aerobic plate	Coliform count	Fecal coliform count
	$°F$	$°C$	$(CFU[c]/g)$	$(MPN[d]/g)$	$(MPN[d]/g)$
Meat loaf	135	57	4.3×10^3	93	4
Roast beef	144	62	1.3×10^4	2.4×10^4	Neg[e]
Ham	--	--	1.1×10^6	1.1×10^3	75
Veal loaf	150	66	1.5×10^5	20	7
Macaroni, meat, and cheese	115	46	3×10	1.1×10^3	2.9×10^2
Fried potato	136	58	2×10^6	1.1×10^3	1.5×10^2
Tuna salad	62	17	1×10^5	2.4×10^2	4.6×10^2
Macaroni, and egg	60	16	TFTC[c]	1.5×10^2	Neg
Macaroni	--	--	3×10^3	23	9
Macaroni and egg	50	10	6×10^5	1.1×10^3	2.9×10^2

[a] Less than or equal to 10^5 CFU/g, 10^2 coliform organisms/g, 10^3 S. aureus/g, and no fecal coliform. All samples contained less than 10 S. aureus/g
[b] From Silverman et al (27)
[c] Colony forming unit
[d] Most probable number
[e] Negative
[f] Too few to count

One index, the aerobic plate count, has been extremely useful as an indicator for the presence of hazardous organisms (9,10) in processed foods and can also serve as a measure of potential shelf life for raw foods (11,12). Hobbs (10) has suggested that it is adequate as a sole index. Others (13,14, 15), however, consider the aerobic plate count of limited value.

The fact that food items may exceed a microbiological constraint does not mean that they are dangerous. To prove this would require additional testing for the presence of specific hazardous organisms. In most instances, monitoring measures the extent to which a food system is approaching a hazardous condition. It can also locate those operations responsible for contamination. Because it is a biological measurement, and microbiological tests take time, its ability to predict is limited.

It should be noted that acceptable levels of contamination for foods ingested raw might be unacceptable for cooked foods.

III. SPOILAGE MICROORGANISMS

The microorganisms mainly responsible for typical spoilage of refrigerated fresh foods are presented in the first column of Table IV. Of these, certain of the *Pseudomonas* are the most active. In fact, only certain members of each of these genera are capable of significant spoilage activity (16,17,18). Once processed, the indigenous microflora of the raw materials are selectively altered and typical spoilage may be delayed, replaced by atypical biochemical activity, or prevented entirely (19).

In general, spoilage organisms must be present in large numbers, usually over 10^7 cells/g or cm^2 before typical spoilage aroma or food degradation occurs. The actual concentration required will depend upon those factors that regulate growth and metabolic activity: oxygen, pH, Eh, temperature, etc (6,20).

TABLE IV. Microorganisms Commonly Causing Spoilage

At refrigeration temperatures (psychrophiles)	At higher temperatures[a] (mesophiles, thermophiles)
Pseudomonas	*Streptococcus*
Moraxella	*Lactobacillus*
Acinetobacter	*Clostridium*
Flavobacter	*Bacillus*
	Enterobacteriaceae
	Molds
	Yeast

[a]*Generally in the absence of competition from psychrophillic organisms*

IV. FACTORS WHICH REGULATE MICROBIAL POPULATIONS

In order for hazardous or spoilage organisms to present a problem in a feeding system, a number of conditions must be met (Table V).

The food must become inoculated with the organisms either in the raw material or during processing, packaging, or serving. The organisms should be able to multiply or survive in the food; the possibility for multiplication is often increased after competitive microflora are eliminated (21). The favorable temperature growth range and required time will vary with the organism and food, but at the extremes of the growth range, the time required for replication becomes too large to be of significance. If these conditions result in sufficient multiplication of an infectious organism or the production of a toxin, then a food poisoning incident can be prevented only by subjecting the food to a sufficiently high temperature to destroy the dangerous organism or the labile toxin. Thermal processing would, of course, have no effect on a heat-stable toxin or a microbial spore. These, then, are the factors to look for when examining a food service system to determine whether or not microbial growth-promoting or sustaining loci exist. If they do, appropriate measures must then be taken.

Many effective commercial operations control the microbiological quality of their raw materials. Recently, the states of Oregon and New York suggested microbiological standards for raw ground beef, and Canada has indicated its intention of imposing standards.

Oregon proposed criteria of an aerobic plate count (APC) level of 10^6 CFU/g and an $E.$ $coli$ standard of 50/g for raw ground beef. New York State has set standards of 10^6 CFU/g and 10 $E.$ $coli$/g. Although this approach has been criticized(22,23)

TABLE V. *Factors Regulating the Presence and Quality*
          of Microorganisms in Foods

Level of contamination
Microbial spectrum
Water activity, pH, Eh, solute concentration, oxygen concentration
Temperature-time
Repair mechanisms
Additives

---

it has also been defended as an effective mechanism for ensuring a more wholesome consumer product, (e.g. many people consume raw hamburger as steak tartare).

The intrinsic factors of foods, i.e. water activity, pH, Eh, and chemical composition are of vital importance since they usually characterize a food, and for a given food item, will establish the rate and extent of microbial growth. Difficulties arise when a food item is atypical and undesirable microorganisms can grow. As examples, fermented products, which depend upon a low pH and whose pH is raised due to the addition of neutral ingredients, or dried products, which depend upon a low water activity and are too nonhomogeneous or are allowed to absorb water.

Probably the most important extrinsic factor is temperature. All food systems depend upon properly processed foods, maintained properly refrigerated at, or below 40°F (4.4°C), or above 140°F (60°C).

The growth of pathogens and spoilage organisms can be prevented or drastically curtailed by low-temperature storage. Microorganisms are capable of growth in the temperature range of -7 to 80°C (20). The optimal growth range for psychrophiles is 10°C with a maximal of 35°C; for mesophiles, 30-37°C with a maximal of 43°C; and for thermophiles, 45-50°C (6).

The shelf life of perishable foods can be significantly extended and safety maintained by storage in the latent heat zone of 28°F (-2°C) rather than 32-45°F (0-8°C) (12). Elmswiler *et al* (25) suggested that ground beef can greatly benefit by storage at 29°F (-1.7°C) in an oxygen impermeable film.

Specific temperature constraints are based upon accepted standards, and that these and the general guidelines should be readily attainable by existing equipment. Constraints used by the author for the military are presented in Table VI. It is often necessary to impose time constraints in conjunction with temperature (26). For example, Silverman *et al* (27) required that cooked items be chilled within three hours of preparation and be displayed for no more than three hours at 55°F (Table VI). Some constraints were based on quality considerations rather than microbiological hazards, and involved limitations on shelf-life.

Cooking temperatures of 160°F (71°C) or greater are generally acceptable and are widely used (28), but lower cooking temperatures for processing certain items may improve quality without appreciably decreasing safety. For example, recommended cooking temperatures of 125-145°F (52-60°C) for rare roast beef will be acceptable for certain cuts of beef if internal contamination by aluminum nails (used for improving thermal distribution), thermometers, deboning, or folding is avoided, and postprocessing handling minimizes contamination (29).

TABLE VI.   Time and Temperature Constraints for Entrees
and Vegetable Items for Military Systems

Stage	State	Temperature		Time	
		^{o}F	^{o}C	Hours	Days
Purchased	Fresh	≤ 45	7		
	Frozen	≤ 0	-18		
	Canned	-	-		
	Dehydrated	-	-		
	Cured	≤ 45	7		
Processed	Cooked[a]	>165	74		
	Cooked frozen	≥160,0	71,-18	3[f]	
	Cooked chilled	≥160,≤45	71, 7	3[b]	
	Chilled	55[c]	13	3	
Stored[e]	Heated	≥140	60	5-8[d]	
	Chilled	≤ 45	7	3	to 21
	Frozen	≤ 0	-18	28	to 180
Served	Heated	≥140	60	5	
	Chilled	≤ 55	13	3	

[a]With the exception of rolled roasts, which may be cooked to
an internal temperature of $140^{o}F$ ($60^{o}F$)

[b]This indicates the maximum time allowed for chilling

[c]If displayed for more than 3 hours the temperature should
not exceed $45^{o}F$ ($7^{o}C$) and pertains mainly to salads

[d]Maximum time allowed for storage at the serving temperature

[e]Precooked entree items and salads

[f]Time to reach the desired temperature after cooking

Due to recent outbreaks of salmonellosis, the U.S. Department of Agriculture now requires precooked roast beef to be exposed to either $145^{o}F$ ($63^{o}C$) or its lethal equivalent (30). For processors who desire a "rarer" roast beef 15 additional and specific time – temperature combinations below $145^{o}F$ ($63^{o}C$) are allowed. Restrictions are also placed upon the type of processing and monitoring equipment. While the use of cooking temperatures below $160^{o}F$ ($71^{o}C$) can improve quality, the benefits may be marginal for certain products (26,31,32) and the practice is not recommended for a variety of products in food service systems (33). Mercuri *et al* (31) found that federal regulations requiring precooked turkey rolls to be heated to 160°F (71°C) were not stringent enough since Eastern type rolls required a treatment to 180°F(82°C) to reduce coliforms and enterococci, and 199°F (93°C) to reduce the standard plate counts to acceptable levels.

Food processed to eliminate the heat-labile psychrophiles can also become more stable during subsequent refrigerated storage (Table VII). Little or no multiplication occurred dur- during 9 days at 40°F for heated items. Storage at 40°F, however, did not prevent microbial growth in raw salad items unless vinegar was present (34).

TABLE VII. *Microbiology of Chilled Prepared Items during Refrigerated Storage*[a]

Food item	Microorganisms (per gram)					
	Mesophiles			Psychrophiles		
	0	4-7	7-9	0	4-7	7-9
Chicken pot pie	210	–	80	175	–	50
Pork spareribs	65	35	35	30	30	45
BBQ frankfurters	95	25	20	45	10	10
Corn beef	20	16000	60	20	7300	25
BBQ beef	25	10	20	10	10	15
Roast beef	725	1000	15000	625	900	13000
Salisbury steak	4200	–	3100	625	–	5400
Fried chicken	4400	–	80	2600	–	65
Cucumber salad without vinegar	–	1.2×10^{6}[b]	35×10^{6}	–	420000[b]	31×10^{6}
Cucumber salad	–	14000	2550	–	13000[b]	1300
Carrot salad	440000	350000	3.6×10^{6}	410000	360000	2.7×10^{6}
Waldorf salad	310000	10000	7800	300000	10000	7300

[a]*From Rowley et al (34)*

[b]*Three days at 40°F*

In food service systems,temperature is also a critical factor for reheating and serving. Brown and Twedt (32) found that neither *S. aureus* nor *S. typhimurium* were able to grow on roast beef cubes held at 50°C or 51.1°C. *Clostridium perfringens* did multiply over the initial 18 hours at 51.1°C but then rapidly decreased. At 53.3°C, *C. perfringens* merely declined. Brown and Twedt suggest that holding temperatures below 60°C (140°F) could safely be employed. Angelotti *et al* (35) considered that food heated to 150°F (66°F) and held for 12 minutes would be free of *S. aureus* and *Salmonella*. They did not evaluate *C. perfringens*. In practice, it is more effective to speify product temperature rather than depending on oven temperature and cooking time (26, 36).

It should be emphasized that hazardous organisms grow best or near neutral pH in nutritious, highly hydrated foods, without excessive salt. Meats, poultry, fish, shellfish and dairy products fit into this category and are therefore classed as "hazardous foods" by public health authorities. The detection of a hazardous organism in food does not guarantee that subsequent growth will occur. The presence of acid, inhibitors, competitive growth by other organisms, adverse temperatures and so on, will either alter growth or prevent the synthesis of specific metabolites (21, 37).

An often neglected consideration in microbiological analysis is that of recovering injured cells (38). Every processing stress, i.e. drying, heating, radiation, chemicals and refrigerated storage, will damage microorganisms. Recovery of these damaged cells by selective media is frequently lower and misleading as to the presence and viability of hazardous organisms. Accurate enumeration requires techniques such a preincubation in a noninhibitory medium.

One must be aware that microbiological end-product analysis may not be a true indication of the microbiological quality of the initial raw materials. Low counts in the final product may be the result of excessive thermal processing (39) or, in the case of frozen foods, the result of wide temperature fluctuations during storage or in the rate of freezing (40).

It has been the experience of some authorities (27, 41-44) that acceptable products can be produced in marginal environments. Processing can also improve the microbiological quality of the initial raw materials (39), but should not be used for "laundering" unacceptable raw ingredients (43).

The military system includes facilities that process food in systems comparable to many civilian counterparts.It includes centralized food preparation facilities, in-house preparation, and precooked frozen food operations. Some of the situations encountered are extreme. Typical internal temperature constraints used by the author in innovative military feeding system studies are listed in Table VI and have proven effective and practical, and generally follow the U.S. Army and Air Force SR 40-5 (45, 46) and the Food and Drug Administration's Food Service Sanitation Manual (46). Properly staffed and monitored systems meeting these constraints produce cooked foods having microbiological levels within the microbiological requirements stated in Tables III and VIII. The latter constraints (Table VIII) were designed for a precooked,chilled food system and the proposed scheme is described in Fig. 1. The labor requirements for conducting this program proved to be excessive. By monitoring temperature and time of the processing, transportation, and storage, conducting an extensive sanitation program, and with minimal intermediate and end-product analysis, almost all of the entree samples were within the imposed constraints, and, while lower compliance occurred for vegetable and soups, no foodborne disease incidents occurred. It should be noted that this is an in-house system and that the items were also monitored during reheating. These data verify the suggestion of Olson (48), that if the monitoring system is properly designed and conducted, end-product analysis in an in-house, contained system, can be minimal.

Thermally processed foods will show an appreciable decrease in their microflora (Fig. 2) (49). Interestingly, in order to meet internal constraints in the finished product, the aerobic plate count has to be decreased approximately 1.5 logarithmic cycles (to 10^5 CFU/g) in contrast with at least 3 for fecal coliforms (to 0 MPN/g). Typically, normal processing, without subsequent recontamination,will reduce the microflora to proper levels,but only if the initial population is also at reasonable levels. Attempts to reduce excessive initial concentrations of organisms by processing can only result in an inferior product.

V. MONITORING TECHNIQUES FOR ENVIRONMENTS

Regulatory agencies and spoilage considerations usually dictate the extent to which indices and tests must be conducted. An effective microbiological control program should include a systems approach, since microbiological populations should be controlled from the raw material to the finished product, and the entry of hazardous organisms prevented. This will require an effective measure of control over the procesing parameters, personnel hygiene,and environmental sanitation.

A variety of techniques are used for assessing the conditions in a food production facility that may affect the microbiological quality of the food it produces (Table IX). These techniques monitor factors that vary in their contribution toward microbiological contamination levels in foods. It is difficult to assess the importance of factors such as

TABLE VIII. *Microbiological Compliance of Food Items Cooked in a Central Preparation Facility*[a]

Food item	No. of items	No. of samples	Total aerobic Count	Entero-bacteriaceae	Staphylococcus aureus	Clostridium perfringens	% Complying[b]
Entree	31	123	123	122	122	122	98
Vegetables	13	29	25	25	29	29	83
Soups	5	9	9	8	9	9	89

[a]In order to comply the samples should not exceed: total aerobic plate count $= 10^5/g$; coagulase positive S. aureus $= 10^2/g$; C. perfringens $= 10^2/g$. enterobacteriaceae $= 10^3/g$;

[b]Percentage of samples complying with all of the microbiological criteria.

aerosols and surface contamination in public health, since even in the more critical hospital environment there are differences of opinion concerning their significance (50, 51).

Environmental monitoring, though, is extremely important in evaluating established sanitizing procedures, and experience has demonstrated its value in both process control and the prevention of contamination. The monitoring systems should be designed to minimize sanitation abuses by imposing specific constraints, and the effectiveness of monitoring techniques can be increased by making them quantitative, and minimizing dependence upon visual inspection (44).

As discussed above, accurate, dependable control and the monitoring of temperature and time as a food item is processed and/or served in a facility are major requirements. Care must be exercised in properly planning the use of equipment to prevent delays in processing, to ensure each piece of equipment is properly sanitized after use, and that the time-temperature guidelines for each stage in the process are followed. A num-

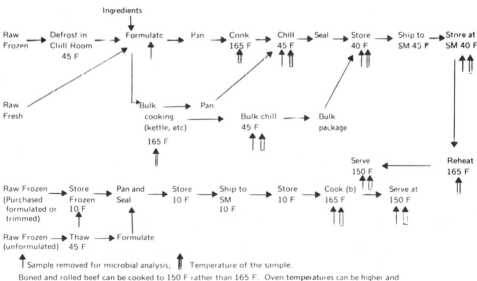

FIGURE 1. Flowchart for meat and meat formulations, soups, and gravies showing processing steps, allowable temperature constraints, stages at which it was proposed that temperatures be monitored and the item sampled for microbial analysis.

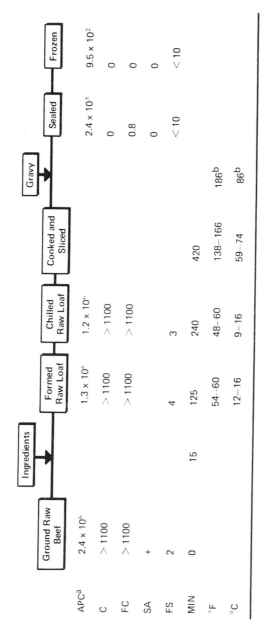

FIGURE 2. Microflora during processing of precooked frozen meat loaf (49).

ber of commercial products used for monitoring are described in Figure 3.

Temperature indicators, known as paper thermometers, or temperature recorders (A,B,C, and D) are effective monitors of temperatures attained by china during washing (44, 52). They contain crystals that release dye when their melting point is exceeded, are rapid and economical, and were found to be sufficiently accurate in detecting problems in conveyor speed, as well as water temperature in pot and dishwashing operations.

For relating storage temperature to time for processed foods, the use of indicators (E and F) has been proposed and is under study (53). Indicators are inexpensive and can be

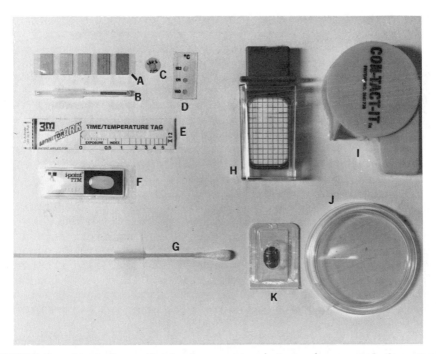

FIGURE 3. Examples of simple commercial devices used for monitoring sanitation and temperature: temperature indicators which employ salts with specific and sharp melting points (A, B, C and D); time-temperature indicator (numerical) (E); time-temperature indicator (colorimetric) (F); swab (G); sampler (H); contact tape (I); Rodac plate (J), and analyzer of chlorine concentration (K).

TABLE IX. Examples of Devices Employed for Assessing
            Environments

Parameter assessed	Devices
Temperature-time	Thermometer, timer
	Paper thermometer
	Recorder
	Temperature-time indicator
Sanitation	Visual examination
	Rodac plate
	Swab
	Contact tape
	Air sampler

extremely useful for precooked frozen and chilled storage for
indicating the approach to the termination of shelf-life.

   The RODAC (Replicate Organism Detection and Counting) plat-
ing technique (J), using an agar contact plate for evaluating
sanitary procedures is rapid and convenient. Another contact
device employs sterile adhesive tape (I). After sampling a surface, the tape is pressed against an agar plate, which is then
incubated. For both the Rodac and the adhesive tape, each locus
of contamination will result in the growth of a colony on the
agar surface/ For curved or irregular surfaces, inappropriate
for testing by Rodac plates, a swab technique is usually employed. The swab (G) has a tip consisting of either cotton or
alginate. A surface is sampled by rubbing a moistened cotton
swab over a known surface area and either dispensing the cotton
in diluent or dissolving the alginate in a citrate or hexameta-
phosphate solution. After that, appropriate dilution aliquots
are spread on agar plates and the microorganisms enumerated as
colonies.

   The requirement for agar plates is eliminated by employing
a sampler (H). Appropriate aliquots are diluted in the container into which the sampler is immersed. The sampler will
absorb a known quantity of liquid, which will dissolve growth
nutrients within the sampler, supporting growth of organisms
entrapped on the membrane surface.

   The chlorine content of a water supply may be ascertained
accurately by kits or estimated less precisely by a simple
sampler (K).

The present standards for Rodac plates vary with the facility and agency involved. The debate about the specific criteria to apply to Rodac plate and swab testing was reviewed by Jopke *et al* (54) who noted that criteria varied from an average of less than 10 CFU/plate for floor cleaning procedures in hospitals, to 30 CFU/plate for hospital dishwashing operations, to 50-100 CFU/plate for field service operations (55). Patterson (56) who surveyed food plants in Britain, considered a maximal count of 50 CFU/cm^2 for cleaned surfaces and 1000 CFU/cm^2 for working surfaces as reasonable. One reason the difficulty in establishing constraints exists is the absence of definitive data relating microbial levels acceptable for sanitation to the probability of causing infections, although this probability has been suggested by Jopke *et al* (54) and is the unstated basis for certain regulations. It is believed that while swabs may be more effective than Rodac plates in quantitating organisms on surfaces (57) and the Rodac more accurate, both often fail to recover the majority of cells present. In the author's laboratory, monitoring techniques are used only to ascertain the effectiveness of sanitizing operations and not to estimate the actual degree of contamination by hazardous organisms.
Microbial contaminants have been found to be distributed non-uniformly on equipment surfaces. Moreover, certain surfaces on particular pieces of equipment will tend to be less effectively cleaned. A good monitoring system will concentrate mainly on these problem surfaces. The use of monitoring techniques has demonstrated that any surface can be satisfactorily sanitized, and can be maintained in a sanitary state if soil is effectively removed, and acceptable sanitizers are employed. In fact, for many surfaces, efficient washing, rinsing, and drying is extremely effective for reducing microbial populations (58). Frequent difficulties arise when the use of sponges and towels is not rigorously controlled. Visual evaluation has been found to be of limited effectiveness in evaluating the sanitary state of surfaces (27, 44). As seen in Table X, many surfaces that were found to be visually acceptable and, in fact, exceeded the monitoring constraints, were unsatisfactory. Other surfaces that were judged to be unsatisfactory by Rodac analysis were visually satisfactory.
Personnel are reservoirs for a wide number of microorganisms (59). The data in Table XI show that human skin harbors a considerable number of microorganisms. Perspiration, skin flaking, and respiration all tend to create aerosols (33, 60, 61). While extensive research has been reported on aerosols in food plants (62), no standards have been proposed. Although aerosols from waste disposals have been found by Jopke *et al* (63) to contaminate cleaned glassware in its vicinity, aerosols are not considered to be an important factor in environmental sanitation or infection in a food system (49). Bryan and McKin-

TABLE X. Comparison between Visual and Rodac Plate Evalu-
          ation of Surfaces

Number of surfaces visually evaluated	Satisfactory as evaluated by Rodac plates (%)[a]		Unsatisfactory as evaluated by Rodac plates (%)[a]	
	Visually satisfactory	Visually unsatisfactory	Visually satisfactory	Visually unsatisfactory
44	62	38	47	53
20	78	22	59	41
23	79	21	22	78
7	100	0	0	100
23	68	32	0	100
7	100	0	50	50

[a]The percentage was obtained with Rodac analysis as the
denominator. A surface was satisfactory if, of the number
of plates used to test a surface, one half or more of the
plates contain 50 CFU/plate or less, and none exceed 100
CFU/plate.

ley (33) do emphasize the need for wearing gloves when handling foods.

VI. INNOVATIVE TECHNIQUES

A number of monitoring devices have been developed to increase the efficiency of laboratory procedures and to aid in
decision making concerning the acceptability of food items.
Aerobic plate counts can be simplified by the Stomacher-Drop-
lette technique (64) and by the spiral plate technique (65),
or they can be eliminated by the use of indirect procedures
such as the radiometric and calorimetric methodology (66), op-
tical or impedance scanning devices (67), the measurement of
Redox potential (68), the use of a Coulter counter for enumerating microcolonies (69), and a carbon dioxide detection device
(70). The problem of adapting these techniques for other indices and enumerating or detecting the presence of hazardous
organisms still remains. Microorganisms can also be semiquan-
titated on nonselective and selective media by a simple dip-
ping device (available from the Millipore Corporation, Bedford,

TABLE XI. Examples of Microbial Populations on Human Skin[a]

Site	Plate count
Forehead	348
Nose	TNTC[b]
Upper lip	TNTC
Behind ear	TNTC
Under chin	TNTC
Upper arm - lateral	42
Elbow - lateral	8
Forearm	41
Wrist - lateral	TNTC
Hand - lateral	224
Palm	Pseudomonas

[a]Data from Ulrich (60)

[b]Too numerous to count

Massachusetts or Corning Diagnostic Research, Corning, New York).

VII. QUALITY CONTROL PROGRAMS

Recently Silverman (71) noted two distinct types of systems: (1) the industrial production facility, where specialized, in-line equipment is devoted to the production of specific products, and (2) the in-house feeding system, with its limited production facility; which is integral with its distribution system and tends to serve a large variety of food items. Systems also exist that contain attributes of both systems, and some in which the production facility is geographically separate from the serving sites. Obviously, each of these systems has distinctly different problems in production, safety, and spoilage. Nevertheless, the principles outlined previously will apply to their quality control programs.

An example of an organization chart for a microbiological and sanitation control operation is presented in Figure 4. In this scheme, the quality control manager has no direct authority over clean-up operations or insect and pest control, but does have direct access to the plant manager and is of equal

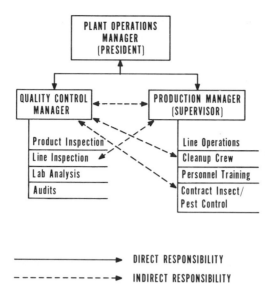

FIGURE 4. *Suggested organization chart for a quality control program (suggested by the Frozen Food Institute).*

stature with the production manager.

The industrial production system uses structural procedures and specialized, highly automated equipment, and a detailed quality control (QC) program can be imposed on the materials and equipment involved. This type of program lends itself to conformity to the FDA's hazard analysis-critical control point (HA-CCP) quality assurance systems (72). The technique of HA-CCP is a system approach to minimizing the overall risk in a system (HA) by pinpointing those CCP operations that potentially represent the greatest hazards (73).

In contrast, an in-house system, characteristic of certain hospitals, universities, airlines, cruise ships, military installations, and penitentiaries, produces menu items with limited, more conventional, multipurpose equipment. Material flow is often difficult to schedule and a QC program for these facilities is usually limited to good manufacturing practices (GMP) for specific applications.

Even the least sophisticated system, however, can take advantage of convenience food items and minimize food preparation operations that tend to tax sanitation.

Actually, the HA-CCP program is not novel, and examination indicates that it is a formalized program of established principles that essentially identifies the more dangerous operations (CCPs) and forces the manufacturer to monitor them by using GMP, supplemented if necessary by microbiological analy-

It is necessary to first define the production facility and then to conduct a hazard analysis. The ingredients and their flow through the facility are analyzed and the CCPs are identified. The system must not subsequently be altered without permission, and monitoring is the responsibility of the processor. To fully understand the basis for HA-CCP, it should be realized that not all food materials have the same hazard (74, 75, 76). In the NAS and ICMSF reports, (74, 76) foods are placed into categories based upon their relative potential for creating a public health problem. A processed food product usually consists of ingredients possessing different degrees of hazard potential. By identifying potential problem areas and effectively monitoring sanitation, temperature, water quality, and the quality of the raw material, and by making certain that the raw material is segregated from the finished product, an effective quality assurance program can be put into effect (75).

The exact microbiological constraints for a food will depend upon experience but do include a degree of arbitrariness. The recent and thorough study for applying statistical models to microbial constraints (76) replaces the present approach that uses some sort of average microbial count for defining acceptable products, by an attribute plan that includes the degree of hazard and the typical associated microflora in a systems approach.

The degree of hazard in the ICMSF study grades 15 cases with case 1 having minimal impact, and case 15 being the most severe hazard. These cases are then assigned microbiological constraints, examples of which are presented in Table XII. A distinction is made between a two and three class plan where, in the two class plan if, of n units sampled, a number greater than m is exceeded in c units, the sample is rejected. A three class plan makes the further distinction that no sample may exceed a value M. This plan places the more stringent constraints upon the most hazardous systems, and upon those organisms associated with them. It recognizes that certain foods are produced, distributed, and consumed with their associated organisms, in ways that can tolerate a higher risk than other foods. It also recognizes that for certain organisms, a minimal risk should be tolerated. The use of averages is also avoided.

Microbial indices are employed for different purposes in cooked and raw foods. Many foods, such as salad ingredients, are ingested directly and often contain large concentrations of organisms. These same indigenous organisms, however, if present after processing, often indicate post processing contamination. This is illustrated in Table XII. Fresh vegetables have no SPC constraint and are allowed *E. coli* limits ($m = 10$, $M = 10^3$) higher than that for the cooked entrees ($m =$

TABLE XII. Examples of Sampling Plans and Microbiological Limits as Proposed by the ICMSF[a,b]

Product	Test	Case	Class	n	c	Limits per g m	M
Breaded precooked fish	SPC[c]	2	3	5	2	10^6	10^7
	Fecal coliforms	5	3	5	2	4	4×10^2
	Staphylococcus	5	3	5	2	10^3	2×10^3
Fresh vegetables (to be consumed raw)	E. coli	5	3	5	2	10	10^3
	Salmonella	11	2	10	0	0	$-$
Blanched, frozen vegetables	SPC	4	3	5	3	10^4	10^6
	Coliforms	4	3	5	3	10	10^3
Entrees, precooked and frozen	SPC	5	3	5	2	10^5	10^6
	Coliforms	5	3	5	2	10^2	10^4
	E. coli	5	3	5	2	3^{d}	10^2
Comminuted meat, frozen	SPC	1	3	5	3	10^6	10^7
	Salmonella	10	2	5	1	0	$-$

[a] Taken from Mossel (6)

[b] n, number of units sampled; c, number of units that can exceed a microbiological level m; no sample may contain a number higher than M.

[c] Standard plate count

[d] No positive tube in three-tube MPN method

3, M = 10^2) with an SPC for the latter of 10^5 (*C = 2, M = 10^6*).
The probability of ingesting pathogens in fresh vegetables is
also minimized by the severe *Salmonella* constraint. Breaded,
precooked fish, being in case 2, a lower hazard category, is
allowed higher microbial limits. It would not be useful to impose a coliform constraint on fresh vegetables due to their
normal presence in high numbers.

The statistical basis for selecting the number of samples
and defining the risk involved is expressed in an operating
characteristic (OC) curve. The OC curve describes the relationship for the probability of accepting or rejecting a shipment
or lot of food in relation to the number of defective samples
present. It is useful in defining the risks involved when deciding the number of samples to be selected since the larger
the number of samples the smaller the risk.

The proposed regulations by Canada of its ground meat outlets uses a three class plan for aerobic plate count, *E. coli*
and *S. aureus*, but a two class plan for *Salmonella*. The aerobic plate count has *n = 5, c = 3, m = 10^7*, and *M = 5 x 10^7*.

It is seen that regulatory agencies and industry are still
searching for theories and techniques that, while not unduly
penalizing processors, will afford maximal protection to the
consumer.

VIII. REFERENCES

1. Anon. *Fed. Reg. 39*, 35438 (1974)
2. Bryan, F. L. *Food Technol. 28*, 52 (1974)
3. Bryan, F. L. *J. Milk Food Technol. 35*, 632 (1972)
4. Evans, D. G., Evans, D. J., and Gorback, S. L. *Infect. Immunity. 8*, 731, (1973)
5. Koupal, L. R. and Deibel, R. H. *Inf. Immunity. 11*, 14 (1975)
6. Mossel, D. A. A. *in* "Critical Reviews in Environmental Control" p. 14, CRC, Cleveland, Ohio (1975)
7. Morrison, A. B. *J. Milk Food Technol. 39*, 218 (1976)
8. Thatcher, F. S. and Clark, D. S. "Microorganisms in Foods." Univ. of Toronto Press, Toronto, Canada (1968)
9. Seligmann, R. and Frank-blum, H. *J. Milk Food Technol. 37*, 473 (1974)
10. Hobbs, B. C. *Food Technol. 31*, 90 (1977)
11. Elliott, R. P. and Michener, H. D. "Factors Affecting the Growth of Psychrophilic Microorganisms in Foods" *Tech. Bull. 1320*, USDA, Washington, D.C. (1965)
12. Smith, D. P. *Food Technol. 30*, 28 (1976)
13. Levine, M. *Food Technol. 15*, 1 (1961)

14. Silliker, J. H. *in* "Microbiological Quality of Foods"
     (Slanetz, L. W., ed.) p. 102, Academic, New York (1963)
15. Corlett, D. A. Jr. *Food Technol. 28,* 34 (1974)
16. Jay, J. M. *J. Milk Food Technol. 35,* 467 (1972)
17. Freeman, R., Silverman, G. J., Angelini, P. and Meritt, C.
     R., Jr., and Esselen, W. B. *Appl. Environ. Microbiol. 32,*
     222 (1976)
18. Barnes, E. A. *J. Sci. Food Agric. 277,* 777-782 (1976)
19. Silverman, G. J. and Goldblith, S. A. *Advan. Appl. Micro.
     7,* 305 (1965)
20. Ayres, J. C. "Reducing Food Spoilage and Deterioration"
     CRC, Cleveland, Ohio (1971)
21. Peterson, A. C., Fanelli, M. J., and Gunderson, M. F. *in*
     "Freezing Preservation of Foods" (Tressler, D.K., Van
     Arsdale, W. B., and Copley, M. J., eds.), Vol. 4, 4th
     ed. Avi, Westport, Connecticut (1968)
22. Winslow, R. L. *J. Milk Food Technol. 38,* 487 (1975)
23. Goepfert, J. M. *J. Milk Food Technol. 39,* 175 (1976)
24. Carl, K. E. *J. Milk Food Technol. 38,* 483 (1975)
25. Elmswiler, B. S., Pierson, C. J. and Kotula, A. W. *Appl.
     Environ. Micro. 31,* 826 (1976)
26. Tuomi, S., Matthews, M. E. and Marth, E. H. *J. Milk Food
     Technol. 37,* 457 (1974)
27. Silverman, G. J., Powers, E. M., Carpenter, D.F., and
     Rowley, D. B. "Microbiological Evaluation of the Food
     Service System at Travis AF Base" *Tech. Rept. 75-110
     FSL,* U.S. Army Natick Res. Labs., Natick, Massachusetts
     (1975)
28. Longree, K. "Quantity Food Sanitation" Wiley, New York
     (1967)
29. Bryan, F. L., and Kilpatrick, E. G. *Am. J. Pub. Health 61,*
     1869 (1971)
30. Anon. *Fed. Reg. 43* (138), 30791 (1978)
31. Mercuri, A. J., Banwart, G. T., Kinner, J. A. and Sessonis,
     A. R. *Applied Micro. 19,* 768 (1970)
32. Brown, D. F. and Twedt, R. M. *Appl. Micro. 24,* 599 (1972)
33. Bryan, F. L. and McKinley, T. W. *J. Milk Food Technol. 37,*
     420 (1974)
34. Rowley, D. B., Tuomey, J. M., and Wescott, D. E. "Fort
     Lewis Experiment: Application of Food Technology and
     Engineering to Central Preparation" *Tech. Rept. 72-46 FL,*
     U.S. Army Natick Labs., Natick, Massachusetts (1972)
35. Angelotti, R., Fotor, M. J. and Lewis, K. H. *Appl. Micro.
     9,* 308 (1961)
36. Canale-Parola, E. and Ordal, Z. J. *Food Technol. 11,* 578
     (1957)
37. Christiansen, L.N. and King, N. J. *J. Milk Food Technol.
     34,* 389 (1971)

38. Busta, F. F. *J. Milk Food Technol. 39*, 138 (1976)
39. Surkiewicz, B. F., Hyndman, J. B. and Yancez M. V. *Appl. Micro. 15*, 1 (1967)
40. Yeterian, M., Chugg, L., Smith, W. and Coles C. *Food Technol. 28*, 23 (1974)
41. Surkiewicz, B. F., Groomes, R. J. and Padron, A. P. *Appl. Micro. 15*, 13 (1967)
42. Tompkin, R. B. *Food Technol. 27*, 54 (1973)
43. Peterson, A. C. and Gunderson, R. E. *Food Technol. 28*, 37 (1974)
44. Silverman, G. J., Powers, E. M. and Rowley, D. B. "Microbiological Analysis of the Food Preparation and Dining Facilities at Fort Myer and Bolling Air Force Base" *Tech. Rept. 75-53-FSL*. U.S. Army Natick Res. Labs., Natick, Massachusetts (1975)
45. Department of the Army. "Medical Services, Preventive Medicine" *AR 40-5*. Washington, D.C. (1974)
46. Department of the Air Force. "Food Service Frozen Food Pack Meal Program" *SAC Regulation 146-1*, Washington, D.C. (1974)
47. Anon. "Food Service Sanitation Manual" *Public Health Service Bull. No. 934*, Food and Drug Administration, Washington, D.C. (1962)
48. Olson, J.C. *J. Milk Food Technol. 31*, 335, (1968)
49. Silverman, G. J., Carpenter, D. F., Munsey, D. T. and Rowley, D. B. "Microbiological Evaluation of Production Procedures for Frozen Pack Meals at the Central Preparation Facility of the Francis E. Warren Air Force Base" *Tech. Rept. 73-37-FSL*. U.S. Army Natick Labs., Natick, Massachusetts (1976)
50. Jopke, W. H., Sorenson, S. D., Hass, D. R. and Donovan, A. C. *Hospital Progr. Rep.* (1974)
51. Shaffer, J. G. *Health Lab. Sci. 11*, 57 (1974)
52. Scalzo. A. M., Dickerson, R. W. Jr. and Read, R. B. Jr. *J. Milk Food Technol. 32*, 20 (1969)
53. Kramer, A. and Farquhar, J. W. *Food Technol* 30, 50 (1976)
54. Jopke, W. H., Sorenson, S. D., Hass, D. R. and Donovan, A. C. *Hospital Progr.* June (1976)
55. Anon. "Procedure for the Bacterial Examination of Food Utensils and/or Food Equipment Surfaces," Public Health Service Bull. No. 1631, *Tech. Inf. Bull. 1*, USDHEW, Washington, D.C. (1967)
56. Patterson, J. T. *J. Food Technol.* 6, 63 (1971)
57. Angelotti, R., Wilson, J. L., Litsky, W. and Walter, W.G. *Health Lab. Sci.* 1, 289 (1964)
58. Maxcy, R. B. *J. Milk Food Technol.* 38, 192 (1975)

59. Skinner, F. A. and Carr, J. G. "The Normal Microflora of Man" Academic Press, New York (1974)
60. Ulrich, J. A. *Ind. Micro.* 14, 137 (1972)
61. Kloos, W. E. and Musselwhite, M. S. *Appl. Micro.* 30, 381 (1975)
62. Heldman, D. R. *J. Food Sci.* 39, 963 (1974)
63. Jopke, W. H., Hass, D. R. and Donovan, A. C. *Hosp. Progr.* October (1969)
64. Sharpe, A. N., Dyett, E. J., Jackson, A. K. and Kilsby, D. C. *Appl. Micro.* 24, 4, (1972)
65. Gilchrist, J. E., Campbell, J. E., Donnelly, C. B., Peeler, J. T. and Delaney, J. M. *Appl. Micro.* 25. 244 (1973)
66. Rowley, D. B., Previte, J. J., Lampi, R. A. and Mikelson, D. A. *Food Technol.* 28, 52 (1974)
67. Cady, P. in "New Approaches to the Identification of Microorganisms" (Heden, C. and Illeni, T. eds.) p. 73, Wiley, New York (1975)
68. Munsey, D. T., Boucher, B. and Silverman, G. J. *Abstr. Ann. Meeting Am. Soc. Micro.* (1973)
69. Suhren, G. *IAMS, Int. Symp. 9th,* Kiel, Germany (1974)
70. Glenn, W. G. and Glenn, M. H. *35th Ann. Meeting. Inst. Food Technol.* (1975)
71. Silverman, G. *J. Milk Food Technol. 39* (1976)
72. Kauffman, F. L. *Food Technol. 28,* 51 (1974)
73. Bauman, H. E. *Food Technol. 28,* 30, (1974)
74. Anon. "Classification of Food Products According to Risk. An evaluation of the Salmonella Problem" *Publ. No. 1683.* Nat. Acad. Sci., Washington, D. C. (1969)
75. Anon. "Prevention of Microbial and Parasitic Hazards Associated with Processed Foods" Nat. Acad. Sci., Washington, D. C. (1975)
76. ICMSF, "Microorganisms in Foods, Volume 2, Sampling for Microbiological Analysis: Principles and Specific Applications" Univ. of Toronto Press, Toronto, Canada (1974)

CHAPTER 23

DESIGN AND OPERATION OF A QUALITY ASSURANCE
PROGRAM IN A MULTI-UNIT FOOD SERVICE OPERATION

Richard N. Schwartz

Quality Control Division
Fairfield Farm Kitchens
Beaver Heights, Maryland

Whether a food service establishment is small or large, the wholesomeness and quality of the food it serves should always be prime concerns. The goal of a quality assurance program should be to prevent problems before they occur. Such a program should be based on critical control points from the receipt of ingredients to the delivery of finished products to the customers.

The quality assurance program of a multi-unit food service operation utilizes the same concepts of good manufacturing practices employed by any reputable food manufacturing concern. There must, however, be greater emphasis placed on the people aspect, since food service operations are typically labor intensive. For any service organization, therefore, quality control of employee attitude and performance is to a large extent the equivalent of product quality control for a manufacturer. Computer manufacturers, for example, can point to a shipment of hardware that has been quality inspected and has passed all performance and quality tests. A service company has nothing as tangible. It must count primarily on favorable impressions made on customers as a result of services properly rendered.

I. TRAINING QUALIFIED PERSONS

After qualified persons have been recruited and trained, it is essential that they be retrained. This will require a commitment on the part of top management to do so. Many times such a commitment is assumed to exist but, in fact, it does not. In

405

Copyright © 1979 by Academic Press, Inc.
All rights of reproduction in any form reserved
ISBN: 0-12-453150-4

that case it is the responsibility of the quality assurance
program to report to the top official of one of the departments
within the organization that there is a lack of employee per-
ception of a management commitment. It is helpful, in that
case, if the head of the quality assurance department is himself a Vice-President reporting directly to the President of
the organization, as is the case at the Marriott Corporation.

Employee training, starting at the Vice-Presidential level,
is essential to the success of a corporate quality assurance
program. Developing food and beverage skills is, of course,
not enough. The quality assurance management, must be trained
in the principles of supervision and management as well as in
counseling and coaching. Emphasis should be placed on motivation, through career progression, and financial reward, through
such devices as bonuses, stock options and/or profit sharing.
The result of these efforts will be a well-trained, properly
motivated employee who will carry out day to day activities
that will improve and maintain the quality that consumers demand.

II. INSPECTION

The quality assurance program should include personnel responsible for the maintenance of food standards and the occasional monitoring of food handling and employee practices. The
prime responsibility for meeting and maintaining quality standards, however, must rest with the operating personnel, i.e. the
regional, district and unit managers. In their inspection of
individual restaurant units, they should use forms similar to
inspection check lists used by regulatory officials. An example of such a form is shown in Figure 1. An official inspection sheet might list approximately 120 items that would be
considered a violation of the law if they do not comply with
it. A demerit system can be used with 6, 4, 2 and 1 demerits
assigned to each item. If the number of demerits received ex-
ceeds a specified amount, the consequences may be serious. The
six demerit items must be corrected within 10 days; the four
demerit items within 30 days and the 2 and 1 demerit items by
the next inspection. If the defects are not corrected, the u-
nit manager might have a serious problem, not only in convincing the local health department as to why his unit should be
allowed to continue operating, but also in explaining to management as to how he could allow his operation to get into such
pitiful shape. The best way to keep this from happening is
through preventative quality control procedures.

VIOLATION	DEMERITS
1. Food covered and protected from contamination	4
2. Suitable thermometers in refrigerators, freezers and walk-in	2
3. Perishables held at $45^\circ F$ or below	2
4. Potentially hazardous foods held below $45^\circ F$ or above $140^\circ F$ after preparation	6
5. Containers of food stored off any floors or clean surfaces	2
6. Frozen food kept frozen until use and properly thawed when used	2
7. Persons with wounds, sores or respiratory infections kept away from food preparation and serving	6
8. Hands washed and clean; sanitized when necessary; clean fingernails	6
9. Clean uniforms; hair nets used on females; hair nets for males when necessary	4
10. Food contact surfaces clean; free of cracks and chips; sanitized when necessary	4
11. Adequate storing of ice dipping utensils	2
12. Toilets clean and free of clutter and filth	4
13. Sanitizing hand cleanser and towels provided at all times in rest rooms and handwashing sinks	6
14. Presence of rodents or flies minimized	4
15. Floors, walls and ceiling clean	4
16. Establishment and property free of litter, etc.	2
17. Milk shake machines cleaned and sanitized daily	6
18. Plastic gloves or sanitized hands used in preparation and handling of raw hamburger	6
19. Raw hamburger stored properly prior to use; covered with approved material; never held at room temperature for extended lengths of time	6
20. Glass at entrance clean of film, streaks and smears	2
21. Tables and seats kept clean at all times	4
22. Refrigerators and walk ins clean, neat, free from mold; temperature at $42^\circ F$ or below	6
23. Freezers clean, neat temperature at $0^\circ F$ or below	6

Figure 1. This figure is continued onto following page.

Figure 1 continued:

VIOLATION	DEMERITS
24. Slicer clean, sanitized between products	4
25. Can opener clean and in good repair	4
26. Refuse stored in proper container with tight fitting lid	2

Was a milk shake sample taken?

    Yes   No

Was a hamburger sample taken:

    Yes   No

Temperature $^\circ$F

FIGURE 1. Inspection sheet using demerit system based on
           6, 4, and 2 points. The seriousness of the
           situation is indicated by the higher number of
           points (or demerits) assigned to it.

III. DEVELOPMENT OF A PREVENTATIVE QUALITY CONTROL PROGRAM

In developing a preventative quality control program, a constant awareness of public health protection requirements must be present. Some of the important points that have to be taught to food service management in order to develop an effective quality control program are:

(1) All perishable ingredients as well as all foods prepared in advance must be refrigerated at proper temperatures. A clipboard should be hung near the freezer and chiller boxes and the temperatures should be recorded morning and evening. This not only provides management with a written record for quality control purposes but also provides an indication of an impending equipment breakdown. Similarly, hot foods should be held above 140°F, and temperature measurements should be routinely taken of hot foods on steamtable or in food warmers to insure that this minimum safe hot holding temperature is being observed.

(2) Special attention should be paid to the quality of the ingredients which are used to make products. The end product is only as good as the ingredients which are used in preparing it.

(3) A strict personal hygiene program must be put into effect and observed. Management must watch for employees with open sores or cuts or bad colds and remove them from any food handling area. When interviewing a prospective employee, managers should try to note his or her personal hygiene habits (example: dirty fingernails, unkempt appearance). Chances are that his or her personal habits will follow the individual to work and it would be difficult and time consuming to break such life-long habits.

(4) Equipment and utensils used throughout the food handling and service areas must be thoroughly cleaned and sanitized. Equipment must be properly washed prior to sanitizing or this step will have little effect.

(5) Raw makeup station and cooked preparation stations should be kept entirely separated. Many cases of food borne illness are due to cross contamination.

(6) Foods should be cooked thoroughly. Partially cooked food held in a poorly operating warmer can result in serious consequences. Most raw foods start out with high bacteria counts or have food poisoning organisms naturally inherent in them. One relies on thorough cooking to destroy these organisms.

(7) One should never store cleansers, sanitizers and other non-food items above food preparation areas. They should be stored in a separate room. Poisoning caused by the accidental introduction of lethal chemicals into food is perhaps the most serious of all types of food poisoning.

IV. IMPLEMENTATION OF QUALITY ASSURANCE PROGRAM

The implementation of a quality assurance program incorporating the points discussed is achieved by the Marriott Corporation as follows:

(1) A periodic inspection program exists involving the Quality Assurance Department at Fairfield Farm Kitchens and the food service operations. Members of the management team in the Quality Assurance Department at Fairfield Farm Kitchens periodically visit the food service operations and offer suggestions on sanitation and food handling. These visits are followed by written reports describing the problem areas found, the complaints made by shop managers and presenting suggestions for improvements. These reports are then circulated to appropriate members of management so that action can be taken.

(2) All Health department inspections are audited by the

central corporate office. This "encourages" the Regional District and Unit Managers to follow up on problem areas and see that they are corrected. By thus following up on health violation reports, chances are lessened of food poisoning incidents which could injure the corporation's reputation and business.

(3) The importance of proper food handling procedures is emphasized in each manager's standards of performance. The yearly bonus he receives and his eventual salary increases are based in part on his adherence to these procedures.

(4) Lastly, each manager is required to attend a concentrated food service management course which stresses the important points of the Marriott Quality Assurance Program. It also qualifies them for registration in states or districts which require manager certification in food service sanitation.

CASE HISTORIES OF SUCCESSFUL
FOOD SERVICE SYSTEMS IMPLEMENTATION

CHAPTER 24

THE 1961 – 1964 NEW YORK CITY SCHOOL LUNCH FOOD SERVICE
STUDY

Thomas Mario

Food Science Associates, Inc.
Dobbs Ferry, New York

I. BACKGROUND AND OBJECTIVES

The Food Service Study, which was coordinated by the writer, was funded by the New York City Board of Education and the Educational Facilities Laboratories (an activity of the Ford Foundation). Both organizations were aware that mass feeding problems in school systems were nationwide and not merely confined to a few metropolitan centers.

The study was started in 1961, its objective being to determine if a huge feeding organization providing 40 million meals a year to 500 elementary schools could take advantage of what were then the newer technologies in the food industry.

Like other mass feeding organizations, the New York City Bureau of School Lunches faced many problems: the budget, personnel recruitment, labor relations, transportation, equipment, and space problems. The Director of the Bureau of School Lunches, as well as personnel of the Bureau, enthusiastically supported the study. The study's program was designed to research the possibilities of what one would now call a "total convenience food system", that is, a food service operation in which conventional cooking on premises, or central cooking with satellite units, could virtually be eliminated. Could corollary problems of dishwashing, potwashing, food sanitation and daily deliveries be simplified? It was hypothesized that the solution lay in the utilization of precooked frozen foods served in disposable tableware.

To get the study under way an experimental food center was set up in a new public school in downtown Manhattan. The center was provided with the necessary instrumentation, power supplies

Copyright © 1979 by Academic Press, Inc.
All rights of reproduction in any form reserved
ISBN: 0-12-453150-4

and personnel. As the coordinator of the study, the writer was
joined by an engineer, an accountant, and other assistants with
experience in mass feeding operations. The study was able to
avail itself of the advice of the New York City Department of
Health and the Bureau of Nutrition. The design of the center
permitted the study of oven performance as well as the testing
of precooked frozen foods especially developed for use in the
school food service program. Foods were evaluated not only for
their weight, composition, flavor, texture, appearance and
other quality factors, but also for their performance in various types of high speed heating equipment. Microbiological as-
says of the foods studied were conducted for the center by outside laboratories.

Several attempts to set up precooked frozen food programs
in schools, such as in Larkspur, California, had been conspic-
uous failures. An apparently successful program along these
lines had been established in some elementary schools in Sweden
where, however, the sources of food supply, dietary habits, and
reconstitution equipment were very different from those existing in the United States.

The study was initially to be completed in one year. It was
expected that large food processors and equipment manufacturers
could be consulted and, by taking advantage of their research
and development capabilities, one would be able to determine
quickly the feasibility of acquiring food and equipment engineered to the needs of the Bureau of Schools Lunches. The buying potential of the New York City school system would be, it
was felt, a sufficiently strong motivating factor to stimulate
industry cooperation. What was soon learned, however, was that
with a few notable exceptions, the research and development
capabilities of many of the largest food processors and equipment manufacturers were limited or nonexistent, that the new
products were frequently developed and marketed on a hit-or-
miss basis, and that most research was quite naturally centered
on products with possibilities of immediate success, such as
frozen dinners for the retail market. There was little interest
on the part of industry in investing research and development
resources in food and equipment whose profit potential was possibly years away. The one year study, therefore of necessity,
grew into a three year study for developing and testing new
food products and engineering new equipment for mass feeding in
school lunch programs.

II. DESIGN OF THE STUDY

The study was undertaken in two phases. The first was concerned with evaluation of the merits of available or new equipment, and sources of food supply that could be used in the development of a frozen food program for schools. The second involved an actual pilot operation of a frozen food program in schools. As soon as adequate equipment and frozen foods were available to permit a beginning, the second phase of the study was undertaken.

A. *Pilot Operation*

The pilot operation involved four elementary schools in downtown Manhattan selected on the basis of pupil lunch loads and facilities. Two were schools without cafeteria kitchens, which were supplied by Bureau of School Lunches' Central Kitchen with soup and sandwich meals. These were the "experimental schools". The soup and sandwich program in these schools were stopped and they were equipped with freezers, reconstitution ovens and hot food holders, and staffed to serve hot lunches using precooked frozen foods. The remaining two schools were operating with cafeteria kitchens serving type A lunches prepared on the premise. These schools were the "control schools". In both groups of schools similar menus were served for identical periods. These included three and two week menu cycles. Every effort was made to control all variables in the operation except the experimental factor, i.e. the type of food served. The experimental schools served precooked frozen foods while the control schools served the same menus prepared on premises from the raw and canned foods normally supplied to cafeterias. In the pilot operation, the major factors studied were:
   (1)   Cost
   (2)   Acceptance of foods by pupils
   (3)   Organizational problems
   (4)   Staffing requirements
   (5)   Food procurement, storage, and distribution

B. *Evaluation of Equipment*

Before the pilot operation could begin, reconstitution equipment was tested. Since no mass feeding program using precooked frozen foods in schools existed in 1961, American made equipment for such programs was not available. However an electric oven had been designed for use in Swedish schools, and a unit was purchased for the study.A number of American oven manufacturers supplied their standard equipment for test purposes.

In all, 19 different pieces of heating equipment were evaluated. They included conventional ovens, rotary ovens, microwave units, quartz ovens, high speed convection ovens and high-pressure steam cookers. Both gas-fired and electrically heated equipment were studied. The main objectives of the tests were to determine whether an oven would reheat precooked frozen food in a uniform manner, and lend itself to easy handling with a minimum of specialized skills. Each oven was evaluated for its:

    (1) Design
    (2) Construction
    (3) Performance in daily operation
    (4) Food capacity
    (5) Operating efficiency
    (6) Cost
    (7) Power requirement
    (8) Power consumption
    (9) Thermal efficiency
  (10) Temperature control

The performance of each oven was tested with a multipoint recording potentiometer equipped with thermocouples which were inserted in frozen food at various locations throughout the oven. Sufficient thermocouple readings were taken to determine the uniformity of heat distribution throughout the oven. The objective of each test was to load the oven to its maximum capacity with food at $0^{\circ}F$ $(-18^{\circ}C)$ and bring it, as quickly as possible, to an internal temperature of $160^{\circ}F$ $(71^{\circ}C)$. Any irregularities in the heat distribution were reflected in the temperature readings. Other factors, such as the shape of the food, its weight, composition, density, texture, specific heat, and position in the reconstitution pan, were considered in each oven test.

III. RESULTS OF THE STUDY

A. *Food*

After canvassing nearly the entire frozen food industry in the Eastern United States, and two years of testing and development, the study was able to procure precooked frozen food on a sustaining basis. During 1961 and 1962 approximately 22,000 test meals were procured and served. The food was purchased following specifications developed by personnel staffing the study, in cooperation with technical personnel from supplier companies. In the judgement of the study team, the food:

    (1) satisfied the nutritional requirements of the Type A

lunch mandated by the U.S. Department of Agriculture
for schools receiving surplus commodities.

(2) met the budgetary limits of the Bureau of School
Lunches

(3) comprised items that could be successfully reheated
in high-speed convection ovens

(4) was adaptable to both bulk pack and preplated meal
system

(5) was highly acceptable to students of elementary
school age

(6) satisfied bacteriological standards recommended by
the New York City Department of Health

(7) was procured from food processing plants capable of
continued production on a scale commensurate with the
needs of the Bureau of School Lunches

(8) was planned for eventual utilization of donated foods
distributed to schools under the National Lunch Program

Based on the food testing conducted, specifications were
developed for those items included in the frozen food program's
menu. The specifications consisted of two parts: (1) a section outlining the general requirements, and (2) individual
specifications for each of the products to be procured. Table I
shows the general requirements, along with a typical product
specifications for meat balls in tomato sauce.

By 1964, two types of precooked frozen foods, complying
with specifications were available to the study. The first
type, illustrated in Table I, was bulk frozen foods packed in
(1) large disposable aluminum pans with foil laminated paper
covers or (2) polyethylene bags and cases, the contents of
which were transferred to disposable pans before reheating.
The second type consisted of complete, individual, preplated
meals. The study showed bulk frozen foods to be lower in cost
by approximately 10 cents per meal, than the same foods packed
in individual trays. While the bulk foods required additional
labor in handling and transferring cooked foods to serving
plates, the complete meal cost, including labor, disposables
and overhead was nevertheless lower when bulk packed frozen
foods were used than when the preplated meals were served.

B. *Reconstitution Equipment*

Of the 19 ovens tested, only two met the objectives of the
test program. The first was the convection oven imported from
Sweden. Since its delivery time ranged from four to six months,
and no local representative was available for servicing
or supplying spare parts, its purchase was not recommended (See
Table II). The second oven was a gas convection oven designed

(text continued on page 437)

TABLE I. New York City School Food Service Study
Specifications for Precooked Frozen Foods
Issued May 1, 1964

General Requirements

Packaging

All cases of precooked frozen foods shall be of adequate
size to hold contents securely and shall not be torn or mis-
shapen when delivered. Open ends of cases shall be sealed by
filament tape. Each case shall be labeled with two Department
of Agriculture approved end labels showing establishment number
and indicating the contents and ingredients. Date of processing shall be indicated prominently on both end panels. Product
letter code shall appear in 3 inch high letters of all four
sides. All polyethylene bags shall be 0.004 gauge. Bulk frozen foods shall be packed in the manner indicated below.

Product letter codes are indicated in capital letters:

Hamburgers in polyethylene bags and paper case:
        "HAM B-1-1/2"
        "HAM B-2"

Fried Chicken in polyethylene bags and paper case:
        "CHIX"

Patties for Meat Loaf in polyethylene bags and paper case:
        "ML-1-/2"
        "ML-2"

Pizzas 48 portions in paper case: "PIZZA"

Frankfurters in 5-lb. waxed cartons with paper separators,
            cartons packed in paper case: "FR"

Fish Sticks in waxed cartons with paper separators, car-
            tons wrapped in heat sealed wax paper, car-
            tons packed in paper case: "FS"

Fish Filets in waxed carton with paper separators, car-
            tons wrapped in heat sealed wax paper, car-
            tons packed in paper case: "FF"

Codfish Cakes in polyethylene bags and paper case or in
            waxed carton with paper separators, cartons
            wrapped in heat sealed wax paper, cartons

TABLE I. *New York City School Food Service Study*
Specifications for Precooked Frozen Foods
Issued May 1, 1964 (cont'd)

---

packed in paper case: "CC"

Meat Balls in Tomato Sauce in Ekco Alcoa #709-55 aluminum
tray or equivalent with 0709 foil laminated,
board cover, 6 trays per paper case: "MB"

Beef and Pork Patties in Brown Gravy in Ekco Alcoa #709-55
aluminum tray or equivalent with 0709 foil
laminated, board cover, 6 trays per paper
case: "BPP 1 1/2"
"BPP 2"

Spaghetti With Meat Sauce in Ekco Alcoa #709-55 aluminum
tray or equivalent with 0709 foil laminated,
board cover, 6 trays per paper case: "SPAG"

Sliced Beef in Brown Gravy in Ekco Alcoa #709-55 aluminum
tray or equivalent with 0709 foil laminated
board cover, 6 trays per paper case: "POTR"

All paper cases containing aluminum trays or food in polyethylene bags shall be of the self-opening type. Open end of
cases shall be sealed by filament tape. If cases are shipped
interstate, they shall be properly labeled in accordance with
regulations of the U. S. Department of Agriculture. If Department of Agriculture labels are not required, each case
shall be prominently labeled or stamped on both ends indicating contents and date of processing.

Delivery

All frozen foods shall be maintained from time of processing to delivery at $0°F$ or lower. No frozen food shall be
packed and held in storage more than 60 days by the producer
prior to shipment. All deliveries must be made in clean,
properly enclosed refrigerated trucks. By properly closed, it
is meant that the trucks must have permanent doors on the rear
and/or sides. Trucks with canvas flaps or coverings, or deliveries from passenger cars, will not be considered as meeting this requirement. Deliveries must be made inside the
building to room to which they are consigned.

TABLE I.   New York City School Food Service Study
           Specifications for Precooked Frozen Foods
           Issued May 1, 1964 (cont'd)

Compliance with Regulatory Requirements

Meats, meat products and poultry delivered under the specifications attached must conform in all respects to the Federal Food, Drug, and Cosmetic Act, the laws of the State of New
York, and the ordinances and regulations of the City of New
York, and must be in prime condition and delivered in a
strictly sanitary manner. Meats and meat products delivered
under the specifications shall have been slaughtered, processed and manufactured in plants operated regularly in accordance
with requirements of the U. S. Department of Agriculture gov-
erning meat inspection. Poultry delivered under the specifications shall have been processed in an official plant operated regularly in accordance with regulations of the Poultry
Branch of the Agricultural Marketing Service of the U. S. Department of Agriculture.

Bacteriological Standards

Bacteriological standards for all foods shall not permit a
total aerobic plate count exceeding 100,000 per gram. Tests
for coliform and staphylococcus shall be negative. A coliform
count not exceeding 10 shall be considered negative. Any
foods which do not meet bacteriological specifications will
not be paid for. Any re-order which is delivered subsequent
to an unfavorable report on bacteriological specifications
must be accompanied by a report from an independent laboratory
certifying that the new shipment meets bacteriological specifications stated above. The cost of such test will be borne
by the vendor. Any storage and handling charges for food that
does not meet specifications shall be charged to vendor.

Specifications for Frozen Meat Balls in Tomato Sauce

Meat balls shall consist of ground beef. Meat shall be
free of all bones, grisle, blood clots, cartilage, bruises,
major ligaments, or extraneous matter. Meat shall be suitably
ground through a plate having holes 3/16 or 2/16 in. in diameter, and shall be free from ice crystals at the time it is
mixed with seasoning ingredients. The ground meat shall be
mixed with bread crumbs (no more than 6 % of the total raw
weight), eggs, onion, either fresh or soaked dehydrated, garlic powder, salt, pepper, and monosodium glutamate. It shall

Table I.   New York City School Food Service Study
           Specifications for Precooked Frozen Foods
           Issued May 1, 1964 (cont'd)

---

be suitably blended before shaping into balls of uniform size,
each weighing 0.45 to 0.5 oz after cooking. Meat balls shall
be lightly dusted with flour and cooked either by frying or
baking or both to an average loss of not less than 18 % from
their raw weight. Any other method of cooking giving equivalent results may be used.   Each   portion of five meat balls
shall contain not less than 2 oz meat after cooking. Meat
balls shall be sufficiently stable to withstand normal handling
and reheating in a high speed convection oven. Sauce shall be
made from fancy grade tomato paste and water or tomato puree.
It shall be suitably seasoned with salt, pepper, monosodium
glutamate, onion, either fresh or soaked dehydrated, garlic
powder, sugar, oregano, and basil, but none of the seasonings
shall be prominent in the finished product. Finished sauce
shall have a tomato solid content of at least 8.5 %. Sauce
shall be thickened with waxy rice flour.   Upon reheating it
shall be free flowing and shall reveal no water separation or
melted fat. Meat balls shall be packed in vinyl coated Ecko
Alcoa container #709, each pan containing 90 meatballs and 24
oz sauce. Meat balls shall be fully immersed in the sauce.

Examination of Meat Balls in Tomato Sauce

Examine	Defect	Minor	Major
Count	weight correct but 89 or 91 meatballs present	X	
	weight correct but count exceeds 90 ± 1		X
Weight	weight of meatball exceeds 40.5 ± 2 oz.		X
Condition	very slight water or oil separation visible in sauce	X	
	excessive water or oil separation visible in sauce		X

TABLE I. *NEW YORK CITY SCHOOL FOOD SERVICE STUDY*
         SPECIFICATIONS FOR PRECOOKED FROZEN FOODS
         ISSUED MAY 1, 1964 (cont'd)

Examination of Meat Balls in Tomato Sauce

Examine	Defect	Minor	Major
	sauce lumpy or too viscous		X
	more than 2 % of meat balls broken		X
Texture	meat balls excessively coarse, dry, fine or cohesive		X
Flavor	slightly underseasoned or overseasoned	X	
	excessively underseasoned or overseasoned		X
	rancid or foreign flavors		X*
Fat Content	fat content by Babcock analysis exceeds 22 %		X
Prohibited materials	bone particles present		X*
	gristle, cartilage, or ligament particles present		X
Foreign materials	hair, dirt, insect, or insect parts, or other extraneous materials present		X*
Bacteriological count	exceeds standards		X*

*Critical defect

TABLE II.   Evaluation Report On Elektro Helios
            Convection Oven

Manufacturer

Aktiebolaget Elektrohelios   United States   ASEA Electric, Inc.
Stockholm, 20   Representative: 500 Fifth Avenue
Sweden   New York 36, N.Y.

General

The Electro Helios oven, Model #32654, was designed and
constructed in Sweden specifically to reconstitute precooked
preportioned frozen food for use in school lunchroom service.
By type, it is an electric convection oven, resistance heated.
This oven has two rather narrow vertical chambers, each containing a removable rack with rows of shelves.   To provide uniform distribution of heat, the Elektro Helios oven incorporates
the following three operational features:

1. Air is heated by resistance units in a plenum chamber
    under the floor of the oven and blown by a propeller
    fan up into two ducts on the sides of the oven.

2. The hot air flows through ducts and emerges through
    perforations in the sides of the ducts, passes over
    trays of food, is exhausted into a central duct through
    grills identical with those on the sides of the oven,
    and is returned to the heating elements.

3. Air is reheated and recirculated following the above
    pattern. A distinguishing feature of the Elektro Helios
    is the short distance in which the heated air travels
    over the trays in each oven section, thus avoiding the
    irregular turbulent air patterns common in convection
    ovens in which hot air is set in motion by a fan in the
    oven chamber.

Auxiliary equipment furnished with the oven includes an especially designed four-wheeled cart or trolley that holds two
racks for placement of trays of food. This equipment facilitates the loading and unloading of the oven, as well as avoids
undue loss of oven heat during these operations. Each rack is
filled with frozen food trays, conveyed to the oven and, in a
single operation, is inserted into the preheated oven chamber.
The reconstituted food is also withdrawn from the oven in a
one step operation.

TABLE II.   Evaluation Report On Elektro Helios
Convection Oven (cont'd)

According to reports, the Elektro Helios oven was used successfully from 1957 until 1963 in an experimental program conducted by the Swedish Board of Education on the use of precooked, preportioned, frozen foods. The ability of the oven to
satisfactorily reconstitute typical American school lunchroom
dishes, different in character from the Swedish diet, as well
as the ability of the oven to reconstitute bulk frozen foods,
however, had not been tested in Sweden.

Specifications

Dimensions: Exterior - 44-9/32" wide, 25-3/16" deep,
              67-1/8' high
              Interior - 23-5/8" wide, (2 compartments,
              11-13/16" wide each), 19-11/16" deep,
              29-29/32" high
              Oven door - 32-3/8" wide, 31-5/8" high

Capacity: 66 individual frozen meals (33 each side),
              7-3/8" x 5-7/8" x 7/8"

              22 bulk pans (11 each side) 10" x 16-½" x 2"

Power
requirement: Service demand - 208 V, 3 phase, 36 A
              Kilowat rating - heating elements - 10.75 KW
                               motor   - 2.00 KW

Weight: 800 lbs

Cost: $ 1392.50, including trolley, two racks and
              shipping charges

Construction of Oven

Oven Body - The outer shell of the oven is fabricated of
grey enameled sheet steel, No. 19 gauge. Inner shell is painted
aluminum sheet steel. Interior of oven is divided into two compartments into which heated air is supplied from grills in wall
ducts. The central duct for return flow of air, separating ov-
en compartments, is made up of identical grills. Each grill
contains 168 peformations, 2 by ¼ inch. Oven door is constructed of an outer and inner panel made of sheet steel with mine-
al wool insulation. Laterally, opening oven door pivots on ex-

TABLE II.   Evaluation Report on Elektro Helios
           Convection Oven (cont'd)

---

posed chromium-plated hinges on right hand side.

Insulation - Between inner and outer shell of oven, there
are 2-1/2 in of mineral wool insulation.

Heating Unit - Heating elements beneath oven chamber are
tubular with coils enclosed in magnesium oxide and surrounded
by a heat-treated material. Beneath the heating chamber is a
centrifugal fan that circulates the air. It is directly coupled to a three phase motor. Electrical wiring for controls
in a cavity at the top of the oven was originally exposed
copper. However, before the oven could be certified for use
in New York City, it was necessary to insulate the exposed
bare wire with porcelain beads.

Vents - The oven is fitted with two chromium-plated vents
at bottom that act equally as outlets for condensation and as
fresh air inlets.

Trolley and Racks - The trolley or cart is of steel tubing,
aluminum painted. Racks are constructed of polished zinc steel
bars and the shelves of stainless steel wire. Racks are constructed to slide over channels in oven bottom, fitted with
removable bronze rollers. Removable drip trays are made of
stainless steel. Oven legs are adjustable.

Oven Controls - The controls are arranged on an instrument
panel above the oven door. A main switch controls the heating
elements that are inoperable unless the oven timer is set. The
latter is a spring wound device adjustable from 0 to 60 minutes controls the fan for air circulation. Controls are arranged in such a manner that the heater cannot be inadvertently
switched on for a longer period of time that the fan. Each
timer has its own pilot light. An oven thermometer calibrated
in centigrade units, is mounted on the control panel, reading
from 80 to 210°C, equivalent to 176 to 410°F. A motor reset
button for the thermal cut-out is located on the upper left
side wall of the oven. Heating temperatures are controlled by
a manually set thermostat with graduated scale dial numbered
from 1 to 10. Equivalent Fahrenheit readings for the thermostat settings are as follows:

1 - 243   6 - 339
2 - 261   7 - 360

TABLE II.   Evaluation Report on Elektro Helios
            Convection Oven (cont'd)

---

3 - 272	8 - 376
4 - 295	9 - 395
5 - 321	10 - 412

Operation of the Oven

Prior to loading with the food, the oven is preheated to $400°F$. This was found to be the optimum temperature for reconstituting frozen food. During the preheating period, racks were loaded with food at $0°F$ or lower. The trolley with loaded racks is rolled to the oven, the predetermined heating time is set on both heat and fan timers, and the racks are inserted in oven. Before the reheating time is completed, another rack is loaded with frozen food. The timer bell indicates when reheating period has been completed, at which time the oven is unloaded, reloaded with frozen food, and reconstituted meals are either served immediately or conveyed to a holding unit for storage until needed.

Capacity of Oven

The Elektro Helios oven has a capacity of 66 individual frozen dinners in 5-7/8" X 7-3/8" trays or 12 bulk-packed trays of frozen food in 9-7/8" X 18-1/4" trays. The preportioned dinners ranged from 7 to 10 ounces or a total of 30 to 37 pounds of food, while the bulk-packed trays varied from 23 to 50 pounds. Thus, the total capacity of the oven is as follows:

Individual dinners	27 to 41 lb
Bulk-packed food	30 to 50 lb

OPERATING EFFICIENCY TESTS

Working Capacity of the Oven. The loading time for the two racks containing 66 individual dinners is approximately 6 minutes. The time for reheating the individual dinners varied from 15 to 25 minutes, with an average of 20 minutes. The oven, therefore, has an average hourly capacity of approximately 200 dinners. The reheating of a variety of bulk frozen foods yielded approximately the same number of dinners per hour.

TABLE II.   Evaluation Report on Elektro Helios
            Convection Oven (cont'd)

Preheating Oven. A test run was made to determine time required to bring the oven up to the operating level of $400^{\circ}F$ in 20 minutes. However, subsequent experiments with the oven indicated that there was faster recovery time and greater temperature stability by allowing a preheating period of 40 minutes. In testing the rate of preheating, the thermostat was set at $200^{\circ}F$ and the heater and fan switched on. When the oven temperature reached $200^{\circ}F$ the power was automatically switched off. The thermostat was then immediately set to $300^{\circ}F$, and the operation repeated. When the oven reached $300^{\circ}F$, the thermostat was reset to $400^{\circ}F$. Test was completed when the heat was cut off with the thermostat remaining at $400^{\circ}F$. Temperature readings were taken every minute using two thermocouples, one placed in the center of the left oven compartment, and one placed in the center of the right oven compartment. Room temperature was $82^{\circ}F$ at start of test. The preheating time test showed remarkable uniformity of temperature in the two oven compartments during the preheating operation.

Time (minutes)	Temperatures $(^{\circ}F)$	
	Left oven compartment	Right oven compartment
1	112	114
2	138	140
3	160	161
4	180	180
5	196	196
6	218	218
7	233	233
8	255	255
9	263	263
10	290	290
11	303	303
12	324	324
13	335	335
14	354	354
15	361	361
16	371	371
17	389	389
18	401	400

TABLE II.   Evaluation Report on Elektro Helios
            Convection Oven (cont'd)

19[a]	413	413
20	406	406

[a]Heat cut off

Factors Affecting Reconstitution of Frozen Food in Trays Covered with Foil Hoods

As tests continued, it became apparent that the aluminum
disposable tray with its foil hood actually became a secondary
oven during the reheating process. The heat of the air space
between the food and the hood is higher in temperature than
the food itself and lower than the heated air circulating outside the tray. The amount of such air space varies with the
type of dinner and its volume. In certain dinners, such as
spaghetti with meatballs, the meat is in contact with the heated bottom of the tray as well as the foil hood top. In dinners
somewhat slack filled, contact only takes place with the bottom
of the tray. All trays used in testing the Elektro Helios were
crimped by hand rather than machine, since such dinners were
not assembly line products. In some instances, the foil hood
was not large enough to allow secure crimping. Both factors
permitted irregular heat penetration. None of the dinners was
covered with the foil laminated cardboard lid, which is a more
secure seal than the loose foil hood. The optimum internal
temperature of the food for serving was $160 \pm 20°F$.

Test of Heat Loss

In judging one phase of the oven's performance, a test for
heat loss was conducted, following the method used by the National Electrical Manufacturer Association and American Standards Association. The approved standard specifies as follows

> "The average watts per square foot of inside oven
> surface areas required to maintain a steady inter-
> nal temperature of $325°F$ above room temperature
> shall not exceed 55 w"

Oven was preheated and operated for a two-hour conditioning period prior to thermocouple readings. Readings were taken
from both left and right hand side oven compartments, at 15-

TABLE II. *Evaluation Report on Elektro Helios*
Convection Oven (cont'd)

minute intervals, for a four-hour period. This test indicates
that the heat loss amounted to 51.05 w/sq.ft. The oven,
therefore, readily meets with the specified standard.

Time	Room Temperature (^{O}F)	Oven temperature (^{O}F)	
		Left section	Right section
10:00	86	395	393
10:15	88	397	398
10:30	85	405	405
10:45	79	401	402
11:00	78	397	398
11:15	87	402	404
11:30	82	397	397
11:45	78	395	397
12:00	80	399	401
12:15	78	398	397
12:30	78	400	395
12:45	80	402	399
1:00	78	396	397
1:15	75	402	400
1:30	83	396	398
1:45	79	393	395
2:00	80	394	395

Power Consumption - 4 hour test

Meter Reading 10:00 AM   —   603.1 W
Meter Reading 2:00 PM   —   615.5 W
                               12.4x.6= 7.44W for 4 hrs.

*TABLE II.   Evaluation Report on Elektro Helios
Convection Oven (cont'd)*

Oven Surface Area

Interior oven surface dimensions (sq.in.) - 2 oven compartments

4 Sides	22" x 31"	2728
2 Tops	22" x 11-1/2"	506
2 Bottoms	22" x 11-1/2"	506
4 Fronts & backs	11-1/2" x 31"	1426

$$5166 = 35.87 \text{ sq ft}$$

Power Consumption Per Square Foot

$$\frac{7440}{4} \ w \ (4 \ hours) = 1860 \ w/hour$$

$$\frac{1860}{35.87} = 51.85 \ w/sq \ ft$$

Standard (maximum loss)   55 w/sq ft

Results of Tests in Reheating Selected Dinners

Individual Chicken Dinners

Number of Dinners - 66

Component	Weight
Oven-baked chicken, edible meat	2.0 oz
Candied sweet potato	2.5 oz
Green Peas	2.1 oz
Total:	6.6 oz

Dinners packed in individual aluminum trays 7-3/8" x 5-7/8" x 7/8", covered with foil hood.

TABLE II.   Evaluation Report on Elektro Helios
            Convection Oven (cont'd)

Thermocouple positions:

1. Left center 1st   2. Right center 1st
   shelf (top)   shelf (top)
3. Left center 6th   4. Right center 6th
   shelf   shelf
5. Left center 11th   6. Right center 11th
   shelf (bottom)   shelf (bottom)

Record of Temperature Changes

Time (minutes)	Oven temperatures (^{o}F)	Temperatures in different thermocouple locations (^{o}F)					
		1	2	3	4	5	6
Before Loading	400						
After Loading	265						
3	287	32	54	34	64	38	44
6	307	37	72	38	68	40	45
9	325	39	87	41	72	42	48
12	327	40	95	49	77	45	50
15	345	44	101	62	82	51	64
18	364	55	112	80	87	55	75
21	370	100	118	112	91	95	83
24	378	145	129	149	118	149	120
27	385	164	142	170	152	178	141

Observations: Slight caramelization of candied sweet potato.
                Peas near rim of plate showed hardening in a
                few instances. Quality of oven-baked chicken
                satisfactory.

TABLE II.   Evaluation Report on Elektro Helios
            Convection Oven (cont'd)

Individual Frozen Haddock Dinners

Number of dinners - 66

Components	Weight
Haddock Filet	2.0 oz
Creole sauce	2.0 oz
Rice	1.0 oz
String beans	2.0 oz
Total:	7.0 oz

Dinners packed in individual aluminum trays 7-3/8" x 5-7/8"
x 7/8", covered with foil hood.

Thermocouple positions:

1. Left front 1st   2. Right front 1st
     shelf (top)   shelf (top)
3. Left front 6th   4. Right front 6th
     shelf   shelf
5. Left front 11th   6. Right front 11th
     shelf (bottom)   shelf (bottom)

Record of Temperature Changes

Time (minutes)	Oven temperatures (^oF)	Temperatures in different thermocouple locations (^oF)					
		1	2	3	4	5	6
Before loading	400						
After loading	279						
3	271	36	33	29	44	37	30
6	280	32	32	34	63	37	32
9	299	33	31	36	86	35	35
12	314	36	36	34	143	47	45
15	335	42	49	39	195	73	68
18	334	62	68	47	212	105	99
21	343	92	102	94	217	140	129

TABLE II.   Evaluation Report on Elektro Helios
            Convection Oven (cont'd)

24	345	138	136	142	215[a]	172	155

(Dinners removed and placed in holding unit at 160°F)

51	173	158	174	154	153	176
59	165	154	163	149	152	175

---

[a]Examination of dinners adjacent to No. 4 indicated temperatures around 160°F. High temperature may have been
caused by loose crimping of aluminum foil hood. Dimensions of foil hood were not large enough to allow secure
crimping in many instances.

Observations: Reconstitution was successful for all compo-
                nents of dinner. Flavor, texture, and color
                satisfactory.

Bulk-Packed Fried Chicken

Number of Portions - 150

Weight of chicken: Total weight with bone   5 oz
                     Edible meat   2 oz

Chicken placed in foil-lined black iron pans, 18-1/4" x
9-3/4" x 1" without foil hood.

Thermocouple positions:

1. Left front 1st   2. Right front 1st
   shelf (top)   shelf (top)
3. Left center 6th   4. Right center 6th
   shelf   shelf
5. Left rear 11th   6. Right rear 11th
   shelf (bottom)   shelf (bottom)

TABLE II.   Evaluation Report on Elektro Helios
             Convection Oven (cont'd)

Record of Temperature Changes

Time (minutes)	Temperatures in different thermocouple locations (^{O}F)					
	1	2	3	4	5	6
5	115	105	105	142	89	98
6	123	107	113	152	99	109
8	123	114	125	170	105	119
9	135	123	137	180	130	123
11	147	132	149	190	145	130
12	169	141	160	196	155	135
14	189	150	177	205	170	146

Observations: Color and flavor of chicken excellent. A few
                 pieces of chicken stuck to aluminum foil, not
                 enough, however, to slow service.

Bulk-Packed Precooked Fish Sticks

       Number of Portions - 105
       Weight of individual fish stick   1 oz
       Number sticks per portion   3
       Weight of edible fish minus breading (3 sticks) 2 oz

       Food reheated without foil hood.

       Thermocouple positions:

          1. Left front 2nd shelf   2. Right front 2nd shelf
          3. Left rear 6th shelf   4. Left rear 6th shelf

TABLE II. Evaluation Report on Elektro Helios
Convection Oven (cont'd)

Record of Temperature Changes

Time (minutes)	Temperature in different thermocouple locations (^{o}F)			
	1	2	3	4
2	60	113	75	65
4	75	127	93	80
6	109	144	139	102
8	138	165	166	130
9	150	176	180	140

Observations: Fish sticks were placed flat on foil lined
trays. Because of tenderness of fish, shing-
ling was not possible. No sticking of fish
to foil lining was observed. Color, texture,
and flavor of fish excellent.

Summary of Results of Reheating Selected Bulk-Packed Foods

Type of food	Number of portions	Reheating time (minutes)	Average re-heating time
Pizza	100	4	
6 oz portion	115	5	4-½
Fish Sticks	150	9	
2 oz portion	72	9	
	144	9	
	103	10	9
Fish Cake	106	10	
4 oz portion	154	12	
	33	10	
	110	15	12

TABLE II. *Evaluation Report on Elektro Helios*
Convection Oven (cont'd)

Fried Chicken	159	14	
5 oz portion	160	14	
	108	15	
	114	15	
	115	15	
	110	15	15
Hamburger			
2-1/2 oz portion	107	8	8
Barbecued Beef			
3 oz portion	100	12	12
Frankfurters			
2 oz portion	40	18	18
Chickenburgers	150	10	
2-1/2 oz portion	114	10	10

Total 2,368

by the study's engineer along with engineers of a local oven manufacturer specializing in custom heating equipment. This oven met all requirements for satisfactory reconstitution and heavy duty use (Figs. 1 and 2). Both ovens circulated heated air over trays of food in vertical chambers. Each oven chamber contained a removable rack on which frozen food could be loaded. The racks were easily inserted into the oven and withdrawn when reconstitution was completed. The minimum capacity of each oven was 66 meals. Thus a school equipped with three ovens could provide approximately 600 meals per hour. In an hour and a half 900 meals could be ready for serving. All hot meals were transferred to holding units until meal time.

C. Sanitary and Microbiological Controls

The study found three methods of control effective for ensuring the wholesomeness of precooked, frozen food:

(1) Plants producing meat and poultry products for the program were required to be under continuous U. S. Department of Agriculture inspection, while plants producing fish products were required to be under continuous U. S. Department of Interior inspection.

(2) Plants were inspected by both a representative of the New York City Department of Health and the Coordinator of the study. No plant was eligible to supply food without the approval of the Department of Health representative. Where changes in equipment and procedures were necessary, such changes were outlined to the management, and no food was accepted until confirmation of such changes was received.

(3) Bacteriological standards were established and incorporated into the food specifications. The standards permitted no food to contain a plate count in excess of 100,000 aerobic bacteria per gram. Tests for coliform and staphylococcus were required to be negative. Random samples of food were taken upon arrival and were tested by a New York City laboratory before the food was served in schools. The service of precooked frozen foods in the case of individual dinners involved no manual handling. In serving bulk foods, the amount of handling was kept minimal. The use of polyethylene gloves by kitchen personnel, the elimination of dishwashing and potwashing, and the use of polyethylene garbage liners provided a high level of sanitation in the operation.

D. Staffing Level

At the time of the study, the Bureau of School Lunches generally followed a formula in its cafeterias that alloted 10 hours of labor per day per 100 meals. In the pilot schools this formula was cut approximately 40 % for the three- week menu cy-

FIGURE 1. The NEVO Thermal Food Conditioner was designed for
the reconstitution of bulk packaged or preplated frozen meals
for the New York City School Lunch Program. (Courtesy of NEVO
Corp., Oyster Bay, New York)

FIGURE 2. The NEVO Holding Cabinet (shown on the left) accom-
modates two oven loads and contains an elevator device which
permits the first load to be rolled into the top section and
then lowered into the bottom storage area. Fully loaded, the
Holding Cabinet contains 48 12 in by 20 in pans or 532 individual hot meals. A 500 pupil school in New York City required
2 NEVO Thermal Food Conditioners and 2 Holding Cabinets.
(Courtesy of NEVO Corp., Oyster Bay, New york)

cle and 43 % for the two-week menu cycle. Whether further reductions would occur in the dietetic and administrative personnel of the Bureau under a frozen food program was not determined. It was the opinion of the study team members, however,
that local dietitians, each of whom then worked one day a week
in each of five schools, could, in a frozen food program, perform the necessary work at each school on a biweekly basis.

E. *Introduction of Menu Cycles*

At the time of the study, menus in the school cafeterias
were varied throughout the year. Variety was based upon food
popularity, availability, cost, and other factors. Variety was
also designed to provide new foods as part of the educational
experience. In the pilot schools, on the other hand, the frozen
food program was based upon menu cycles that were planned to be
repeated throughout the year. Frozen foods do not depend upon
seasonal availability, and while their prices change somewhat
throughout the year, the fluctuations are not as great as in
the fresh food markets. At the pilot schools, both three-week
and two-week menu cycles were instituted and studied. Both cycles included precooked frozen meats, poultry, fish and
blanched vegetables. The menu items chosen were food that had
been served in the first experimental school, where their acceptance and plate waste were studied. They included hamburgers, spaghetti with meat sauce, fried chicken, pizza and other
foods that were found to be highly acceptable to children of
elementary school age. At times, various new foods were introduced and studied for their acceptance. From their observations, members of the study team concluded that new foods could
best serve an educational purpose when their introduction was
coordinated with curriculum activities relating to history, ge-
ography, economics, physiology or nutrition.

In the study team's experience the following administrative advantages were observed in connection with the use of
menu cycles:

(1) The menu cycle permitted food forecasting for an entire year.

(2) Procurement and contracts on a yearly basis simplified buying, warehousing, and distribution procedures.

(3) The tasks of menu writing, as well as menu substitution and the last minute decisions were minimized.

(4) Procedure for storage and service of food in the
schools were simplified.

(5) Inventory control for schools was simplified. The
frozen food inventory in the pilot schools consisted of 63
items as opposed to 105 items in regular school cafeterias.

(6) Training of kitchen personnel was simplified. A
week's training was sufficient for a new cook-manager in charge

of a school serving precooked frozen food.

(7) As menu cycles were repeated, kitchen routines were simplified and cook-managers were able to work efficiently without consulting work sheets.

(8) Regular daily deliveries to schools were confined to milk and bread.

F. Food Acceptance

To test the acceptability of the new precooked frozen foods, a poll was conducted at the first experimental school. Prior to the poll, students at that school had been served fro- zen foods on intermittent days when test runs were being made. On the other school days, they were served the regular food prepared in the school cafeteria. The poll was conducted by teachers in class rooms, and it showed a four to-one preference in favor of the frozen foods. When regular service of frozen foods started in the two experimental schools, lunch room par- ticipation at the first school increased from 400 to 500 daily, and at the second school, from 300 to 400 daily. Principals of both schools, as well as lunch room aides, reported on the pop- ularity and high acceptance of the new frozen food lunches.

G. Warehouse and Distribution

Food for use in conventional on premise cafeterias was de- livered from numerous sources, including the Bureau's own cen- tral warehouse, as well as local distributors and dealers. Un- der the new program, frozen food purchased from processors was shipped to a central warehouse from which, at intervals of a week or more, deliveries were shipped to the schools in refrig- erated trucks. This centralized method of warehousing and dis- tribution not only reduced deliveries, but was responsible for lower food costs due to the elimination of the distributor's costs for the delivery of individual items. Thus, pizzas pro- duced for the New York City program in Newark, New Jersey, were stored in the frozen food warehouse, and were delivered to the schools along with products packed in Red Hook, New York, Cro- zet, Virginia, and Portland, Maine. The pizzas for the frozen food program thus cost 8.8 cents each, while the same pizzas from the same plant, delivered by a frozen food distributor cost the regular school cafeteria 12.3 cents each. In the frozen food program the cost of warehousing, and distribution accounted to about a half a cent per meal.

H. Equipment Costs

An analysis of the costs of heavy duty equipment and small

movable equipment for on-premise cafeteria, serving between
500 and 700 meals per day, showed that it was $23,300 in caf-
eterias built during the period of study. In contrast the cost
of kitchen equipment required for a cafeteria serving precooked frozen food was $17,300.

I. Space Requirements

A comparison was made of the space requirements for an on-
premise cafeteria capable of serving between 500 and 700 meals
per day and cafeterias designed for serving precooked frozen
foods. It showed that a typical cafeteria with on-premise
cooking facilities required 1169 sq ft, while the two pilot
schools converted to the use of precooked frozen meals required 814 sq ft and 920 sq ft, respectively. The latter footage
included space for the storage of disposable ware required.

J. Comparative Meal Costs

The data summarized in Tables III and IV permit a comparison of costs under the frozen food program and on-premise food
preparation. The figures are based on a comparative study of
both types of schools during two-week and three-week menu cycles and identify the costs of food, labor, and disposable aluminum and paperware supplies required in the experimental
schools. The cost of tableware and small utensil replacement
was not estimated for the control schools because of the difficulty of obtaining long term costs for these items. However,
if they, as well as administrative expenses, had been included,
the net saving in the pilot schools would have been even greater than shown. The analysis shows a savings of $ 1764, on the
three-week menu cycle and a saving of $ 756 on the two-week cy-
cle. Table IV shows a saving of approximately 7 cents per meal
when the cost of precooked frozen meals were compared to the
city-wide cafeteria cost per meal.

IV. RECOMMENDATIONS

Since the study indicated that the use of frozen foods in
the elementary school lunch program could reduce the cost of
hot meals served by seven cents per meal, it was recommended
that the Board of Education give serious consideration to the
adoption of a policy implementing a frozen food program for
the elementary schools. Theoretically, the saving shown could
be extended to the forty million meals per year that were prepared in the elementary division. It was considered reasonable to assume that similar savings could accrue to the junior

TABLE III. School Lunch Operating Costs in Control Schools, Experimental Schools and City Wide On-Premise Kitchen Elementary Schools[2]

	Three-week menu cycle		Two-week menu cycle		City wide on premise kitchen schools
	Control schools	Experimental schools	Control schools	Experimental schools	
COST OF FOOD					
Opening Inventory	$ 1799.68	$ 2085.58	$ 1158.65	$ 2176.38	$ 27,372.32
purchases during period	+ 3109.30	+ 2106.15	+ 2166.43	+ 1073.08	+ 2,854,852.88
	4908.98	4191.73	3325.08	3249.46	2,882,225.20
Closing inventory	- 1742.36	- 1518.77	- 1421.64	- 1336.70	- 27,474.84
Purchased food consumed	3166.62	2672.96	1903.44	1912.76	2,854,750.36
Donated food consumed	+ 590.62	+ 246.09	+ 548.44	+ 199.93	+ 1,213,396.70
Total food consumed	3757.24	2919.05	2451.88	2112.69	4,068,147.06
COST OF LABOR					
Cook managers and school lunch helpers	2491.77	1227.85	1534.97	828.69	2,461,446.72
Vacation and holiday pay	211.04	107.78	127.24	72.15	149,200.11
Social security	101.94	50.54	65.00	34.13	89,399.74
Uniforms	53.46	27.20	34.63	18.44	54,255.43
Total labor cost	2858.21	1413.37	1761.85	953.41	2,754,302.00
COST OF NON-FOOD SUPPLIES					
Aluminum and paperware	17.23	560.43	12.55	419.12	
Household supplies	27.39	4.00	17.44	2.69	
Total Cost of non-food supplies	44.62	564.43	29.99	421.81	
TOTAL COST OF OPERATIONS	$ 6660.07	$ 4896.85	$ 4243.72	$ 3487.91	$ 6,822,449.06
Total number of lunches served to children, teachers and employees	14,738	12,019	9,575	9,020	14,714,705

[2]
Costs data for experimental and control schools were collected during the 1963-1964 school year, while city-wide costs are based on the 1962-1963 school year. Cost data for experimental schools are based on the use of bulk-packed frozen foods.

TABLE IV. *Cost per Lunch in Control Schools, Experimental Schools and City Wide On-Premise Kitchen Elementary Schools[2]*

	Three-week menu cycle			Two-week menu cycle			City-wide On-premise kitchen schools
	Control schools	Pilot schools	Difference	Control schools	Pilot schools	Difference	
COST OF FOOD	0.25493	0.24286	(0.01207)	0.26153	0.23422	(0.02731)	0.27647
COST OF LABOR							
Cook managers and school lunch helpers	0.16907	0.10216	(0.06691)	0.16373	0.09187	(0.07186)	0.16728
Vacation & holiday pay	0.01432	0.00897	(0.00535)	0.01357	0.00800	(0.00557)	0.01014
Social security	0.00692	0.00420	(0.00272)	0.00694	0.00378	(0.00316)	0.00608
Cost of uniforms	0.00363	0.00226	(0.00137)	0.00369	0.00204	(0.00165)	0.00369
Cost of employee's meals	0.00980	0.00544	(0.00436)	0.01062	0.00411	(0.00651)	0.00940
Total labor cost	0.20374	0.12303	(0.08071)	0.19855	0.10980	(0.08875)	0.19659
COST OF NON FOOD SUPPLIES							
Aluminum & paperware	0.00117	0.04662	0.04545	0.00133	0.04646	0.04513	
Household supplies	0.00186	0.00033	(0.00153)	0.00186	0.00030	(0.00156)	
Total cost of non-food supplies	0.00303	0.04695	0.04392	0.00319	0.04676	0.04357	
TOTAL COST PER LUNCH	0.46170	0.41284	(0.04386)	0.46327	0.39078	(0.07249)	0.47306

[2] see footnote, Table III

high schools and high schools that served the Type A lunch.[1]

[1]
Editors' Note: In 1966, after two years' additional test-ing, the New York City Board of Education adopted a policy of instituting the frozen meal program in all new and renovated elementary schools. In the years since the program was imple-mented, as labor costs increased, the economics changed to fa-vor individual preplated frozen meals over bulk-packed frozen foods. By 1976 several hundred schools were utilizing either preplated meals or bulk-packed frozen foods. Bulk packed meals accounted for 60,000 school lunches daily and individual preplated frozen meals for 170,000. The total of 230,000 frozen meals represented about 30% of the lunches served in New York City public schools daily.

CHAPTER 25

NEW YORK STATE DEPARTMENT OF MENTAL HYGIENE
SUPPLY SUPPORT SYSTEM

Robert W. Jailer

Planning Research Corporation
Systems Sciences Company
Englewood Cliffs, New Jersey

Harold Ratner

New York State Department of Mental Hygiene
Albany, New York

I. ANALYSIS, DESIGN AND IMPLEMENTATION OF THE SYSTEM

A. Background

Early in 1966, a team of consultants[1] undertook a systems analysis and design effort in institution support services for the New York Department of Mental Hygiene. By the end of December 1965, the New York Department of Mental Hygiene was operating 36 mental hospitals and schools for the mentally retarded, with a total patient load of approximately 100,000 and the equivalent of 30,000 staff members who required full time support in terms of, at least, food supply. The institutions themselves ranged in size from about 150 patients to approximately 13,000 patients, and were scattered across the entire state of New York from Long Island, through the New York Metropolitan Area, to the St. Lawrence River, and west to Buffalo.

[1]*Planning Research Corporation, working with Case & Co. (management consultants), Amman & Whitney (architects and engineers), International Food Consultants, and Food Sciences Associates.*

Copyright © 1979 by Academic Press, Inc.
All rights of reproduction in any form reserved
ISBN: 0-12-453150-4

At the time the study began, the institutions were operating on an essentially independent basis as far as supply support and food systems were concerned. Thirty-four of the 36 institutions had their own warehouses for food, clothing, and housekeeping supplies. The other two were supported from warehouses of nearby institutions.

The group of institutions was operating approximately 20 individual small- to medium-size bakeries. Some of these supported only the institution on the same site, while others shipped bakery products to nearby institutions. A few bought commercial bakery products. Approximately 12 of the institutions were making their own ice cream in small ice cream manufacturing units; the remainder purchased commercial ice cream. Six of the institutions ran centralized root and tuber vegetable preparation lines; the remainder prepared their vegetables in kitchens.

There was some degree of centralization in the system in terms of management of overall food usage through an annual food plan: standardized formulas for food preparation and bakery operations, central control over institution clothing and housekeeping supply levels, and some centralized fiscal management. Other than these, and a central system for management of supply of certain tranquilizers, the remainder of the supply operations in the system were handled locally.

The essentially decentralized system operated reasonably well. The Department of Mental Hygiene used two measures of effectiveness of its supply support operations: patient benefit (which was primary, although not readily quantifiable) and cost. From the viewpoint of patient benefit, the system looked reasonably good. The nutrition services operation was assuring a balanced diet, with good quality food, and provisions for special diets wherever medically prescribed. From a cost viewpoint, the system was running on a relatively low budget compared with similar systems in other states, and no major budgetary problems were being encountered. From the viewpoint of the then-current operations, there was no immediate need for a new system. However, the Department of Mental Hygiene's program, planning for the treatment of mental illness and mental retardation was undergoing a major overhaul; planning was in the transition stage from the large to the small institution. While there was no expectation of a significant increase in the number of patients over the 10-year planning horizon, the Department was anticipating the construction of 22 new institutions, and the phasing down of others during that period.

The study undertook the investigation of whether the Department should continue to build individual warehouses for each new institution that was not close enough to an existing

institution to obtain warehousing support, and whether it
would be necessary to build additional small institution
bakeries, vegetable preparation lines, and other support facilities. The alternative was some degree of centralization in
all these functions. Centralization for the new institutions
alone was obviously not the answer, since they were geographically scattered in a manner very similar to the existing
institutions. Consequently, the study had to consider whether the entire system should go to a new form of food and
other supply support, or should continue with its decentralized support operations.

    In assigning the consulting team to this problem, the
Department specified some study boundaries. Some of these
were obvious while others were not. Food was to be a primary
consideration, including both the supply of foods to the
kitchens in the institutions, and the operation of bakeries
and other nonkitchen food preparation. Other types of supply
could be added to the system if it was found advantageous.
Patient benefit was to take precedence over the economics of
the recommended system. While the Department could not
specify a level of benefit quantitatively, it was agreed that
the new system would not degrade the existing benefits to the
patient, and would increase them wherever possible.

    Other bounding conditions included operation of the system
in conformity with New York State law, and design of the
system primarily for the Department of Mental Hygiene institutions (although in parallel with a portion of the work, a
study was undertaken of extending the services of the system
to some 30,000 or 40,000 people in other institutions such as
the state corrections system, the state narcotics addiction
control system, other state hospitals, and all other state
operated residential institutions, except for the state university).

    The system study was to consider all commodities used by
the Department other than a few for which statewide distribution arrangements that crossed department lines had been
made. Essentially, this included fluid milk, gasoline, and
fuel oil. The system was to be operated by civil service
employees. The study was originally constrained to "stop at
the kitchen door." The supply system was to deliver items to
the kitchen but not concern itself with what went on beyond
that point (this restriction was later relaxed to include data
from individual kitchens in management operations).

    The system was to be an internal Department of Mental
Hygiene operation, although it could support other agency
institutions if it did not interfere with the Mental Hygiene
support operations. It was to be designed for minimum changes
in the interfaces between the Department of Mental Hygiene and

other state agencies such as the Department of Audit and
Control, the Division of Budget, and the Office of General
Services. Because of the transitional nature of the planning-
for-the-future program of the Department of Mental Hygiene at
the time the study was undertaken, it was necessary to include
provisions for maximum flexibility in the system. This was
noted emphatically during the first six months of the analysis, when the Department's projections for patient population
and patient distribution over the ten-year study period
changed twice.

B. Analytical Approach

The consulting team's analytical approach consisted of
four major stages: (1) an analysis of present system operations, (2) a synthesis of alternative system designs and
analysis of these alternatives, (3) selection and optimization of the system to be recommended, and (4) development of
the detailed design of the recommended system.

The point of departure for the study was an analysis of
the then-existing support operations of the Department to
provide baseline data for the analysis of service requirements. The first step was the study of the basic operational
management philosophy of the Department, the relationship
between the institutions and the central office, and between
the Department's management and the management of other state
agencies that it operates.

This led to analysis of the details of the Department's
means for determining requirements for acquisition of and
distribution of all patient-oriented and institution-oriented
material, including a study of food manufacturing and preparation operations; food being the primary area of concern. The
analyses included detailed studies of the Department's annual
food plan, and its translation to the required amounts and
scheduling of food delivery to the institution warehouses and
to individual kitchens. They also included studies of food
costs and sources, warehousing and distribution problems,
requirement determinations, and information flow from the
institutions to the Department's central office to the
State's purchasing agency.

For nonfoods, the study covered an analysis of the rates
of usage of all classes of commodities: determination of the
commonality of use of individual items and classes of items
among the institutions, an analysis of the weight and volume
handling problems of the present level of demand for the
various nonfood commodities, a study of the warehousing
throughput of the individual institutions, analyses of present

distribution problems, and many other factors. Both the food
and nonfood portions of the work involved on-site sampling
studies of institution operations, facilities, management,
and a complete survey of existing warehouses and bakeries.

The relationship between the Department of Mental Hygiene
and other State agencies was studied in detail, with special
emphasis on the working relationship between the Department of
Mental Hygiene and the State's purchasing agency, and the
relationship between the Departments of Mental Hygiene and
Corrections, since the latter supplied many of the Department
of Mental Hygiene's clothing and housekeeping supplies from
its industrial operations. In addition, fiscal, budget, and
other state agencies involved in institution supply and
supply management were studied.

This process developed the major data base for the remainder of the study. Quantitative data requirements were established for both food and nonfood commodities, on the
performance and cost of Mental Hygiene food manufacturing and
processing operations, on the requirements for information
flow in mangement, and on the basic dimensions of the distribution requirements.

C. Analysis of Alternative Systems

The next stage of the design of the supply support system
was to study possible means of providing each of the individual services and products required to meet the total Department needs. In this portion of the work, designs for
alternative means of supplying the Department's requirements
in terms of distribution, food manufacturing, and management
were explored.

The functions of the subsystems necessary for the total
system were first determined from an analysis of the requirements for support services at the institutions. The study
then proceeded to determine the range of possible subsystems
and component types that could meet these requirements. A
decision to buy the materials to be manufactured or to contract for the services to be supplied, especially for food,
was included as an alternative to each subsystem where applicable. Within the range of each possible subsystem spectrum,
a single point or series of points were selected that represented the specific characteristics of the class of operation
under consideration.

There were many choices among some of the subsystems for
a total system as complex as the one required for the Department of Mental Hygiene. Thus, a plan for a logical sequence
for this type of successive suboptimization analysis was

necessary if the work was to proceed in an orderly manner.
The problem was the selection of a starting point for the
analysis that would allow rejection of obviously unsuitable
subsystems early in the analytical process so that detailed
studies for a manageable number of alternatives could be
concentrated on.

Consideration of the requirements for support services
indicated that the types of alternatives to be considered
could be divided into six major groups:

1. distribution system
2. bakery
3. ice cream preparation
4. vegetable and other food preparation
5. butcher shop and meat supply
6. miscellaneous small subsystems, including dry mix
manufacturing and coffee roasting

Of these, the only group that interacted completely with all
other groups was the distribution system, which included both
warehousing and transportation. Thus, the starting point
chosen for the analysis was a study of the major alternatives
in the distribution system design. In exploring the range of
possible distribution system designs, only three clear-cut
cases appeared immediately: (1) a continuation of the then-
current decentralized operations, (2) a centralized system,
and (3) a contracted system for food, with all other types
of supply decentralized.

Analysis of the geographic distribution of institutions
then in existence and planned for the future, of the distribution of patient population among these institutions, and of
the road network available for distribution operations,
allowed identification of two types of systems falling into
the range between a single distribution center operation and
a totally local operation that represented typical alternative solutions.

Thus, five definitive subsystem types from the viewpoint
of warehousing and distributing food were analyzed: (1) a
central distribution system, (2) a regional distribution
system, (3) a neighborhood system combining supply support
for institutions that were near one another, (4) a totally
decentralized local system, and (5) a contracted food system
with decentralized non-food supply.

The first of the alternatives to be eliminated was the
contracting of food service. None of the major food service
contract organizations would bid on the required institution
food service at the nutritional and quality levels then in
effect within the range of then-current costs for Department
operations.

In selecting among the four alternative types of Department-operated distribution systems, the analysis considered patient benefit, operating costs, and capital costs as the three primary criteria. In the analysis, patient benefit was held to the required level by using cost factors that would permit purchase and/or manufacture of the required quality of food, and a distribution system that could provide the necessary level of service. Operating costs were broken down to procurement, transportation, warehousing and stockroom labor, food manufacturing, and management. Capital cost comparisons considered the number and size of facilities required and the extent of trucking operations as preliminary indicators of the capital investment required in each case.

Analysis indicated that major factors in operating costs were a trade-off between lower porecurement costs for car lot and truckload commodity purchases and the increased distribution costs for warehousing and transportation as the extent of centralization increased. Studies of procurement costs in other centralized systems indicated that savings over the then-current practices of 15-20% or more were possible. Analysis of distribution costs in similar systems indicated that distribution typically costs about 5% of the cost of commodities for the level of service required. Accordingly, from an operational cost viewpoint, the more centralized the system to be developed, the greater the cost advantage. Further, a centralized system would have the major portion of its management personnel concentrated in one point, reducing the total staff salaries considerably.

From a capital investment viewpoint, the central system appeared to have an edge over regional or local systems because of the necessity for the construction of new warehouses and bakeries for the new institutions, and the rehabilitation of existing warehouses and bakeries that was required over the 10-year study period.

On an overall basis, considering both operational and capital costs, a centralized system with new distribution facilities could be shown to be economically advantageous over more decentralized operations. Accordingly, the central distribution system for food and nonfood commodities was selected as the basis for the system design. The analysis of alternatives for bakery, ice cream, vegetable preparation, dry mix preparation, butchering, and other support subsystems proceeded in a manner parallel to that for the distribution system. These studies resulted in similar conclusions; centralization offered better opportunities for both operating and capital cost savings, and for maintenance of quality in system operations.

Preliminary detailed analyses, however, indicated that a completely centralized system, operating from a single warehouse and food preparation complex, to supply the needs of the entire set of institutions in all parts of the state would result in problems of delivery reliability. It would also require excessively long round trip driving times, with a necessity for frequent overnight breaks.

A study of the transportation functions indicated that the institutions fell roughly into two major groups: a metropolitan New York City and Long Island area group, containing approximately two-thirds of the patient population, and an upstate group containing the remaining third. Transportation operations for the downstate area would be primarily city traffic type deliveries over relatively short distances for the supply of primarily large institutions. Upstate transportation operations, on the other hand, would be primarily open-road, utilizing high-speed highways for most of the long distance hauling, serving institutions that were on the average smaller than those downstate.

Thus, the most practical centralized warehousing, food processing, and distribution system appeared to require two distribution warehouses. Analyses of transportation routes, driving times, institution populations, vehicle requirements, etc., indicated that one of the distribution and food processing centers should be located near the northern edge of New York City on the road network leading to the large institutions on Long Island. The other should be located along the New York State Thruway, near Rochester.

When this determination had been made, the analysis then proceeded to consider the design of the individual functions required for the operation of the total food and nonfood distribution system. A series of studies of the various alternatives for bakery system design, ice cream, vegetable preprocessing, dry mix manufacturing, butchering operations, etc., including a study of the possibility of buying at least a portion of the Department's food requirements as preprocessed convenience foods, were then conducted as a series of suboptimization analyses.

Once the framework of the distribution system had been established and the analysis had proceeded to these various food preparation operations, it was found that there was little operational or cost inter-relationship between these types of subsystems. After the distribution system pattern had been established, the work proceeded along the lines of the food preparation system. During the process of fitting the subsystems together, it was found necessary to readjust some of the planned details of transportation and distribution of subsystem operations to permit optimization of food manufacturing, especially in the case of bakeries.

The analysis for the distribution of nonfood commodities was given the lowest priority in the study. During the preliminary studies it had determined that the basic form of the system would be designed around food. With the possible exceptions of drugs and other items required for the medical care of the patient, food was determined to be in the commodity directly affecting patient benefits to the greatest degree. Further, from a gross viewpoint, food was the highest cost commodity in the operation of the system.

Preliminary studies indicated that a considerable portion of the commodities other than food required for institution support could not be included in any support services distribution system, either because they were not compatible with food for warehousing and distribution, or because the volume and commonality of demand could not justify warehousing at all. Thus, commodities such as paints, lubricants, plumbing and electrical supplies, and automotive supplies were eliminated from consideration for inclusion in the system. The remaining high volume supplies, primarily clothing, housekeeping materials and small equipment, tranquilizers, and electric light bulbs, were found to be compatible with food from the viewpoint of warehousing, distribution, and similarity in demand.

D. System Design

The final system recommended to the Department of Mental Hygiene consisted of two distribution centers, each with a bakery, two vegetable preparation plants, one dry mix plant, and one ice cream plant. The analyses indicated that a central butchering operation would be more expensive and more difficult from a quality control viewpoint than the procurement of precut meats. It was also found that the Department's coffee roasting plant could not produce coffee of the quality that was commercially available at the same price. Accordingly, these two portions of the food preparation system were recommended as totally purchased operations.

E. System Flexibility

The flexibility of the recommended system design was tested before the implementation phase was well under way. Approval of the system design and appropriation of the required capital funding took considerably longer than had been anticipated. During that time, real estate values, especially in the New York City area, started to rise at a

rate that had not been anticipated, and the site tentatively
selected for the New York City distribution center became so
expensive that the available funding would not permit its
acquisition. An alternative was found from an unexpected
source. The United States Army's Schenectady General Depot
was in the process of being closed, and a group of large warehouses had been declared surplus. These were offered to
other Federal agencies and no takers were found. They were
then offered to state and local governments via the Federal
Department of Health, Education, and Welfare for public
health, education, and other similar purposes. One of these
warehouses was ideal from the Department of Mental Hygiene's
viewpoint. It was very close to the New York Thruway, had
adequate space for both warehousing and food preparation, had
very broad column spacing which permitted flexibility in
interior arrangements, a clear overhead of more than 20 feet,
more than adequate floor loading limits, and available rail
and truck docks. The Department applied for it and acquired
it at virtually no cost. The only major repairs required
were to the roof and heating system.

However, the warehouse was not located near Rochester,
but to Schenectady, very close to Albany. The whole distribution system analysis was repeated with a Schenectady location for the upstate distribution point to determine the
effect on the downstate warehousing location requirement. It
was found that a downstate location on Long Island, east of
New York City, would permit system cost optimization at
approximately the same levels as the previous arrangement,
and a site already owned by the Department of Mental Hygiene
in Central Islip was found available. Reanalysis of the suboptimization of the other systems indicated that the system
could be operated effectively from Schenectady and Central
Islip, and the implementation proceeded accordingly. Thus,
the budget problem was overcome by taking advantage of some
of the flexibility built into the system design.

F. Management System

As the basic structure of the operational portion of the
Supply Support System began to take shape, work was started
on the design of a management system. The concept of management that was recommended was one of centralization of
control. In the system design this was accomplished by
assigning overall system management to an Albany central
office staff, assisted by a computer in routine, time-
consuming operations. The automated management information
system was designed to allow the central management to do the

many things that are necessary for control of a large, geographically dispersed system by providing the required information on its operations rapidly in usable form.

The central management only extended to routine operations in the classes of supply that most directly affected the patients' welfare: primarily food, clothing, and housekeeping supplies, the Department's food manufacturing and pre-processing operations, and the distribution of the commodities. Control of institution-unique, nonroutine, and maintenance supply remained with the individual institutions.

In the initial operational system design phase of the project, only the broad outlines of the management system design were completed. Once the operational system design had been approved, and as the details of the system implementation were being developed, the final design of the management system was fleshed out, and its implementation started in parallel with the operational system.

The management system was designed as a highly automated management information and control system, operating primarily from the Department's central Albany office. Provisions were made, however, for routine data inputs to the computer system directly from distribution centers, and the direct transmission of reports and shipping orders from the computer center to line printers at the distribution centers.

The Supply Support Management System was organized as a group of six subsystems.

1. Requirement Planning, that developed food commodity requirements, on a long-range basis, by conversion of the information contained in the Department's master food plan to commodity requirements.

2. Procurement Request, that developed detailed requirement data for the food and nonfood commodities handled in the distribution centers.

3. Open Order, that maintained a data base on the state contracts available to the system for procurement of food and nonfood commodity stocks for the distribution centers. It initiated computer records on each new contract let by the state, determined the warehouse stock indicator levels for the commodities procured under the contract, and revised inventory control indicators to allow proper functioning of the inventory control operations. It also performed scheduling and status reporting functions for commodities on order.

4. Menu Processing, that converted the information on institution menus and estimated feeding population data into

food commodity orders for warehouse shipment of the food
required to the institution kitchens.

5. Transaction Processing, that handled data on all
transactions related to warehouse inventory and its procurement in the system. It also maintained data on the current
status of contracts, purchase orders, and stock inventory.
It performed inventory management functions, generated reports
on all commodities with stock levels that had passed any of
the inventory control indicator levels established in the
Open Order section of the system, and provided data on the
usage of commodities on an institution and distribution
center basis.

6. File Maintenance, that provided internal support for
the other subsystems in the management system by maintaining
the master system files.

The automated and manual management operations in the Supply
Support Mangement System, from the long-range projections of
requirements for commodities in the distribution centers to
the billing of the institutions for commodities delivered,
were designed to be handled as a series of sequential and
interrelated functions. On a simplified basis, the functions
can be considered in two groups: (1) the generation of data
for the projection of requirements, specification of contracting needs, and the scheduling of production in the system's
food manufacturing facilities, and (2) the filling of institution needs, warehouse inventory control, and the accounting
and billing necessary to maintain the financial integrity of
the overall system.

As an adjunct to the centralized management information
system, the project staff designed a computer operated
institution supply management system that interfaced with the
central system and reduced the paperwork load on the individual institution business offices.

The basic philosophy in the design of the Supply Support
Management System was modular. Some of its more complex
functions, especially the portion of the system that converted individual institution menus and feeding population
data to warehouse order pick instructions, could be bypassed
in the initial implementation of the physical system. These
could be activated later, after sufficient experience had
been gained with the operational portion of the system and
the remainder of the management system to allow the Department to introduce this complex operation.

G. *System Implementation*

The design for the physical system implementation was time-phased by individual commodity class to permit the Department to obtain experience with similar groups of commodities before proceeding to more difficult operations. Initially, nonperishable food stocks were warehoused and distributed. As more experience was attained and the more complex portions of the physical system came on line, refrigerated and frozen foods, bakery products and other system-manufactured food items were added to the operational list. Nonfood items were gradually phased in as the food portion of the distribution system was developed.

As is almost inevitable with a complex computerized management system to be implemented in parallel with a complex physical operation, it was found necessary to make changes in the management system programming, as the system implementation proceeded. Some of these changes were due to a Department change in the procedures and equipment in its computer center. Others were necessitated by problems of data input and changes in details of institution operations. Most of these, however, were instituted after the system design and implementation work of the consulting team had been completed.

II. CURRENT STATUS

The Management Information System established in 1970 by the state of New York, Department of Mental Hygiene, for its entire food service operation, presently serves 63 mental hygiene institutions with a population of approximately 60,000 and an annual raw food budget of over 33 million dollars. Food products are manufactured and distributed from the two large centers that also distribute purchased food. Utilizing a Master Food Plan and monthly feeding population reports from each institution, the computer programs calculate quantities, requisition food by commodity, generate deviation reports to monitor actual requests, printout local purchase reports for each institution, prepare order pick documents for the distribution centers, and provide for commodity substitution for out of stock commodities.

At present, two other New York State Departments use the Management Information System to some extent. The system is capable of providing yearly projected, long and short range

budgeting (including daily per capita costs by diet type),
nutrition, recipe, and menu reports.

The success of the system is believed to be due to the
combined input from systems analysts, programmers, nutrition-
ists, dietitians, and industrial engineers.

CHAPTER 26

A CONVENIENCE FOOD SERVICE PROGRAM
IN A 300-BED GENERAL HOSPITAL

Sanford Kotzen

Franklin Square Hospital
Baltimore, Maryland

I. BACKGROUND

Franklin Square Hospital, until December 1969, was a 171-
bed acute general hospital located in a section of Baltimore's
inner city that had deteriorated significantly in the post-
World War II years. The hospital was founded in 1898 but its
future was threatened by the extensive demolition of residential structures to the north of the hospital to make way
for Baltimore's east-west highway. The hospital, because of
a large proportion of charity and bad debt patients, and a
declining patient census, had few liquid assets. The year
1965 was determined to be the year of decision. It was
decided, if financing were available, to relocate and build a
new facility.

II. THE CHALLENGE

The hospital qualified for the proceeds of a $4 million
bond issue from the State of Maryland. In addition, it
raised $1.8 million in two capital fund campaigns, had some
modest assets of its own and received a Hill-Burton grant of
$725,000. Thus the parameters were set. There was $5,300,000
available for construction. In a 300-bed hospital, this
translates into $17,666 per bed. The total project cost could
not exceed $7,500,000 including the land, architect and
engineering fees, other consultants, equipment, interest, and
insurance during construction. A construction cost of
$17,666 per bed represented just about 1/2 the going rate for

461

Copyright © 1979 by Academic Press, Inc.
All rights of reproduction in any form reserved
ISBN: 0-12-453150-4

a complete community teaching hospital in an urban area bid
in the fall of 1967. These, however, were all the funds
available for the construction and if the hospital were unsuccessful in inviting bids within these limitations, the project
would have been aborted. Knowing this, the architect, the
hospital administration, and the Medical Staff undertook the
project with a singleness of purpose--to succeed. Early on,
some hard and fast decisions were made.

1. The hospital would not be a monument to any one or
group of people except the public it served.
2. Nothing would be taken for granted and consequently
the need for each and every area of the hospital had to be
justified.
3. There were to be no frills in the building. The
common traffic or circulation areas were designed to prevent
a single usage and to keep their overall percentage at a minimum, reaching a figure 32% below the national hospital
average [1].
4. The building had to be designed to permit easy expansion and alterations.
5. The building had to be designed to be cost effective
in its operation. A low construction cost would not be
allowed to result in a high operating cost during the life of
the building.

III. THE APPROACH

After consulting the chiefs of the medical staff, the
hospital department heads, and on occasion, consultants, all
major design decisions were made by the architect and the
administrator, as chief executive officer. Considerable help
was furnished by the Director of Medical Education. An arbi-
tration mechamism was provided in case of conflicting view-
points: the Building Committee of the Board of Trustees was
to have been the arbitrator. Fortunately, this safeguard was
never needed! It was felt that the fewer people and commit-
tees in an organization are involved in the decision making
process the more effectively cost could be controlled.
Each area of the hospital was scrutinized to see if it
withstood the initial test of necessity and cost effectiveness. In so doing, it was found that there were certain
areas that raised real questions: the laundry, the school of
nursing and dormitory, the kitchen, and the milk formula
room [2].
The laundry in the old hospital had been closed about
five years prior to relocation in order to gain an employees'

locker room and lounge. Linen was sent out to a nearby commercial laundry, which provided good service at reasonable prices. Consequently, the decision was made to continue the practice. The elimination of the laundry saved approximately $144,000 in the initial construction cost of the hospital.

The Diploma School of Nursing, which had been maintained since 1901 at a high cost to patients, was offered to a neighboring community college. The students now receive an Associate in Arts degree, while gaining their clinical experience at Franklin Square Hospital and other local institutions. Thus, the hospital has the benefit of exposure and recruitment without any of the expense. Capital costs estimated at $750,000 and operating costs as well were eliminated.

The milk formula room was another area required by the Maryland State Health Department. Most hospitals by 1965 were buying formula processors or drug companies, a practice found to be superior from many aspects. Yet, the regulation requiring one was on the books. A decision was made to get the regulation changed and, after overcoming a good deal of inertia and experiencing much frustration, permission was granted to eliminate the milk formula room at a savings of $22,000.

The next area was, of course, the kitchen. In addition to questioning its ability as a hospital to prepare gourmet food, and overcoming the usual complaints about food quality, the administration realized that if it could have a Dietary Department without a kitchen, it would save approximately $405,000 in capital costs. In the aggregate, the savings through the elimination of these four nonpatient areas was $1,321,000 or 25% of the construction cost.

The hospital was familiar with the Kaiser Hospitals on the West Coast and Hawaii and their convenience food programs. Representatives visited two institutions in New Jersey that had done some pioneering with convenience food—the Rahway Hospital in Rahway, New Jersey and the Pollock Pavillion of the Jersey City Medical Center. With this background as encouragement, the hospital's dietitian, its architect, its food service manager, and the administrators traveled to California at various times to visit Kaiser hospitals at Belleflower, Harbor City, Hayward, and Santa Clara. The dietary personnel at these hospitals demonstrated the state of the art and how it had progressed as each new hospital was built. The conclusion was reached that this could be done successfully on the East Coast where there were more food processors available [3]. To prove the point, however, for a period of about one year before the hospital relocated from downtown Baltimore to eastern Baltimore County, a move of some ten miles, experimental luncheons were conducted every Tuesday in the diet lab of the old school of nursing. A

microwave oven was intalled and various food processors would
put on a demonstration luncheon using their products for
about five to ten persons, including at various times representatives of the Medical Staff, the Board of Trustees, and
hospital department heads. After each luncheon, those who
sampled the food filled out a questionnaire and returned it to
the Food Service Manager. On this basis, the first list of
suppliers for the food service operation in the new hospital
was generated.

IV.   IMPEDIMENTS TO OVERCOME

It began to appear that the route of the Kaiser Hospitals,
which had done such great pioneering with convenience foods
from 1955, would be followed at Franklin Square. It was
decided to have two microwave ovens in each 34 bed nursing
unit installed in a food staging area. There was to be a
central food receiving, storing, assembling, and holding area.
In addition, there was to be office space for dietitians,
dietary aids, a dietary steward, and a secretary.
    There were many, however, who needed to be convinced.
First, the Board of Trustees. This was not a difficult task
since the funds necessary to include a kitchen could not be
generated. The medical staff was the most willing group to
accept the change. Dietary personnel had feelings of insecur-
ity and were rife for the typical unfounded rumors which circulated. With the marked increase in the size of the new
hospital, however, they were all offered positions as aids,
maids, or other positions compatible with their skills. The
chef was named dietary steward and came to the new hospital
as an insurance policy.
    The big challenge was selling the concept to the Nursing
Department. In the old hospital, nurses were a scarce commodity and were usually overworked. The additional task of
processing a tray in the microwave oven, dispensing a beverage,
and taking a tray to a patient presented an obstacle. The
Director of Nursing quickly sized up the problem, realizing
that, unless nurses would undertake this activity, the system
would not work and the new hospital could not operate. With
her low keyed approach, she was able to sell the concept
effectively, and another obstacle was overcome.
    Another problem area involved the various codes and regu-
lations that had to be met. Since the hospital had applied
for Hill-Burton construction funds, it had to comply with the
appropriate regulations and requirements. The mere mention
of a convenience food operation at the Public Health Service's
regional office caused raised eyebrows. It became necessary
to prepare a document about 1 in. in thickness delineating
all facets of the operation including the sources of

processed food. Even financial statements from potential food processors were required. This done, permission was given to proceed, but, with one provision: the Dietary Department had to be located on an exterior wall in case the system failed and a conventional kitchen had to be built.

The difficulties were far from over, however; the State Architect in the Division of Licensure of the State Health Department reviewed the plans and required all the divisions of the Maryland Department of Health to sign off on all respects of the plans. The Bureau of Consumer Protection of the Environmental Health Services viewed convenience food operations as a gag that would ultimately disappear. The principal objections were

1. Lack of control over food processing, particularly in the case of out-of-state food processors.
2. Nutritive losses of the frozen food during processing.
3. The method of defrosting convenience food.
4. The manner in which defrosted food would be transported from the Dietary Department to the Nursing Stations.
5. Who would reconstitute the food in the food staging area?
6. How the personnel would be garbed while processing the meals.
7. Whether entrees would be purchased preplated, or assembled in the Dietary Department.

By enlisting the support of various nationally recognized experts in frozen foods, the Department of Health finally relented. However, this did not end the problems. As in any program, when technology improves, products change causing modifications in procedures. When the health authorities realized that the program was changing slightly, the Hospital was threatened with the loss of approval. For example, it was originally thought preplated entrees would be purchased; but it soon became apparent that the number of food processors of this type were scarce. It also became apparent that one would have to stock numerous combinations of meat, vegetables, and starches to meet the requirements of a selective menu.

When a change was made to bulk frozen food, the size of the slab became an issue. It seems that there was a question about the extent of bacteria growth during the thawing period. As a result of these and other problems, the new hospital had been opened a year and a half before its Dietary Department was finally licensed by the State Health Department!

V.   THE REAL TIME OPERATION

On December 9, 1969, the hospital reopened in its new
location.   The tray assembly line began to roll and meals
were delivered to the food staging area on each nurses
station.

The meal assembly process is relatively simple.   The
entree items for lunch and dinner are removed from the storage
freezer the day before they are required.   The items withdrawn are based upon patient selections from the selective
menu and other factors learned from experience.   The products
are brought up to a temperature of about 38°F (6°C) in a
refrigerator.

The next morning, between 8:30 and 9:45, lunch is assembled.   The trays are placed in tray carts, covered with a
plastic bag, and stored in a holding refrigerator until about
10:45 a.m. when they are transported to the floors.   To avoid
contamination, each individual food item on the tray is
covered before placement on the tray cart, disposable banquet
covers being used on the entrees.   Dinner is assembled from
10:45 to about 11:45 a.m.

The dietary personnel's responsibility for the tray ends
when the tray cart is delivered to a food staging area.   At
meal time someone from the nursing staff prepares the trays
and hands them out to other nursing personnel for delivery
to the patients.   Preparation consists of removing the tray
from the cart, and placing it on the counter under a microwave oven.   While the chilled entree is heated, the beverage
is prepared and set on the tray.

The breakfast is assembled in the Dietary Department from
1:00 to 2:15 p.m.   Trays are placed in the carts stored in
the holding refrigerator until 7 a.m. the next morning for
delivery to the food staging areas.

There is one food staging area in each nursing unit and
it is only 75 square feet in size.   It contains a refrigerator that holds the 34 trays required for the nursing unit.
There are two microwave ovens, a hot water dispenser, a sink,
ice maker, and an undercounter refrigerator.   The entire area
was designed so that one person can process the trays and hand
them out.   Interestingly, the concept for this unit was born
at an altitude of about 30,000 feet; the hospital's architect
observed stewardesses serving over a hundred passengers in a
short time span from a compact area.   In concert with the
hospital's dietitian, the idea was refined until the food
staging area was developed.

Shortly after opening the new hospital, problems started
to develop.   Newly recruited nurses from some of the other
24 Baltimore metropolitan area hospitals felt that preparing

and serving trays was demeaning. Instructions were not followed and some plates were heated too long or even heated
twice.

A key part of the new system was the total use of disposables, right down to the serving tray. Much had to be learned
about disposables. For example, while several disposables
looked similar, some were not designed for microwave ovens.
Even within those that were, some batches were acceptable
and others were not.

The limitations of specific foods had to be mastered. It
was found that bacon can melt and shrivel some disposables,
and that boiled eggs explode. The timing buttons on the
microwave ovens had to be reset to meet the needs of the menu.

To make matters worse, at the time the new system went
into operation much publicity was given to leakage from
microwave ovens. A monitoring program has been in effect
since then and to date there has been no significant leakage.

Patient complaints about food are also monitored continuously. It is now possible to pinpoint a new nurse who has
failed to follow instructions, or who is fighting the system.
On the whole, however, the nurses fully support the system and
there is an inservice training program for new nurses, to
minimize the improper handling of the food.

The Dietary Department has a grand total of 28 full time
equivalent personnel, compared with the old hospital, which
had 45 for 171 beds. The average for a 300-bed hospital
would be, with a conventional food system, 70. In addition
to providing meals to patients, the department maintains two
vending machines catering to interns and residents around the
clock. The department also caters three to four functions per
day ranging from coffee and buns to complete meals, requiring
one full time equivalent.

The department vends about 1250 plates per month, which
the Dietary Steward handles along with the task of purchasing
and removing the next day's food requirement from the freezer.
He also handles most of the catering. The dietitians also
spend considerable time giving dietary instructions to
patients.

In 1971, when the Food Service Manager left, an industrial
engineer was assigned to study the Dietary Department's staffing patterns versus productivity. His studies resulted in
upgrading the Chef to Dietary Steward, with increased responsibilities, and in not replacing the Food Service Manager.
It was also found that personnel on the tray assembly line
were being overworked and as a result of these studies, additional personnel have been added, turnover has decreased, and
errors and complaints have been reduced. An improved
Inventory Control System was also instituted which cut inventory by 50%.

VI.   BENEFITS DERIVED

The operational problems mentioned were all a part of an educational process.   By now the Franklin Square Hospital has a rather sophisticated program.   Patient complaints are at a minimum.   With the cooperation of certain food processors, it has been possible to assemble all of the modified diet requirements.   The menu provides a wide selection of food.   A 14 day cycle menu is used although the average patient stay is 7.4 days.   There are 61 entree items for regular diet and 31 items for special or modified diets.

The Dietary Department itself, is quiet; it does not experience the peaks and valleys of activity found in a conventional hospital.   It is air conditioned and pleasant in summer.   The turnover of personnel was average for the hospital, at 14% for the past year.   The department can cater meals for special visitors or small groups on short notice. Food can be served in any area of the hospital after being heated in the microwave oven in the Dietary Department. There is virtually no food waste during preparation, and food theft is reduced to a minimum.   From the patient's point of view, this system offers total flexibility in the meal hour. While most patients eat at the popular times of day, the occasional patient who prefers an early or late dinner can have it with no inconvenience to hospital personnel.   Patients out of their rooms for a diagnostic procedure can have their complete meal when they return.   The three daily meals are served at the usual mealtime hours.   Additional nourishment is offered at 10 a.m., 2 p.m., and 8 p.m.   The 10 a.m. nourishment, however, is limited to those on liquid or similarly modified diets.

Nursing has found that delivering the diet tray offers some definite advantages.

1.   Nurses have the opportunity to see the patients while bringing them something pleasant, rather than unpleasant medications, or giving them injections.
2.   Nurses can coordinate preparing patients for their meals with the actual delivery of the meal.   These two events previously could not always be coordinated, much to the displeasure of the patient.

Wine is served with the evening meal if the patient so requests and if the doctor approves.   There is a selection of red, white, and rosé domestic wines.   While this nicety is not original with the Hospital, it is receiving greater acceptance [4].

VII. SPACE ALLOCATIONS

The Dietary Department for our 300-bed facility contains only 1456 square feet. Storage areas within the department are as follows:

freezer	476 sq. ft.
defrosting and dairy refrigerators	221 sq. ft.
holding refrigerator for trays	98.7 sq. ft.
storage area	460 sq. ft.

In addition, there are eight food staging areas on the nursing units, and a ninth in the Intensive Care Unit. They contain 75 square feet of space each.

VIII. STAFFING

There are 31 full and part time employees, totalling 28 full time equivalents. This complement includes most of our Dietary Department's housekeeping personnel requirements. Taking a norm of 70 employees for a conventional 300-bed hospital, the Franklin Square's labor force has been reduced by 60% [5]. The hospital's experience appears significantly better than that of other hospitals using the convenience food system.

When the Food Service Manager left after two years of operation, the Chief Dietitian took over complete responsibility for the Department, and has managed it ever since. The former Chef, who now carries the title of Dietary Steward, was given additional responsibilities in purchasing, inventory control, catering, and vending.

The personnel and medical staff eat in the main dining room with meals furnished from vending machines. A commercial vending operator maintains all but two machines. There is no vending cost to the Hospital and mark-ups and profit are kept within reasonable limits. The Hospital now derives a modest income from the operation but, according to The Cost Review Commission, it is insufficient to pay the rent on the vending area. The new addition will feature a larger operation with vending for off hours but with a manual employee cafeteria for meal hours, and a visitors' coffee shop. Both will utilize convenience foods.

When the present dietary operation started in December 1969, 14 food processors supplied convenience food for the regular diets; today there are 16. Of these, all but one have supplied the hospital from the outset. Initially there were

four suppliers for special or modified diets; now there are
six and only one of the original four is no longer involved.

In addition to frozen and canned foods, the hospital buys
from local sources the usual dairy products, baked goods,
scrambled eggs and omelets, desserts such as puddings and
jello, and most salads, except lettuce and tomatoes which it
assembles itself.

Dietary costs for the fiscal year ending June 30, 1975
were

food	$4.16
disposables	.98
labor	2.50
housekeeping	.18
printing, etc.	.09
average dietary cost per patient day	$7.91

When these figures were subjected to the prescribed accounting
treatment of the Maryland Health Services Cost Review Commission to reflect outpatient volume as well, and ranked with
the 25 Baltimore Metropolitan area hospitals, the Franklin
Square Hospital's dietary cost was the seventh lowest.
Stated in another manner, 18 of the 25 hospitals had a
higher dietary direct cost [6]. Since Franklin Square has a
smaller area than conventional dietary departments, its overhead cost should also be the lowest, but indirect cost comparison figures, however, are not available.

The Hospital Cost Analyses Service certifies cost of Blue
Cross, Medicare, and Medicaid in the state of Maryland. Its
accounting treatment differs somewhat from those of the
Franklin Square Hospital and the Health Services Cost Review
Commission. However, as it is recognized as being well
qualified in the field of hospital accounting, its cost findings for Dietary Comparisons are both valid and interesting.
Its figures, shown in Table I, also represent direct cost
only.

Once again, it can be demonstrated by impartial authorities reviewing the cost of Maryland hospitals, that the convenience food concept produces a favorable dietary cost as
compared with the conventional food service system. In this
instance too, overhead cost is not available. In 1971 the
Franklin Square Hospital was 31% lower and in 1973, 30%
lower than the average for its size. Even though the Nursing
Services is responsible for preparing and delivering trays,
nursing hours per patient per day are in the lowest quartile
in the State of Maryland [8].

TABLE I.   Dietary Cost per Patient Day

Year	Institution	Salaries	Other	Total
1967	Franklin Square	$2.35	$2.31	$4.66
1967	4 similar metro. hospitals	2.25	2.26	4.51
1967*	5 larger metro. hospitals	2.60	2.73	5.33
1969	Franklin Square	4.10	2.82	6.92
1969	4 similar metro. hospitals	2.64	2.92	5.56
1971	Franklin Square	1.68	4.09	5.77
1971	5 similar metro. hospitals	4.49	4.02	8.51
1973	Franklin Square	2.14	3.97	6.11
1973	5 similar metro hospitals	4.86	4.31	9.17

* These hospitals are the basis for comparison in 1971 and 1973.

The hospital operates on an annual budget that the Dietary Department must develop and have approved by the administration and the Board of Trustees. It must anticipate all expenses and be able to explain monthly budget variances. The Department submits monthly and yearly reporting statistics that have been developed, and furnish the administration with meaningful information. These monthly reports furnish such basic information as: patient meals served, catering functions, vending, percent of modified diets, diet instruction, and diet changes.

IX.   THE FUTURE

The Franklin Square Hospital is currently embarking on a $21,500,000 expansion program that will double the size of the hospital, adding another 160 beds. The Chief Dietitian, when asked what direction the Hospital should take in patient feeding, recommended that the present program be continued. The convenience food system fulfills all of the requirements

FIGURE 1. Patient meals at Franklin Square Hospital are heated in microwave ovens by nursing personnel immediately prior to delivery to patients.

of the Hospital and will therefore be perpetuated in its
expansion plans.

X.   SUMMARY

The new system has provided patients with a wider dietary
selection at a reasonable cost. With the use of disposables,
no patient ever questions the cleanliness of the wrapped food
or plastic flatware. Isolation patients no longer feel that
they are the object of discrimination. In short, the convenience system, combined with the use of disposables, has been,
and will continue to be, the ideal system for Franklin
Square Hospital.

REFERENCES

1.   Souder, James A., "Estimating Space Needs and Costs in
     General Hospital Construction." American Hospital
     Association (1963).
2.

3.   Flynn, Helen W., "Food Delivered Cold, Served Hot from
     Nurses Stations." *Amer. Hosp. Assoc., 37,* Dec. 16, 1963.
4.   Lumm, Marjorie, "Wine Brightens the Hospital Diet and the
     Hospital," *Hospital Forum,* December, 1969.
5.   Rinke, Wolf J., "Three Major Food Systems Reviewed and
     Evaluated," *Food Service, 50,* Feb. 16, 1976.
6.   Maryland Health Services Cost Review Commission, General
     Services Centers, Dietary, Metropolitan Area Hospitals
     Budgeted Expenses, Divided by EIPDS, January 16, 1976.
7.   Based on information released by A. R. Holmes, Executive
     Director, Hospital Cost Analysis Service, March 19, 1976.
8.   "Hospital Administrative Services." American Hospital
     Association, Jan. 1976.

CHAPTER 27

THE MARRIOTT CONVENIENCE FOOD PROGRAM

Richard N. Schwartz

Quality Control Division
Fairfield Farm Kitchens
Beaver Heights, Maryland

The Food Service divisions of the Marriott Corporation have become very dependent on centrally prepared food over the past 45 years. There are many advantages, as well as some pit- falls in this concept.

The Marriott Corporation was founded in 1927 by J. Willard Marriott, Sr., in Washington, D.C., with the running of a sin- gle nine-seat root beer stand. The soft drink business was great in the summer time but slow in the winter. The Marriott family could not accept this kind of waste, so they began serv- ing tacos and tamales, which eventually led to the offering of medium-priced family food in clean and pleasant surroundings. The root beer stand evolved into the first Hot Shoppe; then in- to a chain of them. As the chain grew, the principles of oper- ation remained the same: close family supervision of all de- tails; benevolent and paternalistic labor relations; a flair for promotion; a good product for the family trade.

By 1964, Marriott had 45 Hot Shoppes, mostly in the Wash- ington, D.C. area. The Marriotts had a reputation for putting out a consistent, reasonably priced meal, satisfying a large segment of the eating-out public. One of the ways in which this was achieved was through the close supervision of prepared products in the kitchen. It was not unusual to see Mr. Mar- riott himself in the kitchen making suggestions on food hand- ling. Early in the life of the organization, it was recognized that food consistency ranked very high, next to pleasant serv- ice and pleasant surroundings, in keeping people coming back to the Hot Shoppes. In 1930, the first central commissary was started to achieve the goal of consistent products. The first products manufactured were mainly base items, such as beef and gravy bases, chicken base, cream sauce base and a variety of

Copyright © 1979 by Academic Press, Inc.
All rights of reproduction in any form reserved
ISBN: 0-12-453150-4

soups. The underlying concept was that if an initial base was
used during final preparation, then the consistency of the
products being served would be maintained. As time progressed,
the number of manufactured items increased to include commi-
nuted meats, such as hamburger and sausage, portion cut meat
products, ice cream in bulk and single portion units, baked
pies, soft rolls, hard rolls, danish pastries, sheet and layer
cakes, chopped lettuce, cole slaw and a full line of salad
dressings.

In 1967, Marriott outgrew the initial commissary and built
a multimillion dollar complex which now supplies even more convenience foods to the Marriott chain. The new commissary was
created to provide a central source of supply for both manufactured and purchased food and supplies to the Marriott Corporation's operations, and to provide a satisfactory net return on
the investment made in the facility. A new technology was also
introduced through the new commissary, i.e. the freezing of all
freezable convenience foods. Initially soups, gravies and
bases were handled, refrigerated, in large stainless steel
pails. This led to the packaging in dairy-type containers,
still in a refrigerated form, and finally, utilizing the capabilities of the new commissary, to frozen products in pouches
or trays. This practice eliminated some of the problems that
were encountered in regard to shelf life and bacteriological
control using the refrigerated concept.

Essential to the central supply concept is the requirement
that food and supplies be purchased from the commissary at or
below competitive sources, that operations be provided with
standardization and control of specifications for all items,
and that all purchasing and delivery functions be simplified at
the unit level. Other advantages include the ability to "custom make" products to the exact specifications and need of operations.

At the present time, the convenience food line and bakery
products make up approximately 90 various items, all of which
are prepared at a central location. The items are manufactured
using a variety of food handling and preservation techniques,
with the exception of thermal sterilization. These products
are used by a great many Marriott operations, including a large
number of institutional and commercial cafeterias.

The shift to a complete convenience food program in a cafeteria operation is of necessity an evolutionary development.
Ideally, it should start at the facility planning stage when
decisions are made as to the amount of space to be allotted for
food preparation and storage, and the type of equipment to be
purchased for food handling. Adequate freezer and cooler space
is a prerequisite for a convenience food program. Many of the
older existing units, however, are totally inadequate with respect to freezer space. Work space in the food preparation area

and the number of kitchen personnel needed, decrease in a change from direct preparation to increased convenience food usage.

There appears to be a fine line, especially during times when there is a down turn in business, where it is feasible to utilize the employees normally helping on line and on tables, to do some of the food preparation work. There is a tendency during these times to revert back to in-house preparation.

A typical Marriott cafeteria menu, utilizing centrally prepared food products would be implemented as follows:

1. Salad - uses pre-mixed chopped lettuce and trimmings in a bulk plastic bag.
2. Soup - concentrated and packed in trays. Requires addition of equal parts of water and heating.
3. Gravy, Spaghetti Sauce and Flavored Bases - packed in plastic trays. Heat and serve products.
4. Entrees - packed in half steam-table size aluminum pans. Heat and serve products.
5. Desserts - custard pies: thaw and serve
   - frozen fruit pies: bake and serve
   - layer cakes: thaw and serve

The utilization of these products makes it possible to reduce the kitchen work and the number of kitchen employees required. Furthermore, this enables management to concentrate on important areas such as customer service, public relations and personnel training, all of which are vital to the food service business. Whereas managers in conventional free standing restaurant units must spend a great deal of time ordering many supplies from various vendors, meeting salesmen and shopping for the best prices, these worries are almost totally eliminated using the central food preparation concept.

Marriott has found that the advantages of a convenience food program are many. Ranking high is the overall control that can be attained over the uniformity of quality and portion control. This is largely due to the ability to incorporate the highest levels of technical competence, management competence and culinary skills in a central facility. Marriott's manufacturing center, located in the Washington, D.C. area, employs approximately 600 people. Included among these are professional research and development, engineering, quality control and manufacturing management personnel. This staff has brought to Marriott the latest in technical knowhow in utilizing the most efficient methods of manufacturing available to the industry. Another advantage inherent in the central facility concept is centralized procurement which permits costs to be lowered because of volume purchases, while providing the quality and reliability factors necessary to run an efficient operation.

A real test of the system presented itself to Marriott with the opening of the "Great America" theme park in Santa Clara, California. The primary function of the theme park is to provide for family entertainment, but running a close second is mass feeding. Needless to say, everything that had been learned in the past in running ice cream parlors, fast food operations, specialty dinner houses, cafeterias and sit-down restaurants was utilized in providing the very best food and service possible in a theme park. Centrally prepared convenience foods played a major role in helping the theme park division of the company to achieve that goal. No less than 25 items, prepared in Washington, D.C., are shipped to the West Coast for use in food service at the park. The availability of proven products, at a known quality level and at a known price, proved to be of considerable value in providing food service successfully at "Great America". The task would have been truly awesome without it, considering a seasonal type operation, manned by seasonal unskilled employees.

Looking back, it is difficult to imagine the Marriott Corporation surviving without the type of food service system it now employs. There is, however, one prerequisite that is vital to the maintenance of the central commissary concept: it is top management's total committment to its effective use. There are also pittfalls to overcome which require close supervision from top corporate management. One of the most important is preventing sloppy facility management because of the captive customer syndrome. It is very easy to become complacent with respect to the quality, service and reliability factors, to say nothing of the overall cost of doing business. Marriott has experienced several ups and downs regarding the above-mentioned factors. Total convenience food programs have been started in various establishments and have failed because of economic and political problems. Marriott, however, has gained considerable insight by using these failures to gain experience and thus achieve the leadership position which it now enjoys in the food service industry.

INDEX

A

Acinetobacter, 383
Aerobic plate count, 381, 382, 390, 400
Airline food service, 27
AMFare System, 14
Anaerobic plate count, 381
Annapolis, *see* RAFT System
Appert, Nicholas, 4
Appetizers, 74
ARA, 9
Armour and Company, 11
Ascorbic acid
  in broccoli, 372
  in brussels sprouts, 368
  in cabbage, 369
  in cantaloupe, 370
  in chilled foods, 377
  in cole slaw, 370
  in cucumbers, 370
  holding losses, 370
  in orange juice, 366
  in peas, 366
  in potatoes, 364, 367
  in prepared foods, 372
  in spinach, 369
  transportation losses, 370
  in vegetables, 364, 366

B

Bacillus, 383
  cereus, 380
Baked goods, 72, 253
Block diagram, 245
Boil-in-bag pouches, 11
Boiling water cooker, 72, 73

Broilers, 75
Bryan Foods, 110

C

Canning, *see also* High-temperature/
  short-time sterilization
  conventional, 82
Canned foods, 82
  storage, 246
Cans/no. 10, 82, 85, 101
Career ladder, 183–184
Carotene, in peas, 366
Central food preparation facility, 19, 24–
  25
  designing, 243–260
Central States Can Company, 104
Cereals, 72
Chemetron System, 277–279
Chilled foods, 80
  Nacka System, 82, 123
  Kap-Cold System, 82, 123
  microbiology, 387
  time and temperature constraints, 385–386
Chrysler Zeder, Inc, 11
Clostridium, 383
  botulinum, 380
  perfringens, 380, 388, 390
Cold food production, 251
Coliforms, 381, 382, 400
Computers
  food management information systems,
    164–174
  in menu planning, 155–175
  in nutritional auditing, *see* Nutritional
    auditing

.